Women
at
Gettysburg
1863

Revisited

Eileen F. Conklin

This book is respectfully dedicated to
the women who served at Gettysburg in 1863
and to
Betty E. Fry
(1920 - 1990)
A twentieth century Gettysburg woman
of the same caliber.

To live in hearts we leave behind is not to die.

Copyright © 2013 Eileen F. Conklin

Printed and bound in the United States of America

Published by   Thomas Publications
                P.O. Box 3031
                Gettysburg, Pa. 17325

ISBN-978-1-57747-174-5

Women of War

We hear of men and heroes
Whose flashing swords are keen,
Who on the field of battle
"Drink from the same canteen"
Who at the post of danger
With the front unbroken stand
And in the hour of peril
Will guard our native land.
But who will tell the story
Of love's sublimest law
Of choicest treasures given
By Women of the War?

by Sybil[1]

Contents

Introduction

he Battle of Gettysburg is, unarguably, the most written about conflict of our nation's Civil War. Historians continue to rehash and even reinterpret that sacred ground, and Civil War enthusiasts can recite not just tactics and maneuvers, but have calculated how much ammunition was spent and how many pounds of horse manure was left behind. The enduring fascination with Gettysburg is perhaps understandable. This battle, with the highest casualties of the war, is largely regarded as the turning point, the beginning of the Confederacy's military decline.

Eileen Conklin was a Licensed Battlefield Guide at Gettysburg National Military Park in the 1980s. She quickly noticed that, despite all that has been written about this most-studied moment, and about the officers and troops who endured it, nothing of substance had been written about the women who witnessed the event, who participated in it, and who risked their own lives to tend to the wounded and dying. This dearth of information seemed particularly glaring in light of the fact that primary sources existed documenting women's participation. There was more to the story of women at Gettysburg than poor Jennie Wade, but no one had bothered writing it.

So Conklin began researching the women of Gettysburg, and the women who came to Gettysburg. She found diaries and letters and memoirs. She found descendants. Her decade of persistence culminated with *Women at Gettysburg – 1863*. This unique and literary volume intertwined the story of the battle with the narrative of women who were in the middle of it. Finally, the long-forgotten women who had been so essential to the war effort, and so indispensible in saving the lives of the men on the front, were written into the historical record. *Women at Gettysburg – 1863* was a groundbreaking work.

The original publication contributed enormously to the explosion of interest in the topic of women and the Civil War, an interest that has spawned a number of books exploring women's experience of the war, not to mention an annual conference on the subject held by the Society for Women and the Civil War, which Conklin founded. Visitors to National Parks now hear the stories of the both men and women. The graves of nurses are being found and marked. Monuments are being dedicated. Genealogists are seeking out their female Civil War ancestors along with the males.

It is most fitting that *Women at Gettysburg – 1863* is republished during the Civil War sesquicentennial. Conklin updated the original work, with new information from archival sources and photographs never before published, most from private collections. Her tireless efforts have resulted in a book even better than the first, a book that honors the women of Gettysburg by faithfully telling their stories, and in the process gives readers an unforgettable portrait of feminine courage.

DeAnne Blanton

Preface

"Next to the Supreme Ruler, women were the soldier's mainstay."[2]

"Truly woman's influence over the destiny of a nation was never more earnestly proclaimed, or sincerely acknowledged and felt, than during the late struggle."[3]

ore facts have been documented about the battle of Gettysburg than any other battle in the War Between the States. There has been research and debate on the numbers of men, cannon, and horses present; the number of small arms used and shots fired. This battle has been studied, analyzed, written about, and lectured on from the strategy of the commanding generals down to the smallest detail. Every aspect has been covered but one, that is, the women who served at Gettysburg.

The 1860 census recorded nearly fifteen million adult women, white and black, North and South, in the United States. Almost all of them would be affected to some degree by the terrible conflict yet to come. Though women's history is intertwined with men's history, it is often a separate experience. The men of the Civil War era came to fully appreciate and in many cases honor the women's war efforts. Today, except for a repetition of a sprinkling of names, these efforts have been forgotten or overlooked in historical analyses. Books on this war of America's greatest upheaval report the actions of men. As the history of men's actions and experiences are important and worthy of close study, no less so are the actions and experiences of the other half of the population. How many women can be found in history texts for our daughters to emulate and for our sons to respect?

An impressive number of women were involved in the battle of Gettysburg. In analyses of the battle there are some references to the townswomen's narratives but their personal stories have not been told. And what of the women who came up with the armies and the women who arrived in the aftershock to deal with the human wreckage of the battle? Who were they? Why were they there? What did they do? How did they feel?

This work is a compilation of war experiences of some of the women who served at Gettysburg. It is a small offering to serve as an example of the women present whose stories cannot be told or have not yet been found. These are the tales of the war as experienced by American women playing an integral part in American history.

> .... [W]e simply mean to present her as a historical fact in the "four years" encounter with the focus and opinions of the world; we know her value in the simplicity and privacy of life, but we cannot take her out of the war. She was amoung its resources ... Men were finally conscripted for the army ... That gap for practical energy was filled by whom, and what? All women were not merely hospital nurses, kindly householders, mothers and teachers—what were the other women doing? .. The quality of that womanhood, like molten metal under white heat, poured into shapes by the exigencies of the times ... Write these stories![4]

In the almost twenty years since this work was first published there has been an explosion of interest in women's experiences during the war. Books, articles, research, presentations, dedications, conferences, education, societies; have brought forward knowledge and recognition of many, many forgotten names and stories.

"The Artist's Tribute to the Selfless, Patriotic Women Who Contributed to the War Effort" from *Harpers Weekly*, September 6, 1862.

Acknowledgments

here are a number of people I would like to thank for their connection with this project:

Marie Melchiori for her generous and knowledgeable help at the National Archives and for her efforts on behalf of Mary Tepe. Ed Guy for introducing me to Lucinda Horne and Mrs. Mary Crawford for taking care of Mrs. Horne's history and gravesite. Mr. Art Kennell for sharing his research on Elizabeth Thorne. Louise Arnold-Friend and Randy Hackenburg at the Carlisle War museum for their help and interest. Joyce Meeks without whose long time encouragement I would not have begun writing. Bill Willmann who introduced me to the wonders of computers therefore allowing this work to be completed before the 21st Century. Cathy Hartland and Lina MacMichael for their time reading the manuscript. Mrs. Nell Baynham, Mrs. Elizabeth Crim, and Mr. Harvey Hancock for their limitless generosity in sharing their ancestor's history. It is a great pleasure and privilege to have met them. Kathy Harrison and Bob Prosperi for their ready cooperation at the Gettysburg National Military Park, and also the many researchers, librarians, and historians across the country who contributed to this work.

Many thanks go to my husband, Artie, for his support and advice, and to my family, for allowing these forty women to live with us for the past seven years.

Without two very special people this book would not have been completed. Deb Novotny's invaluable suggestions and critiques, her knowledge and love of history, her enthusiasm for the project, and most of all, her friendship make her as much a part of this book as the women whose histories are recorded in it.

And lastly, bur foremost, my heartfelt gratitude to a woman whose friendship changed my life by her example of kindness and love for humanity. If I wrote the soul into this book, she was the heart. Her loving support and complete faith in my ability to do justice to this subject never wavered. I will always love and honor the memory of my dear friend, Betty Fry.

As I write this updated edition it saddens me that many of these dear people are gone from my life. But many others have since come into the wide net this book has cast. Remarkable people who have shared research, family histories, raised funds to dedicate gravestones, plaques, and statues; have held memorials, ceremonies, conferred state recognition or named their groups in memory of a woman in this volume. All the new friends and acquaintances made since the first publication have enriched my life immeasurably. I began researching this book when I was a Licensed Battlefield Guide at Gettysburg in the 1980s and invested years of my life in it. I did not know then how people would respond or where it would go, if any place. I was pleasantly shocked at the reaction. So many people took the time and made the effort to carry on recognition of these women. God bless the reenactor.

Since 1993, Thomas Publications has continued to publish my work. I would like to thank the entire Thomas Publications staff. They are honorable, generous people and it has been a sincere pleasure to work with them. But for independent publishers like Dean Thomas, so much history would not be known or recognized. And the women in this volume would have remained forgotten, their service unremarked and lying in unmarked graves.

The Campaign

he battle of Gettysburg was on July 1, 2, and 3, 1863 which was about midway through the Civil War. At that time the country had been engulfed in war for more than two years with many Southern victories in the eastern theater. The Confederate Army of Northern Virginia and the Union Army of the Potomac had faced each other across the Rappahannock River in Virginia for the pervious six months where they had fought two major battles; Fredericksburg in December 1862 and Chancellorsville in May 1863. Both were Confederate victories although the latter cost the South the life of Lieutenant General Thomas "Stonewall" Jackson. The loss of Jackson effected a major reshuffling of the Confederate army with new commanders in untried positions and is one of the many "ifs" of the battle of Gettysburg.

In the western theater of the war the Confederates were faring poorly both near Chattanooga, Tennessee and at Vicksburg, Mississippi. One of the reasons, though not the strongest, for invasion into Northern territory by the Confederate army was the hope that by threatening important cities such as Washington or Philadelphia, Union forces would be withdrawn from elsewhere throughout the South and thus ease military pressure. More importantly, the strain on the South's resources to support the army, which had caused hungry women to riot in Richmond two months earlier, would also be relieved. The Confederates' desperate need for supplies—clothing, horses, and food, could be filled in the North's land of plenty.

Stimulating the Northern Peace Party was another reason for invasion. It was the political reason, in addition to the moral and military ones, for General Robert E. Lee to lead what has been called a "civilized invasion" where private property and citizens would be protected. Also, there was still a possibility that a victory north of the Potomac would gain either English or French recognition of the Confederate States of America. These reasons for invasion, however, did not obscure the ultimate goal of both armies which was each to destroy the other.

The Gettysburg Campaign began on June 3, when General Lee commenced moving his army out of Fredericksburg, Virginia, marching west to the Blue Ridge Mountains, then north through the Shenandoah and

"Southern Women Feeling the Effects of Rebellion and Creating Bread Riots" from *Frank Leslie's Illustrated Newspaper*, May 23, 1863.

Cumberland valleys. The Army of Northern Virginia consisted of approximately 70,000 men roughly divided into three corps: the I, II, and III.

The Union army broke camp at Falmouth, Virginia on June 12, the last elements pulling out on June 15. The Army of the Potomac consisted of approximately 97,000 men roughly divided into seven corps: the I, II, III, V, VI, XI, and XII. The Federals moved up through Frederick County, Maryland, keeping themselves between the Confederate army and Washington, D.C.

Women marched with both armies serving in their various capacities as matrons, laundresses, nurses, vivandieres, or in some cases as soldiers. However, many Union field nurses were evacuated at Falmouth to accompany the wounded to Washington hospitals and to remain "until we should see where the next blow should fall."[5]

One nurse described the passing of the army:

> They have gone, they have all passed by, nothing can be seen of them now but a long line of flashing bayonets, passing close under the brow of yonder hill. First went a few miles of cavalry (interspersed with batteries of artillery), the rattling of whose sabers always announce

their approach before you hear the tramp of their horses. If you happen to be near them as they pass, you will hear them jesting in merry tones, or singing snatches of rollicking songs. They go out ready to do or die and whatever else happens, you may be pretty sure that the cavalry will not disgrace us. Next went their ambulances, painfully suggestive of broken limbs, fearful sabre gashes, and bullet holes through the lungs; worse things than these sometimes, but we must not think of them now. Then their trains of baggage and supply wagons winding along for several miles, and this is the last we see of the cavalry.

A few hours pass, and looking far away over the hills we see a long, dark line in motion, and experience tells us that it is a body of infantry. As they come out of the shadow of the hill, their bayonets begin to gleam, so that now, in the sunshine, they look like a line of blazing lights, and come pouring on, officers riding at the head of their commands, colors and battle-flags waving on the air, some of them pierced and torn almost to shreds, but borne all the more proudly, and guarded the more sacredly for that. Presently, other columns, from other camps and winding around other hills, come on, but all moving in one direction…As they come nearer, you see that many of them have attached to their knapsack-straps, tincups, frying-pans, tinpails, coffee-pots, and some loaf of bread on the bayonets. They seem in good spirits, and, like the cavalry, are singing and joking. But under all this appearance of alacrity you may be sure there is much anxiety, and, in many hearts, a fearful looking forward…

"Glorious fellow!" exclaimed the General, as part of his command was marched by. He was thinking how gallantly they had behaved on many a fiercely-contested field, and how well he might rely on them to follow wherever he should lead in future. "Poor fellows!" said, at the same moment, a woman in sympathizing tones. She was thinking of fearful sights in crowded hospitals, cruel wounds, amputated limbs, pale faces, and brave, faithful hearts, worn out with excess of anguish.

So they pass for many hours, and after them come their trains of ambulances, baggage and supply wagons, and lastly, a herd of cattle, proportioned in numbers to the rations they are to serve. Now, at length, they are all gone…The stillness is painful. We sit down mournfully, and wonder where our friends are gone, and what is on the *tapis* now; for our dear and noble souls have gone out to-day, and many such we have seen go out to return no more. In our hearts we pray for them, and then look out to see what signs of the weather, and hope it will not rain.[6]

In a campaign made memorable by heat, forced marches, thirst, dust, exhaustion, and bursts of precipitation, the armies moved parallel on their separate routes. The Confederates marched with exuberance and confidence; they were an army used to victory. The Union men, though no less willing to fight, were chagrined by their complete defeat at Chancellorsvile and uneasy under the incompetent leadership of Brigadier General "Fighting Joe" Hooker who still commanded the Army of the Potomac early in the campaign. However, the Gettysburg Campaign had a different tone for the Union men. As they came onto Northern soil, they marched, for the first time, into the role of defenders. One Northern woman noted, "They…knew when they crossed the line into Pennsylvania for they were met with such kindness."[7]

In an effort to ascertain Lee's intention, the Union cavalry clashed in several major encounters with the Confederate cavalry who were covering their army's flanks in counter-reconnaissance. One such encounter resulted in the largest cavalry battle fought on American soil, that of Brandy Station, Virginia, on June 9. The Union cavalry demonstrated energy and skill and most importantly the capability to stand up to the Confederates, a stance which had been previously lacking. The fact that the Confederate cavalry commander, Major General J.E.B. Stuart, had been completely surprised at Brandy Station caused him personal and public humiliation. Stuart's embarrassment may have influenced his later decisions on his Gettysburg Raid in an endeavor to reestablish his reputation.

Continuing north, the Confederates routed out Union garrisons along the way; at Berryville, Virginia, on June 13, and at Martinsburg, [West] Virginia, on June 14. The battle of Winchester, Virginia, took place on June 15. At Berryville and Martinsburg the Union garrisons escaped with little fighting and little loss. At Winchester, however, half the Federal command was lost and the Confederates captured a good amount of choice materiel. On a more specific scale, the battle of Winchester began a tale of tragic irony involving a woman in far off Gettysburg.[8]

At the time of the battle Belle Boyd, the "Secesh Cleopatra" as she was dubbed by the Northern press, was home near Winchester between her stints in Washington prisons. She described her experience on June 15, 1863:

> I followed close upon the rear of our [Confederate] army, and when the attack upon Winchester commenced I was but four miles distant from the scene of action. When the artillery on both sides opened fire, the familiar sound reminded me of my own adventures on a former battlefield, and I resolved to be at least a spectatress of this. I joined a

4

**Belle Boyd watched part of the battle of Winchester on
June 15, 1863 until she was fired on by artillery.**
(*Miller's Photographic History of the Civil War*)

wounded officer, who though disabled from taking an active part in the
fight, where, by his crippled condition he would have hindered his men,
was yet able to accompany me some way. Accordingly we rode together to an eminence which commanded an uninterrupted view of the
combat. Here we sat for some short time, absorbed in the struggle that
was going on beneath us...But this calm feeling was not of long duration. I was mounted upon a white horse, which was quite conspicuous
to the artillery men of a Yankee battery which had been pushed up to
within three-quarters of a mile of the spot that we had selected for our
watch-tower...the guns of the battery were turned upon us.

By this time the officer of whom I have spoken and myself had
been joined by several citizens, ladies and gentlemen, who were attracted by curiosity and anxiety to witness the fight. They were for the
most part mounted on emaciated horses and mules which had been over-
looked by the Yankees when they retired, and they one and all seemed
to consider me as the perfect security for themselves. I shall never
forget the stampede that was made when a shell came suddenly hissing
and shrieking in amoung us. I joined, *con amore*, in the general flight;
for I had seen enough of fight to prefer declining with honor the part of
a living target, when exposure, being quite useless, becomes an act of
madness. The battle was not of long duration. The terms were too
equal to leave the issue long in doubt."[9]

Winchester would change hands over seventy times during the war.
(U.S. Army Military History Institute - MOLLUS)

About ten days after these encounters and as both army's movements picked up speed, General Stuart took much of the cavalry and left
the Confederate army to commence his ill fated Gettysburg Raid. The
Confederate cavalry rode around the rear of the Union army, and then
north, moving on the Union right flank. This took Stuart within miles
of Washington, D.C. and caused panic in the city. His men were faced
with obstacles that prevented them from rejoining Lee until the night of
July 2, the second day of the battle. Their absence deprived the Army
of Northern Virginia of its eyes and ears and in many opinions was the
major reason for Confederate defeat at Gettysburg.

In the summer of 1863 in the midst of recent Union depredations
and house burnings in the area, Judith McGuire, a Southern refugee in
Virginia, confided to her diary:

> There are rumors that our army is in Pennsylvania. So may it be!
> We are harassed to death with their [Union] ruinous raids, and why
> should not the North feel it in its homes?...I don't want their women
> and children to suffer; nor that our men should follow their examples
> and break through and steal. I want our warfare carried on in a more
> honorable way; but I do want our men and horses to be fed on the good
> things of Pennsylvania; I want the fine dairies, pantries, granaries, mead-
> ows, and orchards belonging to the rich farmers of Pennsylvania, to be
> laid open to our army; and I want it all paid for with our *Confederate
> money, which will be good at some future day.* I want their horses taken
> for our cavalry and wagons, in return for the hundreds of thousands that
> they have taken from us; and I want their fat cattle driven into Virginia
> to feed our army.[10]

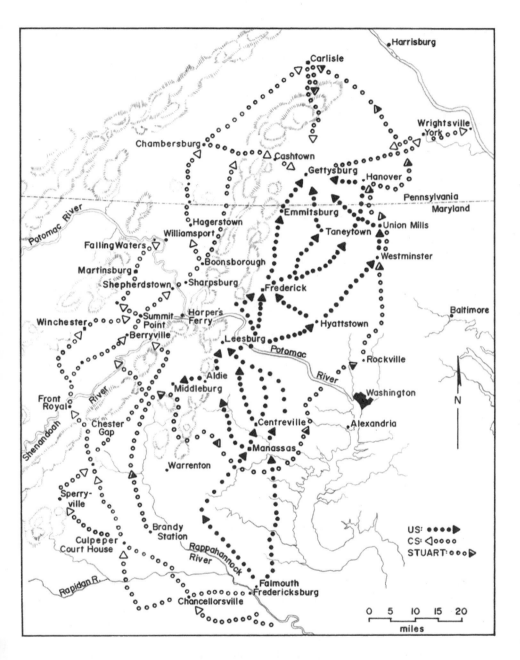

The Routes of the Union and Confederate Armies to Gettysburg
(Map by John Heiser)

Coincidentally, this was exactly what occurred. Before crossing the Mason Dixon line Lee issued General Orders No. 72, which detailed instructions in the seizure and payment of supplies and prohibiting "any damage or destruction to private property."

Mrs. McGuire noted this in her diary: "I am glad to see that General Lee orders his soldiers to respect private property, but it will be difficult to make an incensed soldiery, whose house have in many instances been burned, crops wantonly destroyed, horses stolen, negroes persuaded off, hogs and sheep shot down and left in the field in warm weather—it will be difficult to make such sufferers remember the Christian precept of returning good for evil."[11]

Despite Mrs. McGuire's reservations, on June 27 as the Confederates were deep into Pennsylvania, Lee was justified, with few exceptions, in issuing General Orders No. 73 congratulating the men on their conduct. This order was issued the day after a Confederate brigade has passed through Gettysburg on their march north.

The women in Pennsylvania were fortunate to see only a glimpse of what invasion meant. In 1863 a Virginia woman wrote: "The country would have to be overrun for two years before Pennsylvania could know what the Virginians knew of war."[12]

In the wee hours of June 28, Brigadier General George Gordon Meade assumed command of the Army of the Potomac from Hooker. Meade would be in command for only three days before one of the most decisive battles of the War Between the States commenced. That same day the Confederate vanguard arrived in Carlisle, Pennsylvania and late that night Lee learned from a spy that the Union army was in Frederick, Maryland, and that Meade was now in command.

The Army of the Potomac was scattered south and southeast of Taneytown, Maryland when Meade set up his headquarters there on June 29. That same day Lee sent orders to the Confederate commands which stretched from Chambersburg to Wrightsville to concentrate towards Cashtown which was eight miles west of Gettysburg. The next day, June 30, a Confederate brigade on their way to Gettysburg to obtain shoes, came upon a large body of Union cavalry engaged in the reconnaissance of the area. Neither wanted a confrontation at this time so both sides merely retired to warn their respective commanders of the presence of the enemy.

July First

The women of Gettysburg well remembered the morning of the first day of the battle:

> After days of suspense we were on duty early in the morning occupying our porch ready to reply or ask the usual question, have you heard anything of the Rebels? I heard two cavalrymen talking that morning and one of them said, "Well, the ball is about to open."[1]
> About 9 o'clock we were still standing about our doors, wondering what would happen next, when lo' the sound of the first gun, then another and another.[2]
> I got up early this morning to get my baking done before any fighting would begin. I had just put my bread in the pans when the cannons began to fire, and true enough the battle had begun in earnest, about two miles out on the Chambersburg pike...No one knew where to go and what to do.[3]

I hurried through with my morning work...Everything...was quiet and not a soldier in sight; in fact the stillness was oppressive, and this at a time of day when ordinarily the sounds from the farm yards are the loudest...We started out the ridge road towards the Chambersburg pike...[to] see if we can find out what is going on...After walking about a mile we came to a number of mounted pickets standing by the roadside...One of them told us that they were anticipating an attack at any time and wanted to know if we had seen any rebels about. Almost in answer to the question came a cannon shot off to the right which you can be sure startled us, as the shell seemed to fly almost over our heads...As if by magic thousands of men rose from the earth in the directions in which we had been going, in the fields to the right and left of us, and my old friend [an uncle] and I made a hasty retreat for home, the roar of the battle adding terror to our flight.[4]

By 5:00 a.m. on the morning of July first, two divisions of the Confederate III Corps were on the Cashtown Pike marching towards Gettysburg where Union cavalry waited expectantly. The Confederate skirmishers pushed back the Union pickets from Herr Ridge. They then used that eminence to deploy a brigade on either side of the pike. The Union cavalry was deployed along McPherson's Ridge. They had prepared to fight dismounted as infantry and were armed with single shot breech-loading carbines. Their commander had sent word back to the Union army advising of the enemy's approach in force and requesting the infantry to come up at all possible speed.

At about 8:00 a.m. two Confederate brigades moved down the sides of Cashtown Pike to attack the Union cavalry on McPherson's Ridge. The steadily weakening cavalry line held off the Confederate infantry for about two hours when a division of the Union I Corps arrived on the field to relieve them. The I Corps was commanded by Major General John F. Reynolds, a man much admired by both armies. Reynolds was deploying this body of infantry when he was killed by a Confederate bullet.

South of the pike the Confederates were surprised by the Union's famous "Iron Brigade" which ran up their front and flank. The Federal men captured a number of Tennesseans and Alabamians plus Brigadier General James Archer, the first Confederate general to be captured since Lee took command of the Army of Northern Virginia.

As the Confederate brigade was being outflanked on the south side of the pike, the opposite happened on the north side. There the Confederate men overlapped the Union infantry who then retreated to Seminary Ridge. The Confederates advanced rapidly in chase until a reserve Union regiment rushed them with a murderous fire. Many of the Confederates fighting on the north side of the pike dropped down into the railroad cut that led into town. The cover the cut afforded was so steep that it turned into a trap. The Union men appeared at the edge of the cut and captured about 200 Mississippians.[5]

A short lull followed the repulse of the first Confederate wave. The remnants of the attacking Confederate brigades pulled back to Herr Ridge and the Union infantry adjusted its line on McPherson's Ridge.

The other two divisions of the Union I Corps came up onto the field and deployed on either flank of the existing Union line on McPherson's Ridge, mostly extending it in a northerly direction. The Confederate artillery bombarded the Union line in earnest while two fresh Confederate brigades deployed once again across the Cashtown Pike but this time with another division of the Confederate III Corps moving up behind them in support.

In obedience to Lee's order to concentrate, two Confederate divisions of Major General Richard S. Ewell's II Corps were moving down the roads from the north toward Gettysburg. At about 12:00 noon one of these divisions commanded by Major General Robert Rodes reached the field, arriving under cover of the woods on Oak Hill. They set up their artillery and enfiladed the flank of the Union line at McPherson's Ridge. This Confederate division's infantry attacked a section of the Union I Corps line which was deployed behind a stone wall. The Union men rose up from behind the wall firing such effective volleys that the Confederates fell dead in rows.

Any advantage the Confederates may have had at this point was negated by the arrival on the field of two division from the Union XI Corps, one commanded by Brigadier General Alexander Schimmelfennig and the other by Brigadier General Francis Barlow. They had marched through the town of Gettysburg and because of the Confederate presence on Oak Hill, deployed onto open fields in a line one-quarter mile northeast of the Union I Corps line. The XI Corps, commanded by Major General Oliver Otis Howard, consisted largely of foreign soldiers. So many different languages were spoken that one of the batteries issued commands in the form of hand claps. This corps had an unenviable reputation because of their break and stampede at Chancellorsville the previous May. Any hopes that they may have had to dispel this reputation at Gettysburg were dashed as the other Confederate division coming down from the north burst into their flank and rear. Their line was completely untenable and they broke once again. While trying to rally his men, Union General Barlow was grievously wounded. He was left of the field to be discovered by Confederate Brigadier General John Gordon.

Gordon related the famous Gordon-Barlow incident in his *Reminscences:*

> …He was Major General Francis C. Barlow, of New York, and of Howard's Corps. The ball entered his body in front and passed out near the spinal cord, paralyzing him in legs and arms. Neither of us had the remotest thought that he could possibly survive many hours. I summoned several soldiers who were looking after the wounded and directed them to place him on a litter and carry him to the shade in the rear. Before parting, he asked me to take from his pocket a package of letters and destroy them. They were from his wife. He had but one request, to make of me. That request was that if I should live to the end of the war and should ever meet Mrs. Barlow, I would tell her of our meeting on the field of Gettysburg and his thought of her in his last moments. He wished me to assure her that he died doing his duty at the front, that he was

willing to give his life for his country and that his deepest regret was that he must die without looking upon her face again. I learned that Mrs. Barlow was with the Union army and near the battlefield. When it is remembered how closely Mrs. Gordon followed me, it will not be difficult to realize my sympathies were especially stirred by the announcement that his wife was so near him. Passing through the day's battle unhurt, I dispatched at its close, under flag of truce, the promised message to Mrs. Barlow. I assured her that if she wished to come back through the lines she should have safe escort to her husband's side...[6]

Unknown to Gordon, Barlow survived. Gordon's cousin, who had identical initials, was killed later in the war, thereby convincing Barlow that his compassionate enemy had not survived. Fifteen years later, to their great surprise, they met at a dinner in Washington, D.C. This is a story that has been questioned over the years yet still survives as a part of the battle's story.

The collapse of the XI Corps right flank dominoed down the rest of the line. The Confederates advanced all along their line with great vigor and almost in unison attacks were renewed against the Union I Corps line. The I Corps line dissolved bit by bit, rallied briefly at the Seminary, but by 4:00 p.m. was in full retreat.

The XI and I Corps streamed through the streets of Gettysburg, the infantry offering spurts of resistance with stronger shows by the artillery. The Confederates pressed the retreating men closely. The crush was made worse by ambulances and army wagons moving through the streets. Union men ran down blind alleys or hid in houses to escape the pursuing Confederates who captured many prisoners.

Gettysburg townswomen described their view of the retreat: "...General Howard's troops of the XI Corps retreated through the town to Cemetery Hill past our house. They were followed closely by Confederate troops...As the two lines of soldiers ran past, firing as they went, we watched through the cellar windows. Oh! What horror filled our breasts as we gazed upon their bayonets glistening in the sun and heard the deafening roar of musketry."[7] "All was bustle and confusion. No one can imagine in what extreme fright we were when our men began to retreat."[8]

General Lee had come up to Gettysburg and watched the melee from the cupola of the Seminary. It was about 4:30 p.m. The capable Union Major General Winfield S. Hancock had also arrived on the battlefield by that time. He directed the deployment of the remnants of the

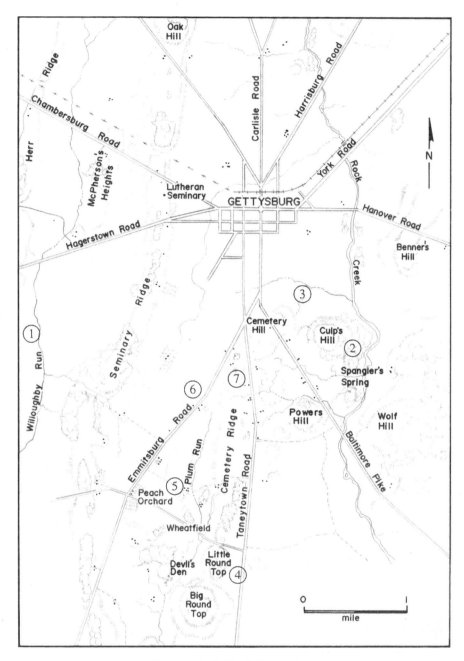

The Battlefielf of Gettysburg

(Map by John Heiser)

1. Plank Farm (Plank)
2. Culp's Hill (Barlow)
3. East Cemetery Hill (Spencer)
4. Weikert Farm (Pierce & Tepe)
5. Trostle Farm (Etheridge)
6. Rogers House (Miller)
7. The Angle (Unknown)

XI and I Corps along Cemetery and Culp's Hills which stood southeast of town. These eminences were the rallying points for the retreating Union infantry and were later the anchor of the Union line. The Confederates did not carry through with an assault against these hills, thus allowing the Union to develop a strong defensive position. The Confederate's failure to continue their momentum on the first day is another great "if" in the battle of Gettysburg.

There were approximately 30,000 Confederates engaged in the first day's battle and well over 19,000 Union; about 5,000 of whom were captured. The decisions made on July 1 were made by junior officers of both armies and committed both commanding generals to a battle at Gettysburg. The ten roads running into town like a spoke of a great wheel were another deciding factor. Marching on any one of these roads, whether to reconnoiter as the Union cavalry did or to concentrate as the Confederates were ordered, eventually led the men to Gettysburg. The timely effects of these arrivals created the great swings in the battle of the first day.

Gettysburg was the Adams County seat with a population of about 2,400 in 1863. The town boasted two institutions of higher learning; the Lutheran Seminary and the Gettysburg College, plus an academy for boys and two private schools for girls. Production of carriages was the main trade in town. Some of the whites and most of the blacks in the area left for fear of capture by the invading Southerners. Since a good number of the white men left, many of the townspeople who remained during the battle were women. Most hid in their cellars during the actual fighting, but many came up to assist in working with the wounded. Their lives and their town would never be the same.

There was much activity during the night hours of the first day. Lee send out a squad of eight riders with sealed orders and instructions to find Stuart. Meade rode up from Taneytown and arrived to inspect the Union lines sometime before dawn. With the exception of Pickett's Confederate division which remained in Chambersburg, Pennsylvania, and the great Union VI Corps which was on a forced march from Manchester, Maryland, the remaining units of both armies came up through the night and early morning.

And during that first day the armies' medical personnel had begun their indescribable ordeal at Gettysburg, which for some would last nearly until the end of the year.

Elizabeth Plank

Gettysburg Civilian

"Now don't be frightened; this house will be a hospital and you can expect many wounded."[1]

Lizzie Plank lived on her parents' 220 acre farm in 1863. J. Edward Plank, who was probably her brother, worked the farm.

Lizzie recalled:

> [There were] all kinds of rumors…that soldiers were coming and a battle would be fought…sometime in the afternoon on June 30, 1863…[two men sitting on the roof of the barn]…looking west, saw a long dark fence, upon closer observation they saw the line move and small objects glittering in the sunlight. It really was the Confederate army.
>
> The next morning [July 1] the first excitement was the burning of the barn on the Fairfield Road, next a house near the Springs Hotel, and the farmers began leaving their homes with their horses. [Lizzie's relative took] three, going over the Mason & Dixon line to friends in Maryland.

Lizzie described the farm and the shock of enemy intrusion. The farm was located,

> about three miles west of Gettysburg, situated on the west bank of Willoughby's Run. The house was a large brick with two large halls, one on the first floor and one on the second, each opening into four large rooms with kitchen off…[T]he firing of guns was heard and the roar of cannon. Not long after this, an ambulance arrived at the farm house and without any ceremony forced open the front door and carried in a wounded officer and placed him in the guest's room and the best bed in the house. Now, the family hearing the racket and thinking of the baby asleep upstairs, rushed up, where they were met by several orderlies or doctors…While other men were driving a staple in the ceiling and with a rope and pulleys made a swing for the officer's wounded foot, tearing the sheets and linens into bandages for the emergency. Now it was not long before all the beds were filled with wounded, and the floor covered with straw carried from the barn, all over the floors in the halls, on the porches, in the out building, on the barn floor and every place were wounded—hauled there in ambulances, on wagons,

gun machines and every way possible, and using the Garner Organ room for surgical or operating room. Many limbs and arms were amputated and their wounds dressed, while the battle raged. As the horses tired out [from] ambulance [work], the were turned into the wheat and oats field near the house to rest and fed on the growing grain, unfortunately two wounded horses died in the yard back of the house. Now these horrible sights were too much for the family to bear so they were advised to leave their home for awhile, so taking a few articles of clothing, they also went to their friends in Maryland.

The Plank farm became Confederate Major General John Bell Hood's division hospital site where 1542 wounded were taken for care. After the battle, 515 were left when the Confederates evacuated the area. One of the outer buildings was used as a dead house.

Lizzie continued:

> These wounded soldiers were left at this hospital, five or six weeks after the fight. Every morning they buried their dead in shallow graves in the orchard. Finally they were all removed and the family…came home. Can you imagine the home it was? The yard and garden fence were gone, the flower and garden beds were as the mud roads, the poultry, hogs and cattle were consumed for food, the fences and part of the building were used for camp fires, the floors of the house were strewn with blood soaked straw, also the flies and vermin of the dog days.

The Plank Farm still stands today.
(Author's collection)

16

Elizabeth Plank explained her suspicion that "...there was a woman doing service in that battle of Gettysburg hospital...At this hospital there were two doctors, one very well built, and a man of fine personality. This name cannot be recalled. [This was Dr. T.A. Means of the 11th Georgia.] The other–John R. Bodly of Georgia, was a smaller man of kind disposition and bore many characteristics of a woman, and often spoken of, by the family, as 'the woman doctor.' These two doctors were constant companions."

Thomas A. Means is in the 1860 census for Taylor County, Virginia soon to be West Virginia. He was 23. There was only one other person in the household, Caroline Means, age 22. Whether a wife or a sister, whether they were all each other had, whether she could have gone to war with him is sheer speculation.

Whether Bodly was a woman in disguise has not been verified, but narratives of wounded soldiers on the Plank farm told of two Gettysburg women, Mary and Sally Witherow, who cared for the Confederates, and of three "grand Christian women from Baltimore."[2] The latter were most likely part of the group of Southern women who organized relief for Confederate wounded after the battle.

Arabella Griffith Barlow

Wife of Union General Barlow

*"We called her the 'Raider'...Her great activity and inex-
haustible energy showed themselves in a sort of roving work,
in seizing upon and gathering up such things as her quick
eye saw were needed."*[1]

On June 2, 1863, ten days before the Army of the Potomac began
pulling out of Falmouth for the Gettysburg Campaign, General Barlow
wrote his mother from Division Headquarters: "Yesterday Gen. Howard
and his brother and Edward [Barlow's brother] and I and Arabella rode
over to the 2nd Corps to see a brigade celebration on the anniversary [of
the battle] of Fair Oaks."[2] A month later Barlow would be near death
and Arabella would be searching Gettysburg hospitals for him.

Barlow was grievously wounded on what is now called Barlow's
Knoll while fighting with the XI Corps on July 1. Confederates moved
him into the relative safety of the woods, then left him with a supply of
water. He carried on his person two letters concerning his commission
with the Freedman's Bureau. He destroyed these along with other papers he carried. Barlow never made mention of meeting or requesting
anything from Confederate Gen. John Gordon. Nor did Barlow, a man
known for sometimes brutal honesty, take the opportunities presented
to deny the meeting.

Barlow was moved first to the farm of Josiah Benner on the Harrisburg Road where he was examined by three Confederate doctors.
On July 2 he was moved to the home of Jane Smith and examined
again by a captured Union doctor. The prognosis of all doctors was
identical; Barlow had no chance of survival. Miss Jane Smith, whose
home was near the Almshouse in Gettysburg, wrote: "Brigadier
General Barlow (Federal officer) brought in this afternoon wounded
in yesterday's battle—perhaps mortally."[3] Here he visited with other
Confederate officers. Whether it was Gordon or another officer who
instigated notifying the wounded general's wife, word was sent to
Arabella behind Union lines by either Confederate General Early
and/or General Ewell.

Daniel Skelley, a Gettysburg civilian, recalled: "On the evening of the 2nd [July] on Chambersburg Street we were halted by two Confederate soldiers who had a lady in their charge. She was on horseback and proved to be the wife of General Barlow who had come through Confederate lines under a flag of truce looking for her husband who had been severely wounded on July 1…"[4]

General Barlow wrote home: "On Thursday morning I moved into another house just inside the town where an elderly lady and her daughter were very kind to me. I found some books there and passed Thursday and Friday [July 2 and 3] very comfortably under morphia…The ladies and some of our wounded in the house did what nursing I required."[5]

Arabella eventually found her husband. She took "care of him, and of other wounded, during the dreadful days that followed, during which the sufferings of the wounded from the intense heat, and the scarcity of medical and other supplies were almost incredible, and altogether indescribable."[6] One grateful woman remembered Arabella in a private letter, "She was with my cousin the night before he died, after Gettysburg, ministering most tenderly to him."[7]

When the Confederates left the area Barlow was again moved to a house on Baltimore Street, an accommodation most likely organized by Arabella. He would spend some time in a Baltimore hospital afterwards but was soon brought back to Sommerville, New Jersey where his wife's careful nursing brought him back to health.

Arabella Wharton Griffith was born on February 29, 1824 to Ann Marie Wallace Howell and William Griffith and was baptized in Sommerville, New Jersey. The couple had three children, John born December 1820, Arabella, and Edward in February 1826. The same month Edward was born, the Griffith's marriage ended. William had been engaged in some disastrous business projects and lost a great deal of money. Law suits followed. Four months after the divorce, William was declared "lost at sea" and was gone from the family life.

At around age six Arabella was sent to live in Burlington, New Jersey with her mother's cousin, Miss Eliza Bradford Wallace. She stayed in Miss Wallace's household for some years as she is listed in the 1830 and 1840 census. Arabella was enrolled in St. Mary's Hall in Burlington in 1837 but was not in the first graduating class of 1844. However, there were at least two other schools in the area she could have attended. In March of 1846 Arabella's brother, John died at age

25 and the following year death claimed her younger brother, Edward, at age 21.

In 1846 Arabella left for New York and by the time of impending war was in Manhattan residing with the Nevius family probably as a governess. Peter J. Nevius was a wealthy merchant and ship broker, socially prominent with ties to Somerville. Arabella moved in sophisticated circles of artists and prominent socialites cultivating long lasting friendships with such as George Templeton Strong, the famous New York diarist and lawyer and his wife Ellen. The couple would later become executive officers of the United States Sanitary Commission. Another couple, Judge Charles Daly and his wife Maria, would greatly influence Arabella's future husband's career. She met artists Eastman Johnson and Winslow Homer, had contributions published in the *New York Tribune* and followed the feminist and reform movements. George Templeton Strong wrote of Arabella in 1855: "Tea at Lydig's tonight, where the Rev. Mr. Weston and Miss Arabella Griffith, of whom I've heard so much from the Lydigs; certainly the most brilliant, cultivated, easy, graceful, effective talker of womankind, and has read, thought and observed much and well."[8]

On April 20, 1861, Arabella Wharton Griffith married Francis Channing Barlow at St. Paul's Church in New York. The ten year difference in their ages mattered not at all to the couple but because of Barlow's youthful appearance and slight built, she was thought to be his mother on occasion. Francis had enlisted in the 12th N.Y.M. the day before the marriage and shipped out day after.

On July 9, 1861 Barlow wrote to his mother: "Arabella is in Washington for the present until we see what we are going to do—she may follow us on here if we encamp in a civilized place."[9] By mid July she was still in Washington and her husband's regiment returned home.

After months of lobbying for a commission, Barlow enlisted in the 61st New York as a Lieutenant Colonel in November 1861 and wintercamped near Alexandria, Virginia. Arabella went to "Burlington where the sickness of Miss Wallace, called her suddenly."[10] On December 24, 1861, Barlow wrote from camp: "Miss Wallace is dead…[she left "her adopted daughter, Arabella, $25 and some furniture, the rest of the estate went to the church and a benevolent fund]…Arabella will come here at once."[11] Arabella stayed the winter of 1861-62 in a local house near her husband's camp. Barlow wrote: "The house is close to the Camp and the bugles and drums would wake you up at 6 a.m. but they don't get up until near 9 a.m…" His distaste for Virginia people and towns was reflected in his observation: "The table is poor and the whole housekeeping disorderly and unpunctual and Virginian."[12] Arabella had a small room without a fire, but there was little complaint as their hosts refused to accept any payment from their guests.

By April 1862 Barlow was a full colonel. The Army of the Potomac commenced the Peninsula Campaign that spring [March-July 1862] and the couple separated. Barlow wrote his mother after individual battles. On June 2, 1862 after describing the battle of Fair Oaks [May 31 to June 1] he asked: "Will you have two copies of this made and send one to Arabella and the other to Bliss [his law partner]. Send Arabella's first and at once. I can't write three copies…" and on July 2, 1862 after the Seven Days Battles [June 25 to July 1]: "Send this by mail at once to Arabella and telegraph her at once that I am safe and unhurt."[13]

By the end of the Seven Days Battles Arabella had joined the Sanitary Commission as a nurse and arrived at Harrison's Landing on June 2 to care for the wounded. "In the Peninsula campaign she was one of those ladies who worked hard and nobly, close to the battle-field…."[14] Arabella was at Harrison's Landing for a week before Barlow found her. On July 12 he wrote: "She is at the large Harrison House which is used as a hospital. The ladies have a very pleasant and well furnished room to themselves and it is very pleasant…."[15] But by August Barlow com-

"Berkeley," the Harrison House at Harrison's Landing.
(Virginia State Library and Archives)

plained of the hospital's atmosphere: "...the heat was most intense and stifling, and the flies, mosquitos [*sic*] and other bugs numerous and vigorous."[16] Arabella stayed at Harrison's Landing until early September. Barlow wrote from a camp near Rockville, Maryland, on September 6, 1862, "...on reaching camp...I found Arabella who had followed me."[17]

The Antietam Campaign [September 1862] commenced and the Army of the Potomac caught up with the Army of Northern Virginia at the bloody battlefield of Antietam on the 17th. Arabella appeared while the battle still raged and later wrote to a friend that she had arrived on the scene "to see Col. Barlow brought in from the battle of Sharpsburg 'Mortally wounded' as the surgeon there said [he was hit in the groin by a spherical case ball]...We came from the little hospital in Keedysville [the School House Hospital] to a charming little quiet farm house [the Samuel Deaner house] a mile from the village where we have pure air good nourishing food and every incentive to get well...."[18]

George Templeton Strong, on the battlefield attached to the Sanitary Commission, saw Arabella and noted, "In the crowd of ambulances, army wagons, beef-cattle, staff officers, recruits, kicking mules and so on, who should suddenly turn up but Mrs. Arabella Barlow, nee Griffith, unattended, but serene and self-possessed as if walking down Broadway. She is nursing the colonel... and never looked so well. Talked like a sensible, practical earnest, warm-hearted woman...."[19]

It took Barlow seven months to recuperate from the wound he received at Antietam. He was back with the army as Brigadier General of a division in the XI Corps on April 16, 1863. Arabella joined him on the 24th in time for the Gettysburg Campaign.

Barlow's painful convalescence after Gettysburg was followed by two months of recruiting in New York and New England and he returned to field duty in Virginia on April 1, 1864. On May 18 he wrote, "Arabella is at Fredericksburg 10 miles off but I have not and cannot see her."[20]

The town of Fredericksburg, Virginia, and its people suffered greatly during the war. In 1864 it was one vast hospital. A friend and sister laborer described Arabella's work:

> At Fredericksburg she had in some way gained possession of a wretched-looking pony, and a small cart or farmers wagon, with which she was continually on the move, driving about town or country in search of provisions or other articles as were needed for the sick and wounded. The surgeon in charge had on one occasion assigned her the task of

preparing a building, which had been taken for a hospital, for a large number of wounded who were expected immediately. I went with my daughter to the building. It was empty, containing not the slightest furniture or preparation for the sufferers, save a large number of bed-sacks, without straw or other material to fill them.

On requisition a quantity of straw was obtained, but not nearly enough for the expected need, and we were standing in a kind of mute despair, considering if it were indeed possible to secure any comfort for the poor fellows expected, when Mrs. Barlow came in. 'I'll find some straw,' was her cheerful reply, and in another moment she was urging her tired beast toward another part of town where she remembered having seen half a bale of the desired article earlier in the day. Half an hour afterward the straw had been confiscated, loaded upon the little wagon by willing hands, and brought to the hospital. She then helped to fill and arrange the sacks, and afterwards drove about town in search of articles, which, by the time the ambulances brought in their freight of misery and pain, had served to furnish the place with some means of alleviation.[21]

Many a fractured limb rested upon a mattress improvised from materials sought out and brought together from no one knew where but [that] earnest sympathizing woman.[22]

Arabella left with the last hospital transport out of Fredericksburg to Port Royal, then on to White House Landing, all hospital sites, where she worked in the latter with another nurse, Cornelia Hancock. In June 1864 Arabella and Cornelia spent a week at the front after the battle of Cold Harbor [June 3]. Hancock wrote, "I left White House Station at the urgent solicitations of Mrs. Major General Barlow to visit the front with the view of establishing a feeding station for the wounded on their road in from the front hospital to the rear hospital."[23]

The Army of the Potomac crossed the James River on June 14, 1864, to lay siege to Petersburg, Virginia. One of the army doctors remembered Arabella at this place: "Mrs. Gen. Barlow, who had been with us a few days at the Tyler House [a hospital site at Cold Harbor] visited us again at this point, and was kept busy in preparing milk punch, which she administered to the wounded with her own hands."[24]

Arabella fell seriously ill at this time and went back to D.C. for better medical treatment than she could receive at City Point. As soon as she improved she returned to the front and her husband. But a re-lapse soon indicated the need to return to D.C. Wracked with fever, Arabella said good-by to her husband on July 6.

On July 15, 1864, General Barlow wrote to his mother: "Arabella has been seriously ill but the fever is broken and in time she will be well again."[25] Nine days later to his brother: "Arabella is sick in Washington and I fear dangerously. She is all run down with fever."[26]

The following notice appeared in the New York *Herald* on July 31, 1864: "Died in Washington, July 27, 1864, Mrs. Arabella Griffith Barlow, wife of Brigadier General Francis C. Barlow, of fever contracted while in attendance upon the hospitals of the Army of the Potomac at the front."

An army doctor described Mrs. Barlow's decline:

> Her exhausting work at Fredericksburg, where the largest powers of administration were displayed, left but a small measure of vitality with which to encounter the severe exposures of the poisoned swamps of the Pamunky [where White House was located] and the malarias districts of City Point [hospital site on the James River]. Here, in the open fields, she toiled with Mr. Marshal and Miss Gilson, under the scorching sun, with no shelter from the pouring rains, with no thought but for those who were suffering and dying all around her. On the battle-field of Petersburg, hardly out of range of the enemy, and at night witnessing the blazing lines of fire from right to left, among the wounded, with her sympathies and powers of both mind and body strained to the last degree, neither conscious that she was working beyond her strength, nor realizing the extreme exhaustion of her system, she fainted at her work and found, only when it was too late, that the raging fever was wasting her life away. It was strength of will which sustained her in this intense activity, when her poor, tired body was trying to assert its own right to repose. Yet to the last, her sparkling wit, her brilliant intellect, her unfailing good humor, lighted up our moments of rest and recreation. So many memories of her beautiful constancy and self-sacrifice, of her bright and genial companionship, of her rich and glowing sympathies, of her warm and loving nature come back to me, that I feel how inadequate any tribute I could pay her worth.[27]

Miss Helen Gilson, the nurse mentioned above, wrote a friend about two weeks after Arabella died: "You say I am getting familiar with death. Yes; but death wears its most solemn aspect when it touches our individual lives. Sometimes it makes terrible voids in our hearts. I groaned aloud last night, so heavy was my heart, when I knew I should not again see Mrs. Barlow."[28]

Arabella Wharton Griffith Barlow was buried alongside her brothers in the Old Sommerville Cemetery in Sommervile, New Jersey. In 1996 a plaque was laid at her gravesite due to the efforts of the Somerville American Legion. I had the honor to provide the inscription. It reads "Arabella Barlow served as a nurse during the Peninsula, Antietam and Gettysburg Campaigns. In 1861 she married General Frances Channing Barlow whom she twice nursed back to life from grievous wounds. She nursed at hospital sites at Fredericksburg, Port Royal, White House and City Point 'with no thought but for those who were suffering and dying all around her.'"

Arabella Barlow's tombstone simply reads:
Arabella Wharton Griffith, wife of Frances C. Barlow,
died at Washington, D.C. July 24, 1864.
(Deborah Novotny)

Frances Haralson Gordon

Wife of Confederate General Gordon

"O, John, how can I stay away from you…I wonder if it is generally known that I am not with you…"[1]

Fanny Gordon's presence in her husband's command throughout the war was so consistently noted that she was conspicuous by her absence at Gettysburg. "…[S]he was found ever near behind the lines, ready to minister to every call that came…Unused to hardships, she faced privations and danger undaunted and was the ministering angel in attendance upon the sick and wounded and in closing the eyes of the dying, with a prayer on her lips for the surviving mothers far away."[2]

No one, including her husband, knew where she was. In General Gordon's open, loving letters to "My Own Precious Wife" written during the Gettysburg campaign, his ignorance of her whereabouts troubled him greatly. On June 7 he wrote to her: "I am exceedingly anxious to hear from you My Darling. I want to know where you are."[3] General Gordon located a "safe" house in Shepherdstown, Virginia, where Fanny could stay and wrote on June 20: "You would be so much nearer to me—if I should be wounded you could be with me so soon."[4]

On June 23 when General Gordon's command was just over the Pennsylvania line he again wrote: "I have no idea where you are…" but guessed she may have been in Staunton, Virginia, where he had previously suggested she go. All the letters the General wrote to Mrs. Gordon were returned to him that day as no one else knew where to forward them. Only five letters from the Gettysburg campaign survive in the Gordon papers. The letter of the 23rd expressed his "sad disappointment" and "depression of spirit" that his letters were returned and that no more mail would go south from the Confederate army because "the danger will be too great." In what could well have been his last communication to his wife, General Gordon began a section, "My *angel,* God only knows how much I love you, "that evolved into a ten page testament of love, ending with "*My sweet girl, My Fanny*—goodbye."[5]

Finally, sometime between July 7 and 10, the General received a letter from Mrs. Gordon. It was in this letter she expressed her wish to

Photo circa 1853 of a young Fanny between two of her sisters.
(Hargrett Rare Book and Manuscript Library)

come to Hagerstown, Maryland, but since the Confederates were in retreat from Gettysburg at that time, he suggested she come only as far as
Martinsburg. "If you come there go to the family of Mrs. Boyd—mother
of Miss Belle Boyd."[6] Presumably the couple was reunited as soon as
possible.

In sharp contrast to Arabella Barlow's life which could provide the
plot of a tragic Victorian novel, Fanny Gordon's story had all the necessary ingredients of a romantic legend.

Frances Rebecca Haralson was born September 18, 1837 in
LaGrange, Georgia. She was the third of four daughters of Clara and
Hugh A. Haralson; her father was an attorney and state congressman.
By all accounts Fanny was a tomboy and possessed an adventuresome
spirit. She married John B. Gordon, a 22 year old lawyer, on her seventeenth birthday. "The courtship was fast and furious…'Fanny, he [the
General]once laughingly asked in the presence of guests, 'was it two
weeks that I knew you before we were engaged?' 'No, John,' she corrected, 'it was three weeks.'"[7] The Gordon's marriage took place at the
bedside of her dying father. In the next five years their union produced
two boys: Hugh born in 1855 and Frank born in 1857.

When war was imminent this devoted couple was faced with an agonizing decision. General Gordon explained:

The struggle between devotion to my family on the one hand and duty to my country on the other was most trying to my sensibilities. My spirit had been caught up in the flaming enthusiasm that swept like a prairie fire through the land...But what was I to do with the girl-wife and the two little boys? The wife and mother was no less taxed in her effort to settle this momentous question. But finally yielding to the promptings of her own heart and to her unerring sense of duty she ended doubt as to what disposition was to be made of her by announcing that she intended to accompany me to the war, leaving the children with my mother and faithful 'Mammy Mary' [a slave who brought up Fanny and remained with her after the Gordon's marriage]. I rejoiced at her decision and had still greater reasons for rejoicing at it afterwards, when I felt through every fiery ordeal the inspiration of her near presence, and had at need, the infinite comfort of her tender nursing."[8]

Although she saw them as often as possible, the separation from her children was always hard on Fanny. In a letter near the end of the war, she lamented, "I want my child so much...I want my boy."[9]

By July 1861 Mrs. Gordon was in Culpepper, Virginia, with her husband's unit, the 6th Alabama, and at Christmas that year she "superintended the preparation of this famous Christmas beverage [egg nog]."[10]

In June of 1862 there was the military rush to reinforce Confederate Brigadier General John B. Magruder who faced the threat of Union Major General George B. McClellan's large army at Yorktown, Virginia. Long trains raced Confederate soldiers toward Richmond. The Gordon's train crashed head on with another. John Gordon described the scene: "Nearly every car on the densely packed train was telescoped and torn in pieces; and men, knapsacks, arms, and shivered seats were hurled to the front and piled in a horrid mass against the crushed timbers and ironwork. Many were killed, many maimed for life, and the marvel is that any escaped unhurt. Mrs. Gordon, who was with me on this ill-fated train was saved by a merciful Providence, without the slightest injury. Her hands were busied with the wounded, while I superintended the cutting away of debris to rescue the maimed and removed the dead."[11]

Both Gordons endured the Seven Days Battles [June 25 to July 1, 1862]. Fanny's uncle, Major S. Lewis, described his niece's reactions to the fighting at that time:

The battle in which Mrs. Gordon's husband was then engaged was raging near the city with great fury. The cannonade was rolling around the horizon like some vast earthquake on huge crashing wheels. Whether the threads of wedded sympathy were twisted more closely as the tremendous perils gathered around him, it was evident that her anxiety became more and more intense with each passing moment. She asked me to accompany her to a hill a short distance away. There she listened in silence. Pale and quiet, with clasped hands, she sat statue-like, with her face toward the field of battle. Her self-control was wonderful: only the quick drawn sigh from the bottom of the heart revealed the depth of emotion that was struggling there. The news of her husband's safety afterward and the joy of meeting him later produced the inevitable reaction. The intensity of mental strain to which she had been subjected had overtasked her strength, and when the excessive tension was relaxed she was well-nigh prostrated; but a brief repose enabled her to bear up with a sublime fortitude through the protracted and trying experiences which followed the seven day's battles around Richmond.[12]

All the women following the armies had to deal with the anxiety of battle. Some faced it with remarkable coolness and others, like Fanny, never got used to it. Fanny endured her personal anxiety through the strength and solace she found in her religious faith. In a letter to her husband during a battle late in the war she wrote:

…[S]ince I began to write the cannons have begun to boom. It is a fearful sound to me, but let us pray O God answer the prayers that are lifted this day for deliverance. The battle is not always to the strong. O Lord in Thee do we put out trust…You tell me John to pray that God's spirit may be present with you at all times. I do my darling. I pray that even more than for your safety. My constant prayer is that God's spirit may dwell in your heart always and that by it you may be directed in all that you do & then I pray that his protecting wings may be spread over you & around you & that in the hour of battle you may be unharmed. Sometimes in my prayers I have sweet assurances that God will hear & answer me. Even now while I write and the cannons are booming, my heart is lifted in prayer to God & I feel that though they may be bursting around the form of my loved one, yet, God will cover his head and bring him safely through it all. O John let us cultivate a spirit of perfect trust in God. How long O God how long shall this last?[13]

The Gordon's worst trial came late in 1862. At Sharpsburg [battle of Antietam—September 17, 1862] Mrs. Gordon nursed her husband, "the broken shape of a man" who suffered five gunshot wounds, the last of which hit him directly in the face. He was not expected to live. The General remembered:

> Mrs. Gordon was soon with me. When it was known that the battle was on, she had at once started toward the front. The doctors were doubtful about the propriety of admitting her to my room; but I told them to let her come. I was more apprehensive of the effect of the meeting upon her nerves than upon mine. My face was black and shapeless—so swollen that one eye was entirely hidden and other nearly so. My right leg and left arm and shoulder were bandaged and propped with pillows. I knew she would be greatly shocked. As she reached the door and looked, I saw at once that I must reassure her. Summoning all my strength, I said: 'Here's your handsome (?) husband; been to an Irish wedding.' Her answer was a suppressed scream, whether of anguish or relief at finding me able to speak, I do not know. Thenceforward, for the period in which my life hung in the balance, she sat at my bedside, trying to supply concentrated nourishment to sustain me against the constant drainage. With my jaw immovably set, this was exceedingly difficult and discouraging. My own confidence in ultimate recovery, however, was never shaken until erysipelas, that deadly foe of the wounded, attacked my left arm. The doctors told Mrs. Gordon to paint my arm above the wound three or four times a day with iodine. She obeyed the doctors by painting it, I think, three or four hundred times a day. Under God's providence, I owe my life to her incessant watchfulness night and day, and to her tender nursing through weary weeks and anxious months.[14]

The General carried a facial scar for the rest of his life from this battle. Fanny referred to it as "John's Yankee dimple."

Mrs. Gordon rode about the camps on her husband's horse. Sometimes housing was procured for her, other times she tented. Mammy Mary would bring the boys up when the army went into winterquarters and whenever else it was practicable. Mrs. Gordon's presence, however, was not enjoyed by everyone.

[Confederate] General [Jubal] Early, hearing of her constant presence, is said to have exclaimed, "I wish the Yankees would capture Mrs. Gordon and hold her till the war is over!" Near Winchester [Virginia], as the wagon-trains were being parked for the night, he discovered a conveyance unlike any of the others that were going into camp. He immediately called to his quartermaster in excited tones: "What's that?" "That is Mrs. Gordon's carriage, sir," replied the officer. "Well, I'll be

_____! If my men could keep up as she does, I'd never have to issue another order against straggling.

Mrs. Gordon was fully aware of the general's sentiments, and had heard of his wishing for her capture; and during a camp dinner given in honor of General [Richard S.] Ewell, she sat near General Early and good-naturedly rallied him about it. He was momentarily embarrassed, but rose to the occasion and replied: "Mrs. Gordon, General Gordon is a better soldier when you are close by than when you are away, and so hereafter, when I issue orders that officer's wives must go to the rear, you may know that you are excepted." This gallant reply called forth a round of applause from the officers at the table.[15]

Yet as late as October 1864 Fanny wrote: "Have you seen anything of Genl. Early or heard any news of his ill natured remarks?"[16]

In September of 1864 at one of the battles of Winchester, Fanny was nearly captured.

As the fighting was near Winchester, through which Mrs. Gordon was compelled to pass in going to the rear, she drove rapidly down the pike in that direction. Her light conveyance was drawn by two horses driven by a faithful negro boy, who was as anxious to escape as she. As she overtook the troops of [Confederate General Robert E.] Rodes' division, marching to the aid of [Confederate General Stephen D.] Ranseur, and drove into their midst, a cloud of dust loomed up in the rear, and a wild clatter of hoofs announced, "Cavalry in pursuit!" General Rodes halted a body of his men, and threw them in line across the pike, just behind Mrs. Gordon's carriage, as she hurried on, urged by the solicitude of the "boys in gray" around her. In crossing the wide stream, which they were compelled to ford, the tongue of the carriage broke loose from the axle. The horses, went on, but Mrs. Gordon, the driver, and carriage were left in the middle of the stream. She barely escaped; for the detachment of Union cavalry were still in pursuit as a number of Confederate soldiers rushed into the stream, dragged the carriage out, and by some temporary makeshift attached the tongue and started her again on her flight.[17]

Fanny was able to reach Winchester and a safe house. General Gordon described the next time he saw her:

> To my horror, as I rode among my disorganized troops through Winchester I found Mrs. Gordon on the street, where the shells from [Union General William T.] Sheridan's batteries were falling and minie

balls flying around her. She was apparently unconscious of the danger, I had supposed that, in accordance with instructions, she had gone to the rear at the opening of the battle, and was many miles away. But she was stopping at the house of her friend Mrs. Hugh Lee, and as the first Confederates began to pass to the rear, she stood upon the veranda, appealing to them to return to the front. Many yielded to her entreaties and turned back—one waggish fellow shouting aloud to his comrades: "Come, boys, let's go back. We might not obey the general, but we can't resist Mrs. Gordon." The fact is, it was the first time in her army experience that she had ever seen the Confederate lines broken. As the different squads passed, she inquired to what command they belonged. When, finally, to her question the answer came, "We are Gordon's men," she lost her self-control, and rushed into the street, urging them to go back and meet the enemy. She was thus engaged when I found her. I insisted that she go immediately into the house, where she would be at least partially protected. She obeyed; but she did not for a moment accept my statement that there was nothing left for her except capture by Sheridan's army. I learned afterward that her negro driver had been frightened by the shells bursting about the stable, and had not brought out her carriage and horses. She acquainted some of my men with these facts. With the assurance, "We'll get it for you, Mrs. Gordon," they broke down the fences and brought the carriage to her a few moments after I had passed on. She sprang into it, and, taking six-year-old Frank and one or two of the wounded officers with her, she was driven rapidly away amidst the flying missiles from Sheridan's advancing troops and with the prayers of my brave men for her safety. [18]

Fall faded into another lean winter for the Confederates. The General related how his wife made the Christmas of 1864 a merry one.

Mrs. Gordon, on leaving home four years before, had placed in her little army trunk a small package of excellent coffee, and had used it only on very special occasions—"to celebrate" as she said, "our victories in the first years, and to sustain us in defeat at the last." When I asked her on the morning of December 25, 1864, what we could do for a Christmas celebration, she replied, "I can give you some of that coffee which I brought from home." She could scarcely have made an announcement more grateful to a hungry Confederate. Coffee—genuine coffee! The aroma of it filled my official family with epicurean enthusiasm before a cup was passed from the boiling pot. If every man of us was not intoxicated by that indulgence after long and enforced abstinence, the hilarity of the party was misleading.[19]

In 1864 Fanny was with her husband but for two exceptions; the battle of Cold Harbor [June 3, 1864] when she was only able to visit him, and, she did not accompany him on Early's Washington Raid [June through August 1864]. But she was present through the Petersburg Campaign [June 1864 to March 1865] which consisted of several major assaults and a good deal of action both north and south of the James River. On March 25, 1865 General Gordon planned and led the attack on Fort Stedman. He described Fanny's efforts: "For hours Mrs. Gordon sat in her room in Petersburg, tearing strips of white cloth to tie across the breast of the leading detachments, that they might recognize each other in the darkness and in the hand-to-hand battle expected at the Federal breastworks and inside the fort."[20]

A resident of Petersburg, Mrs. S. J. Grant, described the city during the time that Fanny spent there:

> During the siege the church bells could not be rung, for the Yankees would commence firing at the church steeples. Later preaching in the churches had to be stopped altogether, as the cannonading would commence just at the hour for services. Funerals had to be conducted in the homes, and burials were made in the farthest churchyards as the cemetery was too near the lines…Things became so hot and the soldiers so numerous, and there was …much distress and sickness in the city…Many little children died from heat and exposure during the siege…before the city was evacuated, things were comparatively quiet, with less cannonading, but we knew Lee was withdrawing his troops…On Sunday night our troops began to march out of the city. No one went to bed, and all night we could hear the tramp, tramp, tramp of passing feet. All else was quiet save for the picket-firing along the lines. [21]

General Gordon, too, marched out of Petersburg with the Confederate army and the "depressing realization" that the end was near. "But another burden—a personal woe—was weighing upon me. I had left behind me in that city of gloom the wife who had followed me during the entire war. She was ill. But as I rode away from Petersburg during the dismal hours of that night, I found comfort in the hope that some chivalric soldier of the Union army would learn of her presence and guard her home against all intruders."[22]

The civilians of Petersburg were no less apprehensive. Mrs. Grant explained: "…we were kept in suspense, not knowing what the Yankees would do when they took possession…With the dawn

Mrs. Fanny Gordon, circa 1865.
(Hargrett Rare Book and Manuscript Library)

on Monday the city was filled with bluecoats, and all day long the stream of soldiers, wagons, and carriages passed up the main road…[Union General] Grant had given orders that citizens in their own homes were not to be molested."[23]

"Under such conditions was Fanny's third son born—John B. Gordon, Jr…General Grant soon learned of this woman's tragic situation. Her name, of course, was quite well known to him…Mrs. Gordon was assured that her household would be guarded by sentries charged to protect her with their lives."[24]

On April 12, 1865, three days after Lee's surrender at Appomattox, Fanny received a telegram from her husband: "I am well and will be in Petersburg in a few days." The next day as he traveled closer, he again telegraphed: "Let me know by telegraph how you are. I will be down tomorrow."[25]

When General Gordon reached the Petersburg house where Fanny was "…he found an armed guard of Federal soldiers around his house. 'We are here by General Grant's orders to protect General Gordon's wife from intrusion at this time,' said the officer in charge, 'You cannot pass.' 'Well, I'm just Mrs. Gordon's husband,' admitted the soldier…"[26]

"I found Mrs. Gordon rapidly recovering, and as soon as she was able to travel…we began our arduous trip homeward, over broken railroads and in such dilapidated conveyances as had been left in the tracks of the armies."[27]

"The long, long journey back to Georgia. Fanny was twenty-seven, veteran of a score of battlefields. Her husband at thirty-three was the youngest officer of his rank…Their Atlanta home, Sutherland, was the refuge of Fanny and General Gordon."[28] In the war's aftermath of total despair, ruin, and loss, the Gordon's true wealth remained intact.

John Gordon embarked on a long political career after the war as a U.S. senator and the governor of Georgia, always with Fanny at his side. "He never failed to try and make her the partner of his triumphs and popularity. At many of the reunions the old veterans accorded her as great an ovation as they gave the commander."[29] Fanny was also active in Southern women's memorial associations. The Gordons were blessed with two more children: Frances, born in 1868 and Caroline, born in 1873. However, in 1884 they suffered John Jr.'s death, the boy who had been born in Petersburg. Fanny enjoyed a life with the General for over fifty years, "…his every spare moment was devoted to her and that home. Every spring he planted Cape-jasmines. Every winter they died."[30]

"Sutherland," the home of Fanny and General Gordon.
The structure suffered a fire in 1898 and was restored while the
Gordons still lived there. This photo was taken after the restoration.
(Hargrett Rare Book and Manuscript Library)

John B. Gordon died in 1904. Fanny survived him twenty-seven years. She was one of the founders of the United Daughters of the Confederacy and remained active in other Confederate organizations then accompanied by her children and grandchildren. In the spring of 1931 Fanny fell ill for about a week, then slipped into a coma. "Until the last she retained her faculties and delighted in relating her experiences when, as the young wife of the General, she was 'among those present' at a number of battles in which he was engaged."[31]

Fanny Gordon died on April 28, 1931 at the age of 93. She was buried in Oakland Cemetery in Atlanta next to the General. "…[H]er gentle, gracious memory will always linger, inseparately interwoven with the history and most cherished ideals of the South…"[32]

> "The tender graces of a day that is dead
> And the sound of a voice that is still." [33]

This photograph was taken on Mrs. Gordon's last birthday.
(Hargrett Rare Book and Manuscript Library)

The state of Georgia honored its Confederate women with three monuments. They are located in Macon, Thomson, and Rome. This photo is a detail of the one in Rome.

(Hargrett Rare Book and Manuscript Library)

Fanny Gordon was a founder of the United Daughters of the Confederacy. This monument honors the "true daughters of the Confederacy," and was erected in 1973 in the Oakland Cemetery where Mrs. Gordon and the General are buried.

(Hargrett Rare Book and Manuscript Library)

Lucinda Horne

Nurse, Co. K, 14th South Carolina

*"I have often thought that had it not been for this good woman
I might be numbered with the many whose bones have been
left in Virginia..."*[1]

The 14th South Carolina was in the last division to leave
Fredericksburg, Virginia, on the Gettysburg Campaign. Descriptions
of the march found in these veteran's narratives were similar to the
other soldier's accounts: "most oppressive heat," "men fainted," "hardest
rain possible," "much rain and mud." Another predominant theme was
the pride in the conduct of the Confederate invaders: "I felt perfectly
clear in the asserting, that no invading army ever showed themselves so
tender of the property, persons and feelings of the inhabitants as we did.
The citizens were amazed at our moderation."[2]

As part of McGowan's brigade [commanded by Colonel Abner
Perrin], the 14th South Carolina fought the Federals along Seminary
Ridge on the morning of July 1 and played an important part in the
break of the Union I Corps line and subsequent rout through town. Their
losses were great: brigade casualties at 647, the 14th's at 252.

A veteran of Company K said, "This was the most disastrous battle
of the war to our company. Its casualties on that day [July 1] were equal
to all the rest from that time to the close of the war. As well as my
memory serves me, we went into battle with 43 men. Thirty-seven were
killed or wounded, only six being able to march back to Virginia."[3] "I
remember three, at least, died of their wounded at the Field Hospital in
less than 26 hours."[4] The 14th's wounded were taken to their division
field hospital down near Marsh Creek on Chambersburg Pike. Laboring in that field hospital was Lucinda Horne of South Carolina.

"Always just before a battle she would find out where the field
hospital would be and she was always there to minister to the wounded
and dying."[5] Both Lucinda's husband and son, who were members of
the 14th, came through the battle of Gettysburg unscathed; they were
not so lucky elsewhere. "...[H]er ministrations were not confined to
her own loved ones, but many a mother's boy was comforted, and his
dying hour made easier, by her presence."[6]

The Horne family lived near Kirksey in Edgefield County, South Carolina before the war. Lucinda was approximately 46 years of age, Cornelius [nicknamed Neal], approximately 40 and their only son, William, about 20. William enlisted in Co. K of the 14th in August 1861: Cornelius followed in November 1861. "Her whole being wrapped up in the lives of her husband and son, she also volunteered and went to the front with them. She remained with them until close of the war, undergoing all the hardships incident to a soldier's life."[7] "She was an earnest Christian woman, and her motive in submitting herself to the hardships of war seems to have been a desire to do good. [Lucinda] was an unassuming and modest woman from the ordinary walks of life…"[8] as were the men in Co. K "who had no aristocrats among them. They owned but few slaves, but were sturdy yeomen, and did their own work."[9] [Lucinda] lived among the men in the ranks…and worked with her hands, doing the humble tasks of cooking and washing.…"[10]

"She was with her husband and son in [the army's] hard marches [and] always on hand when the regiment went into camp and prepared their scanty meals. When in winterquarters she took in washing besides her own, thus making some money, which added to their supplies. Her husband and son wore cleaner clothes and which were nicely patched by her industry through her love for them." Lucinda always referred to her husband as "he," as if there were no other man to whom the pronoun could apply. "She was loved and respected by every member of McGowan's Brigade."[11]

The 14th South Carolina spent their initial months of duty guarding the coast. In May of 1862 they became part of Gregg's Brigade and with five other brigades formed Major General A. P. Hill's famous "Light Division." By January 1863 they would be commanded by Brigadier General Samuel McGowan and would be known by that name until the end of the war.

The regiment participated in the battles around Richmond in June and July 1862. "The battle of Frazier's Farm [June 30, 1862] was among the most complicated affairs I ever witnessed. The Fourteenth regiment was long and furiously engaged. Without knowing what was going on, except that a fire came upon them from the front, they kept up an incessant fusillade till after dark, yielding no inch of ground."[12] The casualties in the 14th were 11 killed, 65 wounded. Lucinda's husband was among the wounded.

"She went on up into Virginia, and really suffered with the boys. She knew what it meant not to be well fed, and to have felt keen cold, as she sat in her little tent. Whatever was the lot of her husband, she shared it. Many a boy has been doctored on and made well by Mrs. Horne, and when she could get things to cooks for them, she was untiring in her efforts for them.

She really loved the boys as she called them and at one time helped them in some of their foraging, although she told them they must not do such things again. One of the boys had slipped off and got some chickens…from a nearby farmyard. He was about to be caught up with, and slipping the chickens to Mrs. Horne, asked her to save him.

She was seated on a box in a tent sewing. She seized them and thrust them under the box, and sewed right on. An officer came in asked the solder if he was guilty of having two chickens on his person.

He said, "Search me, sir, and you will see for yourself." The officer then said, "Then you have hid them in the tent," and asked Mrs. Horne's permission to search which she cheerfully gave, and sewed steadily on. The officer glanced about and then walked out. The chickens were given to the soldier."[13]

The Hornes marched along with their regiment to participate in the battles of Second Manassas [August 29-30, 1862], Ox Hill [September 1], the capture of Harpers Ferry [September 15], Sharpsburg [September 17], and Shepherdstown [September 20]. Afterwards they camped around Berryville and Winchester, Virginia until November 22 when they commenced a 175 mile march made in twelve days to Fredericksburg. After the battle of Fredericksburg [December 13, 1862] they went into winterquarters. Because of Jackson's death after the battle of Chancellorsville [May 3, 1863], the army was reshuffled and McGowan's Brigade was turned over to the command of Colonel Abner Perrin.

After Gettysburg the Horne Family continued to share the fate of the 14th through the fall and winter of 1863 and summer of 1864. "I remember…while we were in line of battle near Petersburg in September, 1864, we had a fight at a place called Jones Farm and in this battle her [Lucinda's] son William was wounded, and the kindhearted mother was ready to wait on her only son. She went with him to the hospital in Richmond and nursed him so as to be able to return home with him."[14] William was indeed seriously wounded and was admitted to Jackson Hospital in Richmond on October 2, 1864. He stayed there until issued a passport on December 21 for a wounded furlough to South Carolina for 60 days. Lucinda went with him. Cornelius was also "sick at field infirmary" from September to December 1864 and was hospitalized at Jackson Hospital in Richmond from October 7 to 16 with neuralgia. The family would not be reunited until the following year.

It is not known when Lucinda and William returned to the 14th. Cornelius was paroled at Appomattox Court House on April 9, 1865 and Williams' incomplete war records show he was admitted to the U.S.A. Transport Hospital in New York City on June 23, 1865 and sent home sometime the following month.

"After the war Mr. & Mrs. Horne and their son were living happily together when the son was so unfortunate as to be thrown by a mule he was riding, and the fall so injured his wound as to cause his death [July 16, 1885]. The son had married sometime before his death."[15] The following year, Willie, one of William's children, age 7 died. Cornelius and "Aunt Cindy" as she was known, took up peddling at this time. They would travel back and forth to Augusta in a covered wagon purchasing pottery and selling it throughout Edgefield County. "On one occasion they undertook to cross Half Way Swamp Creek when the water was too deep and they came very near drowning. Providentially, they escaped with their lives and but little damage to their goods."[16] "Mrs. Horne met with a reunion of the old Fourteenth Regiment at Greenwood, South Carolina in August 1891 and she was unanimously elected an honorary member of the same...."[17]

Lucinda Horne died on February 29, 1896 at age 82. She was buried in Chestnut Hill Cemetery in Saluda along with her granddaughter, son, and later her husband. "To the Confederate Veterans of Edgefield

The Horne family plot at the Chestnut Hill Cemetery outside of Saluda, South Carolina. Lucinda's stone, erected by veterans, is the tall one on the right.
(Author's collection)

and Saluda Counties, South Carolina belongs the honor of being the first organization to raise a monument commemorative of the heroism and noble deeds of a woman during our dark days of war."[18] Lucinda's monument was unveiled in July 1897. "For many years a volley was fired over her grave on Confederate Memorial Day."[19] In December of 1905 the Lucinda Horne U.D.C. Chapter #947 was formed and remained active for many years. In 1972 the Saluda County Historical Commission erected a plaque honoring Mrs. Horne at the entrance to the Chestnut Hill Cemetery.

The stone over Lucinda Horne's grave, erected by grateful veterans, reads:

> She followed her husband and only son throughout
> The Confederate War Illustrating the uncomplaining endurance,
> the sublime physical and moral heroism, the unwavering patriotism,
> devotion, the unsubdued spirit of Confederate women.
>
> History reposing at the base of this humble tomb will challenge the
> admiring attention of all coming generations.

**The dedication in the early 1900s of the monument to
South Carolina's Confederate women in front of the State House
in Columbia, South Carolina.**
(South Carolina Library, University of South Carolina)

Mary McAllister

Gettysburg Civilian

*"We locked the doors and went upstairs and thought we could
bar them out. But soon the wounded ones came in so fast
and they took them in different houses and into the church"*[1]

Miss Mary McAllister [age 41] lived on Chambersburg Street with
her sister and brother-in-law, Martha and John Scott. The building
housed their residence and their general store. Chambersburg Street
was one of the main arteries for the Union retreat through town on July
1; Mary and her sister were in the thick of it. John Scott had kept his
post at the telegraph office until the Confederates entered Gettysburg.
Then he left town.

Mary described the first wounded man she encountered: "The soldier was on a white horse...The blood was running down out of the
wound over the horse...They got him off the horse and they let the
horse go. They brought him into our house and Martha and I put him on
the lounge, and I didn't know what in the world to do."

Mary and a neighbor, Mrs. Weikert, then went across the street from
the Scott house to help the wounded in Christ Lutheran Church. This
church was one of the first sites where the wounded were gathered.

> They carried the wounded in there as fast as they could. We took the
> cushions off the seats and some of the officers came in and said, "Lay them
> in the aisles." Then we did all we could for the wounded men. After a
> while they carried in an awfully wounded one. He was a fine officer. They
> did not know who he was. A doctor said to me, "Go bring some wine or
> whiskey or some stimulant!" When I got outside I thought of Mr. Guyer
> near the church. "Well," I said, "Mr. Guyer, can you give me some wine?"
> He said, "The rebels will be in here if you begin to carry that out." "I must
> have it," I said. "Give me some." I put it under my apron and went over to
> the church with it. They poured some of it into the officer's mouth. I never
> knew who he was, but he died.
>
> Well, I went to doing what they told me to do, wetting cloths and
> putting them on the wounds and helping. Every pew was full; some
> lying, some leaning on others. They cut off legs and arms and threw

43

Across the street from Miss McAllister's house was the Christ Lutheran Church where she helped look after the wounded. This church was one of the first hospital sites of the battle.
(GNMP)

them out of the windows. Every morning the dead were laid on the platform in a sheet or blanket and carried away.

Mary McAllister came across one young man who had four fingers nearly severed off. "He said, 'Lady, would you do something for me?' The surgeon came along and he said, 'What is the use doing anything for them?' and just took his knife and cut off the fingers and they dropped. Well, I was so sorry."

Another soldier asked her to fetch a Mason in town, but she was too frightened to accommodate him. The fraternity of the organization of Masons was often called upon by the wounded or dying during the war, regardless of what color uniform the sufferer wore. If one Mason found another it was almost a guarantee that help would be provided.

The church was full and just then…[a] shell struck the roof and they got scared, and I was scared. I wanted to go home…Well, they begged me not to go, but I went out and there the high church steps were full of wounded men and they begged me not to try to cross the street. Our men were retreating up the street. Many wounded ones who could walk carried the worst ones on their backs. I said, "Oh, I want to go home." So they let me go at last. I struggled through the wounded and dead and forgot the horror in the fright.

Mary crossed the street to her home unscathed. "When I came to the door it was standing open and the step was covered in blood. 'Oh,' I thought, 'All are dead!' and I ran through. I could hardly get through for the dining room was full of soldiers, some lying, some standing. Some ran in to get out of the shooting. The Rebels were sending grapeshot down the street and everyone who was on the street had to get into the houses or be killed…"

Colonel Henry Morrow of the 24th Michigan who had a slight head wound was one of the soldiers in her home. Mary asked him,

Mary McAllister stands in the doorway of her sister's house on Chambersburg Street. On July 1 she "came to the door, it was standing open and the step was covered with blood."
(Adams County Historical Society)

"Can I do anything for you?" He said, "Yes, if you would just wash this handkerchief out." I rushed to get water and I washed it out and laid it on his head." Another officer in the house was Lieutenant Dailey of the 2nd Wisconsin. "He was so mad when he found out what a trap they were in. He leaned out of the kitchen window and saw the bayonets of the rebels bristling in the alley and in the garden. I said, "There is no escape there." I opened the kitchen door and they were tearing the fence down with their bayonets. Dailey…says, "I am not going to be taken prisoner, Colonel!" and he says to me, "Where can I hide?" I said, "I don't know, but you can go upstairs." "No," he says, "but I will go up the chimney." "You will not," said the Colonel. "You must not endanger this family." So he came back. He was so mad he gritted his teeth. Then he says to me, "Take this sword, and keep it at all hazards. This is General Archer's sword. He surrendered it to me. I will come back for it." I ran to the kitchen, got some wood and threw some sticks on top of it.[2]

Col. Morrow says to me, "Take my diary. I do not want them to get it." I did not know where to put it, so I opened my dress and put it in my dress. He said, "That's the place, they will not get it there!" Then all those wounded men crowded around and gave me their addresses. Then Lt. Dailey had another request. "Here is my pocketbook. I wish you would keep it." Afterward I did not remember what I did with it, but what I did was to pull the little red cupboard away and put it back of that. In the meantime Martha had gone upstairs and brought a coat of John's. She said, "Here, Colonel, put this coat on." But he would not take the coat she brought him. He would not stoop to disguise himself and he gave the others orders that they were to give their right names when they were taken prisoner…Then came a pounding on the door. Col. Morrow said, "You must open the door. They know we are in here and they will break it." By this time the Rebels came in and…demanded his sword….

A young Union soldier said to Mary,

"Do write to my mother. I am slightly wounded, but I guess they will take me prisoner." I had all these addresses, but I mislaid his and did not find it until two months afterward. Then I wrote to his mother and the same day she got a letter from him and it seems he had escaped…He was one they took prisoner in the dining room along with Col. Morrow and the rest…the Rebels said, "Those that are not able to walk we will not take; we will parole them." But they said to these wounded men, "Now if you ever fight you know what we will do." But the wounded ones did not pay much attention to that. Then they took away as prisoners all that could walk.[3]

The next thing then was to get these wounded fixed. Then the firing ceased for the evening. That was the time we went upstairs to get some of the wounded ones in bed and to get pillows to make the others as comfortable as we could. Five surgeons came in and one of them said, "Now if you had anything like a red flag, it would be a great protection to your house, because it would be considered a hospital, and they would have respect." Well, Martha thought of a red shawl she had. She got it and I got the broom and we hoisted the front window and were just fixing it on the broom when six or seven Rebels came riding up the street firing and yelling. Well, we did not know what we were doing. They halted at the church [Christ Lutheran where she had been that morning] to say something to the wounded men on the high church steps who had gathered out of range of the firing, and in a few minutes a pistol went off and we saw they had shot a man. He was down then and when we looked, he was lying with his head toward the pavement. And those men on the steps said, "Shame! Shame! That was the Chaplain." Those on horseback said, "He was going to shoot." But the wounded men said, "He was not armed." They had a good many words and then they rode off again, shooting as they had come.

A man kept a little store in Mrs. King's [a neighbor]...but he left town and the Rebels tore off his old bay window on the first evening of the battle. Mrs. King was scared, for she was in the house with her mother and her little children...At night, when it was quiet, there was a Rebel patrol on the street. It was a cloudy, ugly night and Mrs. King said, "We will go over there and ask them to give us a guard." So we went to the church where they had headquarters in the yard. I do not think they were in the basement, for that is where they took the limbs of the wounded ones. Mrs. King said, "Is there an officer among you?" That minute they sat down their guns and were polite. One says, "Come out, Captain!" "Well," Mrs. King said, "your men are breaking our doors down, and I have an old mother that is very feeble, and little children and we want a guard." He said, "Are any of you boys willing to guard these women?" Two stepped front and said, "We will go." They all laughed and said, "You have a snap of it."

They began to lay their blankets down in front of our door and Mrs. King asked them if they had had anything to eat and they said they had not. So she went in and got the biscuits and bread she had and gave [it] to them. It was very damp and I invited them to lay their blankets inside the hall. No, they said, they would rather not. I think they were a little suspicious right away. We began to talk a little. They said, "Well, now, we are Pennsylvanians, too, born and bred in Pennsylvania." I said, "Is that possible?" "Yes," they said, "we were both edu-

47

cated in Washington College, Pennsylvania, and if you had lived in the South you would have been as we are." They were nice men. You could tell they were gentlemen, and we were not molested anymore.

This was the way we had to sleep—Martha and four children lay crossways on a bed in the front room because every other place was full of wounded. I sat on a chair with a shirt folded to lay on the window sill, with the window hoisted. There I slept for three nights, with my head on my arms.

Well, we went through that night as best we could. Next day, the second day of the battle, we went to work—for the Rebels, too. Martha did what she could and I undertook to bake bread. I went on the street and the wounded begged so hard for bread and butter that I started to go…to try to find milk or butter. [Mary went to a neighbor's house on the corner who had refugeed to the countryside.] I knew they had cows in the stable…I said, "I believe I will go milk those cows." But though some women had already milked the cows, they gave me part of a bucket of milk. Just at the…gate lay a dead man, and there were wounded men on the hard pavement. "Oh," they said, "give us a little milk." Well, by the time they all had some, I had hardly a pint left. I gave it out as I came along. Martha said, "Did you get any milk?" I said, "Yes, a little." Indeed we had not much of anything and we were hungry. About all I lived on was strong tea and crackers…which I had hid in the attic and the wounded men could take a few of these. And so we had to live along until the country people began to bring things in after the battle.

"Next, then, the wounded officers upstairs were making me go for some liquor." Mary procured a canteen full of whiskey at a drug store and while she was there an artillery shell burst through the store's front door. She delivered the whiskey to the officers. "…[T]hey took the whiskey and divided it and you can tell it brought song. So I never went for any more."

The wounded ones downstairs were the ones I was most interested in. All this time one poor man suffered awful. He was struck with a bullet and it came around. You could see it in his back. I went into Mrs. Belle King's where there was a good many surgeons and I begged them to come over and look at this man. But they would not come and I threatened to report them and one of them sassed me a little. [Mary finally returned home with a local doctor.] We had no light. The gas was out and we had no lamps. So Martha thought of twisting paper and dipping it in lard. I held the lighted paper while the doctor [extracted the bullet and] gave it to the man and said, "There, take that and put it in your knapsack for a keepsake." The man said, "I feel better already!" I put wet cloths on the wound.

Mary took the small amount of food left in the general store.

In a corner of the basement I threw some pieces of bacon on the floor and piled some old sacks over them. The Rebels had full sway through here, but the Rebels were actually good to us. They…got cod fish and wanted us to cook them and Martha did. The other Rebels came and went down to the basement. This was after they had taken the wounded out of the basement to the church. They did that at night. Well, I had barrels of molasses in the basement—a whole lot of it. The Rebels drew out that molasses in crocks and carried it out. At last I went down with a bucket and I said, "You must give me some of that molasses." Well, they said they needed it worse, but they took up my bucket and drew it full, though they objected. Mrs. King would sass them like everything, and she said, "Well, I see you are not very particular about what kind of molasses jars you use." "If you were as hungry as we are," they said, "you would not care."

Five surgeons stayed with us. They told Martha she would have to cook for them. So every now and then I would get this side meat from the basement and we baked cake with some shortening; baked it on a griddle on top of the stove. As fast as I got it baked, they ate it up.

"On the evening of the second day's battle a Rebel came and said he was going to guard us." Mary's Pennsylvania Confederate guards only appeared at night. This Confederate along with another got "sassy" and taunted the wounded soldiers. Mary ordered them out but they refused to leave. She then went out to the street and stopped a Confederate officer. The officer ordered the men to leave and then stayed to supper.

"Next day [July 3] a couple of men came in and called for something to eat. Martha had baked pie and brought one into the hall to the table there. She set it down, with a knife, and said, 'Now you cut it the best way you can.' He cut it and said, 'You eat a piece.' She said, 'Do you think it is poison? The women here don't poison people.' But he would not eat it; he was afraid it was poisoned."[4]

Mary went to her warehouse on the third day of the battle for more molasses and met up with some hungry and abusive Confederates who had arrived there first. She again sought the help of an officer who took the offenders out with an assurance to her, "If any other comes in here and annoys you, send up to Middle Street where I have my headquarters. I will see that you are not molested."

> The wounded men in our house told us on the afternoon of the third: "We know our men, and those cannons, and we are getting the better of them. Don't be scared, for we believe they are whipped." That night Lee's wagons began to go out. Our Rebel guards had come each night and lay at our door and I heard them all night long. The evening of the third day Mrs. King brought out a lot of biscuits again and she said to them, "Now eat some." They said they had had a right good supper. "Well, then," she said, "put them in your knapsacks. You can eat them on your retreat." "Oh," they said, "we are not going to retreat." There was some talk about [Union General George B.] McClellan coming with a big army. "Why, yes," Mrs. King said, "McClellan will be here before morning with a big army." [This was untrue.] They took the biscuits and put them in their knapsacks and lay down to rest. I went in the house and was at my post there when these wagons began to go out. I wakened Martha and said, "I believe the Rebels are retreating." "Oh, if it is only true," she said, "for I am hardly able to go it." After awhile a man came running down the street and he wakened these guards and he said, "Get up, get up, we are retreating!" I felt like saying goodbye to them, but it would have seemed like mockery.[5]

"By morning [July 4] they were all cleared out [of town], and when we came down there was nobody about, only what were wounded. I went out and Mrs. Horner [a neighbor] came out and began scraping off her pavement of mud and blood. And the first thing we knew, a Union band began to play and I think I never heard anything sweeter, and I never felt so glad in my life." That morning Colonel Morrow appeared to reclaim his diary. He had been brought to the Gettysburg College as a prisoner and escaped by putting on a green surgeon's sash and mingling with them. In the effort to return to Mary's house, Colonel Morrow became lost and wound up hiding in Judge Will's house, the same house that would host Abraham Lincoln five months later. Mary returned Colonel Morrow's diary and also gave him General Archer's sword with the trust that he would give it to Lieutenant Dailey should they meet again.

The day after the battle, barricades were set up across the town streets and the sharpshooters of both armies sprayed the streets with bullets. Mary went out for food for the wounded. At a neighbor's she was warned of the danger and the words had no sooner been said than the man was shot in the leg. In the end she obtained some meat, bread, and butter at another neighbor's. "This shooting went on nearly all day on July 4, but we heard that they really had retreated. But those sharp-shooters did keep our men back. They took most of the wounded out of the house and over to the church and we attended to them as well as we could."

On July 5, Lieutenant Dailey showed up at Miss McAllister's house. He had been marched out of town with some other prisoners and during the night when his guard slept, Dailey literally rolled away to freedom. He did eventually receive Archer's sword.

Mary's narrative ends with a story of a woman she took into her home a few days after the battle. The woman was one of the many relatives who journeyed to Gettysburg to find their wounded loved ones already beyond their reach.

As with most civilian women's narratives at Gettysburg, Mary McAllister noted the good behavior of the enemy. And like most women in both the North and South, she rose unquestioningly above her personal politics to give succor to any needy human being, regardless of what side he was on.

Anna Garlach

Gettysburg Civilian

*"In the retreat of the first day there were more people in the
street than I have ever seen at any time…In front of our house
the crowd was so great that I believe I could have walked
across the street on the heads of the soldiers."*[1]

Anna Garlach lived on Baltimore Street in Gettysburg in July of
1863. The household consisted of her parents and four children. Her
father, Henry, was a woodworker whose shop was adjacent to the house.
Anna was 18 years old, the eldest of her siblings. She and her brother,
Willie, who was 12, her sister Katie, and her 6 month old brother Frank
were all present on June 30, the eve of the battle. That evening they fed
some Union cavalry. One of the guests was Ferdinand Usher of the 12th
Illinois Cavalry, who would die the next day, recorded in history as one
of the first casualties in the battle of Gettysburg.

On the morning of July 1 Anna's father left home to observe the
battle from Cemetery Hill. When he attempted to leave his observation
point, he was halted and accused of being a spy. The Union soldiers
would not allow him to return to town. Mr. Garlach stayed in the countryside and did not arrive home again until a couple of days after the
battle. This was a source of much additional anxiety for the family
throughout the battle. Anna's sister, Kate, also left home on the first
day with some neighbors to find a safer haven.

Anna observed the controversial actions of Union General Alexander
Schimmelfennig during the three day battle. The General was hiding in
her back yard—a unique occurrence to be found in a civilian narrative.
This is Anna's view of the event:

> I have heard persons speak of cowardice when referring to General
> Schimmelfennig during the battle days…but I could see nothing cow-
> ardly in what he did…He did the only possible thing he could do. Any
> other course would have meant capture and perhaps prison.
>
> General Alexander Schimmelfennig was in command of the First
> Brigade of the Third Division of the Eleventh Corps. He reached here
> on the morning of the first day with his brigade and went into line north

of the town and was among the last to retreat through the town hotly pursued by the enemy.

General Schimmelfennig was mounted and in retreat on Washington Street. At that time there was an alley running from Washington Street which ended at the barn of my father Henry Garlach and connected with another alley north to Breckenridge Street but had then no outlet south. He turned down this alley and found that his only outlet in either direction was toward the Confederates.

The Rebels were at his heels and when he reached our barn his horse was shot from under him. He jumped over the alley fence into our yard and ran toward Baltimore Street, but the Rebels were in possession of that street and he realized that he must be captured.

There was an old water course in our yard at the time, now converted into a sewer and for 12 feet from [the] street it was covered with a wooded culvert and General Schimmelfennig hurriedly crawled out of sight under this culvert.

He remained there until after dark. It was night when my mother went out of the house, following the path to the stable, for the purpose of feeding our hogs. Along the pathway was the woodshed and against the shed and running some distance from it was several ranks of wood and in front of the wood two swill barrels. We have been using wood from the rank nearest the barrels and there was a space between barrel and the rank of wood big enough to hold a man. As mother went up to the barrel the General said, "Be quiet and do not say anything."

He had taken of the wood and built a shelter over head to better hide himself.

It was remarkable that he was not captured. The Rebels had torn down fences from Breckenridge Street southward through yards and there were Rebels on all sides of us and movement of his in day time might have been seen from a number of points.

On the second day mother make a pretense of going to the swill barrel to empty a bucket. In the bucket however was water and a piece of bread and instead of going into the barrel they went to the General in hiding. Mother was so afraid that she had been seen and the General would be found that she did not repeat this.

General Schimmelfennig was in hiding between the barrel and rank of wood from the evening of the first day to the morning of July 4th. That last night everything grew so quiet and as soon as there was light we got up and mother hurried down and out, anxious to know what had become of the man.

He was already out of his hiding place before she reached him. When I first saw him he was moving across our yard…He was walking stiff and cramped like. At the fence were a number of Union men and they proved to be some of his own men. They thought he had been killed and when they saw him they went wild with delight. I saw them crowd around him and some kissed his hand. They seemed beside themselves with joy.

That was the last we saw of General Schimmelfennig at that time.

Anna's main responsibility during the battle was the care of Frank, the Garlach baby. Her mother's main concern was the safety of the people in her house. By the night of July 1 there were an additional 11 people in the Garlach house, all neighbors seeking safety. "After dark…Mother made beds on the floor and we slept there. She was afraid if we occupied beds, bullets would come in the windows and reach us."

During the early morning of the second day Mother [and] brother Will fixed up our cellar to live in…Our cellar had a foot or more of water in it…In the yard amoung the lumber were blocks of wood which were to be chopped down for rungs of chairs. Mother and Will rolled into the cellar a lot of these logs and stood them up and then put boards across the logs so as to be out of the water. There were two banks of ground in the cellar, at either end, and these Mother fixed by covering with boards and with a board path to various parts of the cellar. Then she put one family on one bank, another family on the other, and a third one on the platform of boards over the water. The baby and I were placed near the cellar steps. Each party knew the place he or she was to occupy and Mother had an ax behind the cellar door to cut our way out if anything happened.

We stayed in the kitchen most of the time except when there was firing, then we would go into our places in the cellar. We would get an occasional peep out of the door and windows but could not go outside of the house for we would have been a mark for the sharpshooters of both armies.

On the night of the second day firing on Culp's Hill kept us in the cellar until very late. When it stopped we came out of the cellar and tried to get some rest on the kitchen floor. We prepared our meals at night.

We were in the cellar on the third day when a soldier burst in the front door and started upstairs. Mother went up out of the cellar, caught him by the coat as he was going up to the second floor, and asked him what he was doing there. She was told that sharpshooters were going to

Post war photo of Anna Garlach .
(Adams County Historical Society)

use the house. She held on to him saying, "You can't go up there. You will draw fire on this house full of defenseless women and children." He insisted that he must use the house for sharpshooters and Mother insisted that he should leave the house. To this he answered that it would be instant death for him to leave the house.

Mother said he could stay but must not fire from the house. After awhile he said he would go. He discharged his gun out of the front door, and in the smoke darted out and got safely across the street...

Another time Mother again succeeded in preventing sharpshooters from taking possession of the house...As every point occupied by sharpshooters became a special target, our house was repeatedly hit.

One day Mother and brother Will went to the garret to see what they could from the small window toward the south covered by a board with handle. They pulled it back far enough to see out. They must have been seen, for shortly after they had replaced the board and were descending the steps, bullets entered the garret.

During the battle we carried all the water for [the] big family from a hydrant in the yard...This work was done at night and usually Rebels carried for us all the water we needed.

On the night of July 3rd we were aroused by some [Confederate] soldiers who asked to be allowed to go in the shop where father made coffins. They said [Mississippi] General [William] Barksdale had been killed and they wanted to make a coffin for him. Mother told them that if they went into the shop and made a light the house would be a target. She told them there was plenty of wood outside in the yard and they could help themselves to as much of it as they wanted, and then they should go to a shop down in town. They agreed to this...They began the coffin that night but the retreat was ordered before it was finished. [The coffin would eventually be used for the remains of Jennie Wade, a female civilian killed during the battle.]

Anna finished her narrative with the memory of how her mother sent food to the wounded until the hospitals were closed and told of their own patient, Adjutant Roberts of the 17th Maine, who recuperated from an amputation at the Garlach home.

Rules of war gave direction to soldier's actions and goals. Civilians thrown into the shock of battle were left to their own devices. The women who endured the battles of the Civil War were faced with the responsibility of protecting their homes and the people under their care while engulfed in a type of violence that defied civilized humanity. While some were handicapped by terror, they usually acted with great good sense and often with individual acts of heroism.

Elmina Keeler Spencer

Matron, 147th New York
First Army Corps, First Division, Second Brigade

"I never believed I should be harmed by shot or shell."[1]

Elmina Spencer rode horseback on the march to Gettysburg with her regiment. By that time she was an accomplished equestrian having had much practice foraging for the sick and wounded. "The sick were taken forward in ambulances in charge of Mr. & Mrs. Spencer. She rode by the side of the wagons on her horse only resting when the trains were parked."[2] "Mrs. Spenser's horse carried besides herself, her bedding, clothing, and 350 pounds of supplies for the sick. She had two knapsacks and two haversacks and materials to make tea, coffee, and beef broth…"[3] "With unconquerable spirit and heroism she marched with the regiment taking her supplies needed for the footsore and exhausted soldier and restored his drooping energies on that weary and toilsome march, often assisting him by taking upon her horse his coat and blanket, which otherwise would have been abandoned on the way."[4] Enroute an ammunition wagon exploded and the driver was badly burned. Elmina was separated from her bedding which was used to wrap the driver and from her husband who remained with the victim. The night before the battle she slept alone in a tented bed erected from the rubber blankets contributed by some of the regiment for her comfort.

On July 1 Mrs. Spencer was close enough to the town of Gettysburg to hear the gunfire. She pressed forward to a barn near the battlefield and set up her camp kettles. "They occupied a barn where she made coffee for the soldiers. Wounded from the XI Corps were brought in and to get them off the field they had to cross between two lines of artillery firing."[5] "Soon orders came to go back…for security and the news that General Reynolds was killed, the 14th Brooklyn and 147th [New York] nearly destroyed. Mrs. Spencer decided to go forward to care for the wounded…she cared for the wounded on the field during the first day's fight."[6] "Her conduct on the battle-field of Gettysburg exposed to the bursting shells from both armies, furnishing succor to the wounded from supplies furnished from her stores which she always

**Elmina Spencer was an accomplished forager and horsewoman.
She would ride between 30 and 40 miles a day seeking supplies.**
(Oswego Historical Society)

carried with her on her horse for emergencies, is a matter of history and places her in the foremost ranks of heroic women."[7] "As they went towards the battle they found their regiment stationed on a hill above them [East Cemetery Hill] and halting they made a fire and prepared refreshments which they gave to all they could reach. While working here the Surgeon of the First Division came hurrying past, and peremptorily called on Mrs. Spencer to go and help form a hospital."[8]

"...[A]t dark [she] went with the wounded to a little white church on the Baltimore Pike 4 miles from Gettysburg and helped the surgeons form [a] hospital."[9] "They had 60 wounded undergoing every variety of suffering and torture. The church was small, having but one aisle, and the narrow seats were fixtures. A small building adjoining provided boards which were laid on the tops of the seats, and covered with straw and on these the wounded were laid."[10] The supply train was 14 miles behind the lines so the men were fed with the remaining supplies Mrs. Spencer had carried up from Falmouth.

By July 5 there were

over six hundred [Union] besides 204 Confederates [at this hospital site]. Our [wounded] men were in the fields and the houses surrounding—for all of where she cared, gathering supplies of food and other comforts. She rode her horse sometimes twice always once per day to Gettysburg, a distance of four miles to get stores for the inmates of said hospital. And thus she worked night and days, while in town for the wounded, and on her return for those in her hospital until that and all the field hospitals were broken up and [the] General Hospital was formed just outside the village.[11]

During this time Mrs. Spencer saved the life of a patient who had been shot in the mouth and throat, the bullet leaving a great open hole when it exited. He had been given up for dead but through careful and constant nursing she was gratified to see him eating normally by the time she left Gettysburg to accompany some wounded back to New York. "...When the General Hospital was broken up [and] its New York men sent home, she went with them on the cars and cared for them until they reached their destination. [Elmina stayed in New York to gather] more supplies from the people of that state. On her return she was appointed state agent with $25 per month to furnish her food and other contingent expenses. Government received her labors also. Her own regiment was cared for whenever she could reach them."[12]

Elmina Keeler was born in Mexico, New York on September 15, 1819 and spent her childhood in Oswego. She married Robert Spencer in 1840. They both were teachers connected with the public schools in Oswego. Mr. Spencer was a member of the Democratic party's faction opposed to the war and his age exempted him from military service. However, after Antietam [September 17, 1862] with so many homes in Oswego mourning their dead, he resolved to enlist and Elmina went with him.

The 147th left Oswego enroute for Washington Sept. 29, 1862. Robert Spencer was an enlisted soldier of that regiment and Elmina Spencer as a matron of same. The evening of October 1st the regiment arrived in Washington and was conducted to the Soldiers Rest for the night—[Elmina spent that first night on a bench outside the Rest] before morning the cars brought in the wounded from the battle of Antietam. Their wounds had been hastily dressed on the battlefield and were becoming very painful. Mrs. Spencer with her husband's assistance, washed the wounds, re-adjusted the bandages, fed the men and made them as comfortable as possible for the balance of the night. In the early morning October 2nd the regiment was ordered to move to Camp Chase near Arlington Heights. The heat was very oppressive, intensely hot, and several of the men were stricken down, some senseless, others seemingly slight, amoung [sic] the last was her husband Mr. Spencer.

Mrs. Spencer seemed to bear the heat remarkable well and during the next three years seemed to bear a charmed life.

On reaching the camping ground the hospital tent was immediately put up and Mr. & Mrs. Spencer were installed, he as Ward Master, she as matron. There and then she commences her great work for the Union. The regiment remained only a few days and was then removed to…about five miles from Washington. The hospital was filled with sick and dying men—Mrs. Spencer and her attendants had all they could do night and day. Supplies were needed and she gathered them from the Ladies Aid Society in Washington, the Sanitary [Commission], Christian commission and the people abroad to whom she appealed and so she continued to work until the orders were given to send the sick to the different hospitals…After the sick were thus disposed of the regiment broke camp and proceeded to Falmouth to hold post. The women were not allowed to go with the regiment so Mrs. Spencer remained in Washington until such time as the orders relayed and she could be allowed to join her husband again.

While waiting the first battle of Fredericksburg [December 13, 1862] occurred. She repaired to the Patent Office, the temporary hospital and labored there while her services were required. She then went to Oswego [and] busied herself collecting supplies for the soldiers. At last she received letters with orders and requests from [the] Surgeon and Colonel for her to return at once as her help was badly needed in the hospital, men were dying daily with fevers, and the inmates were suffering for care.

On arrival after various trials for a pass she at last received one…for herself and supplies, reached the regiment at Belle Plain and found the hospital in bad condition.

[She] had been there but a few days when orders were received to break camp and the inmates of the hospital [moved] to Wind Mill Point where [the] government was establishing a mammoth hospital for the disabled of the Army of the Potomac."[13]

Elmina was appointed matron of the First Division and held that position for six months. Mr. Spencer was attached to the Medical Purveyor's Department. In June of 1863 both returned to the 147th for the Gettysburg campaign.

After the battle of Gettysburg both Spencers' positions were changed. In 1863 the state of New York created Agencies for the Relief of Sick and Disabled Union Soldiers in the Service of the United States; the Army of the Potomac being Agency #5. Elmina was in charge of this agency along with a Reverend Igen. Her new position carried a good deal of power and responsibility. She was subject to orders from the Surgeon General of the Army, held New York credentials, and a permit from General Grant to allow her to pass through all Union lines in all places. The Medical Purveyor of the Army of the Potomac had Mr. Spencer discharged because of his propensity to sunstroke. He re-enlisted in the regular army as a Hospital Steward attached to the Purveyor's Department. Both Elmina and her husband worked through this department "which followed the army, she was thus carried to the front in time to care for the wounded…"[14]

When Elmina returned to the army from New York in this position,

she was sent by Surgeon [Brigadier] General [Joseph] Barnes with the Purveyor's Dept. to Brandy Station to distribute supplies. She brought to our hospital at Culpepper [Virginia] stores of pillow ticks and such supplies as were needed for our sick ones. The regiment was again ordered to move. The Purveyors Dept. went to Alexandria while the army moved on. The battle was at the Wilderness [May 5-7, 1864]. Mrs. Spencer had gone by the order of the Surgeon General with supplies to Rappahannock Station where the telegraph wires were cut by the enemy and the engine was reversed and the train sped back to Alexandria (her home in that place was the warehouse where the purveyor's goods were kept. Those boxes made partitions for her room. Her time, when there, was filled by visiting the hospitals—many of our soldiers remember her welcome visits and the delicacies she carried them). The whereabouts of the battle had been ascertained and when she reported to Surgeon General [on] the return of cars, he ordered her to Wharf #4 to take the first [hospital] transport. She took the first steamer for Belle Plain on which she found a number of Theological students and Christian Commission men—the boat arrived at daybreak at the wharf and she with others went on shore to feed the wounded who were just arriving in ambulances and government wagons.[15]

In a letter dated November 7, 1864, Elmina recalled her experience at Belle Plain:

I stood on the dock with my basket and haversack filled with rations. We arrived early in the morning. The Sanitary boat with her stores, delegates, and ladies lay beside us. Slightly wounded soldiers who had been able to walk from the field were moving slowly toward the boats with hungry, anxious faces. These were fed with crackers and other food. As soon as I could land I went from the boat to the shore with my rations thinking I might make a little coffee or tea for some of them. I met Dr. Babcock our State Medical Agent moving from one wounded man to another, dressing their wounds and cheering them with kind words. After feeding my rations I went to another portion of the field and found ten theological student delegates of the Sanitary Commission employed in making coffee in camp kettles. The kettles hung upon a pole resting [in] crotched sticks driven into the ground as standards for the poles. I offered my service to stir, dip or serve in any way. My services were gratefully received and we all worked with a will. Some cut wood and brought it, some brought water, some kept the fire, others with pails and cups to distribute to our hungry wounded men.

We worked until dark and far into the night. We fed six thousand men including those brought in by ambulances, with their drivers and attendants. In the afternoon it rained without ceasing. The rain descended in torrents. The wounded lay upon the ground surrounding us by thousands; some under bushes for shelter; others without shelter

The dock at Belle Plain Landing, Virginia.
(Library of Congress)

except for blankets; more with no covering of any kind. It was impossible to make shelter in such short time. We were thankful that we could feed them. Often when passing from one to another I have heard, a grateful "God Bless you." Often I passed a soldier lying in the mud and rain with his arm or leg cut off or a wound in his body he would say in answer to my inquiry, if he had tea or coffee: "Yes, I've done well. Thank you. But you lady will get your death in this rain. How can you go through this mud to wait on us?" Their cheerfulness to me was surprising. I stood in the mud that day over the tops of my boots while preparing food for the wounded. The sanitary [Commission] had but one tent erected. That sheltered their stores. At 11 o'clock it occurred to me that I had no place to sleep.

One of the men who had been assisting me said he would go and ask a driver to give me a place in his wagon. One of the drivers readily assented and left his wagon for my use—finding room for himself with another teamster. I got into the wagon, wrapped my shawl about me, sat myself on the bottom of the vehicle, placed the mule saddle at my back and for the first time since morning settled myself for rest. I could not sleep, my clothes were saturated with rain and mud. My bones were aching with wet and fatigue yet I did not feel discouraged. How could I? When I thought of the thousands lying around me, crippled, wounded, some dying. I found myself in prayer for my suffering countrymen.

At dawn I felt rested and ready for another days work. In going from the wagon to our cooking place I experienced the difficulties of walking through Virginia mud. I found many of our wounded lying in beds of mortar. All that the ambulances could they placed on hillsides. The wounded continued to come to be cared for. Miss Dix with her lady nurses came and after a while passed to Fredericksburg. The government kitchen issued supplies to thousands furnished by the Sanitary Commission when short of meat, bread, sugar, coffee, etc. I stayed here in charge of the cooking. There was so much suffering and need for my services. My shoes were worn out and I needed clothes, but we were working in an emergency.[16]

When night came again the students offered her a place in the tent that covered their stores. She took two small strips of board (that had been part of a cracker box) put them on the muddy ground, then put her empty haversack on that so as to make it a little softer, and that was her bed the second night…She was furnished a tent, a bed of straw was placed therein and there she rested the third night. It was impossible for her to remove her shoes and stockings on account of the coating of mud encrusting them. Her shoes were no protection, now only in name, the soles were held but by the toes and heels, as the thread of which they were made had been destroyed by constant contact with mud and water.[17]

Mrs. Spencer continued in her letters:

May 25th [1864], we left Belle Plain for Port Royal. The wounded were arriving in large numbers. We found an old building for fuel and started our fires and we worked all night distributing coffee. That day Col. Coyler, Inspector General of the Army had stoves brought into the building and five cauldrons outside and sent 28 men to assist in the work. Two cauldrons were filled for coffee, one for soup, two for meat. With these facilities we cooked enough meat to feed all who came.

Just before leaving for White House Landing which was to be our next base…[I was] placed in charge of the cooking on the government barge to oversee it and at the same time, see to my work as Agent for N.Y. From the barge we fed the first wounded that came to White House from the field [battle of Cold Harbor, June 3, 1864]. After a day or two our stoves and cauldrons were brought on shore and we fed our thousands again. We called it the Government kitchen and from it regiments including those from N.Y. were supplied with nourishment…we fed them all…[18]

Sophronia Bucklin, a government nurse, remembered Mrs. Spencer at White House Landing and called upon her for help:

...on the ground [was]...a New York State agent, by the name of Mrs. Spencer—a noble woman, who did her work of mercy well. She occupied one of the log houses, vacated by the negroes, on the brink of the river. Her stores had been brought on the medical purveyor's boat, the stoves erected, cooks detailed, and the food sent wherever a scanty supply existed...I went to Mrs. Spencer for help at near noon...when no breakfast had been sent in for the men, who, after feasting one day, were fasting now for a day and a half, and immediately two men were called, and they, with Mrs. Spencer and myself, repaired to the famishing soldiers with all the food we could carry in our arms.[19]

White House Landing was a Union base for hospital and supply. Northern women served as nurses and cooks here.
(MOLLUS)

Mrs. Spencer wrote:

We came to City Point [Hospital] June 10 [1864]. Here again was plenty to do. The wounded were still coming in. The ground was covered with them and our labors were no lighter. Our hospital was finally established. Our Medical Purveyors boat moved around upon the Appomattox River. The Government kitchen was kept in action and I stayed until the hospital kitchens were in good order, and our hospital ready to receive patients from field hospitals or battlefields. From that time my labors were mostly distributing to needy soldiers at the front, field hospitals and rifle pits. In general hospitals I am not needed so much although I visit them and distribute a portion of my supplies to them. They have their surgeons, ladies and ward masters while at the front [they] have to struggle on alone with only their regimental surgeons.[20]

Nurse Bucklin observed Mrs. Spencer at City Point: "Mrs. Spencer was located…directly on the bank of the river, where the wounded passed daily in being brought from the front. She fed hundreds each day and was allowed to draw Government supplies in addition to what was furnished her by her own State. She had eight men detailed to cook and distribute, and the noble woman seemed unwearied in her extensive work of mercy…She often went to the rifle-pits to distribute supplies of tobacco whilst the bullets of the enemy were dropping around her."[21]

At City Point, "she visited General Hospitals to discover all N. Y. State soldiers and be of service to them. She rode horseback 20 to 40 miles a day about Petersburg and Richmond. One day with her black hat and feather, looking quite like an officer on her mount, a sharpshooter fired at her. The bullet lodged in a tree just back of her. She dug it out with her knife and carried it for a souvenir."[22]

Although not shot, Mrs. Spencer did suffer one wound at City Point. "…[W]hen in the explosion of our ammunition boat at City Point, I sat on my horse about 65 feet from the boat. When it exploded pieces of shell, cannon balls, human flesh, and sticks of timber over and about me—no escape in any direction."[23] Miss Bucklin remembered: "Mrs. Spencer…was on her horse upon the elevation above, and the balls flew quite thickly about her, and even upon her; and, although her stay-springs were broken, and herself bruised from head to foot, no portion of the skin was rent. Looking up, at the sound, she said she saw a clear path in the sky, and reined her horse toward the opening.[24] Shrapnel had glanced off a stay in her corset which saved her life but caused temporary paralysis of her legs.

Elmina Spencer stayed at City Point until after the war and until all the wounded were evacuated. She then served in Washington hospitals until June 15, 1865, when she returned to Oswego with her husband.

After the war Mr. Spencer was unable to earn a living as his health had suffered from his army service. The couple moved to Kansas in 1873 in hopes of a new start. Within two years, Elmina not only lost her husband, mother, father, and mother-in-law, but her house was burned down by a prairie fire. It was then that she applied for a pension which

City Point munitions wharf after the explosion of a munitions boat.
(Library of Congress)

was granted at $8 per month. In the early 1880s she returned to Oswego where the local Congressman took it upon himself to have her pension increased to $20 per month. Mrs. Spencer's pension records are full of depositions and petitions by grateful veterans.

Mrs. Spencer was honored at the head of her regiment in all gatherings and her name was listed along with the men of the 147th on their regimental monument erected in Oswego. A bust of Elmina Spencer resided in the Capitol Building in Albany. In 1893 she was a guest speaker at Gettysburg when the 147th's monument was erected there.

Mrs. Spencer died on December 29, 1912 at age 93, and was buried in Rural Cemetery in Oswego. In 1921 when the women of that city instituted a "tent" of female descendants of Oswego Civil War soldiers, they named it in honor of Elmina Keeler Spencer.

July Second

arriet Hamilton Bayly who lived on a farm outside of Gettysburg, related her morning of July 2.

...Thursday, I packed a market basket full of bread and butter and wine, old linen and bandages and pins, for I belonged to a society which prepared such things and mounting a family horse that had been blind for several years, with my niece behind me, I started towards the town and scene of the first day's battle. When nearing the field of battle I met a Confederate officer, who I was told later was [Brigadier] General [Albert] Jenkins, and telling him my purpose he told me to follow him. Before we had gone far a courier came for General Jenkins and we never saw him again. But on I went; as far as I could see there were men, living and dead, and horses and guns and cannon, and confusion everywhere. There was no fighting that morning. Getting down into the valley I found our wounded lying in the broiling sun, where they had lain for 24 hours with no food or water. A zigzag fence was standing on the side of the road and in it's [*sic*] angles were many who had taken shelter from the sun and to avoid being trampled on. The very worst needed a surgeon's care but while my niece gave food to the hungry and wine to the faint, I looked after their wounds. I would cut open a trouser leg or coat sleeve until I found the wound and then put on a fresh bandage. One of the first I touched was a poor fellow hurt in the back. I cut open his coat from the waist up and found the cloth he had put on the wound had become so dry with clotted blood that I could not loosen it—and had no water. A wounded comrade lying near said, "Madam, there is a little tea in my canteen that I have been saving; maybe you can loosen it with that."

I had been hearing the pitiful cry of "water," "water," all around me, and when I found these men had none for 24 hours I rose up in my wrath and turning to the Rebels who were walking around me, I said, "Is it possible that none of you will bring water to these poor fellows?" An officer heard me and finding that what I said was true, he ordered a lot of men to mount and bring all that was necessary. They said that the wells of the nearest houses were pumped out, but in strong English, with stronger words thrown in, he sent them off with canteens strung over them, and I directed them where to go to find a good spring. Soon we had plenty of water.

While busy at work a German surgeon came along, saying that he had been directed to look after the Union wounded. As he could not speak English, nor I German, I was content to hear his expressions of "goot," "goot," when he examined the work I had done. He was as gentle as a woman in his touch and it did me good to see how tenderly he handled those wounded men.[1]

By the morning of July 2 the famous "fish hook" battle lines had been drawn. The Union hook curved around with its right flank at Culp's Hill to Cemetery Hill with the shank of the hook continuing up Cemetery Ridge until its left flank rested on Little Round Top. The Confederate line curled around the base of Culp's and Cemetery Hills, through the town of Gettysburg and its shank ran along Seminary Ridge which was about one mile west of Cemetery Ridge. The Confederate line ran about five miles in length, the Union line about three miles and had the advantage of the interior line.

All morning skirmishers from both armies kept up a brisk fire, spiced by the occasional boom of artillery. Both commanding generals rode their lines: Meade to inspect the line and anticipate attack and Lee to gather information to ascertain where and with whom he could launch the best offensive. Lee concluded on an oblique attack by the Confederate I Corps against the Union left flank. He also called for a diversion by the Confederate II Corps facing Culp's and Cemetery Hills that could expand into a full scale attack depending on circumstances. The Confederate III Corps, centered between the two other flanking corps, prepared to enter the attack enechelon if practicable. Threatened action along the entire front could negate the advantage of Meade's interior line. Pickett's Division, the last Confederate unit to come up, arrived on the field in mid-afternoon and was held in reserve. The effort to keep the marching columns of the attacking force from observance by the enemy resulted in some confusion and countermarching in which much time was lost. It was not until about 4 p.m. that the Confederate artillery opened fire, the usual prelude to an infantry attack, on the Union left flank.

Meade was on his line's left flank at 4:00. He was furious with his III Corps commander, Major General Daniel E. Sickles. The III Corps was not, as had been ordered, deployed along Cemetery Ridge from the II Corps line to Little Round Top; the latter location was supposed to be the extreme left flank of the Union army. On his own accord, the III Corps commander had marched his line forward in a westward move-

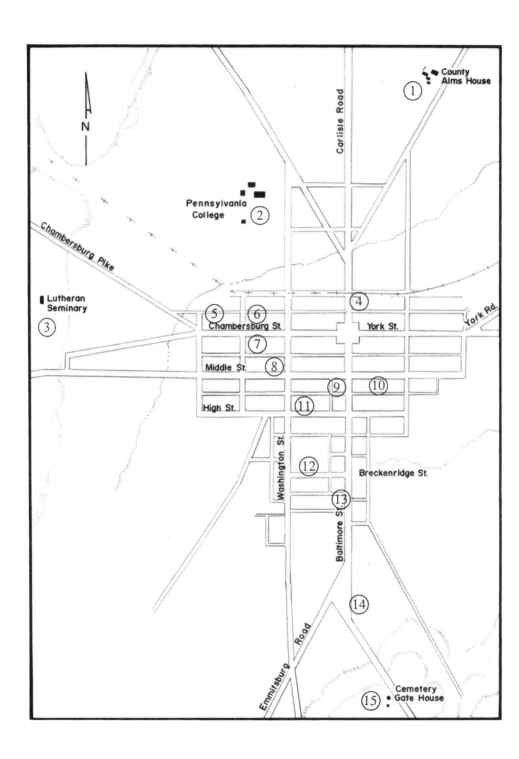

County
Alms House
①

Carlisle Road

Pennsylvania
College ②

Chambersburg Pike

Lutheran
Seminary
③

⑤
⑥ Chambersburg St.
York St.
④
York Rd.

⑦

Middle St.
⑧

⑨
⑩

High St.
⑪

Washington St.

⑫

Breckenridge St.

⑬

Baltimore St.

⑭

Emmitsburg Road

Cemetery
Gate House
⑮

ment to Devil's Den, up though the Peach Orchard, and along the Emmitsburg Road. Sickles created a half mile gap from the main line on his right and his left hung in the air, easy prey for a flanking movement by the Confederates. Behind the Union line, the great VI Corps had arrived after a grueling, record breaking 34 mile march. When the last elements of this corps reached the field some of the men went directly into battle. The bloodiest fighting at the Battle of Gettysburg had begun.

When the Confederate infantry commenced their attack on the Union left flank, there were no Union units on Little Round Top to defend it. The 15th Alabama was the extreme right of the attacking Confederate line. The Alabamians climbed the crest of Big Round Top against impossible terrain and sharpshooter's fire and they could see the whole Union line stretched out along Cemetery Ridge. They used precious moments to rest from their exertion and lack of water. At the same time, Union Brigadier General Gouverneur K. Warren, who was also aware of the vacancy on Little Round Top, rushed about looking for troops to deploy on it. An order to a division commander of the V Corps was intercepted by another Brigadier General who took it upon himself to take his men to the slopes of Little Round Top. Warren per-

The Town of Gettysburg.
(Map by John Heiser)

1. **Crawford House (Smith & Barlow)**
2. **Pennsylvania College (the Sisters & Goldsborough)**
3. **Lutheran Seminary (the Sisters)**
4. **Adams Express Office (Hall)**
5. **Broadhead House (Broadhead)**
6. **Scott House (McAllister)**
7. **Christ Lutheran Church (McAllister)**
8. **Jacob House (Jacob)**
9. **Adams County Courthouse (the Sisters)**
10. **Methodist Episcopal Church (the Sisters)**
11. **Roman Catholic Church (Myers & the Sisters)**
12. **Wade House (Wade)**
13. **Garlach House (Garlach)**
14. **McClellan House (Wade)**
15. **Evergreen Cemetery Gatehouse (Thorn)**

sonally requested elements of Brigadier General Stephen Weed's brigade, also of the V Corps, to add to the defense. The 15th Alabama descended Big Round Top and wound around the shoulder of Little Round Top, where the extreme left flank of the Union army was held by the 20th Maine. On a regimental scale, the combat between these units is one of the most famous of the battle. Both groups fought until exhaustion, attacking and repulsing again and again, until the Alabamians retreated back up Big Round Top.

On the eastern front of Little Round top the Confederates fared better. The Texans and Georgians hit Devil's Den, a great outcropping of large boulders, known as the "Slaughter Pen" by the soldiers. After several onslaughts to penetrate the maze of boulders, the Confederates controlled the area, capturing four artillery pieces. These Confederates advanced across Plum Run's "Valley of Death" until they were checked by fresh troops of the V Corps. South Carolinians hit a Union brigade situated next to Devil's Den and in front of the Wheatfield. The men of the Union brigade resisted until most of their regiments were reduced to remnants. The Wheatfield changed hands several times leaving thousands of wounded and dead on its field.

An awe-inspiring charge by a Mississippi brigade swept all before them, including the Union brigade in the salient of Sickle's line. The Mississippians drove both Union infantry and artillery back from the Peach Orchard to the Union Plum Run line. All along the Union line as the Confederate I Corps hit the Federals and hurled them back, fresh Union reinforcements would come back across the fields to counterstrike.

The Confederate brigades continued the attack from the Peach Orchard up along the Emmitsburg Road. That third brigade which struck near the center of the Union line turned out to be the last offense unit in the Confederate attack column. They reached the crest of Cemetery Ridge, received no support, and were repulsed with a counter attack.

Attacks and counterattacks were innumerable on this end of the battle line on the second day. Amid much confusion and minimal leadership the foot soldier of both sides showed great stamina and courage. Each sector was hotly contested, the proof being that half of the casualties for the battle occurred on the second day, most of which were in the areas with names synonymous with death and glory: Little Round Top, Devil's Den, the Wheatfield, and the Peach Orchard.

Although Lee had planned for the Confederate II Corps to create an artillery diversion on the Union's right flank followed by a coordinated infantry attack with one on the Union left flank, this did not happen. Historians have long pondered why Lieutenant General Richard S. Ewell, commander of the Confederate II Corps wasted those precious hours.

The Confederate II Corps artillery opened fire at about 4 p.m. on the Union right which was the anchor of the fish hook and located along East Cemetery and Culp's Hills. They were answered by Union artillery and the guns dueled until about 6:30. After sunset the Confederate infantry, who had been in expectant battle formation all day, were finally released into an advance. They pushed through the artillery fire of 22 guns trained on them from the high Union defense line. The Confederates broke through the first Union infantry line at the base of East Cemetery Hill and then the second line halfway up the slope. When they reached the crest, the Union infantry had abandoned their artillerists who steadfastly stood by their guns and engaged in hand to hand combat. Union reinforcements hurried from the center of their line on Cemetery Ridge. Finally, with no support behind them and unaided on both flanks, the Confederates retired back down the slope to the base of East Cemetery Hill.

The Union infantry on Culp's Hill had been stripped away during the day to supplement the forces on the Union left flank. Those remaining had spent the day digging trenches and building barricades of wood and stone, in some places five feet thick. The defenders numbered about 2,000 and stood about as thin as a skirmish ling through their entrenchments. They could hear the roar of battle for East Cemetery Hill behind them as they watched the Confederates advance down the slope opposite them in the twilight.

It was about 8 o'clock when the Confederates proceeded up the slope of Culp's Hill. It was near dark, as Daylight Savings Time was not used, when the Confederates hit the Union trenches. After several hard fought assaults, the Confederates finally overran and lodged in a section of the entrenchments at about 10 p.m. where they remained for the night. The second day's fight was over.

While the men in the lines prepared their dinner, searched for water, and slept, the officers of both armies spend busy hours through the night. General Meade held a council of his senior officers to appraise the day's work and plan for the morrow. His decision was to remain in position at Gettysburg with preparations to be made for an assault on the Confederates in the captured trenches on Culp's Hill.

The Confederate officers were also occupied. Men were being moved from the center of the Confederate line to their extreme left flank. There, the foothold gained in the trenches on Culp's Hill was hoped to be exploited the next day. Confederate artillerists located sites for the guns for the proposed assault on the Union Center. General J.E.B. Stuart, after having been located by the scouts General Lee had sent out, finally reported for duty at Lee's headquarters around 11 p.m. Their meeting was brief. Lee himself was bogged down in paper work organizing the evacuation of the wounded.

Both armies' lines had not changed much although they were now closer in some areas. The Confederates now held Devil's Den, the Peach Orchard, and had control of the Wheatfield. The opposing lines on Culp's Hill were within shouting distance. Despite the ferocity of the fighting, no real gain was made by either the attackers or defenders. Over 33,000 Union men and almost 24,000 Confederates were engaged in battle on the second day. Casualties were high with a heavy loss in general officers.

The atmosphere on the field must have been at a keen pitch on the night of July second. Two days done of terrible battle with the certain knowledge of more to come. Who would win, who would lose? Who would live, who would die? The women of America were no less apprehensive. They waited, as always, for news of the battle and of their men, on both sides of the Mason Dixon line, with aching hearts and fervent prayers to the same God. "…[T]hose lonely evenings; after my two children were asleep I would sit in nervous anxiety. I would picture him that was dearer to me than life lying stark upon some lonely battlefield or wounded on a stretcher. There can be no sorrow like that—it was the sorrow of death itself."[2] "Only those who have felt this anxiety know what it is."[3]

> It was here and like this that the women endured,
> Here alone that they grappled with death
> In a form more horrid than the soldiers encountered
> While facing the cannon's lurid breath.
> They were watchful by day and wakeful by night,
> And like Ruth they most faithfully cleaved,
> And many a lady and lassie died
> Of wounds the soldiers received.[4]

Harriet Patience Dame

Matron, 2nd New Hampshire
Third Army Corps, Second Division, Third Brigade

"We did not go to war for money or praise. When I went it was a horrid affair, even dear old Governor Barry opposed me and would not give me transportation, but I fought them all and went! I was independent of all commissions. My regiment, the glorious of 2nd New Hampshire was enough for me."[1]

Harriet Dame's statement in her pension records sums up her service at Gettysburg in two sentences: "Very soon after our regiment returned from New Hampshire [on recruitment duty] we came to Gettysburg. I remained at the field hospital until all were taken to the General Hospital, then came to Washington." [2] Her contemporaries had more to say.

A soldier of the 2nd New Hampshire described the march to Gettysburg in the wee hours of July 2:

> The night being very dark, and the brigade considerably scattered by its disposition to cover various roads, it was between three and four o'clock [a.m.] before the command was assembled. Without breakfasting, the Second formed column with the brigade and started for Gettysburg.
>
> At the end of each hour a halt of about 10 minutes was made to rest, the sunrise halt being somewhat longer, to enable the men to cook a hasty cup of coffee. It was a weird night march. Dark clouds were scudding across the sky, which let loose an occasional quick, sharp shower upon the hurrying troops. The consciousness of impending battle had by some subtle influence taken possession of the minds of the men. During one of the early morning halts there was heard, away to the north, the indistinct sound of a slow fire of artillery.
>
> It was about half past seven o'clock [a.m.] when the column came into the more open country in the immediate vicinity of Gettysburg."[3]

The 2nd New Hampshire went into battle with 354 officers and enlisted men; by the end of the day their casualties numbered 193. Dame "labored…there in the field hospitals [and] found herself in such a

75

Miss Harriet Dame.
(MOLLUS)

multitude of her old boys, wounded and dying, as would have appalled any but the stoutest heart."[4] One casualty "was full of courage and confident he would be all right in a short time…when brought to the field hospital where he came under the care of Harriet Dame…."[5]

Reverend Adams, a chaplain of the 2nd who joined the regiment after the battle wrote: "I have heard them all tell how she toiled day after day on the bloody field of Gettysburg, sometimes during the battle, between the lines…absorbed and self-forgetful, devoting herself to the relief of our wounded men. And when darkness of night, and the exhaustion of her energies made rest imperative, she would pillow her head on the gory field, and sleep amid the dead and wounded scattered around her."[6]

Harriet Patience Dame was born in Barnstead, New Hampshire on January 5, 1815. She was the youngest of the six children of Phebe and James Dame; her father was both a farmer and a teacher. Harriet was a well educated, responsible young woman and worked in various occupations in the northeastern and western parts of the country. She moved to Concord in 1843 and by 1861 was running a boarding house there.

Harriet remembered:

> When the war first broke out, or was talked of, even, I began to
> look about me to see what a woman could do, should there ever be real
> fighting. When the soldiers began to come to camp I found plenty of
> work among the sick, and my house was at once a hospital. When the
> first New Hampshire regiment (three months men) went out over forty
> women went with them. Some were wives of the soldiers (others were
> not)...In the Second Regiment I had many dear friends. They had en-
> listed for three years...I decided to go with the surgeon of that regi-
> ment, with one other woman, Mrs. Menden. He only wanted two matrons
> as we were called, and paid as matrons (had $6 a month) and with the
> grand old Second New Hampshire Regiment I staid four years and eight
> months.[7]

The women went with the regiment to Washington, D.C., then to
Budds Ferry, Maryland. "Mrs. Menden left us there," said Harriet,
"[there was] sickness in her family, and [she] never returned to the regiment."[8] At Budds Ferry, Harriet was restless.

> I received a letter from Doctor Hubbard, our surgeon when we first
> left home, urging me to join him at Paducah, Kentucky. The prospect
> of a change was very alluring. Anything was preferable to the stagna-
> tion, and I seriously considered the offer. But the familiar faces of the
> boys I had known in their beardless, happy days proved a strong mag-
> net. I consulted our Chaplain, Mr. Parker, telling him of my divided
> ambition, and he counseled me to wait one week. During this time he
> wrote to Colonel [Gilman] Marston, who had then taken his seat in
> Congress, and asked his advice. There was true military atmosphere in
> the answer: "Stay where you are, and do not desert the regiment." I
> obeyed this command and deep down in my heart rose a quiet thanks-
> giving that duty had been so plainly to lead inclination. With this first
> diversion perished every desire that was not prompted by devotion to
> the regiment of my choice.[9]

"She shared with the regiment the fortunes of the Peninsula Cam-
paign [March-July 1862]. Her first night before Yorktown...[Siege of
Yorktown, April 5 – May 4, 1862] was spent in a feed box..."[10]
Dame wrote that the regiment,

> ...went to Yorktown, or where we were daily shelled from Yorktown
> by the rebels. One day I met a scared soldier running out of the woods
> with some cards in his hands; he said, "What are you down here for;

they are shelling the woods!" I said they were shelling the camp. "Well," said he, "you are a fool staying here when you could go home." Poor fellow got kicked by a mule the day before Williamsburg battle [May 4-5, 1862], went home to Concord, told them what a fool I was staying in the Army and suffering what I did. Then came such begging letters for me to come home. I did not go; the scared lieutenant was discharged, and may now be getting a pension for the mule kick; know he had to have a new set of teeth. I was all through the Peninsula Campaign.

...[H]ow anxious Miss Dix [Dorothea Dix, Superintendent of Army Nurses] was for me to go into the hospitals in her service. That was Yorktown...where I first met Miss Dix...She said it was folly my thinking of such a thing as living on the field. I said that was what I came for; and should do so if I lived. She was then and always very kind to me; said any time that I would not stay on the field come to her and she would put me in hospitals as one of her nurses at $23 a month. Think of it, most ministers would refuse such a call; double pay and house to live in.

The Peninsula was fearful. At Fair Oaks we were camped where [Union General Silas] Casey fought a few days before we reached them [battles of Fair Oaks and Seven Pines, May 31 - June 1, 1862]. The dead were not all buried; green flies and odors, I can't think of it without feeling sick. There we were shelled all the time; one and only one shell went through my tent, but it did not burst, and I was not in there; did not know it until I saw the boys looking for it. When they burst over us the pieces used to sing; you could not tell where; Dr. Janvier and I bumped heads dodging some pieces, and were both sure it was at our backs. We were not seriously hurt by the bump.[11]

Miss Dame was remembered at the Battle of Oak Grove [June 25, 1862].

Harriet Dame was there, ministering to the wounded. In a moment of leisure she went to the two stark bodies [brought in from the trenches], and lifting the edge of blankets with which they were covered, saw faces of the two boys who, from old acquaintance, were perhaps closer to her heart than any others in the regiment. "My God," she gasped, "It is Tom Leaver!" She had been a neighbor of the Leavers, in Concord, and had known Tom from boyhood. With her own hands she tenderly prepared the bodies for burial and saw them laid in the ground at the foot of an Oak tree near the hospital.[12]

It was around the time near Malvern Hill [July 1, 1862] that Miss Dame bumped into Confederate pickets and was briefly taken prisoner. The chaplains' previous observation of Harriet's self-forgetfulness was no exaggeration. This would not be the last time she was found behind enemy lines. Since she nursed any wounded man she came upon, no matter what uniform he wore, she was never seriously delayed in her work.

But it was on the retreat to the James that her courage and endurance rose to the height of sublime heroism. The announcement to the sick men in the hospital that those who could not walk must be left behind, fell upon many with all the weight of a death warrant: the horrors of life in rebel prisons were now well known, and to them capture meant death. Harriet Dame resolved to remain with them; but when, nerved by desperation, they rose from their cots, resolved on a supreme effort for liberty, she led them forth upon their doubtful journey. They took nothing with them. One faithful fellow, prompted by a tenderness born, perhaps, of a remembered mother or wife, destroyed her little wardrobe so that rebels should not desecrate it. With her feet encased in a pair of rubber boots, her head protected by a faded tatter of mosquito netting, and bearing a coffee boiler and a supply of coffee, she went forth, the guiding spirit of that party of feeble, tottering men.

Although one man of the squad…died before reaching Harrison's Landing, yet it was to her devotion and inspiring courage that most of them owed their liberty and some their lives. At every halt for rest she would fill her coffee boiler and cheer the lagging spirits of her boys with the reviving decoction. At length, reaching the great tangle of the trains, she encountered Captain Godfrey, the division quartermaster, and while she resolutely kept her own feet to the ground, she fought for her boys, and corners were found for more than one of them in baggage wagons and ambulances.

Along in the night she reached a farm house somewhere near Charles City Cross Roads. "The Provost Guard," she says, "went into the farm house to find a sleeping place for me, but the aggressive and disgusted women of the household refused, under the plea that the house was full. I added my own resolute statement that I had a blanket and would sleep in the empty hall, which I proceeded to do in defiance of the opposition offered by the indignant women, and left the house to tell my men where I might be found. Returning, I was met by a meager specimen of a negro boy, who piloted me to a large room up-stairs, where a bed upon the floor invited me to repose. And, in one moment, sleep for me had knit up the raveled sleeve of care. The war, its cruelty and horrors, all were forgotten, until a small voice piped into my ear; "Missis, you had better get up. They's gwine to fight." And when my heavy lids lifted and the cheerful daylight showed me the situation, my awakening senses realized that the teams were gone, and the army was drawn in line of battle before me, waiting for the rebel attack. My toilet was a delayed luxury. My willing and responsible feet obeyed the bent of my mind, and the two carried me to my boys, whose eager welcome and enthusiastic energy proved them to have been improved by the forced march of the preceding day."[13]

Miss Dame described her condition at Harrison's Landing that summer of 1862:

At Harrison's Landing I was two weeks without a tent or the seeing the face of a woman...I was ragged, only had one gingham dress; left all my things at Fair Oaks, and the soldiers destroyed them; said the rebel women should not have Miss Dame's clothes. Some friends from Washington came down; they sent me a big package. I sat up all one night and made a calico dress to wear; we were to leave the next day; but the rest of the things I never saw again. They were with our baggage and other fine things sent from home by some recruits; were all destroyed in the train...I had some blankets put around trees and a rubber blanket or two over my head to keep the rain off. There I and "Skedaddle" a little dog a man gave me on the retreat, lived at Harrison's Landing No. 2...When I left Harrison's Landing [in mid August 1862] had only a piece of green mosquito netting to wear for a bonnet; while without a tent had hung mine, a frame one, in the ambulance to keep it from some of the heavy rains or showers we had while there. The driver fearing it would even get more wet there had rolled it in a horse blanket. When he brought it to me under his arm in the blanket, I was forced to believe it was decidedly out of even army style and left it for the natives.[14]

Miss Dame left Harrison's Landing on a hospital boat that took the army's sick to New York. She rejoined her regiment right before the battle of the Second Bull Run [August 29-30, 1862] where she again found herself behind enemy lines. This time, however, she was taken to "Stonewall" Jackson's tent. After a few words with the great man himself, she was escorted back to where she'd been found. A poem was written about the event.[15]

Dame wrote: "...we were at the Second Bull Run. When the army fell back I was at a house, used as a hospital, at Centreville, and part of the time at the Old Stone Church [another hospital site]."[16] A soldier of the Second remembered her there: "I can speak of personal knowledge, for I have seen her under fire on many a hard fought field, and when

Westover, the house on the adjoining plantation to Berkeley, was used by the Union officers. Today it is privately owned and fully restored. It was most likely the location referred to by Miss Dame as Harrison's Landing No. 2.
(Library of Congress)

lying on my back shot through the body, unable to move a finger, with as everybody thought, my last breath going out, and with shot and shell raining around us, as if the very heavens were about to fall, she at that time was indeed to me a ministering angel..."[17]

Dame remembered the aftermath of battle at Centreville:

> "When I went there Dr. Riley or O'Riley, a Western surgeon, was in charge at the house, and when our folks sent for me to go with them, he begged our surgeon to leave me until he got off the wounded; the second [N.H.] regiment was camped just outside the village. They not knowing where they were going decided to leave me in Dr. Riley's care; he promised to see that I either joined them or went through to Washington. We got all the wounded off that day, then Dr. Riley "lit" out, leaving me in charge of Surgeon Vollum, a regular army surgeon...; he was at the headquarters; he said I could come up there or remain where I was. Only the colored servants were left at the house where we were;

81

I concluded to stay there, for I was just played out; had not slept much for three or four nights…That night just as I was ready to be food for the *chinches* (is that how you spell bed-bugs?) a long train came from the battlefield…We went to work like rested people…[18] [and fed all the wounded who were then sent on to Washington].

Since the Confederates were so close Harriet and a small medical group tried to leave Centreville. Harriet described this first attempt and eventual success in her efforts to get from behind enemy lines to safety.

> Centreville was in confusion. There were a lot of stragglers, as there always was, after the army left. They had got at the whiskey among the medicines and were decidedly too jolly for comfort. We were about two miles from Centreville when my friend exclaimed, with an oath, "There are the rebels on guard." We were stopped, but not until I had made the man call the officer of the guard…When I was sent back to Centreville with men that were taken prisoners at that camp…we walked back to Centreville. Dr. Vollum had me sent to the house where he was, and that same afternoon another train came from the battlefield with badly wounded and paroled men. The clerks that went from Washington to take care of the wounded were along with that train. They were walking. It was the last train from the battle-field. Many that were left to die were on that train, and several did die before they reached Washington. I told Dr. Vollum I wanted to go with that train. He said, "Come quietly with me, as though you were looking for some one." We

The Old Stone Church in Centreville.
(Library of Congress)

walked along until we got to the end of the train, the head ambulance, and I popped in without leave even.[19]

Harriet Dame was next at the battle of Fredericksburg [Dec. 13, 1862]. "There I liked to die of the cold; did have a tent, but it was so cold there where we camped after the battle, and all the wounded were sent back to Washington and those that were very sick."[20] She accompanied the men back to D.C.

Harriet was asked to organize rooms in Washington for supplies sent from New Hampshire for its men. Dame explained:

> They had several times written to me asking me to come and get the rooms fitted up, then put some one in charge and go back if I wished to do so. I had refused all their invitations and General [Gilman] Marston's request, but when an order came from him for me to report there, saying also the Second Regiment were going home to recruit, I went; was there all winter. We had heaps of things that we distributed among the soldiers at the different hospitals, and found plenty of work all winter; did not go home to recruit with the regiment. Each member of the association had a hospital to visit and make their report every week at the rooms. Most or all of the soldiers that were able to travel wanted to go home, and we would get them furloughed or their back pay or discharge. I assure you we were not idle or making calls except at the hospitals and War Department that winter. I had a strong letter sent me from our governor that I used to shoulder and start off for the War Department. Perhaps some of the men belonging to the association had been there and failed to get what they desired; I generally got what I asked, not that I was young or handsome. We all know youth and beauty can do a heap with some people. I was young, [but] never a howling beauty. If the letter was good enough, why, of course, youth and beauty were not necessary. Very soon after our regiment returned from New Hampshire we came to Gettysburg.[21]

After Gettysburg the Second New Hampshire was among the regiments ordered to guard Confederate prisoners at Point Lookout [prison camp] Maryland. Miss Dame wrote:

> Our governor desired some one to go South and report to him the condition of our soldiers there. The Third, Fourth, and Seventh New Hampshire Regiments were on the different islands in the vicinity of Charleston, S.C. As they, our regiment, were all well fixed at Point Lookout and very little sickness there, the association decided Miss Dame needed rest and she better go.

I sailed from New York on the steamer *Arago* sometime in October, was busy all the way to Hilton Head taking care of seasick women, mostly schoolmarms that were teaching the freedmen in South Carolina and Florida. I visited Morris and Folly Islands where most of the New Hampshire regiments were stationed; went up to Fort Wagner, and were going to Fort Gregg, but they [the Confederates] turned their guns on us at Fort Moultrie and we decided best to quit. I stayed there a few days, then found the plan to take Charleston was given up. Was told *in confidence*, before I left Washington, that there was to be the fight of the war very soon, and Charleston would be ours, &c. Only for that yarn I would not have gone. Returned to Hilton Head and took passage for Saint Augustine. Before leaving Washington, Miss Dix sent word to me not to go South, if I did they would not let me leave the boat, and many other messages; but if I did go on shore, would I, for her, visit and report to her the condition of all the hospitals in that vicinity. I heard there was just starting a large hospital at Saint Augustine, Fla. The men were not willing to go there, said it was so far from home; they did not want to be any further away, especially when sick. I went there and decided that it was a lonely place; the men were right. Met [Brigadier] General [Truman] Seymour, and [Brigadier] General [John] Sprague, from New York…I came up on their boat. They did not think it was a good plan to have a hospital there, and it was soon given up.

A hospital in Beaufort, South Carolina.
(MOLLUS)

While waiting for the boat I visited all the hospitals at Beaufort, and these were a large number. Most of the houses and all the churches were filled with sick and wounded, and the very large one at Hilton Head, and the last of November started for home. The boat *Arago*, the same I went down on, was crowded with sick, furloughed, and discharged soldiers; not any accommodations for them. Only officers were allowed in the state rooms, I was told when I gave mine up to a poor feeble private; how I did long for a big pocket filled with shoulder straps. General Sprague was on board, and with me was indignant at the treatment, but could not blame the captain of the boat, he had his orders to obey. He had all the baggage removed and filled that room with the worst cases; the others went in where the cattle were when we went down. Chaplain Emerson of the Seventh New Hampshire Regiment, Tottingham, an old friend of mine, one of the Post band, and I worked all the time to make the poor fellows comfortable. The captain ordered the steward to give us anything we wanted. When the captain was not around he was a devil, still we got along without killing him. General Sprague told me to report to the Surgeon-General the way the men were treated and he would write a letter to him. When I went and reported the case to [Surgeon-General Joseph] Barnes, he said he had just received letters from New York complaining of the accommodations on the boats, and it would be remedied at once. All boats after that had a hospital fitted up with one or more surgeons in charge.[22]

In the spring of 1864 Harriet Dame returned to her regiment now a part of the XVIII Corps. This corps' hospital was located at Point of Rocks on the Appomattox River. There was a photograph of her in front of the field hospital with her dog, "Whiskey." She also had another dog at this hospital named "Quinine." Harriet remained with the XVIII Corps hospital for the rest of the war. She remembered Point of Rocks: "...all the sick of the regiments were sent there...There was that awful coal harbor [battle of Cold Harbor, June 3, 1864]; three years' men in the Second had about served out their time, but they went into that fight willingly, and so many poor fellows, that in less than a week expected to be at home, were either killed or wounded; what were left and had not re-enlisted went home."[23]

Reverend Adams remembered Harriet at that time: "During the sanguinary conflict at Cold Harbor, she established herself at White House [hospital site], rendering great service to our soldiers, who suffered severely...Miss Dame remained with us, caring for our sick and wounded until we swung around in front of Petersburg."[24]

War time photo taken of Miss Dame at the Point of Rocks Hospital on the Appomattox River in 1864 with her dog "Whiskey."
(Roy Frampton)

The hospital moved by transport to Broadway Landing. Miss Dame told of the nurses' first night there, "The first night there the sick we had on board were sent off with us, and no place to go for shelter; we soon had an old church filled, then we hunted up all we could *hear groaning* and laid them around the church; our chaplain the next morning asked us where we slept; I said, 'In the room with you;' 'Why,' he said, 'I slept under that tree;' 'So did we,' I said, 'on the other side.'"[25]

Again, Reverend Adams remembered Harriet:

> ...at Broadway Landing, she could be seen to advantage—one moment in distributing garments, comfort-bags, cordials &c., from her private tent, at another moving under the large cooking tent, surrounded with delicate and substantial articles of diet, and the large kettles steaming with wholesome and palatable food in a state of preparation. This tent was her throne; but she did not sit upon it. From this place she issued her orders, dispatched her messengers, and distributed luxuries to thousands. Here she not only ruled with system, but with sleeves rolled up, toiled harder that any of her assistants.[26]

Harried simply stated, "The doctors all called me boss woman..."[27] Thus she spent the winter of 1864 and spring of 1865.

Harriet's statement continued:

In June [1865] after *Robert* [E. Lee] surrendered our hospital was all cleared away...I went to my regiment then at Manchester, Va., opposite Richmond. In July we left there for Fredericksburg, and the regiment was scattered over pretty much all of the Northern Neck; headquarters at Warsaw Court House, Richmond County. About all were sick. Never, while with the regiment, did I see as much suffering as then. Many poor fellows who were daily waiting, not patiently, to be mustered out, heard and answered their last roll-call. God is good and gracious and I will put my trust in him, but if they only could have gone home. The 25th of December the old Second, what there was left of it, were mustered out. That ended my services of four years, eight months, and some days without ever have a furlough or sick leave.[28]

Two years after the war in 1867 Harriet procured a position in the Currency Division of the Treasury Department in Washington which she held for the next 28 years. She was president of the Army Nurses Association established in 1884. Harriet journeyed home to New Hampshire for the annual reunions of the Second Regiment. She was entitled to wear three army corps insignia [III, XII, XVIII] and a gold badge given her by her own 2nd New Hampshire. Harriet used the $500 awarded to her by the New Hampshire legislature for her service along with some of her own funds to build a structure on Lake Winnipesaukee for use of the veterans of the Second.

In 1884 she was granted a $25 a month pension by a special act of Congress initiated by a petition signed by over 600 veterans. She had this to say about her pension: "My soldier friends are determined to make a grand effort to have me pensioned. They have been talking about it for years, but I have always said get the soldiers pensioned; let me take care of myself. Now they risen in their wrath and say if I don't keep quiet they will put real army sticking plaster over my mouth. Well, to tell the truth I am tired of hard work, and would not object to living without toiling for my daily bread...Call me Dame River, or harbor, or flat even; get an appropriation to have me repaired. My feet are lame, hands swollen, head aches, &c., &c. Think I need repairs and will sleep."[29] However, Harriet kept working until 1895, when after suffering two accidents, she left her job at the Treasury Department.

Harriet Patience Dame died in Concord, New Hampshire, on April 28, 1900 at the age of 82. She was accorded a full military funeral which was largely attended by veterans and their descendants. She is buried in St. Paul's Cemetery.

In the year after her death the governor of New Hampshire suggested that a portrait of her be placed in one of the state buildings. It was and still hangs on the first floor of the state house. Hers was the first portrait of a woman to hang in the state house. In the 1930s the Daughters of Union Veterans in New Hampshire named their tent #1 after Harriet. Dame school in Concord was named in her honor. In 2002 she was inducted into the American Nurses Association. She is also remembered by her descendants. A great, great, grandniece from Concord says, "Aunt Harriet" is a touchstone for finding out quickly if a Dame is related.

Harriet Dame was honored in various ways yet there was one moving declaration made by a veteran of the regiment in which she served that must have especially pleased her; "[Hers] is a name that will not be found on any official roster of the Second Regiment; but she was with them, she was of them, and was and is honored and respected and loved by her old comrades with a depth of affection that can find no adequate expression in words."[30]

Miss Dame wearing her military medals.
(Roy Frampton)

Amanda Matilda Colburn Farnham

Nurse, Vermont Units, Sixth Corps

"Mrs. Farnham, the dress you wear is abominable, a most abominable dress, and I do not wish any of my nurses to dress in that manner; but you came highly recommended, and I have long known of your work, but I didn't know you wore such a dress."[1]

By the time of the Gettysburg Campaign, Amanda Farnham had been in the army for two years and obtained her own transportation. "In the spring of 1863 I was permitted by the Prov. Marshal Gen. [Marsena Rudolph] Patrick to have a team and wagon of my own on which to carry my personal effects and in addition to this, I carried a large supply of articles for use of the sick and wounded that were furnished by the Christian and Sanitary Commissions...."[2] "[S]he was permitted to keep a two-horse team, to take along supplies on the march. When in camp the boys could usually procure for themselves what they needed, but on the march they often suffered severely. Such articles as shirts, socks, etc., coffee, sugar, condensed milk and canned goods, she [Amanda] carried, and gave where most needed."[3]

Amanda wrote: "in the campaign which began at Falmouth in June and ended in Gettysburg, I aided many soldiers on their hurried and fatiguing day and night marches by taking them on my wagon, and on the last day the 6th Corps march from Manchester, Md. to Gettysburg...I gave up my wagon entirely to such disabled soldiers as could not keep up with the command or find room to ride in the overcrowded ambulances, walking the whole distance myself..."[4] Another soldier on that march recalled:

> It was a weary march from the Rappahannock to Gettysburg, made more so by the night marches, always so tiring. The last day they went thirty-four miles over a stone road, and under a burning sun. It is now simply a matter of history that the Sixth Corps marched from Manchester to Gettysburg from daylight until 4 o'clock p.m., and it was the greatest feat in marching every accomplished by any troops under like conditions. Mrs. Farnham went with them, and most of the way on

Amanda Farnham.
(*Our Army Nurses*)

foot, giving up spare room on her wagon to worn-out soldiers…A ride for an hour for one, and he could walk on again for a time, giving his place to another. Thus many more were able to keep along than would have been without such help. Again, when she found a poor fellow with blistered feet, she gave him a pair of socks to take the place of the holes, all that was left of his own.[5]

Mrs. Farnham stated: "…on our arrival at Gettysburg at sunset of July 2nd, 1863 I went to work with the wounded of the 3rd Corps for the entire night without sleep or rest."[6]

The story of her work all night after such a day, has been told in print many times; how a guard was placed over a certain pump at the request of the ladies of the house, as they feared the well would go dry, and they be obliged to go to Rock Creek, a quarter of a mile distant, for water,— little caring how far the exhausted soldiers had to go. But some of the boys, knowing Mrs. Farnham was near, got her to pump for them; and when complaint was made, the guard said his orders did not include women, so she could get all the water she wanted. In this work, and caring for wounded of Sickles [III] Corps, who filled all the barns and outbuildings on the place, she remained all night long. Few of the Sixth

Corps were wounded at Gettysburg, but she was busy among others, until the division left there.[7]

"From Gettysburg I followed with the Vt. Brigade to Funkstown, Md. where they had a severe engagement with a portion of the rear guard of Lee's army and in which many of the Ver. troops were killed or wounded and by request of many officers of the command I was sent home to Vt. with the remains of some of the killed, and returned to join them again at Warrenton, Va., about the last of July 1863."[8] A member of the Vermont Brigade wrote: "...at Funkstown, the Vermont Brigade suffered severely. Among those killed was an old acquaintance, and she [Amanda] obtained permission to take his body and two others home. She was absent two weeks..."[9] This was the second and last time Mrs. Farnham would go home during the war.

Amanda M. Colburn was born in West Glover, Vermont, Nov. 12, 1833. Her father was a farmer in moderate circumstances, and having only one boy, a share in the out-door work was often given to Amanda. This early training proved of estimable value to her in later years, when a large reserve of physical strength was so necessary to enable her to endure, with comparative ease, the long marches where hundreds of men were overcome, as during the Peninsula, Gettysburg, and other campaigns. At about twenty three years of age she was first married, and it was as Mrs. Farnham that she became so well known in the Army of the Potomac.[10]

"...[F]rom July 1861 to May 1865 and both inclusive, I served in the Hospital Dept. of the U. S. Army under the name and address of *Mrs. Amanda M. Farnham*."[11]

In 1861 Mrs. Farnham returned to her Vermont home 'left alone with her little boy and in poor health." There is no record in Vermont of Amanda Colburn's marriage or birth of a son. Nor has any information of the fate of Mr. Farnham been found. Amanda's brother, Henry, had enlisted in the 3rd Vermont much to his parents' distress. "...[S]he left her child with her parents, and followed her brother; partly to relieve the great anxiety respecting the only son, partly from a desire to help in the struggle just at hand."[12]

"Early in June 1861 I enlisted in the 3rd Regt. Vermont Vols. Inf'ty and was appointed Hosp. Matron of said regiment, and paid as such on the muster rolls of the regiment, for some six months—when by a Genl. Order from the War Dept. 'That no Hosp. Matrons should be paid for

91

further service in the field, from and after that date'—my name was dropped from the rolls of the regiment and pay stopped at that time."[13]

> ...she was dropped from the rolls as matron of the 3rd, for the Government would no longer recognize the position; but she still continued her work, and until the Wilderness campaign in 1864, occupied a different position than most female army nurses, as she did not do regular ward duty, but went from one regiment to another, wherever she was most needed. Day or night it made no difference, she always responded to the call, and would stay until the crisis was passed, or death had relieved the patient of his suffering. But it was to the boys, like her brother, that her heart went out with greatest sympathy. Writing letters for such was a daily practice, and when there was no hope she would record the dying request, and take care of some keepsake to be sent to friends at home.[14]

Amanda stated:

> ...early in the year of 1862 the sickness and mortality among the Vermont troops was alarming and I was requested by many of the Medical Officers of the "First Vermont Brigade" to remain with the command— with which request I complied—and assisted in the care of the sick during the winter.
>
> When the Army of the Potomac left the vicinity of Washington in March 1862 for the Peninsula Campaign, I went with the Vermont Brigade and was with that command, helping to nurse their sick and wounded at the siege of Yorktown [April 5-May4]—and the battles of Lee's Mills [Mechanicsville, June 26] Williamsburg [May 4-5], Gaines Mills [June 27], Goldings Farm [June 27-28], Savage Station [June 29], and Malvern Hill [July 1]. In all above named battles I worked on the field, and in the field hospitals with the sick and wounded—and through the campaign ending at Harrison's Landing, Va. July 2nd, 1862. I marched on foot with the soldiers.[15]

"She not only walked in the rain from Malvern Hill to Harrison's Landing, through mud knee-deep, but also helped the soldiers by the way."[16] A major from New York remember her at this time: "I first saw her on the march from Yorktown to Williamsburg, Va. May 4, 1862, [and] frequently after that during the Peninsula Campaign. Mrs. Farnham always maintained a good reputation in the service in every respect."[17]

Again, Mrs. Farnham: "In Aug. 1862 the sick were sent from Harrison's Landing to Hospitals in the north—and I was sent with a detachment to aid and nurse them while in transit and at this time made a short visit to my home in Vt."[18]

Amanda arrived at "Washington on Sunday the 14th [September 1862], and finding where the army was supposed to be, she tried to get a pass to the front that day but failed. The next morning she went to Secretary Stanton herself, and received not only her pass, but also an order for an ambulance."[19] "I rejoined the army on the 17th day of Sept. 1862 at Antietam, Md. while the battle was in progress, and not readily finding the Vermont Brigade—I went to the field hospital of French's Division—assisting them through the day and most of the following night."[20] Here Amanda performed "her first and only surgical operation. A soldier had been struck in the right breast by a partly spent ball, but with force enough to follow around the body under the skin, stopping just below the shoulder-blade. Taking the only implement she had, a pair of sharp button-hole scissors, and pinching the ball up with the thumb and finger, she made a slight incision and pressed the ball out."[21]

> After the Antietam Campaign was over I went with my old command to Hagerstown, Md. where we were in camp some six weeks,— where I was as usual on duty with the sick—and in the next campaign which ended with the battle of Fredericksburg Dec. 13th 1862. I went with the Vt. Brigade and on duty among the wounded there of that battle.
>
> During the winter following a Div. Hospl. (2nd Div. 6th Corps) was established near White Oak Church Va. and I was appointed by Surg. S. J. Allen Chief Medical Officer of the Div. as Matron in charge.[22]

A hospital steward of the 4th Vermont wrote: "December 13th came Fredericksburg, with all its horrors; The Vermonters suffering severely, and Mrs. Farnham, who was stationed at the Bernard [*sic*] House, worked with the wounded without rest until getting back to the old camps at White Oak Church..."[23]

On May 3, 1863 was the battle of Chancellorsville.

> ...the brigade lost nearly three hundred in killed and wounded,— Mrs. Farnham doing her usual efficient work...Before a battle it became a common thing for soldiers, especially of the Vermont troops, to intrust her with money or other valuables for safe-keeping, until an event occurred after which she dared no longer accept the responsibility. During the battle of Chancellorsville she had an unusual amount of money, which she carried in a belt on her person, and other things of value in a hand bag. After getting into quarters on our side of the river she put up a tent, as it was raining, and, for the first time in several

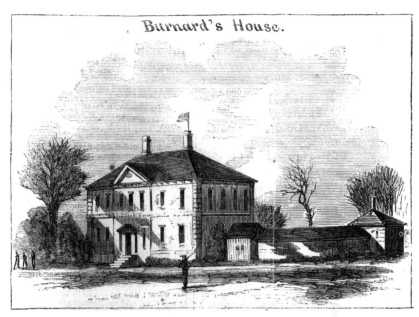

The Burnard House, known as Mansfield, in Fredericksburg, Va.
(Virginia State Library and Archives)

nights, took off the belt and put it with the bag on the ground under the mattress. Probably this was all seen in her shadow on the tent-cloth, by some one watching for that purpose. She had just fallen asleep when she became conscious that some one was trying to get in; but the flap strings had been drawn inside and tied tightly around the pole, so that plan was abandoned, and the robber passed around the tent. Fully aroused, Mrs. Farnham now crept from the blankets, and finding her revolver, awaited results. Her first thought was to give alarm, but she knew that the thief could easily escape in the darkness and return later. As no entrance could be found, he cut a long slit in the tent, to reach through. Up to the time that the knife began its work she had not realized how serious was her situation; now she hesitated no longer, but aiming as well as she could in the darkness, fired. An exclamation and the sound of hurried footsteps was all she heard. The next morning news came that one of the new recruits was sick, having been wounded by the 'accidental discharge of a pistol in the hands of a chum,' and she did not ask to have the case investigated.[24]

After the battle of Gettysburg Mrs. Farnham's narrative picked up in the fall of 1863. "In Oct. I was with our troops on the retreat from near Madison Court House to Centerville [Bristoe Campaign Oct. 9-

Nov. 9] and also in the Mine Run Campaign [Nov. 26-Dec. 1] in Dec. 1863."[25]

In the spring of 1864 General Grant issued an order that affected all army women. An officer remembered Mrs. Farnham at that time. "I communicated to her the order for all women to leave that army [Army of the Potomac] a few days before the campaign of 1864 began."[26] Amanda said:

> A short time before the Wilderness Campaign under Gen. Grant began in May 1864, orders were issued from the War Dept. for all women then in the army at the front, to leave it and to go to the rear, and though many of the most prominent officers of the 6th Corps signed a petition—praying I might be allowed to remain and keep my team—the request was not granted and I was obliged to go—having to sell my team at a great sacrifice and abandon many articles of use and value for want of time and transportation to take them with me. From the front near Brandy Station I went to Washington and in a short time was sent for by Miss D. I. Dix, Supt. of Women Nurses Med. Dept U.S.A.[27]

Amanda "used to like to tell of her first interview with Miss Dix. From the time she entered the army, Mrs. Farnham had worn a dress similar to the ladies cycling costume of the present [1895],—full pants buttoning over the tops of her boots, skirts falling a little below the knee and a jacket with tight sleeves. This dress she had on when she called to present her papers and request. Miss Dix glanced at the papers, then looked Mrs. Farnham over from head to foot, until the situation was becoming embarrassing. Finally she arose…" and expressed her firm opinion of Amanda's "abominable" dress…"though they met many times when Mrs. Farnham wore the same dress, it was not mentioned again…From that time until after the war closed she was one of Miss Dix's trusted nurses, and was charged with duties and commissions at the front that she would trust to no one else."[28] "For compensation I received pay for some six months only at the beginning of the war—and from June 1864 to May 1865 while under the direct orders of Miss Dix at the rate of 12 dollars per month."[29]

It was only a week between the time of General Grant's order and Miss Dix's order for Mrs. Farnham 'to report without delay to Sur. E. B. Dalton of the Sixth Corps at Fredericksburg, Va. where the wounded were being taken from the Wilderness [May 5-6, where her brother, Henry, was wounded][30] and Spotsylvania [May 7-20] battle grounds,

Dorothea Dix,
Superintendent of Women Nurses, Medical Department, U.S.A.
(MOLLUS)

and I remained there until the Field Hospitals were removed to White House on the Pamunkey in June 1864.

It was at the latter place that I first put into practice a plan by which the changes of the wounded—there coming in by the thousands from Cold Harbor [May 31-June 12]—could be washed and saved for use again, and not burned or destroyed as had been done at some former places, and some way by which the clothing and bedding of the wounded should be saved had become a necessity for supplies of this kind were nearly exhausted.

At this time there were many colored women—contrabands—coming into White House Landing who had to be provided with food and quarters by the Quarter Master [*sic*]—and no means had as yet been found to make them other than a burden and hindrance besides they were exposed to the evil influences of camp followers and others who crowded about the Army Supply depots and hospital grounds.

To accomplish the double purpose of finding employment for these unprotected women—and to save and wash the soiled bedding and clothing of the wounded—I had the women detailed by proper authority—and put under my charge—and then I obtained a supply of empty barrels from the depot Quarter Master from which wash tubs were made—and soon had made a beginning of what later on proved to be an important part of the field hospital service.

On the final establishment of the army hospitals at City Point, I was appointed by Miss Dix upon the recommendation of Surgeon E. B. Dalton to take entire charge of this new department at the 6th Corps Hospl. where I remained until the 6th Army Corps left City Point for the Shenandoah Valley under Gen. Sheridan in July [1864]—when I was ordered to report to Dr. McDonald of the 9th Corps Hospl. at City Point—and here I organized and carried into effect the same laundry system as had been adopted by the 6th Corps previously.

I had been on duty with the 9th Corps but a few weeks when application was made by some of the medical officers of the 6th Corps—for me to go and assist in that Dept. ("Valley of Virginia") and I asked for and obtained leave to go....[31]

An officer recalled: "She reported to me on the 21st day of August 1864 during a severe skirmish at and near Pickets House [*sic*] west of and near Charlestown [West] Va. [Shenandoah Valley Campaign, Aug. 7, 1864 to March 2, 1865] showing papers detailing her as Hospital Nurse and assigning her to duty with the 2nd Div. 6th Corps. I then directed her to the field hospital of that division where she did efficient service."[32]

Sometime during the war Amanda Farnham had fallen in love. The man was Marshall P. Felch, a hospital steward of Co. H, 4th Vermont.

I first became acquainted with Mr. Felch in front of Richmond in 1862, [and] saw him occasionally after that in service [as] an army nurse…In Dec. 1864 at City Point…I was at the IX Army Corps hospital in charge of the contrabands. He came to my quarters late in the evening with 3 or 4 of the boys that were sick…When Mr. Felch came to my quarters he complained of a pain in his left side. I said, "What's the matter with you?" He replied, "We have had an awful hard time and I got hurt at Cedar Creek [battle of, Oct. 19, 1864] and feel very much as I did then." I het [*sic*] some rocks and put [them]to his feet and think I gave him quinine and whiskey…[He] was not fully well when he left my quarters for the front, complained of the pain in his side, but I did not give my mind to it as I had so many to look after.[33]

Marshall Felch would suffer intermittent but incapacitating physical problems for the rest of his life.

Amanda went home to Vermont after the war and Marshall followed. "I met him at the depot when he got home...We were married December 16, 1865..."[34] at the First Baptist Church in Boston where they boarded on Blossom Street and Mr. Felch worked in a shoe shop. They decided to move west. The Felchs were in a party of four that went as far as St. Joseph, Missouri and from there Marshall went on alone. "I did not cross the plains with him" said Amanda.[35] Marshall arrived in Denver, Colorado in May of 1866 and obtained a claim in Canon City on June 11, 1866. Amanda joined him that October. The 1870 census shows the couple with four children: Albert, 13, who is almost certainly the child she left with her parents to go to war, Sarah, 3, Edward, 1, and [Webster] Emmerson, 9 months.

Marshall received a pension of $4 and then $8 from July 1865 to August 1881. An invalid request was rejected in 1890. Despite his heart problems and partial paralysis, Mr. Felch became quite a celebrity in his own right. He "produced a definitive Stegosaurus and Alosaurus" from a "bone yard" in Garden City, Colorado. Mrs. Felch was known to provide a dinner for visitors to the site.[36] Amanda requested a pension in 1888 for her services as nurse which passed as a private claim by Congress in March 1891 for the amount of $12.

Amanda Matilda Colburn Farnham Felch died at St. Luke's Hospital in Denver on December 31, 1893. She was buried in Greenwood Pioneer Cemetery, Canon City, Colorado.

Tillie Pierce

Gettysburg Civilian

How often my thoughts were anxiously fixed on my dear ones at home as the troops hurried along toward town. Were they well? Were they alive? Did I still have a home? These, with many other silent inquiries, sprang to my mind without any hope of an answer.[1]

Tillie Pierce was fifteen years old at the time of the battle. A town resident, she watched the Union men file through Gettysburg to the west for the first day's fighting. Shortly after noon her family urged her to leave with some friends for a safer quarters south of town. Tillie refugeed to the "safe" farmhouse of Jacob Weikert which, though located about five miles from the first day's fighting, sat directly behind Little Round Top. With the exception of the actual battlefield, she couldn't have chosen a more dangerous place to stay.

After arriving at the Weikert farm on July 1, Tillie gave water to the marching Union regiments who were approaching the battlefield up from the south. Although Tillie witnessed the explosion of an ammunition wagon and the driver's eyes blown out, it was the scene that evening of the retreating Union soldiers who filtered back to the Weikert's that gave her a glimpse of what was to come.

> [S]ome of the wounded from the field began to arrive where I was staying...some limping, some with their heads and arms in bandages, some crawling, others carried on stretchers or brought in ambulances. Suffering, cast down, and dejected, it was a truly pitiable gathering. Before night the barn was filled with the shattered and dying heroes...Nothing before in my experience had ever paralleled the sight we then and there beheld. There were the groaning and crying, the struggling and dying, crowded side by side while attendants sought to aid and relieve them as they could. We were so overcome by the sad and awful spectacle that we hastened to the house weeping bitterly.[2]

July second "dawned bright and clear" for Tillie. During the morning and afternoon she spent much of her time providing water to the passing soldiers.

This afternoon another incident occurred which I shall ever remember. While the infantry were passing, I noticed a poor worn-out soldier crawling along on his hands and knees. An officer yelled at him, with cursing, to get up and march. The poor fellow said he could not, whereupon the officer, raising his sword, struck him down three or four times. The officer passed on, little caring what he had done. Some of his comrades at once picked up the prostrate form and carried the unfortunate man into the house. After several hours of hard work the sufferer was brought back to consciousness.[3]

At one point in the afternoon Tillie was requested to show some Union officers up to the roof of the Weikert house to observe the field. She also viewed the scene with field-glasses. "The sight I then beheld was wonderful and sublime. The country for miles around seemed to

Tillie Pierce, 1863, at age 15.
(Adams County Historical Society)

be filled with troops; artillery moving here and there as fast as they could go; long lines of infantry forming into position; officers on horse-back galloping hither and thither! It was a grand and awful spectacle, and impressed me as being some great review."[4]

Later that afternoon the second day's fighting commenced.

> [H]eavy cannonading began…just back of the house. This was so terrible and severe that it was with great difficulty we could hear our-selves speak. It began very unexpectedly, so much so, that we were all terror-stricken, and hardly knew what to do.
>
> Some of the soldiers suggested that we had better go to a farm house about half a mile across the fields to the east; and acting on that advice we ran thither as fast as we could.
>
> When we reached the farmhouse…[5] we were permitted to remain but a few moments, for hardly had we arrived at our supposed place of refuge, when we were told to hurry back to where we came from; that we were in a great deal of danger, from the fact that the shells would fall just about the place, whereas the house near [Little] Round Top the shells would pass over us. So there was no alternative but to retrace our steps about as fast as we came.

The "safe" farmhouse of Jacob Weikert located behind
Little Round Top.
(Author's collection)

During the whole of this wild goose chase, the cannonading had become terrible! ...Occasionally a shell would come flying over [Little] Round Top and explode high in the air overhead. It seemed as though the heavens were sending forth peal upon peal of terrible thunder directly over our heads; while at the same time, the very earth beneath our feet trembled...The cannonading, which all the time appeared to be getting more and more severe, lasted until the close of the day.[6]

Tillie recalled the night of July second: "On this evening the number of wounded brought to the place was indeed appalling. They were laid in different parts of the house. The orchard and space around the building were covered with the shattered and dying, and the barn became more and more crowded. The scene had become terrible beyond description..."[7]

Tillie and the members of the Weikert household spent that night feeding the soldiers and assisting the surgeons and nurses.

> One soldier, sitting near the doorway that led into a little room in the southeast corner of the basement, beckoned me to him. He was holding a lighted candle in his hand; and was watching over a wounded soldier who was lying upon the floor. He asked me if I would get him a piece of bread saying that he was very hungry. I said certainly, ran away and soon returned. I gave him the bread and he seemed very thankful. He then asked me if I would hold the light and stay with the wounded man until he came back. I said I would gladly do so, and that I wanted to do something for the poor soldiers if I only knew what.
>
> I then took the candle and sat down beside the wounded man. I talked to him and asked if he was injured badly. He answered:
>
> "Yes, pretty badly."
>
> I then asked him if he suffered much, to which he replied:
>
> "Yes, I do now, but I hope in the morning I will be better."
>
> I told him if there was anything I could do for him I would be glad to do it, if he would only tell me what. The poor man looked so earnestly into my face, saying:
>
> "Will you promise to come back in the morning to see me."
>
> I replied: "Yes, indeed." And he seemed so satisfied, and faintly smiled.
>
> The man who had been watching him now returned, and thanked me for my kindness. I gave him the light and arose to leave.
>
> The poor wounded soldier's eyes followed me, and the last words he said to me were:
>
> "Now don't forget your promise," I replied:

"No, indeed," and expressing the hope that he would be better in the morning, bade him good night.

The sun was high in the heavens when I awoke the next day. I hastened down to the little basement room and as I entered the soldier lay there dead. His faithful attendant was still at his side.

I had kept my promise but he was not there to greet me.

As I stood gazing in sadness at the prostrate form, the attendant looked up to see me and asked, "Do you know who this is?" I replied: "No, sir." He said: This is the body of General Weed, a New York man...."[8]

General Weed, one of the saviors of Little Round Top, would be one of the four Union officers' bodies laid out on the Weikert porch that day.

On the third day of the battle Tillie and the Weikerts left the farm for a short time seeking a safer haven. In late afternoon after the noise of battle subsided, they returned. Tillie was again gripped by shock. "The approaches [to the house] were crowded with wounded, dying, and dead. The air was filled with moanings and groaning. As we passed on toward the house, we were compelled to pick our steps in order that we might not tread on prostrate bodies. When we entered the house we found it also completely filled with wounded. We hardly knew what to do or where to go...."[9] Tillie assisted in tearing all the linen and muslin in the house for bandages. Her memories of the scenes of the amputating benches and the resulting piles of human limbs around the yard were vivid and painful. "...I could have no other feeling that the whole scene was one of cruel butchery."[10]

On July 4 Tillie met a soldier who had seen her family and he assured her that they were safe, a concern that had been constantly on her mind. However, it was not until July 7 that Tillie journeyed back to her home. "As it was impossible to travel the roads, on account of the mud, we took to the fields. While passing along, the stench arising from the fields of carnage was most sickening. Dead horses, swollen to almost twice their natural size, lay in all directions, stains of blood frequently met our gaze, and all kinds of army accouterments covered the ground. Fences had disappeared, some buildings were gone, others ruined. The whole landscape had been changed and I felt as though we were in a strange and blighted land."[11]

Her home was safe but changed and so was Tillie. Wearing the same bedraggled clothing that she left home in six long days before and a new countenance from her experiences, her mother did not recognize her. When Tillie finally spoke, her mother said, "Why, my dear child, is that you? How glad I am to have you home again without any harm having befallen you."[12]

Tillie Pierce attended the wounded in hospitals after the battle. In the years to come she saw the reunions between the Blue and the Gray. In 1888 Tillie wrote: "What in my girlhood was a teeming and attractive landscape spread out by the Omnipotent Hand to teach us of His Goodness, has by His direction, become a field for profound thought, where, through coming ages, will be taught lessons of loyalty, patriotism, and sacrifice."[13]

Tillie Pierce's home on Baltimore Street.

Annie Etheridge

Nurse, 3rd Michigan
Third Army Corps, First Division, Third Brigade

*I entered the military service of the United States in May
1861 with the 2nd Michigan Vol. Inf. Determined to serve
my country as long and as faithfully as my comrade brothers in every duty which a woman could do and I remained
the entire war with the Michigan Regiments the 2nd, 3rd,
and 5th Inf. of the Army of the Potomac—returning home
with the 5th Michigan Veteran Volunteer Inf. (which was
the 3rd and 5th Vol. Inf. consolidated) in July 1865.[1]*

"No history of Michigan in the war would be complete that did not
contain some mention of the noble service performed by Mrs. Anna
Etheridge...She unquestionably saved many hundreds of lives of
wounded men who would have perished but for her timely assistance."[2]

Anna Etheridge, or "Annie" or "Gentle Annie" as the soldiers called
her, was quite well known during the war. Acknowledgements and eyewitness accounts can be found in a variety of regimental histories, newspapers, books, and unpublished papers. Annie was loved and respected
by both the private and the general: "...not one of whom but feels
proud of the fact that he had the high honor to stand by her side in the
ranks of the grand army of the Republic."[3] "Many of us, who still carry
about painful reminders of those terrible scenes, are proud and grateful
to know that we owe our lives to her heroism and self-sacrifice on the
field of battle."[4]

"Her work was in the field hospitals and on the battlefields. It was
in the latter service that she accomplished the greatest amount of good
and displayed a heroism and devotion to her work that have not been
excelled in the annals of war. Often in the very thickest of the fight, she
never flinched for a moment in her noble work of love. Seeking out the
wounded who had been overlooked or not yet reached by the surgeons,
she bound up their wounds with the skill and promptness of a practical
surgeon."[5]

Annie's first battle experience was at Blackburn's Ford, Virginia
[July 18, 1861]. "The Second Michigan charged the enemy position,

the charge carrying them forward with such momentum that two mounted officers rode through the lines and were killed inside the enemy earthworks...Anna rode with the charge...and when the charge was over she dismounted, and under heavy fire, she unpacked her saddlebags and set about caring for the wounded."[6]

"She has for use a horse furnished with side-saddle, saddle-bags etc. At the commencement of a battle, she fills her saddle-bags with lint and bandages, mounts her horse, gallops to the front, passes under fire, and regardless of shot and shell, engages in the work of stanching and binding up the wounded of our soldiers...."[7]

> Where was she during battles? On the field with the regiment or as close to it as possible; binding up wounds in the storm of shot and shell and deadly mines, directing and aiding the wounded to the rear, to find the surgeons. Twice her horse was shot from under her, but she never quailed. The soldier sick in camp, was sure of a visit from Annie, and her ready sympathy and every comfort she could command. And often the encouraging, hopeful words were of more benefit that the delicacies that Annie's loving heart and willing hands found some means of providing. She was 'Our Annie' indeed...sympathizing and comforting us in sickness, sharing our perils on the battlefield and binding up our wounds.[8]

At the First Battle of Bull Run [July 21, 1861] "Annie Etheridge and her big horse were not on the field because the Second Michigan Regiment was being held in reserve, though at the end it was moved to cover the retreat...."[9]

"When not actively engaged on the battle-field or in the hospital, she superintends the cooking at the headquarters of the brigade. When the brigade moves, she mounts her horse and marches with the ambulances and surgeons, administering to the wants of the sick and wounded, and at the bivouac she wraps herself in her blanket and sleeps upon the ground...."[10]

At some point in the early part of 1862 Annie left the regiment. It is not known why but it could have been in response to one of the orders that were issued periodically forbidding women at the front. Sometimes the orders were conveniently ignored or proved unrealistic as soon as the next battle occurred. Whatever the reason was for Annie's temporary absence, she was still in the service of attending the wounded. She worked with other nurses on the hospital transports ships: the *Knickerbocker, Louisiana* and *Daniel Webster*. She also made three trips on truce boats to receive the wounded who had been left in enemy territory. She was back with her regiment by May.

One eyewitness claimed that it was "At the battle of Williamsburg [May 4-5, 1862], while dressing wounds, under fire, she was noticed by [Brigadier] General [Philip] Kearny, who ordered that she be provided with a horse, and told her that he should commend her for a sergeant's pay and warrant."[11] Kearny was killed in a subsequent battle before he was able to make good his recommendation. "For four years she performed these humane services without one cent remuneration or reward from any source whatever."[12]

> At one time the enemy had killed nearly every horse of one of our batteries, several of the caissons had been exploded, and more than half the men shot at their guns. Disheartened, the remainder were about to abandon their pieces, when Annie rode up calmly to the battery so thinned, and smiling, said, "That's right, boys, now you've got good range, you'll soon silence their battery." The boys took courage, remained at their posts, silenced the enemy's battery, and saved their pieces. One of the men, relating the incident, said, that "all the officers in the Army of the Potomac would not have had as much influence over the men as did Annie, on her little roan mare." They say she saved their battery that day.[13]

"At another time she came very near to being captured. Riding in the extreme front, she came within a rod of the enemy's line, but she said she grasped her pistol, (which she always wore in her belt) determined to have a fight before being captured."[14] Several accounts note this near escape but there is no record of Annie ever being captured. She wore two pistols in her belt but there is no evidence that she ever fired them.

Some accounts cite that Kearny's recognition of Annie's service occurred at the battle of Second Bull Run [August. 29-30, 1862]. This seems more reasonable since Kearny was killed at Chantilly [Sept. 1, 1862]. It was at this battle of Second Bull Run that Annie had a ghastly experience.

> Early in this battle she was on a portion of the battle-field which had been warmly contested, where there was a rocky ledge, under shelter of which, some of the wounded had crawled. Annie lingered behind the troops, as they changed position, assisted several poor helpless fellows to this cover and dressed their wounds...a noble

looking boy, to whose parched lips she had held the cooling draught, and had bound up his wounds, receiving in return a look of unutterable gratitude from his bright eyes, and his faintly murmured, "God's blessing on you," when a shot from the rebel battery tore him to pieces under her very hands. She discovered at the same moment that the rebels were near, and almost upon her, and she was forced to follow in the direction of the regiment.[15]

Annie was not at the Battle of South Mountain [Sept. 14, 1862] or Antietam [Sept. 17, 1862] because "the division in which she belonged was temporarily detached from the army and left in front of Washington." 16 But she was back in form for the Chancellorsville Campaign [April-May 1863].

"Anna is of Dutch descent, about five feet three inches in height, fair complexion (now somewhat browned by exposure), brown hair, vigorous constitution, and decidedly good looking. Her dress on entering the battle, is a riding dress, so arranged as to be looped up when she dismounts."[17]

> At Chancellorsville, on the third of May [Annie's birthday] 1863, while commanding a brigade engaged with the enemy and under severe fire, I saw Annie Etheridge riding along my line of battle, she came to me and offered me some hot coffee which she said she had just made. I told her she was in great danger, and directed her to proceed immediately to the rear. She did not seem to appreciate the peril of her position; but replied that she had just come from the front where she saw [Major] Gen. [Hiram] Berry, that if I should be wounded she would be sure to take care of me, and that she was well provided with bandages, etc.[18]

Another soldier observed Annie's visit. "During the severest shelling on Sunday [May 3] morning, she rode coolly up to the spot where the brigade commander and staff were watching the progress of the fight, and insisted on them eating some breakfast and drinking some coffee she had provided. Ordered repeatedly to seek a place of safety, she refused till each one had taken a drink of coffee from her canteen, and a 'hard tack or two if nothing more.' While in the group three horses were shot from under their riders by her side, but she never flinched or betrayed the slightest emotion of fear."[19]

At one point Annie rode to some trenches at the front and made her way along the line with words of encouragement and praise. The men reacted by cheering her. The commotion was duly noted by the enemy who were now aware of the position of the line and a volley was fired. A Union colonel ordered Annie to the rear.

> Anne rode to the rear of the line, then turned to see the results; as she did so, an officer pushed his horse between her and a large tree by which she was waiting, thus sheltering himself behind her. She looked round at him with surprise, when a second volley was fired, and a minie ball whizzing by her, entered the officer's body and fell a corpse, against her and then to the ground. At the same moment another ball grazed her hand (the only wound she received during the war), pierced her dress, the skirt of which she was holding, and slightly wounding her horse. Frightened by the pain, he set off on a run through a dense wood, winding in and out among the trees so rapidly that Annie feared being torn from her saddle by the branches, or having her brains dashed out by violent contact with the trunks. She raised herself upon the saddle, and crouching on her knees clung to the pommel. The frightened animal as he emerged from the woods plunged into the midst of the Eleventh Corps, when his course was soon checked.[20]

A soldier's letter told how Birney's Division followed the Confederates down the Plank Road at Chancellorsville, were surrounded, and had to cut their way out. He went on: "Annie Etheridge...accompanied them on their perilous journey on horseback, and was under fire the whole time; she was perfectly cool, and often dismounted to help the poor wounded soldiers."[21]

Annie was seen the next day.

> Upon a stump sat the form of a woman...Her long black hair had fallen from its coil; no covering was upon her head. A rubber blanket was about her form. It was Annie Etheridge, the heroine of Birney's Division. She had been out all night on the plank road, had been hit through the clothing several times, and now, pale and exhausted, but resolute, she was cheering on the poor fellows, whose life-blood dripped from the stretchers as the carriers sped in rapid procession by her position. Her dark, expressive eyes, clear-cut face, and a firm mouth betokened the courageous, daring woman who won the respect of all alike during those dark and perilous days.[22]

"She shrank from no danger however great, when she could be of service in saving the lives of the men. Frequently under the hottest fire of the enemy, she always displayed the most intrepid coolness and indifference to danger. No man in all the army, from General to Private, periled his life oftener or more willingly than she."[23] "Gen. Barry...declares that she has been under so hot a fire of the enemy as himself."[24]

On May 16, 1863 General Order #48 was issued containing an announcement at its close. "The Brig. Gen. commanding Div. [Brig. Gen. D. B. Birney] announces the following names of meritorious and distinguished non-commissioned officers and privates selected as recipients of the 'KEARNY CROSS'—the Division decoration...This CROSS is in honor of our leader [the deceased Gen. Philip Kearny] and the wearers of it will always remember his high standards of a true and brave soldier and will never disgrace it."[25]

"On the 27th [May 1863], the division was paraded to witness a presentation of the Kearny medals...Among the recipients was Annie

Annie Etheridge wearing the Kearny Cross.
(MOLLUS)

110

Etheridge; and, as she received the medal from the hands of Gen. Birney, there was not a soldier in the division who did not feel that it was a just and fitting tribute to a brave woman."[26]

Annie marched with her regiment to the battle of Gettysburg. "Do not think that 'with the regiment' meant back with the ambulance train and with the hospitals; far otherwise, 'Our Annie' was one of us and always with us, riding her own horse at the rear of the regiment with the surgeon, on the march…at the bivouac and in camp."[27]

"On the march she usually rode a pony, but at night by the bivouac she wrapped herself in her blanket and slept upon the ground with all the hardihood of the veteran soldier. Yet, although sharing thus all the exposures and hardships of the common soldier, with whom she freely mingled, she always maintained the modest reserve and delicacy of the true lady. The soldiers held her in the highest estimation, not one of whom but would have periled his life in her defense."[28]

"I remember her moving softly amongst the wounded kneeling upon the ground beside them and tenderly bathing and dressing their wounds. Her low woman's voice was music to their ears and her kind words of sympathy and encouragement and gentle reproof for undue and danger-ous restlessness seemed almost angelic to the sufferers whose eyes fol-lowed her from place to place as she went from one to another. Her presence alone was of incalculable benefit…she filled a place there that no man could fill…"[29] "I had the misfortune to be wounded twice while in the army and both times had the good fortune to meet her on the field and she dressed my wounds…"[30]

One Pennsylvania officer remembered seeing Annie on July 2. It was late afternoon after the III Corps was pushed back from their ex-tended line. He was one of the re-enforcements running past the Trossel Farm toward the Peach Orchard "amidst cannon shot that was throwing up loose dirt around the farm…While passing the Trosell [sic] House, a woman on horseback and in uniform galloped back from the line of battle, asked for some information, and quickly returned to the front again. She was a nurse of the Third Corps, Anna Etheridge, and was directing the removal of the wounded. She was cool and self-possessed and did not seem to mind the fire."[31]

Annie marched away from Gettysburg with her regiment and after the Draft Riots [July 13-16] accompanied them to New York to quell any further demonstrations. A soldier of the regiment recalled her at Troy, New York. "Annie's tent is besieged with visitors. People come

The Trostle Farm after the battle.
(MOLLUS)

from far in the rural districts to get a sight of the great heroine of so many campaigns and battles. We do not blame them much, for indeed she is a curiosity, as she is one woman in a million who would leave a home of luxury and cast her lot with the soldiers in the field, who are all proud of her, and any man in the regiment would die in her defense, should anyone cast a reproach on her fair name and character. All believe her to be one of the truest of women."[32]

"She takes the deepest interest in the result of this contest, eagerly reading all the papers to which she can obtain access and keeping thoroughly posted as to the progress of the war."[33] "She always refused to enlist as a nurse, saying she would never leave the Third [Michigan]."[34]

During the campaigns in the spring of 1864, an undelivered letter was found on the body of one of the soldiers in Annie's division. It was dated January 14, 1864 and addressed to her.

> Dearest Friend; I am not long for this world, and I wish to thank you for your kindness ere I go. You were the only one who was ever kind to me, since I entered the Army. At Chancellorsville, I was shot through the body, the ball entering my side, and coming out through the shoulder. I was also hit in the arm, and was carried to the hospital in the woods, where I lay for hours, and not a surgeon would touch me; when

you came along and gave me water, and bound my wounds. I do not know what regiment you belong to, and I don't know if this will ever reach you...But should you get this, please accept my heartfelt gratitude; and may God bless you, and protect you from all dangers, may you be eminently successful in your present pursuit. I enclose a flower...it is the only gift I have to send you...I know nothing of your history, but I hope you always have, and always may be happy; and since I will be unable to see you in this world, I hope I may meet you in that better world, where there is no war. May God bless you, both now and forever, is the wish of your grateful friend....."[35]

On April 15, 1864, General Grant issued the order for all females to leave the front. The effectiveness of this order varied in individual cases. In Annie's case her records show that she was in seven battles of the Army of the Potomac from the Wilderness [May 5-7, 1864] up to Cold Harbor [June 3, 1864] and "Before Petersburg" to mid June. A nurse at White House [hospital site] on June 16, 1864 wrote: "I met with Annie Etheridge, who has been in the army for three years. She looks as sunburnt as any soldier."[36]

Annie served on the Hospital Transport *Wenonah* that traveled up to D.C. She returned to City Point and the Second Corps Hospital in early July. A nurse at City Point wrote on July 7, 1864: "I went, day before yesterday, out 6 miles with Anna Etheridge to see some sick in the first Michigan cavalry."[37] On July 13, 1864 a petition was gathered for Annie to "return and remain" with her regiment. It was signed by 286 men, plus their Colonel, the Brigade General, the division's Major General, and the II Corps commander Major General A.A. Humphreys. Yet, on September 12, 1864 she is still at City Point. A nurse wrote: "Last night Anna Etheridge staid all night with me. She is of newspaper renown and is deserving I guess."[38]

Annie was famous by this time. "Among the many heroes and heroines of this present war [who] has [been] developed, there is one...furnishing an example believed to be without a parallel in the history of the sex."[39] "...[I]f England can boast of the achievements of Florence Nightingale, we of America can present a still higher example of female heroism and exalted acts of humanity in the person Anna Etheridge."[40] A romanticized image was published of Annie rallying the troops, waving a flag on horseback. Although there are allusions to her rallying the men and leading the men into battle there were no verifiable examples given. Annie also had poems written about her.[41]

The Hospital Transport *Wenonah* on which Annie Etheridge served.
(Miller's Photographic History of the Civil War)

Having sent gifts of food to her old regiment from City Point all summer, Annie was back in the ranks.

> On the 27th of October, 1864, in one of the battles for the posses-sion of Hatcher's Run and Boydtown Plank Road, a portion of the Third Division of the Second Corps, was nearly surrounded by the enemy, in what the soldiers called the "Bull Ring." The regiment to which Annie was attached was sorely pressed, the balls flying thick and fast, so that the surgeon advised her to accompany him to safer quarters; but she lingered, watching for an opportunity to render assistance. A little drum-mer boy stopped to speak to her, when a ball struck him, and he fell against her, and then to the ground, dead. This so startled her, that she ran towards the line of battle. But to her surprise, she found that the enemy occupied every part of the ground held a few moments before by Union troops. She did not pause, however, but dashed through their lines unhurt....[42]

This appears to be one time that Annie was unnerved.

A nurse wrote home of Annie in March 1865; "[She] is very bare of clothes. She wants thee to buy her a skirt exactly like mine and two pairs of stockings like my old brown ones."[43] Yet a soldier of the regi-ment observed Annie in the spring of 1865: "Then on Sunday too, can be seen Annie in her best dress, sitting on the ground with her own boys

War time image of Annie rallying troops.
(Women's Work in the Civil War)

listening to the men of God. These Sunday meetings, as a general rule are well attended...."[44]

Annie said: "When encamped near Jeffersonville, Indiana July 5, 1865 just before our return home I was presented with an official copy of the battles in which we had participated in nearly every one of which I had been with my command giving my services as nurse..."[45] This copy lists 32 battles. However, with general designations such as "Battles before Richmond (1862), Before Petersburg, and Pursuit and capture of Lee," the true total is higher.

A soldier of her regiment recalled the muster out in Detroit on July 17, 1865: "Noble Annie is with us to the last, and her brave womanly spirit breaks down, and scalding tears trickle down her beautiful bronze face as each of the boys and comrades bid her goodbye."[46]

Information of Annie's pre-war life is both conflicting and confusing. It is agreed that she was born Lucinda A. Blair but three different birthdates can be found. The month and day [May 3] are not in question, but the year is noted as 1832, 1839, or 1844.[47] However, the 1850 census of Wayne County, Michigan, listed Lucinda Anna Blair at eleven years old. Her parents, Cynthia and John, had two other children: Maria, age 6 and Edwin age 4. Supposedly Annie's father died while she was still a child.[48] Sometime between 1850 and 1860 the family moved out of state, either to Minnesota or Wisconsin, according to various sources. Annie was "visiting" in Detroit when she enlisted in the 2nd Michigan. By 1861 Annie had already married twice. Her first marriage was to a David Kellogg, the second to James Etheridge. Any evidence of a husband, however, disappeared by the time of her enlistment. Not one of her war experiences recalled by the veterans mentioned a husband although she was frequently noted as Mrs. Annie Etheridge.[49]

After the war Annie settled in D.C. She acquired a position in the Treasury Department by gathering a good number of character references from army surgeons, officers and a general or two. This was done in 1865 and 1866, so she must have spent little time in the west and headed to the capital soon after she was mustered out. In 1870 Annie married Charles E. Hook, a one armed veteran of Co. H., 7th Connecticut Infantry.

In 1878 Annie was discharged from her job at the Treasury Department to make room for another applicant. Union veteran organizations immediately went into action.

> The call for petitions to re-instate "Anna Etheridge," "Our Anna," who, for four years, braved with us every danger and shared every privation and hardship of a soldier's life, and who so often freely risked her life on the battle-field to bind up the wounds of the fallen and comfort the last moments of the dying, has through petty intrigues, been removed from her position in the United States Treasury. The only reasons given for her discharge were that she possessed a small competence which she has saved from her hard earnings, and that her husband, a one-armed soldier, has a place as watchman at the navy yard at a very small salary. Beggarly reasons, these. Her noble deeds in the dark days of the war entitled her to a place in Government employ as long as she lives. This would be but a small return for the service she rendered the country.
>
> Comrades, an opportunity is now offered us to testify to the grateful love we bear her, and the obligations we owe at her hands. This is to sign a petition for her reinstatement. Let this be done with a prompt-

A post war photograph of Annie with her medals.
(State Archives of Michigan)

ness and heartiness that shall show the gratitude we, as soldiers of Michigan, feel for her kind and loving care on the field of death and in the weary hospital.[50]

Although hundreds of men [and a few widows] from a variety of units throughout the states signed petitions it appears that Annie was not re-instated.

Newspaper articles tell of Annie's trips to Michigan from D.C. for army reunions. Quotes from speeches chronicling her war activities were given. She received glowing tributes and emotional receptions.[51]

In 1866 a request was submitted in Annie's behalf for a pension for her services throughout the war. Included was a deposition by an embittered Annie.

> [I served] upon the "field" as well as in camp hospitals—"under fire" the same as were the soldiers—dressing the wounds of the fallen—caring for the dying and preparing and supplying from the stores in my care nourishment and stimulant which alone could save the lives of many of our brave men.
>
> I received no compensation whatever during the war for any services—they were given entirely at "the front" and most amid the hardships and dangers of the battlefield. In this receiving none (not even what the soldiers received). I was obliged to expend for personal expenses in living—clothing, some even in transportation though *that* it was expected I would be furnished—All of which for four years and three months could but be considerable.
>
> ...I most earnestly and respectfully ask for the rate of $50 per month [privates' pensions ran as high as $72] feeling that the length of my service and the character of the same with the great danger and hardship incurred from which I can never fully recover...My services have never received recognition unless some government employment at low compensation for *very* hard work in the U. S. Treasury where I *earned* more than received can be called such—prior to 1878—since which time I have been denied *even that*.[52]

The pension was approved by Congress on February 9, 1887 for $25 per month.

Annie Etheridge Hook died on January 23, 1913 at Georgetown University Hospital, her husband having preceded her in death three years earlier, almost to the day. On January 27, 1913, she was buried in Arlington National Cemetery, section 15, grave number 710.

Mary Tepe

Vivandiere, 114th Pennsylvania
Third Army Corps, First Division, First Brigade

"Hers was the only face in the vicinity which seemed in any way gay. She was laughing and pointing very unconcernedly, as she stumbled over axes, spades and other obstacles, on her way through the trench! She was wonderfully courageous or else did not understand the danger...the shower of musket-balls, shrapnel, and every sort of projectile falling the in the midst of us was trying to the nerves of our coolest."[1]

There are numerous conflicting stories concerning Mary Tepe. It is thought that she was born Mary Brose in 1834 in France, emigrated to America at about age 15, and at about age 20 attached herself, legally or otherwise, to Bernardo Tepe who was a tailor in Philadelphia. In 1861 when he enlisted in the 27th Pennsylvania, Mary went with him.

Her uniform was similar to that of the women who followed the eagles of France. She wore a blue zouave jacket, a short skirt trimmed with red braid, which reached to just below the knees, and red trousers over a pair of boots. She wore a man's sailor hat turned down.

She purchased a store of tobacco, cigars, hams and other things not issued by the government and sold them to the soldiers. She also did a thriving trade selling contraband whiskey. She carried the whiskey in a small oval keg strapped to her shoulder.

When the regiment was not in action, she cooked, washed and mended for the men.

She drew the pay of a soldier and was allowed 25 cents per day extra for hospital and headquarters services, making her pay $21.45 per month for over two years. Then some friction in the Paymaster's Department about the enlistment of women stopped her pay, but did not dampen her patriotism. She continued selling goods to the soldiers and $5 per pint for whiskey was not an unusual price.[2]

Sometime in 1861 Mary left both the 27th Pennsylvania and Bernard Tepe. A veteran gave this story for the reason: "One night some soldiers among whom was her husband, broke into the vivandiere's tent

Mary Tepe,
in French-styled uniform.
(GNMP)

and stole $1,600. The men were afterwards punished, but the vivandiere decided to quit the regiment. She refused to have anything to do with her husband…[she was] requested to continue with the regiment, but her indignation was so great that she left."[3] It was after she left the 27th Pennsylvania that she joined the 114th Pennsylvania, which was known as Collis' Zouaves.

"She was in the first battle of Bull Run [July 21, 1861], witnessed the slaughter at Fair Oaks [May 1862], and campaigned with McClellan near Richmond [Peninsular Campaign March-July 1862]."[4]

On October 27, 1862, a soldier in the 114th Pennsylvania noticed Mary at a difficult fording of the Potomac. "All were in the same predicament, excepting the staff officers, who were on horseback, and Marie, the vivandiere, who had the forethought to pick up an old mule, on which she safely crossed the river."[5]

At the battle of Fredericksburg [December 13, 1862] she is noted again: "Here, with the surgeons and Marie, the vivandiere, we established the field hospital, and soon after we had quite a number of our regiment, who were wounded, to assist in taking care of."[6] Mary herself was wounded at this battle. "At Fredericksburg she received a bullet in her left ankle."[7]

Mary was back in season for the battle of Chancellorsville [May 3, 1863]. A nurse attached to the Maine troops in the Army of the Potomac described her own crossing of the Rappahannock having come up from the field hospital and she remarked on Mary's presence, "…[S]ince I left this place for the hospital at Chancellorsville, I had not seen a woman, and did not know that any other woman crossed the river at this place while our forces were on the south side, excepting 'Mary,' the vivandiere of the 114th P.V., who was a brave and faithful worker."[8]

After this battle Mary received the Kearny Cross. A comrade in the 114th had this to say about the event:

> We were pleased to find that quite a number of the valiant comrades of our regiment had received medals for meritorious conduct in battle, and particularly in the last desperate contest [Chancellorsville]; but they did not seem to appreciate the special recognition, many regarding it as casting a reflection upon the men who stood shoulder to shoulder with them, and worthy of the same mark of heroism. It was the feeling of the true soldier that prompted them to ignore the exceptional favors, saying, as they did, that they did not consider themselves entitled to any more distinction than those who received no medals. For this reason very few of the medals were worn. Even Marie, the vivandiere, received one, but she would not wear it, remarking that [Major] General [David Bell] Birney could keep it, as she did not want the present. Had it been made of gold, instead of copper, Marie would have set a higher value upon the souvenir. She was a courageous woman, and often got within range of the enemy's fire whilst parting with the contents of her canteen among our wounded men. Her skirts were riddled by bullets during the battle of Chancellorsville.[9]

Mary marched with her unit in the campaign to Gettysburg. One soldier wrote: "On June 12th [1863] the entire 3rd Corps passed us and…a good opportunity was had for watching this command pass in review. In it we had many friends. On foot and marching with the One Hundred and Fourteenth Pennsylvania (Collis' Zouaves) we saw 'French Mary.'"[10]

The field hospital to which Mary would have been attached was located on the Taneytown Road behind the "Round Tops." A hospital assistant described the hospital during the battle:

It was discovered that the hospital was too close to the line of battle, and at this time there was an abundance of work for the operating surgeons and their corps of assistants. The doctors selected another hospital site, along Rock Creek, as a proper place on account of safety and the good supply of water. What we experienced here will never be effaced from our memories. Along this creek was a meadow of several acres. Here they brought all the wounded on this part of the line...The 2nd of July was a day of horror. To and from our hospital the ambulances heaped with the wounded were running all day; some of the men were dead when delivered to the surgeons, and others were more dead than alive; the most of them however, were not dangerously stung by the balls and bayonet thrusts of the enemy. The dead were lying on the field. The surgeons soon had their rude tables erected for amputating purposes...

The wounded could soon be counted by the thousands, and what could these few doctors and their assistants do when there were so many to do for?...[T]he wounded were constantly crying for water. All day, and even during the night, these busy surgeons were amputating limbs in the hope of saving the lives of the unfortunate. Frequently the severed arms and legs reached level with the tables, in ghastly heaps, when a detail of men would dig long trenches and bury them.

...[A]ll this, too, taking place under the intense heat of a July sun! The second day around these tables, the peculiar stench became unbearable. At night we had some opportunity for lying down, in the hope of having rest, but sleep was impossible for the pleading cry for water came from the wounded in every direction...and so it was kept up, this horrid work..."[11]

Mary was photographed on East Cemetery Hill soon after the battle. Why she did not leave the field with her regiment to pursue the retreating Confederate army is not known. Perhaps she stayed to help with the wounded.

Mary was back with her regiment in winter quarters 1863-64 and was observed at Brandy Station, Virginia:

At this time gambling was rife in the army, to a demoralizing extent. Looking over the field could be observed dozens of groups of soldiers squatted on the ground, playing what was called "sweat box." One of the group was selected as banker, sometimes they would break him, but oftener the banker would break them. Hundreds of dollars would often change

**Mary Tepe on East Cemetery
Hill a few days after the battle.**
(GNMP)

hands in a short time, and even our Marie the cantiniere, was tempted to try her luck. Looking on at a party playing, she saw a soldier win a large sum of money in almost no time, so she thought to go and do likewise, and invested with the banker; but instead of winning, Marie soon lost, and was fifty dollars poorer by reason of her experience. She was too sharp to be caught again, and being thoroughly disgusted she played no more.[12]

When the Army of the Potomac took up their deadly occupation again in the spring of 1864, Mary was with them. She was seen at the Bloody Angle during Spotsylvania [May 7-20] by a soldier of another unit. "I looked around. Sure enough there was a woman! She was about 25 years of age, square featured and sunburnt, and dressed in Zouave uniform in the Vivandiere style. She was with two men and they seemed to be looking for their regiment, the 114th Pennsylvania Infantry, they said, which was also know as Collis' Zouaves."[13]

After the war Mary Tepe lived in the Pittsburgh area and married Richard Leonard on April 9, 1872. Leonard was a veteran of a three month Pennsylvania unit and late of Co. K, 1st Maryland Cavalry. In 1893 Mary journeyed to Philadelphia with her comrades to celebrate the anniversary of the Battle of Fredericksburg. In 1897 she filed divorce papers which were not followed through and in 1900 made a will leaving Richard all she possessed valued at $31.35.

"For many years the aged woman had been an invalid and was lately a great sufferer from the rheumatism and a rebel bullet which she still carries in her left ankle."[14] Mary committed suicide in the spring of 1901 by drinking paris green "a caustic pesticide and paint pigment."[15] She died on Rafferty's Hill, Baldwin Township, Allegheny County, Pennsylvania and was buried there in an unmarked grave.

Mary Tepe, however, was not forgotten. Her photograph that was taken after Gettysburg was published in *Military Images* in 1983 spurred more information on the vivandiere to come forth, most being supplied by Marie Melchiori, who has spent years researching Tepe. Around the same time, a couple from the Pittsburgh area, Mr. & Mrs. Russ Baroni, began their quest to locate Tepe's grave. They found it four years later, unidentified, in St. Paul's Cemetery. Mr. Baroni brought the lack of identification to the attention of a local Sons of Union Veterans chapter who took it upon themselves to raise money and erect a stone for Tepe. The stone was dedicated in a ceremony on September 25, 1988.

The Melchioris stand behind Mary Tepe's gravestone.
(Marie Melchiori)

Rose Quinn Rooney

Laundress, Co. K, 15th Louisiana
II Army Corps, Johnson's Division, Nicholls' Brigade

"There is one bright, shining record of a patriotic and tire-less woman which remains undimmed when placed beside that of the most devoted Confederate women: I refer to Mrs. Rose Rooney, of Company K, Fifteenth Louisiana Regiment, who left New Orleans in June 1861, and never deserted the 'b'ys' for a day until the surrender."[1]

Rose Rooney was in her forties when she enlisted in New Orleans on June 8, 1861 as a laundress in the "Crescent City Blues...This company was composed of members of the Pelican Hook and Ladder Company of New Orleans. It went to Virginia unattached and fought at the First Manassas [July 21, 1861 with Shafer's independent battalion] with two other independent companies. In September, 1861 it was attached for one month to the 49th Virginia Infantry. In October, 1861, it was transferred to St. Paul's [Louisiana] Foot Rifles and in May, 1862, was attached to Coppen's [Louisiana] Battalion. In August, 1862, it was transferred to the 3rd Louisiana Battalion [which then became the 15th Louisiana] and appears to have late served with the 1st Louisiana Volunteers. Of its members, 38 percent were foreign born...."[2]

"By late spring [1861] most of the commands destined for Virginia were organized and ready to be shipped out. In addition to the twelve thousand men who made up these units, a sizable number of camp followers went along as well. One New Orleans correspondent that Coppen's Zouaves had the good taste to bring women along with them to Pensacola [Florida] to wash, cook, and clean their quarters...They were described by one observer as being "disgusting looking creatures,' who were 'all dressed up as men.' Rose Rooney, however, was one woman who earned the respect of all the Louisiana soldiers."[3]

"At the battle of First Manassas, she signalized her courage and devotion by bravely pulling down a fence in the midst of bursting shells to let the Battery of the Washington Artillery pass through."[4]

The notorious activities of some Louisiana troops branded any military unit from that state. They were well known for mutiny, drunkenness, brawls, looting, robbery and theft. Most soldiers and civilians, both North and South, dreaded the "Louisiana Tigers."[5] The officers of these units were not exempt from the men's aggression and employed the strongest forms of discipline to maintain control.

Despite their reputations, Louisiana troops excited and impressed people.

> The greatest sight I have yet seen in the way of military was a body of about 600 Louisiana Zouaves, uniformed and drilled it was said in the true French Zouaves style. Most of them were of foreign extraction—the French predominant—but there were Irish, Germans, Italians, Swiss, etc. etc. Their uniforms consisted of loose red flannel pants tied above the ankles, blue flannel jackets, and for headgear a kind of red flannel bag large enough at one end to fit the head and tapering to a point at the other where it was generally decorated with a piece of ribbon. This end fell behind. In this cap, which, you see, did not protect their faces from the sun in the least, they had been wasting for month or two in the burning sun of Pensacola, and of course were as brown as they could get—browner than I ever saw a white man. Add to their costume and complexion that they were hard specimens before they left the 'crescent city' as their manner indicated and you may perhaps imagine what sort of men they were. In fact they were the most savage-looking crowd I ever saw....[6]

Their reputation, uniform, foreign speech, and renowned fierceness in battle all contributed to set aside the Louisiana troops as exotic and extraordinary. Mrs. Rooney must have been an equally strong and unique individual to hold her own with these men for four years of war. During the war one veteran wrote a piece on the Crescent City Blues and said: "This Historical note would not be complete unless or without the allusion to Mrs. Rose Rooney, whose faithfull [sic] service as a Laundress and nurse and Cook deserve special mention. She joined the company at its organization, has constantly accompanied it in all its long and wearisome marches and still remains with it."[7]

Another comrade described the marching route of the 15th Louisiana through the Gettysburg Campaign: "...[T]he 4th of June 1863 it marched with the whole Army for the invasion of Pennsylvania, proceeding by way of Culpeper Court House and Winchester, assisting in the rout of Milroy's forces at the last named place on the 13th of June 1863, crossing the Potomac at Shepherdstown and continuing thro' Hagerstown and Chambersburg, advanced within four miles of Carlisle, being in the Corps commanded by Genl. Ewell. [Even the Tigers were on good behavior during the invasion except for a few drunken toots.] With the whole army it retreated, participating in the hard found battle of Gettysburg July 2nd and 3rd 1863."[8]

The 15th Louisiana was one of the Confederate units that attacked Culp's Hill on July 2nd. Johnson's Division hospitals were around the Hunterstown Road and Rose was most likely nursing in that area.

A Louisiana nurse remembered Mrs. Rooney:

> She was no hanger-on about camp, but in everything but actual fighting was as useful as any of the boys she loved with all her big, warm, Irish heart, and served with the undaunted bravery which led her to risk the dangers of every battle-field where the regiment was engaged, unheeding the zip of the minies, the shock of shells, or the horrible havoc made by the solid shot, so that she might give timely succor to the wounded or comfort the dying. When in camp she looked after the comfort of the regiment, both sick and well, and many a one escaped being sent to the hospital because Rose attended to him so well. She managed by some means to keep on hand stock of real coffee, paying at times thirty-five dollars per pound for it."[9]

Rose Rooney remained with the 15th Louisiana until the close of the war. Her name is on the roster at Appomattox. "The surrender almost broke her heart. Her defiant ways caused her to be taken prisoner."[10] The following is an account of Rose's experience at the surrender and afterwards which was said to be in her own words:

> Sure, the Yankees took me prisoner along with the rest. The next day, when they were changing the camps to fix up the wounded, I asked them what would they do with *me*. They tould me to "go to the devil." I tould them, "I've been long enough in his company, I'd choose something better." I then asked them where any Confederates lived. They tould me about three miles through the woods. On my way I met some Yankees. They asked me, "What have you in that bag?" I said, "Some rags of my own." I had a lot of rags on the top, but six new dresses at the bottom; and sure I got off with them all. Then they asked me if I had any money. One of the Yankees, a poor devil of a rivate soldier, handed to me twenty-five cents of Yankee money. I said to him, "Sure, you must be an Irishman." "Yes," said he. I then went on until I got to the house. Mrs. Crump and her sister were in the yard, and about twenty negro women—no men. I had not a bite for two days, nor any water, so I began to cry from weakness. Mrs. Crump said, "Don't cry, you are

among friends." She then gave me plenty to eat,—hot hoe-cake and buttermilk. I stayed there fifteen days, superintending the cooking for the sick and wounded men. One-half of the house was full of Confederates, and the other of Yankees. They then brought us to Burkesville, where all the Yankees were gathered together. There was an ould doctor there, and he began to curse me, and to talk about all we had done to their prisoners. I tould him, "And what have *you* to say to what you done to *our* poor fellows?" He tould me to shut up, *and sure I did.* They asked me fifty questions after, and I never opened my mouth. The next day was the day when all the Confederate flags came to Petersburg. I had some papers in my pocket that would have done harrum to some people, so I chewed them all up and ate them, but I wouldn't take the oath, and I *never did take it.* The flags were brought in on dirt-cars, and as they passed the Federal camps them Yankees would unfurl them and shake them about to show them. My journey from Burkesville to Petersburg was from eleven in the morning till eleven at night, and I sitting on my bundle all the way. The Yankee soldiers in the car were cursing me, and calling me a damn rebel, and more ugly talk. I said, "Mabbe some of you has got a mother or wife; if so, you'll show some respect for *me*." Then they were quiet. I had to walk three miles to Captain Buckner's headquarters. The family were in a house near the battle-ground, but the door was shut, and I didn't know who was inside, and I couldn't see any light. I sat down on the porch, and thought I would have to stay there all night. After a while I saw a light coming from under the door, and so I knocked; when the door was opened and they saw who it was, they were all delighted to see me, because they were afraid I was dead. I wanted to go to Richmond, but would not go on a Yankee transportation. When the brigade came down, I cried my heart out because I was not let go on with them. I stayed three months with Mrs. Cloyd, and then Mayor Rawle sent me forty dollars and fifty more if I needed it, and that brought me home to New Orleans.[11]

Rose Quinn was born in Ireland in the 1820s. She emigrated to America in the 1840s, most likely one of the thousands of Irish who left during the potato famine. She lived in New Orleans and married Michael Rooney at St. Mary's Church on June 2, 1844. In March of 1845 a daughter, Mary, was born to them and in March 1849 a son, Michael, arrived. Rose's husband, Michael, died on August 28, 1853 from yellow fever during the "Epidemic Summer." By 1860 she appeared to have lost her children also. The only Rooney living with Rose in the 1860 census was one Peter Rooney, age 14. Whether a relative or not,

Peter Rooney enlisted in a state militia unit while Rose left with her regiment in 1861.

Rose's post war life is a mystery until 1888 when a former Confederate nurse wrote: "Mrs. Rooney is still cared for and cherished by the veterans of Louisiana. At the Soldier's Home she holds the position of matron, and her little room is a shrine never neglected by visitors to 'Camp Nichols.' Upon every occasion when the association of A. [Army of Northern Virginia] appear as an association, Mrs. Rooney is with them, an honored member. Neatly dressed, her cap of the real Irish pattern surmounting her face, beaming with pride in the 'b'ys.'[12] In a February, 1891 document from Camp Nichols, a home for Confederate Veterans, she was listed as an occupant receiving $6 per month for unspecified employment. At that time the superintendent's wife was the matron.

In an article on Camp Nichols in 1893, a *Daily Picayune* reporter wrote: One of the chief inmates of the home is old Mrs. Rooney. She followed the boys of the 14th [*sic*] La. during all the war, washing, mending, and caring for them. Now that she is old and alone the soldiers take care of her. She lives in a tiny room off to herself away from the main building where she mends the boys clothes and lives out the

A postcard of Camp Nichols, Louisiana State Confederate Soldiers Home in New Orleans.
(Historic New Orleans Military/Research Center)

129

end of her life in sunshine and peace. Almost any hour in the day one may [visit] and hear Mrs. Rooney fighting her battles over again with some *graybeard* here as she sits and knits in the sun beside her door."[13] And it was the *Daily Picayune* that reported Rose's death from a fall: "On Wednesday, Feb. 27, 1895 at 10:30 a.m. Mrs. Rose Rooney, aged 72 years, a native of Ireland, and a resident of this city for the past fifty-two years. Funeral will take place from the Soldier's Home this (Friday) morning, March 1, 1895 at 10 o'clock."[14] Since the names of the dead are not listed, it can only be assumed that Rose is buried in the Home's tomb for destitute veterans in Greenwood Cemetery, New Orleans. Sadly, this site has been so long neglected, that it has been impossible at this point to even discover who has the responsibility for maintaining it.

Rose Quinn Rooney was born to a country with legendary female warriors and in her adopted country she herself joined a fighting unit whose history was both famous and infamous. Unfortunately, as with so many female American historical figures, most of her own story is lost.

Mrs. Rooney is believed to have been interred in this tomb for destitute Confederate soldiers in Greenwood Cemetery, New Orleans.
(Courtesy Yvette Guillot Boling)

Elizabeth Salome "Sallie" Myers

Gettysburg Civilian

"I went to the church, where men were lying [on] the pews and on the floors. I knelt by the first one inside the door and said, 'What can I do for you?' He replied, 'Nothing. I am going to die.'"[1]

That meeting took place at the Roman Catholic Church on West High Street in Gettysburg where Sallie began nursing on July 2. Her narrative continues: "To be thus met by the first one addressed was more than my nerves could stand and I went hastily out, sat down on the church steps and cried."

"In a little while I re-entered the church hospital and spoke again to the dying man. He was Sergeant Alexander Stewart of the 149th Pennsylvania Infantry Regiment. He spoke of his home, his aged father and mother, of his wife, and his younger and only brother, who had been severely wounded, and was then at home, and asked me to take their addresses and send them his dying message."

Sallie took Sgt. Stewart to her home where "He lingered until Monday, July 6. He had been sinking gradually all evening. About 9 he had a spell of coughing until 10 o'clock, he suffered dreadfully. I held him in my arms until nearly 11 when his head sank back on the pillow and he died with only a slight struggle. [He] was buried in the graveyard of the United Presbyterian Church in which his father had been baptized 63 years before."

Sallie Myers was 21 years old in 1863. She worked in the Gettysburg public school system as second assistant to the principal. She lived on West High Street down the road from the Catholic Church with her parents, four sisters and one brother. Her family, including uncles and cousins, gave 15 men to the Union army during the war.

For a woman, who on July 1, almost fainted at the sight of a horse with head wound, Sallie soon overcame her sensitivity to dress wounds and witness amputations. Her family's home was used for soldiers with serious wounds, mostly from Pennsylvania units. The fact that only two men died of the twelve who stayed there attests to the quality of

Elizabeth Salome "Sallie" Myers in 1863.
(Jim Cole)

**The Roman Catholic Church
where Sallie nursed.**
(GNMP)

Sallie Myers Steward later in life.
(Adams County Historical Society)

care they received. Sallie worked with the wounded in town until they were all removed to the Letterman General Hospital just outside Gettysburg.

On July 16, the father of Alexander Stewart came to claim his son's body. In the following summer of 1864, Stewart's mother and brother, Henry, visited Sallie. A romance developed between Sallie and Henry Stewart. They eventually married in 1867 and moved to Jamestown, Pennsylvania where Henry became a pastor in the Presbyterian Church.

After Henry's death in Jamestown in September 1868 and the birth of their son in October, Sallie returned to Gettysburg. She taught school to provide for her son's education. The son, Henry Stewart, Jr., became a well known doctor and historian in the area.

In the 1880s Sallie Myers Stewart was elected Treasurer of the National Association of Nurses in honor of her work at Gettysburg. She was one of the few members of that organization who was not an enlisted nurse during the war.

Sallie died on January 17, 1922 and is buried in Gettysburg's Evergreen Cemetery. Her tombstone reads:

Salome Myers
Widow of
Rev. Henry F. Stewart
D Co. 149 PA Vols.
Born June 24, 1842
Parted Sept. 20, 1868
Reunited Jan. 17, 1922
Volunteer Nurse of the Civil War
Daughter, Sister, and Wife of a Soldier
Faithful unto Death
Above All A
Mother

July Third

iss Jane Smith wrote: "May I never again be roused to the consciousness of a new born day by such fearful sounds. It seemed almost like the crashing of worlds and I felt that life was rushing by the shores of time as a mighty flood. That the hardy son of New England was laying down side by side with his brother of the far sunny South. The ragings of passion are stilled by the hand that knows no distinction."[1] She and her mother lived in a house on Baltimore Pike, an area that had been overrun by the action of the first day's battle. Besides cooking for Confederate General Ewell and his staff, Miss Smith's house was full of wounded, including Union General Barlow. Two of her most vivid memories of the three day battle were her vigilant watch over a painfully wounded soldier determined to take his life and the shocking frenzy of the battle on the morning of July 3rd.

Before the Confederates were able to exploit their advantage on their left flank, Union batteries opened up on the men in the trenches on Culp's Hill at about 4 a.m. Joined by the infantry, the Federals kept up a furious fire for about seven hours. Because of the terrain, the Confederates were denied the benefit of artillery but their infantry steadfastly returned the favors. The intensity of fire power can be imagined in that the trees on Culp's Hill would eventually die of lead poisoning.

The fighting on the morning of the third is often underrated in the context of the battle. However, great determination was shown by both the Blue and the Gray. Although both lines were securely entrenched, neither side would settle for the role of defender. Both coveted possession of Culp's Hill and some of the desperate charges so bravely made were in reality only suicidal. About 10 a.m. a concerted attack by the Confederates was made against a terrible storm of shot and shell. Some Confederates came within 20 paces of the Union trenches and a great number were felled. The Union then counterattacked, broke the Confederate resistance, and reclaimed the entrenchments. The Confederates withdrew to the base of the hill and a quiet settled over the field.

Towards the center of the lines a sharp contest for the Bliss barn disturbed the quiet. The barn stood about midway between both lines. The Federals ended the contest by burning it down.

During the early afternoon officers made preparations and gave orders, the men in the ranks assembled and waited in the hot stillness for what was to be the grand finale of the battle of Gettysburg.

> Again, the battle began with earthly fury. Nearly all the afternoon it seemed as if the heavens and earth were crashing together. The time we sat in the cellar seemed long, listening to the terrific sound of the strife; more terrible never greeted human ears. We knew that with every explosion, and the scream of each shell, human beings were being hurried, through excruciating pain, into another world, and that many more were torn, and mangled, and lying in torment worse than death, and no one able to extend relief. The thought made me very sad, and feel that, if it was God's will, I would rather be taken away than remain to see the misery that would follow. Some thought this awful afternoon would never come to a close.[2]

At approximately 1:00 p.m., on the afternoon of July 3rd, the heaviest cannonade ever heard on American soil commenced. One hundred seventy guns along the Confederate line on Seminary Ridge opened up on the center of the Union line along Cemetery Ridge. The Confederate artillery fired high, many of the projectiles merely screamed overhead of the Union infantry and tore into Meade's headquarters and supply lines. However, the length and volume of fire were stunning and the magnitude of this two hour cannonade was appropriate to the assault that followed.

The Union gunners answered this onslaught of shot and shell with about 110 guns until they were ordered to cease firing to conserve ammunition for the infantry attack certain to come. Also, some disabled guns were removed from the line. The Confederates read this lessening of fire as a weakening of the Union line and deemed it the proper time for their infantry assault.

A spectacle of two lines of assault columns, each a half mile long, numbering over 12,000 men with battle flags waving proudly, stepped off Seminary Ridge with a determined tread, almost as if on parade. The magnificence of these assault columns was exclaimed by witnesses on both sides. Forward they went, stopping only to remove fences and dress ranks, moving against the ever increasing fire blazing from the Union line. Across almost a mile of open terrain, with their flanks dissolving, and in the face of devastating canister and rifle fire, only a couple of hundred Confederates charged over the stone walls to penetrate the Union line. Here the Federals' fierce resistance was contin-

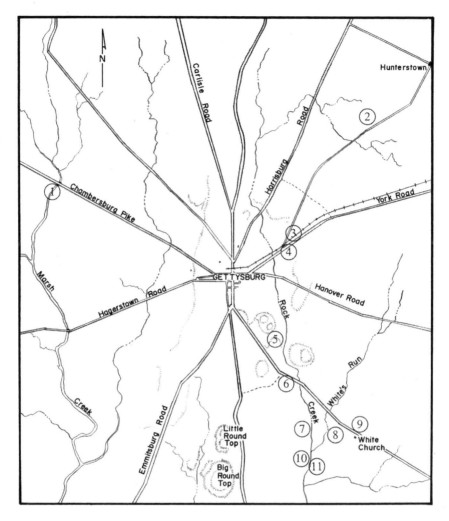

The Gettysburg Battlefield and Surrounding Areas.

(Map by John Heiser)

1. Pender's Division Hospital (Horne)
2. Johnson's Division Hospital (Rooney)
3. Sanitary Commission Lodge (Woolseys)
4. Camp Letterman (Bucklin, Husband, Lee, Hancock,
    Holstein, Goldsborough)
5. XII Corps Hospital (Dada, Bell)
6. Musser Farm (Thorn)
7. II Corps Hospital (Harris, Lee, Hancock, McKay, Holstein,
    Jones, Souder, and the Moores)
8. White Church (Spencer)
9. Beitler Farm (Thorn)
10. III Corps Hospital (Gilson, Husband, Dame, Farnham, Etheridge, Tepe)
11. V Corps Hospital (Fogg)

137

ued on a personal basis. Soldiers ran spontaneously from other parts of the Cemetery Ridge line to help beat back their foe, engaging in hand-to-hand combat; a frenzy of rocks, gun butts, fists, until the chaos fought itself out.

The "High Tide of the Confederacy" had crested. They had attempted to perform the impossible. The Confederates who penetrated furthest behind the Union lines were either wounded, killed, or taken prisoner. With no supports forthcoming, any Confederates who were able to extricate themselves from the mob did so and retreated back across the fields to their own lines, picking up their wounded as they went. There they were met by Lee with words of consolation and encouragement. The casualties were appalling; almost 10,000 Americans in about an hour. Many of the survivors were in shock. Expecting a counterattack, the remnants of Longstreet's Assault [Pickett's Charge] were gathered back into a line and the Confederate right flank was withdrawn to the west side of Emmitsburg Road to consolidate their front.

There had been some cavalry action in the rear of the Union line where J.E.B. Stuart was sent to exploit any advantage gained by the infantry charge. About 6,000 Confederate horsemen collided with 4,000 Union cavalry a few miles northeast of the main battle lines. They were hot into it at the same time the Confederate infantry stepped off Seminary Ridge in Pickett's Charge, but nothing was gained by the Confederate cavalry either. After several fierce charges and countercharges, both sides retired.

On the evening of July 3rd the Confederate hierarchy held a council of war and the decision was made to fall back from Gettysburg to seek a better defensive terrain for the expected attack by the Federals. The men from the lines at the base of Culp's and Cemetery Hills were pulled back so the Confederates were consolidated along Oak and Seminary Ridges. Although none knew if there was to be another day of battle, anxious preparations had begun from Philadelphia to Baltimore to Washington to Frederick. As the two armies remained facing each other across the fields that evening, supplies and medical personnel traveled through the night towards Gettysburg.

Mary Virginia Wade

Gettysburg Civilian

*"If there is anyone in this house that is to be killed today, I
hope it is me, as Georgia has that little baby."*[1]

Mary Virginia Wade was born on May 21, 1843 on Baltimore Street
in Gettysburg. Later her family would move to Breckenridge Street a
few blocks away but she would spend all of her short life in that town.
"Jennie" Wade has the sad distinction of having been the only
townsperson killed during the battle of Gettysburg and is considered
the "citizen heroine" of the battle. Many uncounted civilians lost their
lives because of the war. In this battle, one woman died in the cellar of
her Gettysburg home while giving birth, her family unable to seek medical help during the battle. There is an unverified but oft repeated account of a woman killed on Chambersburg Street by a stray bullet. And
the armies were long gone when several people were killed or wounded
by live shells left on the field. These citizens were no less casualties
than the dead soldiers on the battlefield.

Jennie Wade's family consisted of eight people: her father, James,
her mother, Mary Ann, brothers James, John, Samuel and Harry, and
two girls, Georgia and Mary Virginia. At the time of the battle her
brother James was away in the 3rd Pennsylvania Heavy Artillery and
John was a bugler in Co. B, 21st Pennsylvania Cavalry. Georgia had
married John Louis McClellan in 1862, who was away in the 165th
Pennsylvania Infantry, and was living on Baltimore Street with a new
born baby. Jennie, too, had marriage plans. If Johnston "Jack" Hastings
Skelley, of the 87th Pennsylvania could get leave, they would be wed in
September of 1863.

James Wade had lost his health and it fell to Jennie and her mother
to earn a living for the family.

> Mrs. Wade and Mary Virginia worked as seamstresses maintaining
> a little home on Breckenridge Street, where they were living at the time
> of the war...Virginia Wade was a good looking, hard working, young
> woman whose daily service assisting her mother in maintaining a home
> for themselves and the boys will always remain an honor and a credit to

A portrait of Mary Virginia Wade.
(GNMP)

American womanhood…Virginia Wade and her mother did not have any too easy a time of it making ends meet. They had accepted for board a crippled boy, Isaac Brinkerhoff, age six, whose mother worked out by the week…He was not deformed, but simply unable to care for himself…When Mrs. Wade left the home on Breckenridge Street to be present with her older daughter, Mrs. McClellan, the care of little Isaac Brinkerhoff was intrusted to Virginia.[2]

When the Confederates came through town on July 26, Jennie's brother Samuel, age 12, who was a delivery boy for a butcher, was told to take his employer's horse out of town to save it from confiscation. Samuel was overtaken, arrested, and brought back. After learning of Samuel's arrest, Virginia "remonstrated with the Confederates for having arrested her brother. Failing to secure his release, she immediately went to the McClellan residence—where her mother was in attendance on Georgia Wade McClellan, who had just given birth to a son about half past two—one hour before the Confederates rode into Gettysburg. Virginia desiring to bring about the release of her brother and yet not wishing to disturb her sister, called the mother out of the house explain-

Jennie Wade's home on Breckenridge Street. This house still stands.
(GNMP)

A war time photo of the McClellan house.
(GNMP)

ing to her the circumstances of Samuel's arrest."[3] Mrs. Wade was able to secure Samuel's release but not the horse he was riding.

Since the First day's battle was north and west of town, anyone looking for a safe area would naturally go south or east. "Accordingly, Virginia carried her crippled charge to the McClellan house on Baltimore Street and then returned to the home on Breckenridge for her brother Harry [age 8 and some clothing]. On leaving the house on Breckenridge Street, she locked the door placing the key in the pocket of her gown."[4] The McClellan house was a double house. The McLean family, a mother and five children, lived in the south side. The McClellan side housed Virginia, the two boys, Harry and Isaac, Mrs. Wade, Georgia McClellan, and her newborn son.

Virginia spent July 1st filling the canteens of Union soldiers and giving out bread and water. When the Union army retreated to Cemetery Ridge and Culp's Hill late that day the newly formed lines placed the McClellan house in a dangerous position behind Union lines. Sharpshooters of both armies were active in that area.

> The constant firing by the Confederate marksmen toward these brick walls in the afternoon, evening, and night of July 1st, made rest within, at least in the north side of the building quite impossible. The moaning of the wounded soldiers in the yard outside indeed made the night hideous.

> Mrs. McClellan's bed had been taken down stairs…and placed in the parlor. The mother and her five day's old babe occupied the bed and the parlor room at the outbreak of hostilities. As night came on and danger increased, the three women and three children found comfort in each other's company. Without disrobing the mother reclined on the bed with Mrs. McClellan and the child while Virginia rested on a lounge under the window at the north side of the house. The two little boys did not mind trundle beds on the floor, Harry Wade having hidden under the bureau from time to time as the danger from the shots increased.

> From time to time Confederate bullets found their mark and Union soldiers fell seriously wounded or in death about the McClellan yard; also in the vacant lot to the north. The cries of these wounded men, who were still under fire, prevented the possibility of sleep. And now it may be said to the honor of the American girl that Virginia Wade went out of the house on the evening of July 1st, 1863, and at the risk of her life brought water and cheer to those about who had fallen.[5]

> The morning of July 2nd passed uneventfully, but in the afternoon the patter of rifle balls against the side of the house and occasionally through a window light was interrupted by the crash of a 10-pdr. Parrot

shrapnel shell fired from Oak Ridge, to the north of the town, which came through the slant roof over the stairway on the north side at the east end of the incline. Passing through the wooden roof and the plaster wall, which divided the two houses of the double dwelling, the missile plowed through the brick wall on the south side of the house finally resting in an unexploded condition above the overshoot or outside extension of the roof, where it remained for over fifteen years.

Virginia Wade fearful that the house was being made an object for artillery as well as infantry fire, fainted at the roar of splintering wood and falling bricks upstairs.

The failure of the shell to explode within the house either on the north side or on the south side…was doubtless Providential.

Late on the afternoon of July 2nd as the evening shadows lengthened, an occasional Union soldier would venture to the door of the house, asking for bread. The diminishing quantity did not send away disappointed the few who applied at the door, but it became more and more apparent that there would be need the next day for a goodly supply of that home baked bread…

Accordingly, on the afternoon of the second day, Mrs. Wade and her daughter started the yeast, which was mixed into a sponge on the evening of July 2nd and left to rise, until the morning of July 3rd.

Frequent alarms and desultory firing during the evening and night of July 2nd again prevented normal rest. However, the women reclined as on the night before not knowing what new terrors each forthcoming hour might bring.[6]

Early the next morning, Jennie and her brother Harry fetched wood for baking. The occupants of the north side had a simple breakfast and read the bible.

About seven o'clock the Confederate sharpshooters again began firing at the north windows of the house. Every pane of glass was soon broken, one bullet on entering the front room struck the southwest bed post, then hit the fireplace or wall, finally falling on the pillow at the foot of the bed toward which Mrs. McClellan and the child had been turned as a measure of safety, by the mother of the young women, at the suggestion of Virginia. It was thought bullets might come through the west door and window. The one which came through the north window was, in fact, warm when Mrs. Wade gathered it with splinters from the damaged bed post.

At eight o'clock work preparatory to the making of the biscuits, which had been promised, was begun. Going to her mixing tray Virginia prepared the flour and baking soda for the biscuit. She has just about finished kneading the dough and had asked her mother to start the fire for the baking when a Confederate bullet, presumably from a sharpshooter's rifle at the Rupp Tannery office, penetrated the outer door on the north side, also the door which stood ajar between the parlor and the kitchen, striking the girl in the back just below the left shoulder blade. The heart was hit, the bullet embedding itself in the corset at the front on her body. She fell dead without a groan. It was now about 8:30.

Mrs. Wade turning from her work at the fire seeing her daughter fall, realized after a hasty examination what had happened. She went to the parlor and said to Mrs. McClellan: "Georgia, your sister is dead."[7]

Georgia screamed upon hearing of her sister's death, which brought Union soldiers into the scene. Some broke through the door to investigate and soldiers came down from the rooms above. No one knew how or when these men from upstairs came into the house. It was decided that everyone should move into the cellar on the south side of the house. Since no one was safe to leave the north side of the house, they went through into the south side by the hole left by the Parrot artillery shell. The opening was made larger and through it passed the soldiers, the children, Mrs. McClellan, her baby, Mrs. Wade and Jennie's body. The small procession made its way down to the south cellar. There the family stayed until the early afternoon of July 4, except for Mrs. Wade who "at the suggestion of the soldiers and assisted by them returned by the route they had made through the division in the wall to the room stained with her daughter's heart blood and baked fifteen loaves of bread, the dough for which her daughter, who had been her main support in life, had prepared."[8]

The remaining members of the Wade family buried Virginia in the late afternoon of July 4th in the garden of the McClellan house. She was wrapped in a quilt her mother had made years before and placed in the coffin that had been started by the Confederates for Mississippi General Barksdale in Anna Garlach's back yard. "No preparations whatsoever were made for the cleansing, embalming or redressing of the deceased. She was placed in the coffin with the quilt wrapped around her. The dough which was still on her hands and arms gave mute evidence of the service which she had and was faithfully endeavoring to render the Union Cause."[9] "A photograph of Corporal Skelley was found in the pocket of Virginia Wade's gown along with the key to the house she had left on Breckenridge Street."[10] "There were no spoken prayers and no music, as the girl was laid to rest in the yard of her sister's home."[11]

Virginia Wade was also a main character in a larger tragedy; the tragic irony of Gettysburg's most famous "brother against brother" story of William and Wesley Culp. Wesley left Gettysburg before the war and settled in Virginia married to a Southern woman. William remained in Gettysburg. When the war started, William enlisted in the 87th Pennsylvania and Wesley in the 2nd Virginia. In 1863 after the battle of Winchester on the campaign north, Wesley visited the Union prisoners and found his brother William along with another Gettysburg friend, Jack Skelley, who was seriously wounded. Skelley gave Wesley a verbal message for a special lady in Gettysburg, who, of course, was Jennie Wade. Wesley was unable to deliver the message, however, as he was killed in the third day's action at Culp's Hill. Jennie, then, also died on July 3rd never knowing of Skelley's wounding or of his message. Skelley died from his wounds nine days later on July 12.

The original headstone on Miss Wade's grave in Evergreen Cemetery.
(GNMP)

145

Jennie Wade was to have three grave sites. From the McClellan house she was moved in January 1864 to the German Reformed Church's cemetery. The third and final site was in the Evergreen Cemetery where she was reinterred in November 1865. This cemetery was then, and is now, the local Gettysburg cemetery, and also contains the remains of Jack Skelley and William Culp. Wesley Culp's body was never found.

The dedication of Virginia Wade's gravesite monument erected by Georgia McCllellan and the Women's Relief Corps of Iowa. Mrs. McClellan is in the first row, second from the right. The monument reads:
Jennie Wade
age 20 years 2 months
killed July 3, 1863
while baking bread for the Union soldiers;
Whatsoever God willith must be. Though a nation mourn;
Erected by the Women's Relief Corps of Iowa AD 1901;
With a courage born of loyalty, She hath done what she could.
(GNMP)

In 1882 Mrs. Mary Wade was awarded an $8 a month pension as Jennie's death occurred while working for the Union cause. In 1901 Georgia McClellan, who was then living in Denison, Iowa, visited Gettysburg with the Women's Relief Corps of Iowa. It was this group that was responsible for the large monument erected on Jennie's grave. The flag always flies on Mary Virginia Wade's grave.

Mainly because of a letter found in Jack Skelley's pension file[12] and the fact that Jennie did not show up at patriotic functions [i.e. greeting and singing to the Union troops arriving on the field] when she had family obligations to attend to, Jennie's morals and patriotism have been besmirched over the years. Unfortunately, she has become almost a local joke.[13] Whereas most women of the Civil War have been completely forgotten, Miss Wade has been highlighted for over a century under an unrelenting glare. The ludicrous attitude about her deeds and death do honor to no one. Perhaps her memory could be best served with respect for her actions, recognition of her sacrifice, and permitting her to rest in peace.

Josephine Miller

Gettysburg Civilian

"When the battle was over, her home was found to be riddled with shot and shell, and 17 dead bodies were taken from the cellar; the bodies of wounded men who had crawled into the little dwelling for shelter."[1]

Josephine Miller was 23 years old at the time of the battle. She lived with Peter and Susan Rogers in their house situated on the Emmitsburg Road. The house was in the battle arena on July 2nd when men of Sickles' advance took partial shelter in the house and barn and also on July 3rd through the cannonade and the assault of Pickett's Charge.

[Brigadier] General [Joseph B.] Carr…informed her that a great battle was inevitable and advised her to seek a place of safety at once. She said she had a batch of bread baking in the oven and she would remain until it was baked and then leave. When the bread was baked, it was given to our soldiers, and was devoured so eagerly that she concluded to remain and bake another batch. And so she continued to the end of the battle, baking and giving her bread to all who came. The great artillery duel which shook the earth for miles around did not drive her from her oven. Pickett's men who charged past her house found her quietly baking her bread and distributing it to the hungry.[2]

"She told me…that when her stock of flour was almost exhausted, six members of the 1st Massachusetts kindly volunteered to go out and steal three sacks of flour from General Sickles' commissary stores. In an hour's time they returned with flour, raisins, currants, and a whole sheep, with which a rattling good meal was made."[3]

Susan and Peter Rogers also remained in their house. Susan baked bread alongside Josephine. Both women attended the wounded. Peter stayed in the cellar, observing that the armies seemed unable to fire over the house, but only through it.

"…[D]uring the height of the fray a soldier tottered into the yard and sank upon the grass. Miss [Miller] came out to him. 'Are you tired?' the girl asked. 'Yes, and hungry,' faintly replied the soldier.

Josephine Miler in the doorway of the Roger's kitchen,
and (below) at the reunion in 1886.
(GNMP)

Miss [Miller] rushed into the house and back again bringing bread. 'Here eat,' said she. The soldier answered not. She shook his shoulder and by the motion his face was turned to her. It was that of a dead man."[4]

After having survived the battle, Josephine contracted typhoid fever and nearly died. She was well enough on October 25, 1863, however to marry William James Slyder. Around 1883 they moved to Troy, Ohio.

"Twenty years after the close of the war, General Carr's men and others had a grand reunion at Gettysburg [July 2, 1886]; and learning that Josephine Miller was still living, but had married and taken up her residence in Ohio, they sent for her, paid her passage from her home to Gettysburg and back, and had her go to her old home and tell the story which they all knew so well."[5] At this reunion, Josephine was presented with a gold badge from the men. She was the only female member of the III Army Corps Veteran's Association's last reunion and symbolically cooked a dinner for General Sickles.

Born October 25, 1836, Josephine Miller Slyder died in early 1911 at age 74 in Troy, Ohio. She is buried in Riverside Cemetery.

Female Soldiers

"Remarks: one female (private) in rebel uniform."[1]

The unidentified body of a female Confederate soldier was discovered by a burial detail on the west side of the stone wall at the angle on Cemetery Ridge. A participant of Pickett's Charge, she was one of the 12,000 courageous souls that stepped off Seminary Ridge and marched across a mile of open ground through a hell of enemy fire. The fact that her body was found in such an advanced position is testimony to her bravery. Sadly, the above notation is the extent of acknowledgement she received for having given her life for her country.

At the time this volume was published twenty years ago, this researcher had come across over 60 instances of women disguised as male soldiers fighting in both armies. Those most well known, such as Jennie Hodges, Loreta Janeta Velazquez, and Sarah Emma Edmonds, have been used over and over as examples, as was the tired, oft repeated assertion of a second hand opinion from an anonymous source in Mary Livermore's book, *My Story of the War*: "Some one has stated the number of women soldiers known to the service as little less than four hundred. I cannot vouch for the correctness of his estimate, but I am convinced that a larger number of women disguised themselves and enlisted in the service, for one cause or other, than was dreamed of. Entrenched in secrecy, and regarded as men, they were sometimes revealed as women, by accident or casualty. Some startling histories of these military women were current gossip of army life; and extravagant and unreal as were many of the narrations, one always felt that they had a foundation in fact."[2]

All of this speculation ended in 2002 with the ground breaking *They Fought Like Demons* by DeAnne Blanton and Lauren Cook. *They Fought Like Demons* chronicles hundreds of such women. Such a number can produce a real insight on the who and how and why of female soldiers. This is a remarkable feat and took over a decade of diligence and perseverance as this has to be the most difficult and frustrating research concerning Civil War women's service to their causes. No war library is complete without a copy on the shelf. Blanton and Cook have done a great service to women's collective history and anyone interested in such owe a debt of gratitude to these two ladies.

Demons discovered five female soldiers at the battle of Gettysburg; two Union and three Confederate. One Union woman was Mary Siezgle, "originally went to the front and served as a nurse but decided to stay with her husband in a New York regiment. The only way for her to do so was to put on male clothes and do 'her share of actual fighting.'"[3] The other Union woman was "an unidentified drummer boy who was slightly wounded at Gettysburg was not the 'lad of fifteen' he appeared to be, but a girl of eighteen who refused to give her real name or any other personal information. One newspaper reported that 'She wore a neat suit of soldier clothes and made a pretty boy.'"[4] She "vowed that 'they may do what they please with her, but she [would] never wear women's clothes again."[5] This young woman "was turned out of the army in a quiet way after she recovered. Just as quietly she re-enlisted. She was discovered the second time by accident and was sent on the boat to Fortress Monroe to be dismissed."[6]

The Confederate female soldiers suffered much worse fates. "One was shot in the leg and captured. She was removed to the U.S. Military Hospital in Chester, Pennsylvania, where surgeons amputated her leg in order to save her life."[7] A Union soldier recovering in the same hospital wrote to his parents: 'I must tel you we have got a female secesh here. she was wounded at Gettysburg but our doctors soon found her out. I have not seen her but the[y] say she is very good-looking[.] the poor girl [h]as lost a leg. it [is] a great pity she did not stay at home with her mother but she get good care and kind treatment. it [is] rather romantic to have a female soldier in the hospital and her only to have one leg and far away from home but I hope she will soon get better and get home to her friends.' Union officials...apparently sent this woman to her home in the South rather than retaining her as a prisoner of war."[8]

The other two Confederate soldiers participated in Pickett's Charge. "One of them was severely wounded, unable to move herself from the pasture. That evening, a Union private from New Jersey who was detailed to guard Emmitsburg Road listened to her screams of agony. He later wrote that it was the most awful sound he had ever heard."[9] The remains of the other Confederate woman was found on the field by a burial detail. This last brave soul was the only verified female soldier at Gettysburg for 140 years until *Demons* was released.

Bridget Deavers

1st Michigan Cavalry
Cavalry Corps, Third Division, Second Brigade

"Swinging her soldier's cap over her head, she shouted, 'Arrah! Go in boys and bate the bloody spalpeens and revenge me husband, and God be wid ye.'"[1]

The heroines of the Great War for the Union, like its heroes, have come from every class of society, and represent every grade in our social scale. Ladies of the highest refinement and social polish have left homes of luxury, and devoted themselves, week after week, and month after month, to daily labor and nightly vigils in the wards of great hospitals.

No less praiseworthy and admirable have been the devotion and self-sacrifice of those who were born in less favored circles, and brought with them to the work, if not the elegance of the boudoir, the hearty good will, the vigorous sense, and the unwearied industry of the laboring class.

If the antecedents and manners of Bridget Deavers, whom Sheridan's men commonly knew as 'Irish Biddy,' were not those of what the world calls 'a lady,' she proved herself possessed of the heart of a true, brave, loyal, and unselfish woman who devoted herself, from the beginning to the end of the war, and to the good of the soldier, with such uncalculating generosity, that she deserves and enjoys the grateful remembrance and the unfeigned respect of every patriot who saw anything of her admirable labor.[2]

Another remarkable heroine who, while from the lower walks of life, was yet faithful and unwearied in her labors for the relief of the soldiers who were wounded and who not infrequently took her place in the ranks, or cheered and encouraged the men when they were faltering and ready to retreat, was Bridget Divers, better known as 'Michigan Bridget' or among Sheridan's men as 'Irish Biddy.' A stout robust Irish woman, she accompanied the First Michigan Cavalry regiment in which her husband was a private soldier, to the field, and remained with that regiment and the brigade to which it belonged until the close of the war.[3]

Bridget Deavers, or Divers or Devens, all variations to which she is referred, is one of the most elusive female personages to trace during the war. Although she can be found in all the general war references from

Moore's *Women in the War* to Massey's *Bonnet Brigades* and in several nurses' letters and narratives, there is no record of her or a husband of those names in any census or roster before, during, or after the war.[4] As it stands now, only these writers and eyewitness accounts record her war efforts. Any means of verifying them has not, as yet, been found.

Mary Livermore of the Sanitary Commission remembered her: "Bridget Devens, known as 'Michigan Bridget' went to the field with the First Michigan Cavalry, in which her husband was a private, and served through the war. Sometimes when a soldier fell she took his place, fighting in his stead with unquailing courage. Sometimes she rallied retreating troops—sometimes she brought off the wounded from the field—always fearless and daring, always doing good service as a soldier."[5]

In the commencement of the war, she went out with the first Michigan cavalry, and through the war continued to act with and for that organization. But as she became familiar with the army, and well known in it, she extended her labors so as to reach the wants of the brigade, and even the division to which the first Michigan belonged.

She knew every man in the regiment, and could speak of his character, his wants, his sufferings, and the facts of his military record. Her care and kindness extended to the moral and religious wants, as well as the health, of the men of 'her regiment' as she always called it. In the absence of the chaplain she came to the Christian Commission for books and papers for the men, saying that she was the acting chaplain, and appearing to take a very deep interest in the moral and religious well-being of them all.

It made no difference to her in what capacity she acted, or what she did, so be it necessary for the good of the men.

Acting now as *vivandiere* or daughter of the regiment, now as nurse, hospital steward, ward master, and sometimes surgeon, she was invaluable in each capacity. From her long experience with wounds and disease, her judgment came to be excellent, and her practical skill equal often to that of a physician. In drawing various supplies from the Sanitary or Christian Commission she showed good judgment and knew just what the men really wanted, never encouraging waste or recklessness in distribution, while she was really very kind and tenderhearted.

Her whole soul was in the work of aiding and sustaining the soldier. No day was too stormy or too cold to check her in an errand of mercy. She overcame all obstacles, and battled successfully with all sorts of rebuffs and discouragements in the prosecution of her duties.

When the Christian Commission received letters from home, which was very frequently the case, inquiring for a soldier, if the man was believed to be even in the division to which she was attached, Bridget was the first person to whom application was made. If it was in 'her brigade,' as she called it, she could tell all about him. If in the division, she was more likely to know than the commanding officer of the adjutant, and could generally give all the desired information. Her memory of names and places was truly wonderful.

When the brigade was in active service she was with it in the field, and shared all its dangers. She was a fearless and skillful rider, and as brave as the bravest under fire.[6]

"She became well known throughout the brigade for her fearlessness and daring, and her skill in bringing off the wounded. Occasionally when a solider whom she knew fell in action, after rescuing him if he was only wounded, she would take his place and fight as bravely as the best. In two instances and perhaps more, she rallied and encouraged retreating troops and brought them to return to their position, thus aiding in preventing a defeat."[7]

One of these instances is related:

The battle of Fair Oaks [May 31-June 1, 1862] commenced by a vigorous charge of the overwhelming rebel force upon a single division of McClellan's army, which had advanced across the Chickahominy. As Casey's division, thus attacked, gave way, there was danger that the panic might spread and infect the troops that were hastening to the support. Among these was the Seventh Massachusetts, that, having advanced to within range of the rebel artillery, had just received the order, 'Forward,' that would in a few moments plunge them into the heat of the contest. The obeyed the command but slowly, for the enemy's fire was growing every moment more terrific. Just then 'Irish Biddy' came along, supporting her husband, who had a ball through his leg...[Bridget called upon them to do their duty.]

The effect was instantaneous and decisive. The regiment gave three cheers for 'Irish Biddy,' and three for the seventh. Then joining the tenth Massachusetts, and other troops, they made a gallant and successful charge on the enemy centre.[8]

It appears Bridget was separated at least occasionally from her regiment through the summer and fall of 1864 as she is mentioned in a New Jersey's nurse's letters: [July 18th, 1864, City Point, 1st Div. 2nd Corps Hospital] "Bridget, who lives with me, was very much delighted to

An image of Bridget Deavers in battle.
(*My Story of the War*)

think her floor was scrubbed. She is a woman who has been in the army for three years, done all the marching with regt. and is a splendid hand to work." [City Point, August 15, 1864] "If I am sick Bridgett [*sic*] takes excellent care of me and gets along very well." [City Point, Sept 2nd, 1864] "I will send my ruffles home to be washed and they can come back in the letters. Bridgett wants a plain black net like mine. Mine was very nice. She will pay for it; send the price and we will pay the bill." [City Point, Oct. 17th, 1864] "Bridget was very pleased with her saque. Her tent was a sight to see, all stowed with every thing belonging to me and looked laughable…Bridget does not live with me at present but does everything I want her to." [City Point, Dec. 29th, 1864] "Bridgett washes my clothes. She quarrels with the men too much to be in a winter kitchen. I see that she is made comfortable and has everything she needs."[9]

Bridget was soon back with the First Michigan Cavalry. "In the battle of Cedar Creek [Oct. 19, 1864] she found herself at one time cut off and surrounded by the enemy, but managed, by an adroit movement, to escape capture."[10]

> In actual battle she had two or three horses killed under her, and in the course of the war lost eight or ten in various ways.

As to making something out of the war, she was utterly indifferent to that. At one time a purse of some three hundred dollars was made up and presented to her; but in a few weeks the most of it was gone, having been expended in various purchases for the comfort of her boys. Any money given to her was sure to find its way back again into the regiment, as she would expend it for the benefit of some sick, or wounded, or unfortunate man, or for the purchase of hospital supplies.

Her personal appearance is not prepossessing or attractive. Sleeping on the ground like a soldier, and enduring hardships like the rest, her face has become brown by exposure, and her figure grown athletic by constant exercise and life in the open air. But the heart that beats under her plain cassock is as full of womanly tenderness as that of any princess in purple velvet; and, though her hand is strong and brown, it is as ready to an act of generous kindness as that of Florence Nightingale herself.[11]

In the early part of 1865 a Massachusetts nurse recalled a visit with Bridget:

Mar. 28—Visited, in company with Miss Bridget Deavers, two large camps of dismounted cavalrymen lying along the James River, a few miles from City Point. Bridget—or, as the men call her, Biddy—has

Tents at City Point hospital on the James.
Bridget Deavers was here in 1864.
(MOLLUS)

probably seen more of hardship and danger than any other woman during the war. She has been with the cavalry all the time, going out with them on their cavalry raids—always ready to succor the wounded on the field—often getting men off who, but for her would be left to die, and, fearless of shell or bullet, among the last to leave.

Protected by officers and respected by privates, with her little sunburnt face, she makes her home in the saddle or the shelter-tent; often, indeed, sleeping in the open air without a tent, and by her courage and devotion, 'winning the golden opinions from all sorts of people.'

She is an Irish woman, has been in the country sixteen years, and is not twenty-six years of age.

"Where is that nice little horse you had with you at the hospital last summer, Bridget?"

"Oh, Moseby [sic] captured that from me. He came in while I was lying asleep on the ground, and took my horse and orderly. I jumped up and ran away."

One of the above-mentioned camps consists of men just come in from Sheridan's last raid, having been during the past winter in the valley of the Shenandoah. We found them lying under their shelter-tents or sitting on the ground in front of them, boiling coffee over their camp-fires and eating their rations of salt and pork and *hardtack.* They looked tired and sunburnt, but were every moment expecting horses and a call to 'boots and saddles.'

Having distributed socks, handkerchiefs, towels, and some articles of clothing which we brought for them, and partaken of Bridget's simple fare, sitting on a blanket in front of her tent, we remounted our horses and rode along the river-side to the other camp, which is a more permanent institution.[12]

The hardihood of 'Irish Biddy' was probably not surpassed by any camp-follower during the war.

She sometimes went out with the men on picket, and remained all night on watch. At times, when sickness or hard service had thinned the ranks of the regiment, she would take the place of a soldier, and go out on a scouting or raiding expedition, doing the full duty of a soldier.

At other times the part she acted was more fearless and sublime, taking then the place of an officer, and acting the commander rather than the companion.

One occasion of the latter class shows that Irish Biddy possessed the courage, if not the grace and poetry, of Joan of Arc.[13]

Bridget had one very famous exploit. A Sanitary Commission nurse from Pennsylvania told her version of the tale:

In one on Sheridan's grand raids, during the latter days of the rebellion, she, as usual, rode with the troops night and day wearing out several horses, until they dropped from exhaustion. In a severe cavalry engagement, in which her regiment took a prominent part, her colonel was wounded, and her captain killed. She accompanied the former to the rear, where she ministered to his needs, and when placed in the cars, bound to City Point Hospitals, she remained with him, giving all the relief in her power, on that fatiguing journey, although herself almost exhausted…After seeing her colonel safely and comfortable lodged in the hospital, she took one night's rest, and returned to the front. Finding that her captain's body had not been recovered, it being hazardous to make the attempt, she resolved to rescue it, as 'it never should be left on rebel soil.' So, with her orderly for sole companion, she rode fifteen miles to the scene of the late conflict, found the body she sought, strapped it upon her horse, rode back seven miles to an embalmer's where she waited whilst the body was embalmed, then again strapping it on her horse, she rode several miles further to the cars in which, with her precious burden she proceeded to City Point, there obtained a rough coffin, and forwarded the whole to Michigan. Without any delay Biddy returned to her Regiment, told some officials, that wounded men had been left on the field from which she had rescued her Captain's body. They did not credit her tale, so she said, 'Furnish me some ambulances and I will bring them in.' The conveyances were given her, she retraced her steps to the deserted battlefield, and soon had some eight or ten poor sufferers in the wagons, and on their way to camp. The roads were rough, and their moans and cries gave evidence of intense agony. While still some miles from their destination, Bridget saw several rebels approaching, she ordered the drivers to quicken their pace, and endeavored to urge her horse forward, but he baulked and refused to move. The drivers becoming alarmed deserted their charge and fled to the woods, while the wounded men begged that they might not be left to the mercy of the enemy, and to suffer in Southern prisons. The rebels soon came up. Bridget pleaded with them to leave the sufferers unmolested, but they laughed at her, took the horses from the ambulances, and such articles of value as the men possessed, and then dashed off the way they came. Poor Biddy was almost desperate, darkness coming on, and with none to help her, the wounded men beseeching her not to leave them. Fortunately, an officer of our army rode up to see what the matter was, and soon sent horses and assistance to the party.[14]

Another nurse, Miss Rebecca R. Usher, recorded this event and on April 7, 1865 wrote:

A few days ago I saw Bridget…She had just come in with the body of a captain who was killed in a cavalry skirmish. She had the body lashed to her horse, and carried him fifteen miles, where she procured a coffin, and sent him home. She says this is the hardest battle they have had, and the ground was covered with the wounded. She had not slept for forty-eight hours, having worked incessantly with the wounded. She is brave, heroic, and a perfect enthusiast in her work. Bridget said to me, in her earnest way, "Why don't you ladies go up there, and take care of those wounded men? Why, it's the worst sight you ever saw. The ground is covered with them." "We should like to go," I said, "but they won't let us." "Well, they can't hinder *me*," she said; "Sheridan won't let them."[15]

"Browned by exposure, and with sensibilities somewhat hardened by years of constant service in camp, a character like that of Irish Biddy may fail to interest us for its feminine characteristics, but it must, nevertheless, command our admiration for its strength, its fortitude, its dauntless courage, and the genuine and inextinguishable kindness of heart which led her ever to place the good and the comfort of the men above all demands of safety, and all considerations of personal ease."[16]

Many women stayed on after Lee's surrender. A nurse remembered:

On the 17th [April 1865], accompanied by Bridget Devers, I took a train, going out to the front, with sanitary supplies for some wounded cavalry-men, of whom we had heard that they were in great suffering. The cars, having stopped three or four hours within a dozen miles, pushed on to Ford's Station, where they made a general 'break-down,' and there was no possibility of their getting farther at that time. We stepped out, and making our way through other trains of cars crowded in front and rear, and a promiscuous assemblage of men, horses, wagons, and tents…[The two women stayed in a nearby house that night.] That evening some soldiers came in, who reported that the wounded cavalry-men to whom we were going had been carried to City Point…[The next day they were in an ambulance]…and joined the column as it wound its slow length along. Near Petersburg, spreading themselves over an area of five or six miles, on the same hills, and near the fortifications lately occupied by Lee's army, they encamped. We were furnished with a tent, and soon met many friends who had happily escaped the perils of the late campaign.[17]

Doubtless remembered by that captain's family for rest of their days and by the many soldiers she nursed, prayed with, cooked and laundered for, and the nurses who knew her and of her, we are only privileged a glimpse, as she dropped into our history's pages for four years of war. Her story as yet has no beginning or end. She came into the American Civil War from Ireland via Michigan and leaves with only a few vague references to her joining the regular army after the war and going out west, disappearing as mysteriously as she appeared. She is another example of an American woman lost to American history.

Helen Gilson

Independent Massachusetts Nurse

*"The more this experience comes to me the more I am lifted
into the upper ether of peace and rest; I am stronger in soul
and healthier in body; yet, I never worked harder in my life."[1]*

"[Miss Gilson] went on to Gettysburg, arriving a few hours after
the last day's fight. She worked there till the wounded had been sent to
Base Hospital."[2] A doctor in the Sanitary Commission described his
meeting with Helen Gilson at Gettysburg.

A few days after the battle of Gettysburg...I went out to the field-
hospitals of the 3rd Corps, four miles from town, where twenty-four
hundred men lay in their tents, a vast camp of mutilated humanity...One
woman, young and fair, but grave and earnest, clothed in purity and
mercy...moved in and out of the hospital tents, speaking some tender
words, giving some restoring cordial, holding the hand of a dying boy,
or receiving the last words of a husband for his widowed wife. I can
never forget how, amid scenes which under ordinary circumstances no
woman could have appeared in without gross indecorum, the holy pity
and purity of the angel of mercy made her presence seem as fit as though
she had indeed dropped out of heaven. The men themselves, sick or
well, all seemed awed and purified by such a resident among them.

Separated from the main camp by a shallow stream, running through
a deep ravine, was a hospital, where, with perhaps fifty of our own men,
more than two hundred wounded rebels had been placed.

Under sudden and violent rains, the shallow stream had in a few
hours swollen to such a torrent as actually to sweep away beyond recovery several wounded men who lay, thoughtless of any new peril,
asleep upon its banks. For three days the flood kept at an unfordable
height: and the wretched hospital of the rebels was cut off from medicine and supplies by the impossibility of reach it. A brave young rebel
officer repeatedly swam the torrent with a bag of medicine and small
comforts, the only communication that was had meanwhile. Accompanied by the young woman named above, I found my way, at the earliest
moment possible, to this unwillingly neglected scene. The place was a
barn and stable. Every foot was occupied by wretched sufferers, clad
usually in the ragged gray of the Confederate uniform. There, upon

Helen Gilson.
(*Our Army Nurses*)

heaps of manure, reeking with rain, and tormented with vermin, their wounds still undressed, and many longing for amputation as the hungry long for food or drink, lay fair and noble youth, with the mark of gentle breeding in their fine-cut features, and hunger, despair, and death in their bright and hollow eyes. The surgeons had at last got to work among them; and limbs just cut off (one I recollect well, with the heavy shoed and stocking still upon it) lay in dreadful carelessness, in full view, about the place.

When we had exhausted the little store of comforts we had brought with us, one of the sufferers said to Miss Gilson, "Ma'am, can't you sing us a little hymn?" "Oh, yes!" she answered: "I'll sing you a song what will do for either side:" and there, in the midst of that band of neglected sufferers, she stood; and with a look of heavenly pity and earnestness, her eyes raised to God, sang, "When This Cruel War is Over," in a clear, pleading voice that made me remove my hat, and long to cast myself upon my knees. Sighs and groans ceased; and, while the song went on, pain seemed charmed away. The moment it ceased, one poor fellow, who had lost his right arm, raised his left, and said, "Oh ma'am! I wish I had my other arm back, if it was only to clap my hands for your song."[3]

Here [Gettysburg] as elsewhere Miss Gilson soon made a favorable impression on the wounded men. They looked up to her, reverenced and almost worshipped her. She had their entire confidence and respect. Even the roughest of them yielded to her influence and obeyed her wishes, which were always made known in gentle manner and in a voice peculiarly low and sweet.

It has been recorded by one who knew her well, that she once stepped out of her tent, before which a group of brutal men were fiercely quarrelling, having refused with oaths and vile language, to carry a sick comrade to the hospital, the request of one of the male agents of the Commission, and quietly advanced to their midst, renewed the request as her own. Immediately every angry tone was stilled. Their voices were lowered, and modulated respectfully. Their oaths ceased, and quietly and cheerfully, without a word of objection, they lifted their helpless burden, and tenderly carried him away.[4]

Helen Gilson was a most unique individual. Everyone with whom she came in contact was touched to no small degree. Accounts of the lady suggest the presence of a celestial being.

Miss Gilson had a special manner and technique that were carefully studied by observers, and were described again and again. Though

most of these studies start by being severely professional and imper-
sonal, they end on a very sentimental note. There was apparently something so moving about Miss Gilson's manner and method that no one
could watch her long without becoming lyrical and dewy-eyed. She
had an exquisiteness in all her appointments and arrangements for the
sick and the suffering equaled only by Miss Florence Nightingale herself. The poorer and more neglected a creature was, the more Miss
Gilson would be lavish with perfectly made custards and crisp white
linen delicately fragrant with lavender or cologne.[5]

Helen Gilson was born in Massachusetts on November 22, 1835,
into a family of at least five children and was orphaned by the time she
was sixteen. At age 17 she obtained the position of head assistant at the
Phillips School in Boston which she resigned in 1859 because of ill
health. It was then that she became governess to the children of her
uncle and guardian Mr. Frank Fay of Chelsea, Massachusetts and was
in this service when the war broke out.

> Miss Gilson from the very commencement of the war, gave herself
> to the work for caring of the soldiers, first at home, and afterward in the
> field. In that glorious uprising of American women, all over the North,
> in the spring of 1861, to organize Soldier's Aid Societies she was active
> and among the foremost in her own city. She had helped to prepare and
> collect supplies, and to arrange them for transportation. She had also
> obtained a contract for the manufacture of army clothing, from the
> Government, by means of which she provided employment for soldier's
> wives and daughters, raising among the benevolent and patriotic people
> of Chelsea, and vicinity, a fund which enabled her to pay a far more
> liberal sum than the contractor's prices, for this labor.[6]

When Mr. Fay began his services to the Army of the Potomac, Helen
wanted to go also. She applied to and was rejected by Dorothea Dix so
she went along with Mr. Fay as an independent nurse.

> During nearly the whole term of Miss Gilson's service she was in
> company with Mr. Fay and his assistants. The party had their own tent,
> forming a household, and carrying with them something of home-life.
> In this manner she, with her associates, followed the Army of the
> Potomac, through its various vicissitudes, and was present at, or near,
> almost every one of its great battles except for the first battle of Bull
> Run [July 21, 1861].
> In the summer of 1862 Miss Gilson was for some time, attached to
> the Hospital Transport Service, and was on board the *Knickerbocker*

when up the Pamunky River at White House, and afterward at Harrison's Landing during the severe battle which marked McClellan's movement from the Chickahominy to the James River [Peninsula Campaign, March-July 1862]. Amidst the terrible scenes of those eventful days, the quiet energy, the wonderful comforting and soothing power, and the perfect adaptability of Miss Gilson to her work were conspicuous.[7]

A friend asked her once, "How did you manage to pass through the jealous barriers of official service, and to press your way into the actual work?" She answered simply, "When I reached White-House Landing I saw the transport 'Wilson Small' in the offing, and knew it was full of wounded men; so, calling a boatman, and directing him to row me to the vessel, I went on board."

A poor fellow was undergoing an amputation; and, seeing that the surgeon wanted help, I took hold of the limb, and held it for him. The surgeon looked up, at first surprised, then said, "Thank you:" and I staid and helped him. Then I went on with the next case; he made no objection, and from that time I never had any difficulty there; though, often, in a change of place, I would have to make my way afresh.[8]

She got her first experience in service on battlefields under her uncle Frank B. Fay, who had been a pioneer organizer of battlefield relief, and who became the director of all army auxiliary relief corps. She had attracted such attention by her service in the Transport Service on the Peninsula that thereafter she could get almost anything she wanted from the aid societies for the soldiers, and do what she pleased in relation to the military authorities...Mr. Fay had merged his unit with the Sanitary Commission, and Miss Gilson had been accepted as one of the front-line workers...[9]

Right before the battle of Antietam [Sept. 17, 1862] Helen wrote from Washington:

It is a bright morning here, but our hearts are heavy...The conflict promises to be terrible and decisive. What our arrangements will be, I cannot say. We want to go up to the lines...The corridors of the Capitol are full of beds, and every church and other available place will be crowded with our wounded men. Our women everywhere will surely devote all possible time to this great claim...[Sept. 17] I am in the devastated city of Frederick...Tomorrow I go to the front (Antietam) my coveted desire. Send a box of supplies to Frederick at once, if possible; any thing and every thing, well packed...(At Antietam) Today a message comes to summon us immediately to Harper's Ferry, where they have *no stores* for the wounded. We pass the army lines, and go at once...[Sept. 19] The sick and wounded are lying all along our route in barns, neglected and filthy, their wounds all alive with vermin...have slept in an ambulance or barn for several nights...[back at Antietam] I have been round among the men in all the barns, making gallons of corn-starch, and feeding the worst cases of wounded; those with eyes shot out, tongues shot away, and wounds in the brain...When I arrived on the battle-field, men were lying in all directions, the dying and the dead. With so much to do for the living, we could only pass the dying by, who were past all earthly healing...Three thousand have already been buried, yet you could hardly advance a dozen paces without stepping upon the dead. The doctors tell me I ought not to stoop over the men to fed them, but I *must* do it, it is so much more satisfying to them and so much more like the home ministry...I have had a busy, busy day; let me give you an account of it. This morning we rose at *reveille*, and immediately proceeded to the hospital, which is in two barns across the way. Having but one basin and sponge for the washing of seventy-five sick men, you can imagine the operation a long one; especially as I feel inclined to be so unreasonable as to insist that fever patients should have clean feet. This being over, next comes breakfast; and, considering that we have but one old tin dipper to about every six men, this process is also a slow one. A little corn-starch or gruel must be made for the sickest; then, in many cases, they must be fed; and I find their appetite is much improved by a pleasant chat during the process. Then while Mrs. H was preparing raspberry vinegar, or some other cooling drink, I went to the men bathing their heads with bay-rum, and writing letters for those who were most ill. I have several patients who are being doctored for home-sickness (nostalgia), and I make it a business to talk with such men half an hour each day. It has a wonderfully cheering effect. Then comes the dinner, another long process; and after that, a little nap for the boys; then a chapter, some songs, and a few words of cheer, with constant call for care, meanwhile.

[By November 2nd, Miss Gilson was in Pleasant Valley, Maryland, near Boonsboro]: The valley was bathed this morning in the autumn light, but my heart was dreary and desolate. Nine hundred sick here, and I could not find a place either for myself or stores. Bustle and confusion everywhere; the army marching or cannonading in the distance. Besides looking after myself and stores, I have to provide the forage for our two horses, and rations for the dinner, and most of all, the sick must be cared for...I have been all day with a church full of fever cases. What think you was brought them for dinner? Salt beef boiled (very fat at that), hard-tack, and pea-soup! Thanks to our Chelsea friends,

I could supply crackers for the most delicate. After dinner, I was chaplain again; sang, prayed, and talked with the men. I could not have asked a more attentive audience. When I finished, there were tears in many eyes.

How I wish that some one abler than myself could have spoken to these sick and weary souls! You cannot imagine how receptive the soul of a soldier is, who is prostrate and suffering. Then is the opportunity for influence, to talk with him of home, of his errors, and of the temptations of the army.

I have tested myself sufficiently under shot and shell to know that in danger I can be calm. And that is needed on the field. I am thinking and planning hard. An ambulance is a more comfortable bed than you can imagine. Field-work is wearing. I am exhausted, not having had my clothes off for a week.[10]

A sergeant from an unidentified regiment remembered Miss Gilson:

I first met Miss Gilson in Pleasant Valley, Md. soon after the battle of Antietam.

She was then giving the wealth of her mind and heart to the sick and wounded soldiers, in an old, cheerless log barn we tried to call a hospital. What a beautiful minister of goodness she was! There, on the hard threshing-floor, she could be seen constantly; often sitting beside the sick, speaking those words of comfort, reading those 'words of life,' singing those songs of home, country, and heaven, which earned for her in the army the name of "Sweet Miss Gilson." We all loved her. I am sure she made home dearer, life purer, and heaven nearer, to every one of us. When, as happened so often, some spirit was about to be released from its bonds, she always took a place beside the dying one, and received his farewell messages. Then, with her pale, uplifted face, never so beautiful as when it was looking up so earnestly…she bore the departing soul by the power of faith onward to its rest.

She was brave, too, as she was loving. I have seen her sit silent and unmoved in the midst of a severe cannonade, while soldiers were flying for refuge…In the midst of ignorance unsuited to her, vice that must have been repugnant, and squalor in all its repulsiveness, she moved an angel of mercy, loving and loved. Never was step so light as hers. There was always a brightness at her coming, and sadness at her going.

She had a rare power over the soldier's heart; it acknowledged her sway always. With us, her life was hidden from the world; it lay a constant sacrifice before every needy patriot friend, and rich were we who received its blessings.[11]

"In November and December, 1862, she worked in the camps and hospitals near Fredericksburg, at the time of Burnside's campaign."[12] One man recalled her there: "I first saw her standing at an open door, with two large tin vessels of farina and soup before her, supplying nurses who were carrying refreshments to the wounded, after the first disastrous defeat at Fredericksburg. Never have I forgotten, and never shall I forget, the light of her eyes, and her smile, when, looking up, she gladly greeted me as a fellow-helper, that glance and her first words, revealed to me her generous, devoted heart."[13] Another also remembered her:

> I shall never forget the Sunday after the battle of Fredericksburg [Dec. 13, 1862]. Miss Gilson entered the tent where I was. She had a cheery, hopeful word for each of the poor sufferers; then, standing in the middle of the tent, she said, "Soldiers this is Sunday morning; wouldn't you like to hear something from the Bible?" Then, as she read in her musical voice to those rough men, I could see by the expression of their faces, that dreamy, gentle thoughts of home, and the goodness of God in preserving their lives, stole over them. As she left the tent, one of the men by whose side I was kneeling, his eyes strained to catch the last glimpse even of her dress, turned to me, the tears streaming over his cheeks, and said, "If God ever made an angel, she is one!"[14]

Praise of the method and manner of Helen Gilson's war service was constant and unanimous. "Whatever she did was done well, and so noiselessly that only the results were seen. When not more actively employed she would sit by the bed-sides of the suffering men, and charm away their pain by the magnetism of her low, calm voice, and soothing words. She sang for them, and, kneeling beside them, where they lay amidst all the agonizing sights and sounds of the hospital wards, and even upon the field of courage, her voice would ascend in petition, for peace, for relief, for sustaining grace in the brief journey to the other world, carrying with it their souls into the realms of an exalted faith."[15] "She was sweet, merry, and kind. She nursed and entertained the soldiers with equal skill, and was one of those who had mastered Miss Nightingale's art of domestic perfection under the most unlikely conditions. Hot soup served by Miss Gilson was *hot*, iced lemonade served by her was *cold*. What she made clean was not only clean—it was dainty.

Although not a Sanitary Commission worker, Helen was noted in their reports:

Upon Miss Gilson's service, we scarcely dare trust ourselves to comment. Upon her experience we relied for counsel, and it was chiefly due to her advice and efforts, that the work in our hospital went on so successfully. Always quiet, self-possessed, and prompt in the discharge of duty, she accomplished more than any one else could for the relief of the wounded, besides being a constant example and embodiment of earnestness for all. Her ministrations were always grateful to the wounded men, who devotedly loved her for her self-sacrificing spirit.

We have seen the dying man lean his head upon her shoulder, while she breathed into his ear the soothing prayer that calmed, cheered and prepared him for his journey through the dark valley.[17]

As there were never enough supplies for the sick and wounded, Helen was always seeking help in meeting the needs of the soldiers. "In all her journeys Miss Gilson made use of the opportunities afforded her wherever she stopped to plead the cause of the soldier to the people, who readily assembled at her suggestion. She thus stimulated energies that might otherwise have flagged, and helped to swell the supplies continually pouring into the depots of the Sanitary Commission."[18] A chance meeting on a train with a gentleman from Philadelphia recorded only as "Mr. K." accessed Miss Gilson to a constant source of supplies and as an independent army nurse put her in an uncommon position.

It was late in a wintery afternoon, at the close of that gloomiest year in our national history, 1862, that my attention was drawn to a weary couple seated immediately before me in a railway-carriage on the New York and Philadelphia road.

A gentleman and lady—for such, though clad in worn and faded garments, and covered with the dust of travel, they evidently were— seemed to be returning from some far country, and to be conversing earnestly on some grave and unwonted topic. The lady looked pale and faint, and leaned wearily on the shawls and cushions arranged around the seat of the car for her support; which circumstances, allowing an opportunity for some trifling courtesy, led to a conversation which occupied the remaining hours of the journey.

So casual was my introduction to a friendship which I cherish as one of the most privileged memories of my life; for this lady was Helen Gilson, returning with her guardian, Mr. Fay, for a few weeks of needed rest from her first year's campaign among the field hospitals of the Army of the Potomac.

I soon recognized in her a true and unselfish woman, seeking only the relief of suffering humanity; and I afterwards learned to know her as one of the most heroic Christian characters that our country's great peril had called into active service in her cause.

Mr. Fay and Miss Gilson had just returned from the scene of Burnside's disastrous attack on Fredericksburg, having passed through the whole dreary Peninsular career of McClellan, which ended in his re-embarkation for Washington with the wreck of his army, and the victorious, though bloody battles around Antietam. No marvel that a young woman, brought up amid the comforts of a New England home, should grow tired and faint with the sight of such unparalleled carnage, and the exhausting labors and duties of a conscientious field-hospital nurse.

She told me somewhat of her story during that evening's ride; and afterwards I leaned more of it from herself and her friends, as well as through the pleasant share I took in her subsequent work, by furnishing, together with other of her friends, much needed supplies as could not readily be obtained from the Government or the Sanitary Commission on the field.[19]

What Mr. K proposed was for Helen to receive supplies personally from a standing fund on which to draw. Miss Gilson wrote him:

> ...I am opposed as much as the Commission is to independent labor. I believe strongly in united effort; but circumstances have made me, in some degree, an exception to the rule. Now, in regard to supplies; your offer is a most liberal one, and one that I shall gladly accept...I have never solicited supplies for my own distribution, and I cannot do so now; partly because I fear people may think I disapprove of the Commission, partly because it seems like asking favors for myself. Then, too, *I believe* I desire to work quietly. I believe my only motive in this work is to do good. I pray to the good Father to keep me lowly and humble. I am but too happy if I know I am treading in the footsteps of the Great Teacher...[20]

The potential problems of making an exception to the rule of no supplies being permitted to enter the hospitals under an individual's charge was discussed through correspondence between the Medical Department directors, the Sanitary Commission, and Mr. K. As all were of the same exalted opinion of Miss Gilson, it was decided "Every thing should be done to strengthen her heart and hands."[21]

Helen wrote frequently to appraise Mr. K of the needs of soldiers and receipt of the supplies he had sent, one of which was "The new tent [one which Mr. K had sent out to Miss Gilson specially constructed and arranged for her comfort and convenience on the field] is a little trea-

sure; wherever I may wander I have a home, comfortable and cherished."
After the battle of Chancellorsville [May 3, 1863] she wrote him from
Potomac Creek: "We have now in this corps hospital about twelve hundred patients. We shall remain here until an engagement takes place…"
She conscientiously acknowledged distribution of supplies:

> My supply of milk is exhausted, and none to be obtained in Washington. Please send me more. The porter you sent is being distributed
> and is doing a great work. With the porter came twenty boxes of lemons. My supplies in some articles are running low; nine hundred and
> sixty-one men soon drain a storehouse. I have plenty of brandy and
> crackers, of figs, prunes, and broma. I need sherry and port wine, milk,
> powdered musk (for vermin), mutton, chicken, dried apples, and mosquito-nettings; the last is needed to keep flies from the wounds. I see
> personally to the distribution of all my supplies, sending an order to the
> storehouse for each article needed, which is delivered by my storekeeper,
> a responsible man. Then each day I prepare a special diet for the sickest men, selecting at my own discretion, and send to the kitchen at mealtime with a written order…All stimulants through the hospital are given
> with my own hands, and kept in my possession.

She also told him of her work and her feelings:

> I am working night and day, —cooking, feeding, dressing wounds,
> taking messages of the dying, and praying with them…I have to-day
> held two services and sung in the wards…Last Sunday I rode over to
> Fredericksburg in the morning and went on to that battle-field [part of
> the battle of Chancellorsville, Fredericksburg was the site of a secondary attack] just as they fell. I took the contents of some of their pockets
> and forwarded by express to friends in Massachusetts…We found
> wounded in churches and houses. Remained all day and night working
> for them, and was obliged to retreat hastily the next morning in the
> general flight…Our work is never finished until midnight. Two nights
> ago, hearing that there were two hundred and thirty wounded just outside the town (Fredericksburg) who had been brought in from the Rebel
> lines under a flag of truce, and learning that these poor fellows had
> been living on two "hard tack" apiece for five days, we immediately
> prepared a good supper for them…The ambulances lay half a mile out
> of town, and we were obliged to walk and carry the kettles of food, and
> did not retire till two o'clock in the morning; but the grateful expression of appreciation, and the blessings showered upon us, were compensation enough for our toil, and our sleep was sound and sweet, from
> the consciousness of duty done…No one has the right to stand aside

and say, "I have done my share" till his means or his strength shall fail him...I am so *happy* in being *able* to work for my country. The world does not consider that *I* am the favored one. Many would have done what I am doing if the opportunity had been presented...I have never spent a happier year that the last; and I hope God will continue to me the great blessing of health and strength, that I may still labor in the field.[22]

After having served at Gettysburg into the fall of 1863, Helen spent the rest of that year "in the hospitals on Folly and Morris Islands, South Carolina, when General Gilmore was besieging Fort Sumter. Early in 1864 she joined the army at Brandy Station, and in May went with the Auxiliary Corps [created by Fay to meet individual soldier's needs] of the Sanitary Commission to Fredericksburg...."[23] There were wounded everywhere as the hospitals in Fredericksburg reeled under the burden of wounded form the battles of the Wilderness [May 5-7, 1864] and Spotsylvania [Campaign May 7-20, 1864]. Helen wrote:

> The heart revolts at the thought of describing the state of things here. The sights are terrible and the air is heavy with the horrible odor, not from the wounded alone, but from the accumulation of filth about the city. Every church, store, and dwelling is filled with the wounded and they are constantly arriving from the front twelve miles from here.

A tent hospital on Morris Island.
(MOLLUS)

The slaughter is terrible…It is midnight now, the patients are asleep and we are awaiting the arrival of ambulances from the front, with our wounded from the battle of yesterday. Every hour is important, but with every victory come sad tidings of the fall of some of our best and bravest men…[Four days later] Every house, store and church is crowded with wounded. Farm-houses and barns on the outskirts of the city are filled. Hospital touches hospital. We have never known such an experience. We are all weary, but the sight of the fresh troops which are passing daily to the front invigorates us, and keeps up our working power from day to day. The ambulance trains arrive daily, with hundreds of men, unfed, uncared for, dying. (Miss Gilson's tent was pitched upon the Court-House Square [Fredericksburg]…the whole city was her ward)…I have visited six hospitals to-day. After midnight I went into one of the churches which was filled with wounded. Many of the men were asleep, but more were suffering intense pain. After spending some time there, changing the position of *this* one's limb, placing a pad under *that* stump, &c., a low, devout voice was heard, as if in prayer. Many other sounds filled the old church. Some were groaning in agony; others calling for a nurse; one stout German was swearing in his mother-tongue, and all around us sonorous tones bespeaking others in heavy sleep. But amid all, like the low surging of a distant sea, came to our ears the tones of prayer. We traced the voice, and found it was that of a sergeant, who was lying with closed eyes and clasped hands, his knap-

Burying the dead at Fredericksburg in 1864.
(Library of Congress)

sack for a pillow, and his bed the floor, praying that God would sustain his dear wife in this hour of her calamity, and be a father to the children who he committed to his care. The prayer was most simple and beautiful; and with this dying breath he did not forget his bleeding country. The midnight hours, the flickering light of candles, the arched roof, the altar of the church, the dim Gothic outline of the architecture, with the solemnity of the incident, make it one of the never-to-be-forgotten incidents of our hospital lives.[24]

A doctor wrote of Helen at the hospital in Mayre Mansion in Fredericksburg at this time:

One afternoon, just before the evacuation, when the atmosphere of our rooms was close and foul, and all were longing for a breath of our cooler northern air, while the men were moaning in pain, or were restless with fever, and our hearts were sick with pity for the sufferers, I heard a light step upon the stairs; and looking up I saw a young lady enter, who brought with her such an atmosphere of calm and cheerful courage, so much freshness, such an expression of gentle, womanly sympathy, that her mere presence seemed to revive the drooping spirits of the men, and to give a new power of endurance through the long and painful hours of suffering. First with one, then

The bullet marked Marye Mansion on Marye Heights, Fredericksburg where Dr. William Reed first met Helen Gilson.
(Library of Congress)

175

at the side of another, a friendly word here, a gentle nod and smile there, a tender sympathy with each prostrate sufferer, a sympathy which could read in his eyes his longing for home love, and for the presence of some absent one—in those few minutes hers was indeed an angel ministry. Before she left the room she sang to them, first some stirring national melody, then some sweet or plaintive hymn to strengthen the fainting heart; and I remember how the notes penetrated to every part of the building. Soldiers with less severe wounds, from the rooms above, began to crawl out into the entries, and men from below crept up on their hands and knees, to catch every note, and to receive of the benediction of her presence—for such it was to them. Then she went away. I did not know who she was, but I was as much moved and melted as any soldier of them all. This is my first reminiscence of Helen L. Gilson.[25]

"The army had fought its way from its base on the Potomac, to the new one established for the moment at Port Royal, on the Rappahannock, and as the city of Fredericksburg swarmed with a guerilla-band, our Sanitary Commission steamer 'Kent' swung into the stream to receive the parting shots of those who were just too late to capture our wounded. There were forty cases of amputations on our decks. Miss Gilson knew no rest...."[26] At Port Royal over a thousand blacks of all ages had gathered and were put on a government barge. Helen Gilson spent time there, speaking, praying, and singing with them.

The hospital site was moved again to White House and as the battle of Cold Harbor [June 3, 1864] was being fought, the transport boats docked. Eight thousand wounded poured in from the front. Helen wrote: "This White House is a tremendous field. We are working night and day. When we think of preparing for a night's rest, heavy ambulance-trains arrive loaded with these poor, suffering men, helpless and broken, the dead among the living. The transportation over fifteen miles of bad road in army-wagons is worse than death, they say...We make twenty or thirty gallons of milk punch at a time, and immense cauldrons of soup. But there is no end."[27]

The army's base of operations was moved for the last time to City Point in June of 1864 to weather the campaigns of Petersburg and Richmond [June 1864 to April 1865]. People from Mr. Fay's Auxiliary Corps moved to the battle front and arrived before the medical wagons. "After working among the wounded at Cold Harbor the boat went to City Point, Miss Gilson, with Mrs. General

Barlow, at once went to the front at Petersburg, where the Second and Eighteenth Corps had been fighting."[28] In sight of the trenches, they used her private stores "especially the chloroform, was of great service to the surgeons who were operating in the rear of our line of battle, giving thus relief to hundreds who were under the knife."[29] Helen wrote from this spot: "Last night the battle raged fiercely. We have never heard such musketry firing during the war; and this morning at five, artillery and musketry again. We are only a mile and a half from the battle line, and could see the shells burst from the brow of the hill; but our wounded give no time to witness the battle. I feel *old* and stiff to-day; bending down and dressing wounds on the damp ground makes me feel old.[30]

The black soldiers of the Ninth Corps who had fought at Petersburg suffered high casualties. "In the bloody battle of June, 1864 in Virginia large numbers of these wounded men were brought to City Point, and there dumped. No adequate preparation had been made for them. Many were sick with typhoid and malaria. The weather was hot; the filth and blood indescribable."[31] "These stories of suffering reached Miss Gilson at a moment when the previous labors of the campaign had nearly exhausted her strength; but her duty seemed plain."[32] "When Miss Gilson asked if she might take charge of these men, her friends protested, 'You cannot live through it. You will die.' 'I couldn't die in a better cause,' she said."[33]

"Thus far Miss Gilson's cares and labors had been bestowed almost exclusively on the white soldiers; but the time approached when she was to devote herself to the work of creating a model hospital for the colored soldiers who now formed a considerable body of troops in the Army of the Potomac. She was deeply interested in the struggle of the African race upward into the new life which seemed opening for them, and her efforts for the mental and moral elevation of the freedmen and their families were eminently deserving of record."[34]

> ...[S]he started out alone. A hospital had to be created, and this required all the tact, finesse, and diplomacy of which a woman is capable. Official prejudice and professional pride had to be met and overcome. A new policy had to be introduced, and it had to be done without seeming to interfere. Her doctrine and practice always were instant, silent, and cheerful obedience to medical and disciplinary order, without any qualification whatever, and by this she overcame the natural sensitiveness of the medical authorities.

Miss Gilson carried among sick Negro soldiers exactly the same tender, caressing manner she had always used with the white soldiers, and aroused in them an even deeper gratitude and an almost religious reverence.[35]

A hospital kitchen had to be organized upon her method of special diet; nurses had to learn her way, and be educated to their duties, while cleanliness, order, system, had to be enforced in the daily routine. Moving quietly on with her work of renovation, she took the responsibility of all changes that became necessary, and such harmony prevailed in the camp that her policy was vindicated as time rolled on. The rate of mortality was lessened, and the hospital was soon considered the best in the department. This was accomplished by a tact and energy which sought no praise, but modestly veiled themselves behind the orders of officials. The management of her kitchen was like the ticking of a clock—regular discipline, gentle firmness, and sweet temper always. The diet for the men was changed three times a day; and it was her aim to cater as far as possible to the appetites of individual men. Her daily rounds in the wards brought her into personal intercourse with every patient, and she knew his special need. At one time…nine hundred men were supplied from her kitchen.[36] …[H[er great work now was raising the hospital at City Point from a disgrace to an object of pride.[37]

The nurses looked for Miss Gilson's word of praise and labored for it; and she had only to suggest a variety in the decoration of the tents to stimulate a most honorable rivalry among them which soon opened a wide field for display ingenuity and taste, so that not only was its standard the highest, but it was the most cheerfully picturesque hospital at City Point.

Miss Gilson wrote in June of 1864:

We have one hundred and forty cases of typhoid. We have had no cooking stove and all our gruels, soups, and tea are made by an open fire under a hot sun. We have three thousand men in hospital…Today we have a breathing spell, a fresh breeze has come to our weary bodies. For days the thermometer has been over 100; now we feel cool and refreshed. Still the wounded are there; still the sick come in ; still the army is in front of Petersburg; still they lie in dusty trenches…It is very singular, this new experience with sick colored men. The sick are *very* sick, and seldom recover; the wounded are most imperturbable creatures, uttering no complaint. The dust is intolerable. We have never endured so much…[and in July] It is hot, and we are smothered by the dust. The day has been a hard one. My men in the kitchen are down with fever. I have stood all day over a raging stove making soups and gruels for two hundred men, then later, tea for a hundred more, besides the diet for the convalescents. Yet I have found the time to visit the wards, to read to the men, listen to complaints, and straighten out abuses...These details only show you how much there is to do.[38]

She was, among other things, a heroine among the contrabands. Women who could attach to themselves the devotion of these runaway slaves who cluttered every Union army, and turn them into devoted and efficient workers, were always a power in the army...Gradually people became aware, that one way of dealing with the freedmen was being unobtrusively dramatized for them by a beautiful young woman...She was Miss Helen Gilson.[39]

The conditions in the contraband camps were terrible.

Amid all these labors, Miss Gilson found time and opportunity to care for the poor negro washerwoman and their families, who doing the washing of the hospital were allowed rations and a rude shelter by the government in a camp near the hospital grounds. Finding that they were suffering from overcrowding, privation, neglect, and sickness, she procured the erection of comfortable huts for them, obtained clothing from the North for the more destitute, and by example and precept encouraged them in habits of neatness and order, while she also inculcated practical godliness in all their life. In a short time from one of the most miserable this became the best of the Freemen's camps.[40] She took the forlornest contrabands into service, and turned them out as cleanly, self-respecting maids, cooks, laundresses, and nurses' assistants, all able to work domestic miracles according to her high ideals.[41]

Miss Gilson's work wore on into the next year. In March of 1865 she wrote:

I am tired, tired, chronically tired. Tired to the very marrow of my bones. Last night I tried to answer your letter, but dropped asleep, pen in hand. Last evening from the special diet, I fed three divisions of the hospital. Each case was catered for separately. Each day I have to decide how much beef or mutton is needed; order it, waste nothing, save the pieces of bread for puddings, &c., and at the same time the adaptations necessary in all the cases arising in such a vast hospital, keeping a wholesome and pleasant atmosphere,— make the brain as well as the hand weary...There are stages in our physical and mental development when we think much, not about, but upon ourselves. We *need* these lessons while we are learning to live. After that, an unconscious growth goes on; and with an eye ever raised to Christ, our pattern, and to heaven, our home, we lose ourselves in the attaining; and are hardly conscious of individual life, which is swallowed up in doing and living for others. From this outside life, comes *inward peace*; sweet rest; which is more than peace that comes from looking Christward and heaven ward, let us seek…You spoke of spiritual nearness. I have always believed in it…It is a great comfort to believe in the spiritual presence of those we love, either in this work or the other, when we are homesick and heartsick here; and sweeter still, in the nearness and communion of one who abideth ever and always, ministering to our loneliness, even before we can send up our petitions…I wish I could hear the robins or some spring-bird; it is *so lonely* without them….[42]

"Miss Gilson's love of nature and quick apprehension of its grandeur and beauty, never deserted her. She enjoyed sunset skies and winter storms, the sound of waters and the perfume of flowers, with a keen and loving earnestness…."[43] [This appreciation remained active through the war. In 1864 she wrote:] To-night we went on shore. Such gardens, and such roses! How I wish you had been with us to enjoy them! I saw great bushes laden with blossoms of our favorite Luxemborg rose. Now I rejoice in a bunch of buds; and they *do me good*…They fairly make me *cry*, with thoughts of home. Dear buds! They seem to me living things; and though they fade, they are like a harbinger of the eternal freshness and beauty of immortal life. So even here we have something to cheer us…[and in 1865] It is a lovely moonlight night, but beauty and horror are here strangely mingled. I turn from this scene for a moment, to the quiet beauty of your woodbined home. I read again your letter, and am with you in the library, enjoying the western window the light of fading day. I feel the fresh breeze of evening playing through the rustling vine-leaves; and for a little time I can forget war, and all its fearful surrounds.[44]

A doctor recalled Helen at this time:

I went with Miss Gilson into one of the wards, where she was asked to sing. Joining in some simple hymn, which called forth a response from a few voices in different parts of the tent, and finding how eager the men were for more, she sang a plaintive little song, "Just before the battle, mother," then the most popular song in the army and reproduced a hundred different ways by the soldier or by the bands. There was perfect stillness in the ward, and the melody melted into the exquisite air, "I'm lonely since my mother died." Nearly every man had raised himself on his elbow to catch these notes. Some were wiping their eyes, and others, too weak to move, were hiding their emotion which still was betrayed by the quivering lip, and the single tear as it fell, but was not wiped away. One fine fellow, a Vermont boy, very sick, could hardly speak, when she went up and laid her hand upon his head, and brushed back his fine, soft, black hair. He was a man of delicate mould; and she soon found, in talking with him that although a private in the army, he magnified his position, while it also reflected back its dignity upon him. Homesickness had done its work. He had been in the hospital six months, after the severe exposures of the earlier part of the campaign. He said to me, "Do you know how many men die of homesickness in the army: Oh," said he, "I feel it so much *here*," pressing his fingers over his heart, "and I think it will wear me out."

[In April after a Sanitary Commission agent came with the news of the surrender.] Miss Helen Gilson took Knapp [the agent] to the "contraband quarters," where about a hundred Negroes were living. The shouting had awakened a few; but most of them were "sound asleep." The Negroes looked on Miss Gilson as a "guardian saint," said Knapp, and they obeyed her order to assemble in the tent street at once. Here they learned the news and praised God for their victory and freedom.[45] [She stayed to sing and pray with them.]

Helen moved into a hospital at Camp Lee in Richmond.

As was the case with nearly every woman who entered the service at the seat of the war, Miss Gilson suffered from malarial fever. As often as possible she returned to her home for a brief space, to recruit

Camp Lee in Richmond. After General Lee surrendered, Miss Gilson moved into this hospital until July 1865.
(Virginia State Library and Archives)

her wasted energies, and it was those brief intervals of rest which enabled her to remain at her post until several months after the surrender of Lee virtually ended the war.

She left Richmond in July, 1865, and spent the remainder of the summer in a quiet retreat upon Long Island, where she partially recovered her impaired health, and in the autumn returned to her home in Chelsea.[46] And so, through all the war, from the seven days' conflict upon the Peninsula, in those early July days of 1862, through the campaigns of Antietam and Fredericksburg, of Chancellorsville and Gettysburg, and after the conflicts of the Wilderness, and the fierce and undecided battles which were fought for the possession of Richmond and Petersburg, in 1864 and 1865, she labored steadfastly on until the end. Through scorching heat and pinching cold, in the tent or upon the open field, in the ambulance or on the saddle, through rain and snow, amid unseen perils of the enemy, under fire upon the open field, or in the more insidious dangers of contagion, she worked quietly on, doing her simple part with all womanly tact and skill, until now the hospital dress is laid aside, and she rests with the sense of a noble work done, with the blessing and prayers of hundreds whose suffering she has relieved or whose lives she has saved....[47]

In person Miss Gilson is small and delicately proportioned. Without being technically beautiful, her features are lovely both in form and expression, and though now nearly thirty years of age she looks much younger than she actually is. Her voice is low and soft, and her speech gentle and deliberate. Her movements correspond in exact harmony with voice and speech. But, under the softness and gentleness of her external demeanor, one soon detects a firmness of determination, and a fixedness of will. No doubt, once determined upon the duty and propriety of any course, she will pursue it calmly and persistently to the end. It is to these qualifications, and physical and moral traits, that she owes the undoubted power and influence exercised in her late mission.[48] During the following years, she spent some months in Richmond, working among the colored and white schools, but with declining health she returned to Massachusetts.[49]

Helen Gilson married Hamilton Osgood, who had been connected with the Sanitary Commission, on October 11, 1866. She spent the winter of 1867-68 back in Richmond working in a black orphanage. Back in Massachusetts by April of 1868 she died in childbirth. Her child did not survive either. She was buried in Woodlawn Cemetery in Chelsea, Massachusetts. The monument over her grave was erected by veterans with the simple inscription "A tribute from soldiers for self-sacrificing labors in the Army hospitals." As of 1895 the GAR posts and the Women's Relief Corps were still decorating it.

On her last birthday, she wrote: "Life has been long to me, but God has given me the sunshine of sweet, dear friendships. I thank him for the joy and the sorrow. I love humanity, the world, and I want to live that I may serve and be happy through my work...." She had always said, "Do not try to prolong my life when the time has come for me to die." True to this feeling, when the hour came, she put her hand upon her forehead, felt the damp, and said calmly, "This is death. The door is open, let me go."[50]

Do you remember that Sunday evening in the gloaming, when she came, with her attendant, on horseback, to the Rowe-House Hospital on the Plains, and at our request, standing at the head of the stairs, sang hymn after hymn to our poor wounded fellows? They said it was like the voices of angels. Ay! It was so. She stands for us now at the head of the golden stairway to heaven; and the voice is ever, 'Nearer, my God, to thee; Nearer to thee.'[51]

Miss Gilson is buried in Massachusetts.
(MOLLUS)

183

July Fourth

O n the celebrated day of American Independence, Vicksburg, Mississippi fell to Grant's Union army. Unaware of this crushing blow, the battered armies of the North and South faced each other from opposing ridges at Gettysburg. From Seminary Ridge Confederate sharpshooters had the scope of the town's streets. Union sharpshooters were also active.

One Gettysburg woman recalled: "…our sharpshooters were pushed out to this side of town, and were all around us. We were between two fires, and were kept close prisoners all day, not daring to go out, or even look out of the windows, on account of the bullets fired at every moving object…It has been a dreadfully long day…"[1]

One young woman, Julia Jacobs, did venture out.

By Saturday's [July 4] dawn we learned that the Confederates were in retreat. To the west of the town there was a little run of water at the Hagerstown Road. At that run Confederates had left a line of pickets, whose rifles covered the street intersection at our door. As the Union men rode down Washington Street and crossed Middle Street the watching pickets fired on them. My sister Julia… stood the situation as long as she could. Then she went to the front door our house, from which approaching Union soldiers could see her, and began to call to them as they approached the corner, "Look out! Pickets below! They'll fire on you!" She became a living danger signal and a most effective one. The men, as they caught her words, halted, watched their opportunity and made their passage of the death spot in flying dashes. She saved many lives. After some time, the riflemen at the Hagerstown Road, only three squares away, realized how she was foiling their best marksmanship. They turned their guns on her. They could not hear her cries of warning; but they had seen her standing there, and the actions of their foes— perhaps, too, some warning gestures of hers—made it evident that she was the danger signal. Girl or no girl, she must be silenced. But Julia was not silenced. When their bullets began to frame her where she stood at the threshold of the door, she retreated a few steps in to the hall and called her warning still. We could see the leaves and twigs of our linden trees fly as they were snipped by the bullets; but none of them reached her. For half an hour she warned the Union soldiers, then the need for her steady cry passed.[2]

The Confederates began sending back horses, equipment, and supplies to the South. Their seventeen mile column of wounded began the tortuous journey home with whomever could be reached and moved. The tattered regiments of Pickett's division left the field with about 4,000 prisoners headed for Southern prisons; Lee paroled about 1500 more and sent them back to Carlisle. By the evening of July 4th Lee began to pull his army out of Gettysburg along routes west and south, parallel to his supply and medical lines.

On the fourth of July Meade held a council of war as he was unsure whether the Confederates were retreating or not. Forward elements of the Union army left the field on July 5th and by the 7th all units were in pursuit of Lee's men. Although the pursuit afforded some harassment, Lee was able to reach the area around Williamsport, Maryland and entrench his army in an eight mile long line with their backs to the swollen Potomac River. He waited there for two days for Meade to strike. Finally Meade did attack on the morning of July 14th but he hit only a rear guard at Falling Waters, West Virginia. Lee's entire army had slipped away across the river through the night. The Gettysburg Campaign was over.

Elizabeth Masser Thorn

Gettysburg Civilian

"My husband was keeper of the Cemetery. He had gone to war a year before the Battle of Gettysburg. I was alone at the Cemetery all that year and had to take care of the cemetery myself. My father was with me and helped me some; but there was no other man to be gotten for any money."[1]

Elizabeth Catherine Masser was born in Eicheldorf, Germany on December 28, 1832. She immigrated to the United States in 1854 leaving a man whom she loved in Germany. One of Elizabeth's descendants tells a family story that when the family left Ellis Island, New Jersey, a helpful citizen offered to carry their luggage and made off with it all. Elizabeth married [John] Peter Thorn in September of 1855. In 1856 Peter accepted the job as caretaker of Evergreen Cemetery for $150 per annum. Evergreen Cemetery, the local Gettysburg cemetery established in 1853, would influence the names of two famous places on the Gettysburg battle site; Cemetery Hill and Cemetery Ridge. It was after the couple moved to the caretaker's house that Elizabeth's German lover showed up at her door one day to persuade her to leave with him. As the family story goes, Elizabeth had decided to go with him and was almost gone when her baby began to cry. The German lover left alone.

In 1862 Peter Thorn joined the 138th Pennsylvania which was at Harpers Ferry and Washington, D.C. during the Gettysburg Campaign. In July 1863 Elizabeth was filling in at her husband's job and had her parents, Catherine and John Masser, ages 63, and her three sons; Fred, aged 7, George age 5, and John age 2, all living with her at the cemetery gatehouse. Also at this time, Mrs. Thorn was six months pregnant. The following is her narrative of her experiences during the battle of Gettysburg.

The battle was on Wednesday, the 1st of July, and it was on the Friday before [June 26] that I first saw the rebels. As the rebels came to Gettysburg, we were all scared and wished for them to go.

The 1855 wedding photo of Elizabeth and [John] Peter Thorn.
(Mrs. Nell Baynam)

Six of them came up the Baltimore Pike. Before they came into the Cemetery they fired off their revolvers to scare the people. The chased the people out and the men ran and jumped over fences…I was a piece away from the house…When they rode into the Cemetery I was scared, as I was afraid they had fired after my mother. I fainted from fright, but finally reached the house…They said we should not be afraid of them they were not going to hurt us like the yankeys did their ladies.

They rode around the house on the pavement to the window, and asked for bread and butter, and buttermilk…My mother went and got them all she had for them and just then a rebel rode up the pike and had another horse beside his. The ones who were eating said to him: "Oh, you have another one." And the one who came up the pike said: "Yes, the —— —— shot at me, but he did not hit me, and I shot at him and

187

blowed him down like nothing, and here I got his horse and he lays down the pike." (The man whom the rebel had killed was Sandoe, who had composed a company in Gettysburg).[2]

He turned around to me [and] asked me: "Is that a good horse over there?" It was our neighbor's horse, and I said "No, it ain't. It is a healthy enough horse, but he is very slow in his motions." Well, it would not suit. I knew if the horse was gone the people could not do anything, so I helped them.

Soon they sent to different places where they destroyed the telegraph and the railroads. Evening came on and they had destroyed a good many of the cars, and burned the bridge and seven cars on it. This was the Rock Creek Bridge. We could see the cars drop down from Cemetery Hill. Next morning we heard that there was a small battle at York. Everywhere they destroyed all they could.[3]

We were trying to feed them all we could. I had baked in the morning and had the bread in the oven. They were hungry and smelled the bread. I took a butcher knife and stood before the oven and cut this hot bread for them as fast as I could. When I had six loaves cut up I said I would have to keep one loaf for my family, but as they still begged for more I cut up every loaf for them.

We had all the glasses and tins and cups and tubs and everything outside filled with water. All the time our little boys were pumping and carrying water to fill the tubs. They handed water to the soldiers and worked and helped this way until their poor little hands were blistered, and their bread I had given away on Friday.

Nobody felt like work any more, and on Wednesday morning they came with big forces, and the battle begun above Gettysburg near the Springs Hotel in the morning early on Wednesday.

[On July 1] As I went upstairs so often I saw them come in on the ridge near McMillan's house, near where the Springs Hotel now is they came and got more help. While they were fighting on the ridge the Union soldiers came from all directions.[4]

When our men lost and the rebels had driven them more this way, they put their cannons on Cemetery Hill and throw some shells over toward Coon Town. And as they fired towards the direction of the Poor House they were firing at our own men, but they did not know it, and I heard them say this amongst themselves, that they did not know it.[5]

So at last they came to the Cemetery House and wanted a man to go along out with them (a young boy was there about thirteen years, and I thought he was too young, and my father was too old) I offered myself to go along. He refused at first, but I thought there was danger all around, and said I wasn't afraid, so he said, "Come on."

We walked through flax, and then through a piece of oats, and then we stood in a wheat field. They all held against me coming through the field, but as he said I was all right, and it did not matter, why they gave three cheers and the band played a little piece, and then I walked a little past a tree to where I could see the two roads. I showed him the Harrisonburg Road, the York Pike, and the Hunterstown Road. It was with one of General Howard's men that I went. Then he took me back home. He said, "They will commence very heavy firing now, walk on the other side of my horse." And so as soon as I jumped on our porch he went back again.

I wanted to go upstairs once more to see if our men gained, but when I came on the stairway a shell had cut in the window frame, then jumped a little, then went through the ceiling, so I would not go up any more.

Soon one of General Howard's men came and ordered me to have supper for Gen. Howard. I complained I had no bread, for I had given it all away in the morning. But I said I could make cakes, and he said they were good enough for war times.

They did not come for so long, it was near twelve o'clock. It was Gen. Howard, Gen. Sickles, and Gen. Slocum.

The house was so full of soldiers that the boys had to lay on the floor in the kitchen, on feather beds. And as they saw the children lying there, they said it was very sad.

After they had some supper and I found they were going to leave I asked them if they thought I should leave the house in the night. Gen. Howard rubbed his forehead and said: "Leave the house? Leave the house?" Then he looked towards the others and said: "Comrades, I say stay." Then he said we should take our best things and pack them up and in two hours he would send two men to carry them to the cellar. The he smiled and said: "I guess you call all *best*." But I said: "Some I call better than others." He said they would begin hard fighting about day-break, near four o'clock, and then we should go into the cellar.

About two hours after they left the men came and took the things to the cellar. Gen. Howard said: "When I give you orders to leave the house, don't study about it, but go right away."

About four o'clock we went to the cellar. There were seventeen of us [other civilians]…We were in the cellar about two or three hours. The noise of the cannonading was terrible. At last the door flew open and some said: "This family is commanded by Gen. Howard to leave this house and get as far in ten minutes as possible. Take nothing up but the children and go." They said we should keep [to] the pike, where the soldiers could see us, and that would save us. When we were a little way down the pike a shell bursted back of us, and none of us were killed, but we commenced to walk faster. We went down the pike one and one half miles when we began to feel weak and sick, we were so hungry, for we had eaten nothing that day before we were so scared when the battle commenced. So we went into a farm house to buy bread…but the bread was doughey and we could not eat it. Later we stopped at a farm house, —Musser's.[6] We did not feel like going farther as it was full of soldiers and army wagons and provision wagons.

Near midnight [July 2], when everything was quiet, my father and I undertook to walk home to the Cemetery house. As we left the [Musser's] house we had to pass through a room where the Union soldiers were sleeping, lying in two rows, with only one candle to light the whole room. About the middle of one row a man raised himself on his elbow and motioned me to come to him, my father signaled I should go to him, and he took a picture out of his pocket and on it was three little boys, and he said they were his, and they were just little boys like mine, and would I please let him have my little boys sleep near him, and could he have the little one close to him, and the others near him? And so, he took them and had them lying by him.

When we got to the pike we had an awful lot of trouble to get up, because the guard was not going to let us through. But as they listened to what I had to say—that we wanted to look after our things in the cemetery house—they let us pass. We had fat hogs and we wanted to look after them. When we got to the stable we could hear the wounded men holler and go on, laying around the house,—in the cellar too, and there is where we had carried our *good* things, that Gen. Howard had told us to leave there. We could not get near the house for wounded and dead. They had been brought there from the first day's fight.

My father went to the pig pen and said: "The pigs are gone." My father got a man to take us into the cellar where six wounded men were, and they had our bed clothes all around. We went to the cellar thinking we could get a pillow and quilt, but all could find was my mother's shawl and no pillow. The poor wounded men were crying and going on so that we did not want anything then. They called their wives and children to come and wet their tongues. Then we went down the pike again. We had no trouble with the guards going back. And when we came again to the farmhouse we picked up our little boys out of the soldier's arms, and got ourselves ready, and about three o'clock in the morning we started on another journey, and went down the pike to the White Church, and then it was daylight, and we stopped a little bit there and saw some of our neighbors; then we went into a big farmhouse. We wanted water but there was none to be got, the pumps were all broken, and we were tired and hungry again, and still had nothing to eat.

They had there a big wagon shed where they brought the wounded and took off their limbs, and threw them into the corn crib, and when they had a two horse load they hauled them away.

Another lady and my self went upstairs in the house to where our officers were. We rapped at the balcony door and an officer came out and asked us what we wished. I told him I lived in the Cemetery House and we were driven away from home and had nothing to eat or drink, and we thought we would lay in a complaint.

He laughed and said: "You want to live on the army then?" Then he asked me if I knew Jenny Wade. I told him I did, and he said she was killed, and he asked me if I knew Maria Bennet, and he said she was killed (but that was not true). Then he wrote an order on the – to go to the provision wagon a mile away. We went over and we got our aprons full of coffee, sugar, and hardtack. (I have some of that coffee and sugar yet.)

When we got back we hunted for milk in the cellar and we found two crocks full. I opened a crock. The woman with me could not see, so she got her hand in the soft soap. We took one crock of milk up to our sick people and we hid the other one. But they wanted it soon, and

The gatehouse to Evergreen Cemetery after the battle.
(Library of Congress)

191

when we came in the cellar again somebody else had found it and we had none. But we found the woman's yeast and we bought flour and we baked bread that night. The woman had gone away and had taken the family to Littlestown. (Hen. Beitler lived there.)[7] Then he came home and asked us what we were going to do. And he said he had a barrel of flour nailed in a closet, and so he did. He got a man to help and rolled the barrel upstairs. We were to watch this part and he to give us a dollars worth. So when we had bread in the morning the soldiers found it out. Some came and threw down a dollar for a loaf, and another three dollars. Monday [July 6] we had no bread to give them and they were so hungry they could not wait. We hid two loaves, but we baked the next night again. The house was full of soldiers. In daytime we were watching the sick and wounded, and they were calling for water and screaming all the time.

We saw some of our furniture going on some of our wagons down the pike, and my boys wanted me to go out and stop it.

We stayed at the farmhouse, I believe three nights and then we went home.

This clock was the only item left of the Thorn possessions. It was found hanging on the wall outside the house. Mrs. Nell Baynham, granddaughter of Mrs. Thorn, generously donated it to the Evergreen Cemetery gatehouse.
(Author's collection)

Mrs. Thorn's mother, Catherine Masser, most likely attended to the domestic duties while Elizabeth and her father dug graves.
(Mrs. Nell Baynam)

We were down the country four days and the fifth [July 7] we went home. On the way home we met Mr. McConaughy. He was the president of the Cemetery at that time and he said to me: "Hurry on home, there is more work for you than you are able to do." So we hurried on home. When we looked at the house I could only say "O my!" There were no window glass in the whole house. Some of the frames were knock out and the pump was broken. Fifteen soldiers were buried beside the pump shed. I went to the cellar to look for the good things I had put there on the first night. One chest was packed with good German linen, others packed with other good things,— everything was gone, but three featherbeds and they were full of blood and mud. After I had dragged them out of the cellar I asked an officer who was riding by, if I would ever get any pay for things spoiled like this. He asked me what it was, and I told him bed clothes that were in the cellar, and he said in a very short way: "No!"

So as soon as the pump was fixed I sent for three women and we washed for four days before we got them clean.

Then I got a note from the president of the Cemetery, and he said: "Mrs. Thorn, it is made out that we will bury the soldiers in our Cemetery for a while, so you go for that piece of ground and commence sticking off lots and graves as fast as you can make them."

Well, you may know how I felt, my husband in the army, my father an aged man. Yet for all the foul air we two started in. I stuck off the graves and while my father finished one, I had another one started.

This lasted for days, until the boys sent word, if I couldn't get help at all I should telegraph to some of my friends to come and help me. Two came, but one only stayed two days, then got deathly sick and left. The other stayed five days, then he went away very sick, and I had to pay their fare here and very good wages for their work. By that time we had forty graves done. And then father and I had to dig on harder again. They kept on burying the soldiers until they had the National Cemetery ready,[8] and in that time we buried one hundred five soldiers. In front of this house there were fifteen dead horses and beside the Cemetery there were nineteen in that field. So you may know it was only excitement that helped me to do all the work, with all that stench. And in three months after I had a dear little baby. But it was not very strong,[9] and from that time on my health failed and for years I was a very sickly woman. In my older days my health has been better, but those hard days have always told on my life.

Mr. Art Kennell, now retired superintendent of the Evergreen Cemetery, was not only the caretaker of the cemetery but of its history in which Mrs. Thorn played a noteworthy part. He said: "In my opinion *she* was the heroine of Gettysburg. The men couldn't tolerate the condition of the bodies [yet] Mrs. Thorn buried 13 bodies on the 11th of August. She was never compensated other than her husband's salary of less than $13 a month for burying all the soldiers and cleaning and repairing the gatehouse." Of the 105 soldiers whom she buried in Evergreen, only 50 were reinterred in the National Cemetery. The families of the other dead did not want them moved.

Peter Thorn resigned as Cemetery keeper in 1874 and the family moved to a farm down the road. Peter died in January of 1907. That October Elizabeth joined him. They are both buried at Evergreen Cemetery.

In 2002 the Gettysburg National Women's Memorial was dedicated. It is a larger than life bronze statue of Elizabeth Thorn and stands by the gatehouse.

When the Thorns left the employ of the cemetery, they moved to a farm down the road. This family photo of children and grandchildren shows Mrs. Thorn seated at left.

(Mrs. Nell Baynam)

The statue of Elizabeth Thorn depicts her taking a break from
grave digging, with one hand to her brow, the other protectively
placed on the baby she carried.
(Deborah Novotny)

Isabella Fogg

Maine State Agent and Nurse

"From personal observations I can truly say that Mrs. Isabella Fogg, of Maine, did a great and noble work in the hospital of the 5th Corps, after the battle of Gettysburg; that but for the nourishments and delicacies procured and prepared by her hand and her personal ministrations, the suffering of the wounded would have been much greater than it was."[1]

. Some of the women who performed noble service in various capacities in the Southern and Northern armies had more of a personal stake in the war that others; they had followed their sons or husbands to war. Mrs. Fogg's son, Hugh, was all she had in the world.

The 1860 census listed the Foggs as born in New Brunswick, Canada, but residents in Maine. Isabella was a 38 year old widow employed as a tailoress. Hugh, at a different address, was a servant and 18 years old. Hugh was mustered into Co. D, 6th Maine, in July 1861.

Isabella followed. The Free State Baptist Church of Portland organized the Maine Camp Hospital Association and two of the earliest agents were Isabella and Harriet Eaton. They were pioneers from the state of Maine into field nursing. The partnership did not go well. The ladies were from different backgrounds, held different attitudes and employed different work habits. Isabella displayed an extraordinary amount of energy and would work herself into illness. No surprise that under the grind of field nursing hardships there was conflict. However, they were in complete agreement when writing their superiors about the dismal conditions of the Maine sick and wounded after Antietam and detailing the despicable behavior of the 20th Maine's quartermaster in February of 1863. Eaton wrote the forthright and moving letters, but the only signature was Isabella's. The last letter may have brought about Isabella's departure from the Maine Hospital Camp Association.

Isabella first went to Annapolis where she nursed in the contagious wards from the fall of 1861 to the spring of 1862. After the battle of Williamsburg [May 4-5, 1862], Mrs. Fogg worked on the hospital transport ships, at White House, and after Fair Oaks [May 31, 1862] was finally able to go to Savage Station, two miles from the front. "Just before the campaign culminated in the seven days' fight, her son came down to Savage Station, and gave a moving account of the sufferings of his comrades at the extreme front, where he was stationed. The next morning found Mrs. Fogg in an ambulance, loaded with supplies for the sick, making her way through the Chickahominy Swamp, to where [Major General Erasmus Darwin] Keyes was posted, on the extreme left, and within sight of the spires of the rebel capital.

> On reaching the camp of the sixth Maine, which was in [Brigadier General Winfield Scott] Hancock's brigade of [Major General William "Baldy"] Smith's Division, she found from sixty to seventy brave fellows, who, though sick, had refused to be sent to the brigade hospital, partly from the soldier's dislike of all hospitals as long as he can stand, but mainly because they hoped to be well enough to march through the streets of Richmond, which they confidently expected that great army, then having nearly one hundred and twenty thousand men fit for duty, would enter in a few days.
>
> Here, protected from the burning midsummer sun and the malarious night air by nothing better than a little shelter and 'dog' tents, they were languishing with typhoid fever and chronic diarrhea [sic]; their bed the earth, their fare salt pork and 'hard tack.' The medical officers of the regiment were neither unskilled nor inattentive. Her labors for that day were wholly for these brave sufferers, dispensing the stores which she had brought, cooking palatable food, quenching the fever thirst, cheering the sinking heart with kind and sympathetic words. Their smiling or tearful gratitude was a reward and a stimulus which dispelled fatigue, and made her heedless of the occasional shot or shell that went screaming over the lines."[2]

Mrs. Fogg marched with the army up the James River to Harrison's Landing where she was in charge of the diet for amputation cases until August. She visited the Antietam battlefield hospitals in October and November of 1862, clearly appalled at the conditions.

Isabella went home to Maine to collect supplies and then, assigned with other agents from Maine, distributed them in various hospitals. In December she was back at the front. There is a pass in her pension records dated December 12, 1862 at the Camp near Falmouth: "All Quartermasters attached to this command are hereby directed to afford the bearer, Mrs. Fogg, all facilities in the way of transportation, storage, and any other aid she may require and which it is in their power to

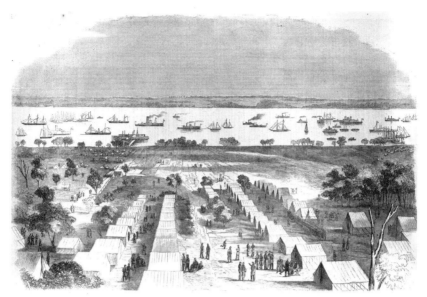

View of the encampment of the Army of the Potomac at Harrison's Landing looking from the house [Berkeley] towards the James River. Here Mrs. Fogg was in charge of diet for amputation cases.

(Virginia State Library and Archives)

afford. Her mission is one of mercy and charity to the soldiers of the army."[3] Here, she nursed through the battle of Fredericksburg [Dec. 13, 1862]. Except for an occasional trip to D.C. to forward supplies sent from Maine and a bout with pneumonia which lasted several weeks, she stayed with the army through the battle of Chancellorsville [May 3, 1863] where she was active in the removal of wounded from Confederate lines. At Chancellorsville Isabella worked not only past the point of exhaustion but at one point under heavy artillery fire. Her work was not unnoticed: General Joseph Hooker wrote of "the valuable services which you rendered in the Hospital Department during my connection with the Army of the Potomac. They were indeed precious..." and General Meade: "[She] gave her time and service as a nurse to the sick and wounded during the whole of the war. While in command of the Fifth Army Corps, and subsequently in command of the Army of the Potomac, I had many opportunities of personally knowing the value of Mrs. Fogg's services...."[4]

On May 27, 1863 Dr. F. S. Holmes, the Surgeon in Charge of the 6th Maine wrote Isabella from their camp in White Oak Church:

Please send by bearer the packages you spoke of. We are, I think, on the eve of another great battle. The articles I received from you before Chancellorsville was [*sic*] the means of saving many lives on the battle-ground of those terrible days. You can never know how thankful I was for them.

Pardon me for saying that the friends of Maine soldiers can never realize how much they are indebted to you for such hazardous, arduous, and untiring watchfulness of the wants of our men; and not only are we made the recipients of your care, but I may add the wounded and sick of the whole army. I do not hesitate to say, from my own observation, that the lives you have already been the means of saving may be counted in the thousands, and I sincerely trust that those of us who may live through this conflict will not be unmindful of their obligations to you in our day of peace.[5]

Isabella Fogg could not obtain transportation to Gettysburg for her supplies so she left them to be forwarded and she arrived on the field July 4. She spent much of time foraging through the surrounding farmland and nursing in the Fifth Corps Hospital which was located by this time at the Michael Fiscel farm which also had wounded from the VI Corps.[6] During this time, her son Hugh who was in the VI Corps, was on detached service as an ambulance driver. Isabella stayed for about two weeks in the Gettysburg hospital, returning to the army and remaining with it through the battles in the latter part of 1863.

Armed with letters and testimonials from no less than 10 colonels of Maine regiments, and various Maine surgeons, officers and chaplains she returned home. "During the winter of 1864 she again visited Maine, and the legislature of that state, much to their credit, voted a handsome sum of money to be appropriated and placed at her disposal for disbursal, according to her knowledge and judgment...."

Isabella returned to the army and labored at Fredericksburg. She wrote of this vast hospital: It was indescribable in this enormous woes, a sight demanding the tears and prayers of the universe...."[7] While her son was in the and out of hospitals in D.C. and Alexandria during the summer of 1864, Isabella served in the great hospitals of the Army of the Potomac. There is a document in her pension records from late August of that year. "The bearer, Mrs. I. Fogg, is the State Agent of Maine with these Armies, whose services for a long time in connection with our sick and wounded have been of the most assiduous and valuable character. She has been exposed to great hardships during her

Isabella Fogg.
(Maine Historical Society)

labors, but has still gone through them with wonderful fortitude. It is our earnest hope that wherever she may go she may meet with the respect, attention and confidence of all those with whom she may come in contact."[8]

In the fall of 1864, on her way home, she received news of her son's wounding. Hugh was shot at the Battle of Cedar Creek on Oct. 19, 1864 which resulted in the amputation of his left leg. Isabella found him at a hospital in Baltimore where she personally nursed him, but then collapsed herself and was sick for about a month. When she was up again she had Hugh transferred to a hospital in Philadelphia where he could be fitted for an artificial limb. Mrs. Fogg went back to the army and worked with Annie Wittenmeyer who, under the auspice of the Christian Commission, set up diet kitchens in the major army hospitals. Isabella was assigned to a hospital in Louisville, Kentucky where she "received very serious and permanent injuries" from a fall.

> She entered the service of the Union from the State of Maine under the auspices of the governor of that Sate in the year 1861 and spend the first year of her service in the Hospitals at Annapolis, where she remained until the movement of McClellan's Army when she went to the extreme front…She remained on duty in the Field Hospitals at the front for about three years serving on twenty nine battle grounds and exposed to the fire of the enemy eight times, and only left her post when compelled to do so by the illness of her son who lost his left leg at the Battle of Cedar Creek…and then under the orders of the Christian Commission, with which association she had connected herself some time previously, she went to Louisville, Ky. and while on duty there in 1865 on the Hospital Boat, Jacob Strader, she fell through the Hatchway (when in her hurry, in the dusk of the evening, to obtain some wine for a dying soldier) receiving an injury in the spine, which rendered her completely helpless for upwards of two years, during which time her sufferings were very great. She being confined to her bed during the whole of this period. She is now left a cripple for life—being unable to walk without a crutch.[9]

Isabella was hospitalized after the fall and received a pension of $8 a month in 1866. The pension was sent to St. Luke's Hospital in Cincinnati, Ohio. In 1867 the pension was increased to $20 and sent to the Hospital of the Good Samaritan in Cincinnati where she had been transferred. Meanwhile Hugh was discharged and pensioned in June of 1865. He married in July 1865. His pension was gradually increased to $24. He was never able to wear an artificial limb. The amputation left the skin flap too short and "bulbous growths" appeared on the severed nerve endings. Apparently he endured no small pain for the rest of his life. He became the caretaker at Leavenworth National Cemetery in Kansas for 11 years and then was transferred to fill the same position at Cave Hill National Cemetery in Louisville, Kentucky in 1879.

Isabella lived in Quincy, Illinois for a few years once she was able to walk. She was living in Washington, D.C. by November 1872. On December 23, 1872 she died in D.C. and was buried in Forest City Cemetery, Cape Elizabeth [now South Portland], Maine. She was 49 years old. Hugh died 7 years later at age 38.[10] Mother and son gave themselves to their adopted country and suffered greatly for it. The results of their service contributed to their early deaths.

In 1993 the cemetery had no record of Isabella's grave site. A researcher I hired in Portland found it by sheer accident. She was buried near a street sign [Central Ave.] in an unremarkable flat area. Her stone was flat, broken, and partially sunken into the ground. It was lonely, sad and forgotten. I tried to interest a Sons of Union Veterans to take it on as a project but it wasn't until interested individuals read this volume that action was taken. In 1994, the sunken grave marker was resurrected, restored and dedicated in a ceremony attended by both Canadian and Maine reenactors and historians. An iron marker recognizing her service was erected in 1995.

Isabella Fogg's restored stone and plaque.
(Author's collection)

Mary Morris Husband

"She made a flag for her tent by sewing upon a breadth of calico a figure of a bottle cut out of red flannel, and the bottle-flag flew to the wind at all times, indicative of the medicines which were dispensed below...."[1]

Mary Morris Husband was well known throughout the Army of the Potomac. To many during the war she was known as "the lady with the apron..."she has a stout serviceable apron nearly covering her dress, and that apron is a miracle of pockets; pockets before, behind, and one each side; deep, wide pockets, all stored full of something which will benefit or amuse her 'boys'; an apple, an orange, an interesting book, a set of chess-men, checkers, dominoes, or puzzles, newspapers, magazines, everything desired, comes out of those capacious pockets."[2]

Mrs. Husband had two sons in the army; John, the youngest, enlisted when he was barely 18 in Co. C of the 72nd Pennsylvania. Henry Morris, age 20, enlisted first in the 23rd Pennsylvania, a three month unit. Henry's subsequent military career was checkered at best.[3] His list of desertions is long and confusing and through his actions Mary became deeply involved in the plight of the deserter. "Whenever she went to the army, one of the first places to which she sought access was the guard-house. The condition of many she found there awaiting sentence, or awaiting trial, was sometimes most pitiful...when not engaged in the care of the sick, she used to visit the various guard houses...and interest herself in the cases of those confined there, many of them unjustly, for the soldiers well know there is but little justice in a military court-martial..."[4] "She began...to take an interest in these cases of trial by summary court martial, and having a turn for legal investigation, to which her early training and her husband's profession [lawyer] had inclined her, and a clear judicial mind, she made each one her study..."[5] "She undertook these cases, one after another, going to the various brigade, division, corps, and department commanders, and if unsuccessful here..."[6] "she took her case to the Secretary of War and, failing here, she repeatedly appealed to the gentle spirit in the White House. Many a life that otherwise would have been unjustly sacrificed was saved by her unflagging zeal and a persistency that would not know defeat."[7]

Mary Morris Husband.
(MOLLUS)

For the first year of the war Mary Husband worked for the Philadelphia Ladies Aid Society and in the military hospitals in Philadelphia. In July 1862 she began her almost incessant labor "three years in the field, either on hospital transports, or as matron of division or corps hospitals."[8] It must have been one of her first trips down to Harrison's Landing when her son John was brought to her. He had fainted on the retreat from Richmond and was brought to the hospital transport ship the *John Brooks*. Mary recalled this:

> [He was] suffering with diarrhea and a compilation of other diseases. I remember now he had a large bump on his right side as large as my fist, bronchitis, and rheumatism. My other son, H. Morris and an-

other comrade brought John…on board the boat. He was then like a dead man and I got permission to…take him to Philadelphia…[A]fter the order was given to send him to Philadelphia on our boat, I perhaps saw less of him than of the other patients who were wounded and dieing [*sic*]. I was a nurse on this boat, a Hospital Transport. After we got to Philadelphia I obtained permission to take him home with me and if he was too unwell to report to the hospital the next day I could report for him. The next day he was unable to report to hospital and I reported for him and obtained for him a two week leave and sent him to the country and I went again to the front.[9]

John never regained his health. He was "discharged by order of the surgeon" in Philadelphia on September 28, 1862.

After a brief stint in a Baltimore hospital as a substitute for a sick matron, Mrs. Husband worked at Smoketown General Hospital after Antietam [Sept. 17, 1862]. A Massachusetts soldier remembered her there: "When I saw Mrs. Husband for the first time, I was impressed by the very capable manner in which she labored. All the patients that could speak were loud in her praises, and those who were too sick to talk look their gratitude and appreciation. For weeks and months she labored from an early hour in the morning till late at night, going from tent to tent, with always a cheerful word for all, never losing for a moment that perfect evenness of temper, and that admirable knowledge of

The hospital transport *John Brooks* where Mrs. Husband found her eldest son "like a dead man."
(MOLLUS)

the wants of the sick, with which on a women is endowed. It was my good fortune to witness on her part several acts of heroism, one of which I mention."

A New York soldier, a mere boy, sick with fever, was discovered also to have diphtheria in its most malignant form. He was at once removed to a tent, put up for the purpose, in a distant part of the grove, away from all others, and a soldier detailed as nurse, who, however, fearing the disease, neglected him. Knowing this, Mrs. Husband took charge of the patient, staying every moment that could be spared from the rest of the sick, for several days and nights, tenderly caring for him like a saint, reading to him from the Testament, and taking his dying message for his mother....[10]

After traveling home with convalescent soldiers, Mrs. Husband returned to the army in early 1863 to nurse at Falmouth in a division hospital in the V Corps.

Immediately after the battles of Chancellorsville [May 3, 1863] she went to United States Ford, but was not allowed to cross, and joined two Maine ladies in the hospital on the north side of the Rappahannock, where they dressed the wounds until dark, slept in an ambulance, and early in the morning went to work again, but were soon warned to leave, as it was supposed that the house used as a hospital would be shelled. They left, and about half a mile farther one found the hospital of the Third and Eleventh Corps. Here the surgeon in charge urged Mrs. Husband to remain and assist him, promising her transportation. She accordingly left her ambulance and dressed wounds until midnight. By this time the army was in full retreat and passing the hospital. The surgeon forgot his promise, and taking care of himself, left her to get away as best she could. It was pitch dark and the rain pouring in torrents. She was finally offered a part of the front seat of an army (medicine) wagon, and after riding two or three miles on the horrible roads the tongue of the wagon broke, and she was compelled to sit in the drenching rain for two or three hours till the guide could bring up an ambulance, in which she reached Falmouth the next day.[11]

Here she was matron of the Third Division, III Corps hospital until the army moved in pursuit of Lee in June of 1863.

"She reached the [Gettysburg] battle-field on the morning of the 4th by way of Westminster, in General Meade's mail-wagon. She made her way at first to the hospital of the third Corps, and labored there till that as well as the other field hospitals were broken up...."[12]

I was surgeon Eleventh Regiment Massachusetts Volunteers, and was well acquainted with Mrs. Mary Morris Husband, a nurse "at the front" in the late civil war; at Gettysburg, Pa. during the month of July, 1863, while she was on duty nursing the Confederate wounded, who were cared for by the Third Corps after the battle at that place; that I was put in charge of the same station, and thus had ample opportunity to know of Mrs. Husband's work as nurse; that she was kind, faithful, and skillful in her management of the wounded, unremitting in her labors, sparing herself neither night or day whenever there was anything she could do to relieve the sufferings of the wounded and sick:[13] ...she devoted herself to the wounded in Camp Letterman. Here she was attacked with miasmatic fever, but struggled against it with all energy of her nature, remaining for three weeks ill in her tent. She was at length carried home....[14]

Unbeknownst to her, son Henry had deserted July 1 near Emmitsburg, Maryland. About a week later he showed up at a General Hospital in Philadelphia with a gunshot wound in the right foot. He was in and out of hospitals with his wounded foot until November 9, 1863 when he deserted and must have been arrested shortly thereafter. He was court martialed and "found guilty of the charge and sentenced to be shot to death with musketry."[15]

Meanwhile Mrs. Husband had been appointed "to serve as relief agent of the [Sanitary] commission at Camp Parole; and in this capacity she performed arduous and valuable service, with the same devotion of spirit and rare executive ability which gave such efficiency to her work for the soldiers during the long years of the war."[16] When Mary learned of Henry's fate, she must have moved with all possible speed as the verdict in his case was "disapproved" by President Lincoln and he was returned to duty December 18, 1863.

The winter of 1864 found Mary in Fredericksburg: "Nurses like Miss Gilson, Mrs. Arabella Barlow, and Mrs. Husband ran special diet kitchens, serving soup, coffee, stimulants, soft bread, and other food for the thousands of passing wounded."[17] She served at Brandy Station where a young nurse remembered her: "I am going to see the third Corps to see Mrs. Husband...She is an old lady I met at Gettysburg and one I admire very much."[18] Mrs. Husband had a smoking tent at Brandy Station which afforded some amusement until it burned down. Nevertheless, Mrs. Husband kept up her business correspondence to the Philadelphia Ladies Aid Society. In early March she wrote:

I will give you an account of the day's work, and each day is much the same. Rise at six o'clock; make my fire; whilst dressing, boil chocolate, make tea. My toast for the patients is brought me from the kitchen; I butter and soften it; poach eggs for some, and stew potatoes for the rest; arrange on plates, and send to the wards. Make milk punch and egg-nog, a tapioca pudding, corn starch, and blanc-mange; visit each patient, the surgeon, and kitchen; give directions for beef tea, soup, &c.; stew tomatoes on my own stove; mash and prepare potatoes for dinner. Afternoon, go to the station to market; buy oysters, eggs, and butter; stop at headquarters and see medical director of division about a cow which was promised us,—hope we may get it; returned and amused and entertained a couple of convalescents in my tent for an hour; then buttered toast, soaked crackers, and arranged the plates to suit the cases, with peaches, jelly, and corn starch; visited the wards, found R., our most dangerous case, suffering; heated whiskey, and applied flannels, also a bottle of hot water to his feet; wrote a letter for him to his family, and finish my day's work by writing to you, stopping now and then to stir fruit which I am stewing. Day before yesterday I visited the first division guardhouse. Some new ones have been brought in—thirty-two in all—most of then in want of stockings. I distributed some, and will see them again in a few days. How the poor fellows gathered around me, glad to receive a few words of sympathy.[19]

Mary Husband went next to serve in the vast hospitals at Port Royal and at White House in June of 1864:

Mrs. Husbands is doing for sick people in the 13 Ohio Cavalry Regt. I do know that thee knows her, thee has heard me speak of her, she lived in that peculiar looking house corner of 18th and Spruce. She is even preferable to Mrs. Lee for a companion for me. She is a woman of the same indomitable perseverance…A tent was erected for our accommodation and soon the same home-like appearance overspread the tenement that had characterized it in our previous encampment, as our table was spread upon the tail board of one of the wagons and our friends, Mr. Doolittle, Mr. Wadsworth, the Capt., Mrs. Husbands, & myself partook of a very good meal…Orders were obeyed and the train was ready to start in thirty minutes and remained in that state and did not move until four in the morning, sleeping as best we could—Mr. Wadsworth, Capt. Harris, Mrs. Husbands, and myself…Mrs. Husbands was taken with an intense nervous headache and to help her with the means at my command was my desire. In the afternoon all moved to the parking ground and the tent was pitched and Mrs. Husbands safely laid upon a bed to rest. Mrs. Husbands is writing…The development was this—that Dr. Douglass came down in the boat to see how we were getting along and Mrs. Husbands, much to my regret, *would* go on the boat to City Point.[20]

A soldier remembered Mrs. Husband at City Point: "I can never forget her kindness to me. Her untiring devotion to the sick and wounded soldier won the hearts of all. She was indeed a mother to us. Night and day she was always at her post, ever ready to relieve the suffering of our brave boys.

Mary Morris Husband.
(*Women of the War*)

"I have no doubt she saved the lives of many by her skill in dressing wounds, and her unceasing attention. No wife or mother could have been more devoted. The daily visit of that good woman to our tent was the one pleasant feature of my hospital life. She was always cheerful, and had a kind word for us all."[21]

Mrs. Husband stayed at City Point in charge of various Corps diet kitchens until Richmond fell. She returned to Philadelphia, created a cabinet in her house full of war mementos, and received visits from former patients for many years.

Mary Morris Husband was the granddaughter of the Revolutionary War financier Robert Morris. She married J. L. Husband, a lawyer, in Philadelphia and had two sons. She appears to have enjoyed a wealthy household.

Mary was 41 when she embarked on her nursing career. After the war John worked for the Freedman's Bureau in Florida and Mary and her husband lived on an orange plantation in that state for a time. Later in life "she lost by misfortune her property, her husband [1881], and by a fall upon the ice has broken her hip, and is now in advancing age thrown entirely upon her own resources for a livelihood...."[22] In 1883 Mary was a clerk in the Pension office and living in Washington, D.C. She received a pension of $25 a month in 1884 by a private act of Congress. Mary Morris Husband died March 3, 1894.

Both sons worked for the Postal Department. John married, had seven children and died in 1916 having endured pain much of his life. Henry never married. He died in 1919 and is buried with his mother at Laurel Hill Cemetery in Philadelphia. Mrs. Husband has a rather large stone over her grave with reference to her war work on it.

Ellen Orbison Harris

Philadelphia Ladies Aid Society's Secretary

"...Am full of work and sorrow. The condition of things here [Gettysburg] beggars all description. Our dead lie unburied, and our wounded neglected...Our wounded in numbers have been drowned by the sudden rising of the waters around, and thousands of them are still naked and starving. God pity us! God pity us!"[1]

Ellen Harris was the Philadelphia Ladies Aid Society's Secretary and Field Agent and was also "their worker among the soldiers." That summer of 1863 Mrs. Harris traveled from Chancellorsville to Falmouth and then to Harrisburg at Pennsylvania Governor Curtin's personal request for nursing services in anticipation of Lee's invasion. But on July 1 She was in Washington. She, like many others, could only guess at the next conflict:

Now a fearful battle impending, where in our beloved State we know not...[and on July 2] A battle is in progress: I fear the results are unsatisfactory. An evident reluctance to forward hospital stores to Hanover or Gettysburg, where the conflict is supposed to rage, betokens a want of confidence in the position or the strength of our forces. [And on July 3] Waked this morning to learn that the peaceful village of Gettysburg was the scene of a terrible battle. I went early to the War department to beg permission to carry forward a car-load of stores; besought with tears the privilege. Experience of the saddest kind have taught me that everything is needed to meet the wants of the battle-field immediately after an engagement. My entreaties were in vain; so I left Washington with a sad heart and harrowing forebodings; reached Baltimore at half past one, p.m.; heard conflicting rumors. The atmosphere seems to be loaded with sighs. Wounded are coming in; can only tell that a bloody battle is in progress, and that the "tide seems to turn in our favor." Most torturing uncertainty rests upon us. I am advised that it is unsafe to venture to the scene of conflict, but must go on; the Lord will carry me there safely, if there is work for me. I leave this at five p.m., carrying some chloroform and few stimulants. I regret now that I did not bring more without permission. The gentlemen employed here,

Ellen Orbison Harris.
(Gladys Murray, Library of Bellefonte, PA)

seem to realize the necessity of forwarding such stores at once; but they are not on hand. [On July 4] Westminster, four clock, a.m. Spent the night on the cars, being ten hours, the only woman; and with a kind-hearted baker and his wife; had an opportunity of comforting some of our wounded with pies and cakes of their manufacture. Large numbers are coming in, all giving the most frightful accounts of the fearful losses on both sides. Have seen hundreds of wounded soldiers from the battle of Wednesday and Thursday [July 1 and 2], whom I cannot name, who greet me with the kindest expressions. Many of them severely wounded, but all cheerful. Generals Hancock and Gibbons have just arrive, wounded on the 3d,; report favorably of our position; speak of the ad-mirable handling of the troops on our side. Brave men, they lose sight of their own sufferings in their zeal for their country. General Hancock has ordered the ambulance which brought him here to carry me back; it rains heavily; the streets are blocked with wagons; may find trouble. Some of the Christian Commission will go with me. My heart fails me; know I go to mourn and lament.[2]

Another nurse recalled Mrs. Harris at Gettysburg: "Mrs. Harris was in the first division of 2nd corps."[3] By the time Mrs. Harris arrived on the field this hospital was located at the Jacob Schwartz farm. Mrs. Harris wrote again on July 10 from Gettysburg:

> Since Saturday, the 4th, I have been on this "field of blood," seeing suffering of the most fearful character. Every hour brought to my view my own boys, maimed and mutilated, whose joyful greetings almost break my heart. The poor fellows, how bravely the bear the loss of members, and such extreme discomforts, which would be hard to bear by men in good health. Abijah, our Abijah,[4] is now dying; lost a leg; was taken off close to the body, I cannot particularize. Thirty-eight boxes of stores from "Ladies Aid" have reached us. We are sending many to Frederick City. We go there to-night. A battle is imminent there…Miss B[5] goes with me. An ambulance has gone on with chloroform, sticking plaster, &c., to be ready at once, should a battle occur. The amount of stores here at this time is very large, more than adequate to meet present wants, indeed prospective ones, except in the matter of bread and butter. We have cut and dispensed four hundred loaves daily, and comforted many.[6]

From Frederick on July 13, 1863, Mrs. Harris wrote to her husband, "My Dear Dr.":

> After a week of unparalleled experiences, even in my woeful history, Miss B, and self left Gettysburg; so many assistants with such a large amount of supplies had arrived, and were arriving continually, we concluded to leave for the advance, to which course we were called by the most touching appeals. Having two ambulances and other facilities, not possessed by many, we felt the call, and so are here…We are now going to the front; one ambulance loaded with medical stores; the other, with food and clothing. Tell Mrs. J.[7] to send no more supplies forward now, everything being so uncertain; will telegraph her…Never has my heart been so sad; and yet we are victorious at all points, but so much fearful suffering and death.…[8]

It is interesting to note that Mrs. Harris felt supplies were adequate at Gettysburg by July 10, while other nurses stated that the soldiers' needs were not met for weeks after the battle. It could have been that she had previously seen such want of necessities that relative to her

Second Corps Field Hospital, Gettysburg.
(MOLLUS)

experiences there seemed an abundance at Gettysburg. She was ever mindful of the lack of preparedness officials showed concerning the inevitable wounded from an upcoming battle. In late August of 1862 she had complained bitterly of this. In a letter to her husband from Hampton Hospital at Fort Monroe, after a friend had visited a battle-field [probably the Second Bull Run, Aug. 29 and 30] and reported that "the state of things there was most distressing," Mrs. Harris wrote: "Everything characterized by the same want of thoughtful care, which was observable in our first engagements. We will not learn by experience. Notwithstanding the immanency of battle known to all, not a *single* preparation had been made to take care of our wounded; all acting as men with lives insured against all risks, – bullet and powder proof."[9] She goes on to say that the only food and bandages supplied were from the civilian boxes sent by aid societies.

Ellen Harris was a most unlikely candidate for field hospital work. In 1860 she was 48 years old, married to a prosperous 70 year old doctor and druggist, with no children to care for. She was described as "A pale, delicate woman, often an invalid for months, and almost a sufferer...."[10] The Philadelphia Ladies Aid Society's "secretary was one of those delicate, fragile, and feeble-looking ladies who are apparently condemned to lives of patient suffering and inactivity by constitutional defect of physical vigor. She was known merely as a lady of warm personal piety, and excellent but mild and unobtrusive sense."[11] It is hard to reconcile these descriptions with a woman who held such an arduous and powerful position for the entire war; in the eastern theater through 1863, then out west in Tennessee, and finally working with the released prisoners of war from Andersonville and Salisbury.

In spite of, or perhaps because of, her physical condition, Mrs. Harris rarely mentioned any problems in her letters. In May of 1862 after a grueling day on board a hospital transport ship she wrote: "Disrobed and bathing with bay rum, was glad to lie down, every bone aching, and head and heart throbbing, unwilling to cease work where so much was to be done, and yet wholly unable to do more. There I lay, with the sick, wounded and dying all around, and slept from sheer exhaustion, the last sounds falling upon my ear being the groans from the operating room."[12] Later, in August 1862 and again on the hospital transport, the *Kent*, she wrote:

> …I would gladly have assisted [with cooking] but was very seasick. It was stormy, our boat leaked, and the atmosphere was loaded with disagreeable odors, so I could only lie still upon a bench in the little aft cabin, and think of what could be done for the poor fellow, if I were only able…[the next morning] I was roused by the water falling upon my face, and awoke to find my boots, my only pair, half full of water, and my clothing all more than moist. This proved rather a *damper*, but if we will help our soldiers, we must suffer with them. The poor sick ones in the adjoining apartment had fared no better. So with gratitude that we had not all been swept away (for the gale had been very severe, and our boat in a leaky condition), I bestirred myself, dried off at the furnace, and my sea-sickness having nearly passed away, got to work, to forget myself and think of others,—a most admirable cure for all kinds of sickness.[13]

In 1863 she wrote: "…often wish for longer days and more strength, there are so many ways of doing good, and bearing the burdens of our poor soldiers."[14]

Sometimes when she went home for short stays but took her responsibilities with her: "I felt impelled to leave Philadelphia before I was restored, feeling anxious about our stores and our soldiers. We found all our co-workers gone, and no one knew what had been done with our stores, many of which I knew could not have been distributed *judiciously* before leaving the "Landing."[15] On these occasions she found either her stores had completely disappeared or were piled safely somewhere far away from the people who needed it.

Many times Mrs. Harris' resolve to leave for a rest were overcome quickly. In a letter dated September 3, 1863, she dreamed of a respite to renew her strength:

> The two weeks preceding had been most trying upon our strength. As I crept into my ambulance all alone, after a day spent in the preparation of food, every nerve and muscle throbbing and a thirst which would not be assuaged by the muddy, fetid water we could command, my determination to seek rest and comfortable quarters away from all the depressing influences of climate and of war's surroundings, more depressing still, seemed fixed, but sleep was mercifully granted, and proved a "sweet restorer," and with the early dawn, plans for relieving and comforting our brave boys occupied my mind, and before I knew it, they were being carried into execution....[16]

That day she went to assist the sick of the Sixth Michigan Cavalry, numbering about sixty which included the surgeon and stewards. They were on the other side of a swollen stream, with no food, medicine or medical attendants. After locating the men, Mrs. Harris' group had to go six miles out of the way to use the closest ford. With minimal implements to prepare even the simplest food, they persevered until everyone was fed. She concluded "...if you could have seen the tears, and heard the thanks of these sick braves, you would not wonder that I remained day after day."[17]

These excerpts do not produce an image of an invalid. Other nurses half her age and in good health spoke more of exhaustion and illness. Whatever infirmities Mrs. Harris endured or overcame, she did not share them in her letters. And it is for her letters that history remembers Mrs. Harris. Her letters of clipped or fragmented sentences were prolific and forceful. Probably due to constant interruptions, they bolt from highly emotional to strictly business. Her descriptions of hospital experiences and death scenes are so moving they can reach across more than a century of time and break your heart. Her earnest and sometimes piercing criticism of anyone, no matter how highly placed, who added to a sufferers lot came from justified outrage. She was writing these letters for publication in the Philadelphia Ladies Aid Society's reports to be read by the women of the North; women whose sons, husbands, fathers, and lovers were the soldiers of whom she spoke. With spontaneous honesty, Mrs. Harris' letters burned and wept and must have taken thousands of women's hearts with them. She was probably the most successful collector of supplies any ladies aid society had.

The Ladies Aid Society, of which Mrs. Harris was secretary, was not confined in its operations to one army, or one class of sufferers. A noiseless channel for the distribution of genuine charities, its principle of action from the time it was organized, in April 1861, till the Proclamation of Peace, was to relieve any suffering, in any part of the land, that arose out of the state of war, and in this noble mission to "sow beside all waters." A signal of distress in any quarter, whether from a provost guard at a fort, the captive in his prison, the soldier on the field, the mutilated but patient hero in the hospital, the refugee from starvation and death, the Cherokee in his devastated fields, the freedman in his destitution, even the bleeding rebel soldier, alike called for the sympathies and shared the bounties of this association.[18]

Deeply religious, Ellen Harris carried out this mission of charity and sympathy to the letter. She spoke of the "enemy" with understanding and love. In August of 1862 she was at the Chesapeake Hospital, Fort Monroe, and recollected the year before when they buried the first dead of the hospital:

> ...[I]n May last [1861], when six soldiers, friends and foes, were carried to their last resting place, in the spot selected a few days previous for a soldiers' burying-ground. When these six were lowered into the earth, the place seemed solitary; only five had been laid to sleep

The Chesapeake Hospital, Fort Monroe.
(MOLLUS)

there. Now some hundreds of little hillocks, with small, wooden head-marks, tell of as many souls gone up…What histories cling about that now sacred spot! How many mothers' hearts, North and South (for many Confederates sleep here), are making pilgrimage to it, as they walk by the wayside, when they lie down and when they rise up, their sorrowful yearnings clustering about the, to them, hallowed spot. Northern and Southern mothers' hearts meet and touch each other oftener than they know; a common sorrow and mingled blood cements them. Would that the blood already shed might prove enough to bind us all together.[19]

At Antietam battlefield: "Testaments, of which we have none now, gave my own, a wounded Confederate having begged me for it. I feel a painful degree of loneliness without it, but could not refuse the request of a wounded prisoner who loves the Savior and will soon be with Him…."[20]

And in Warrenton, Virginia, about a month after Gettysburg:

We have had a most fatiguing and trying service, following our army in its rapid marches, and caring for the sick and wounded, who grew in numbers every stage of our journey. Severe skirmishing going on. We have fed the hungry, and clothed the naked, in barns, by the wayside, in churches, in cars, preparing food *in the streets*…We will lose many of our brave boys, in consequence of the extreme heat and impure water…The weather has been extremely warm, and my hands have hung down, and my heart has fainted. Have had the sorrows of the rebel sufferers, which are neither "few nor small" to carry. Oh, what scenes we are passing through! Scarcely a family in Warrenton but mourns one dead in the Gettysburg fight.[21]

Mrs. Harris' main responsibility and concern was nutrition. While visiting the regimental hospitals around Washington in early 1862 she wrote: "Everywhere we see the want of good cooks. The diet after all is the main thing—better be without surgeons than without good nurses and cooks."[22] "It is well the sick are not behind the scenes,—appetite would be still more fickle."[23] After distributing bread, oranges, and pickles on a transport hospital she wrote: "[They] were seized upon with avidity. And here let me say, at least twenty of them told us the next day that the pickles had done them more good than all the medicine they had taken. So much for pickle treatment…."[24] She wrote more fully on the subject in October of 1862 at the Smoketown Hospital caring for the wounded from Antietam [Sept. 17, 1862]:

Our soldiers have too little vegetable diet, I am convinced. One cause of the disease among our Northern soldiers on first coming into the field, arises from the great change in diet. I believe it to be more prolific of disease than change of climate or water. It is a well-known fact, that the troops from Maine, Vermont, and other far north states, suffer more from the acclimating, and I would add army dieting process, than do those of the border. Within six weeks a regiment from Maine came among us. Before much exposure of any kind, they began to sicken and there are already of that noble regiment three hundred unfit for duty. They ascribe their sickness largely to the meat diet. They have not been accustomed to subsist upon meat; fish, vegetables, and farinaceous food having been their staples. Border State men, having depended more upon animal food, the transition is not so violent. Wish much arrangements could be made for furnishing dried codfish to the army. A very large proportion of the men crave it. We need it much in the hospital. The surgeons would be glad to give it to many. So with herring, mackerel, &c. The desire for change of diet is, I may say, intense. If you could see the eager expression of the wan, hollow-cheeked, sunken-eyed men and youth in our charge here, when bread and milk, chicken soup, toast, bread and butter, or potatoes are carried to them, you would weep, as I do every day many times. These brave fellows, coming out to risk life for us, suffering for the want of this simple fare! It is sometimes almost more than I can bear.

At a field hospital in early 1863 she wrote: "Yesterday we were told that many of them might, humanly speaking, have been spared to bless their families and their country, had proper nourishment been at hand."[25]

Drunken surgeons, a bane many nurses wrote about, were also in Mrs. Harris' letters: "I find still some [soldiers] very destitute, through neglect on the part of surgeons I charge. Had yesterday some of the most painful experiences to which I have been called. Cannot tell it now, though now I shudder as I think of the dreadful intemperance destroying many. Drunken surgeons carry death with them and that in its most horrid form. The surgeons here are free from that vice, but a neighboring hospital is witness of its terrible power to destroy."[26] "…[W]hat agony is meted out to our poor boys, through the intemperance and heartlessness of physicians; and yet there is a great improvement in the character of our medical department…."[27]

If Ellen Harris had an enemy, it was war. After Antietam she wrote a chilling letter to the contributors of the Aid Society:

I was called upon to comfort a broken-hearted wife...who staggered into our tent, speechless and pale with anguish, having just arrived...to learn that her husband...had ceased to live but a few hours before. We comforted her as best we might. Her sorrow was of that silent, touching kind, so sad to witness and so difficult to meet...and this is glorious war! Oh! The fearful significance of that little word. How differently the eye rests upon it, or the ear catches the sound, stripped of the pomp and circumstance distance gave it. Sad partings, forced marches, mortifying reverses, the column of groans and sighs from hospitals, army Judases, mutilated bodies, ghastly death, weeping Rachels and lamenting Davids are in the foreground. Once they were only seen in perspective, the dim haze of time and distance shutting out the hideous features, which now stand out in bold relief all ungarlanded and reeking with a nation's blood. All these are ours, for are we not one people, claiming the same Lord and the same Savior, and anticipants of the same eternal home? You have all been intensely interested in the experiences of the army these last months of rebuke and heaviness, and have thought, I doubt not, that you were in full sympathy with our battle-driven, weather-tossed soldiers. You look over the papers with eager eyes, to learn the movements of different divisions. You read such a division moved to such a point. Your minds are occupied with the probable advantage to be derived from it, and the causes suggesting it. You may be scanning the war news a day or two hence, and notice the change in position of Generals [Abner] Doubleday's and [Rufus] King's divisions, but you will not know that the order to strike tents and march reached them late in the afternoon of Sabbath, a cold, easterly storm, with some snow and much rain prevailing, all off routine camp duty, as they lie in their little, low shelter tents, dreaming of home, or perchance, peering wistfully into the future, so full of immediate interest to them, and thinking of the comrades who so lately bivouacked with them now filling soldiers' graves all around them, are startled by the order, "Up, boys; strike your tents; we are off." Soon all is bustle, the tents struck, are wrung out, and rolled up wet, tied to the knapsack, wet too, haversack, with rations for three days, all wet, thrown round the neck, tent and knapsack, hung with moisture on the back, they fall into line, and off they march; some half-sick, not long out of the hospital, not a few of whom will fall out by the way, and be carried to some cheerless shelter, to suffer, and perhaps to die. Their very sick are placed in ambulances, and left at the nearest hospitals, which in this instance, is Smoketown. It is night, and very dark, the ground is saturated, and the grass wet, when a halt is called. Soon the hills are a blaze with campfires, every few rods a bright flame goes upward, for the rain slacks, and straw, upon which so many of the our wounded of the late battle slept out life, is abundantly scattered over. The scene is brilliant, but oh! the background, how dark! Shiverings, hollow coughs, and whistling, meant to be joyous and long drawn sighs, which will follow close upon a joke or laugh, *but no complaints,* as the brave fellows roll themselves in their blankets, and lie down to rest. By midnight, all is quiet, but we know our sons and brothers are lying around us, on their cheerless beds, the wind whistling and the rain pattering upon the window panes…Day dawns…the soldier must lose no time now, with a vigilant foe close upon us. Up they get, not with the elastic bound of young life, but with the movement of age, muscles sore, joints stiff…and to work they go, make their fires…eat standing, and "in haste"…In a few minutes, they "fold their tents like Arabs, and silently fade away." No music on these marches, no sound but orders given in low tones, and the tread, tread, tread of many feet…The happy, quiet rest of friends at home, whose ignorance is bliss, is at all times envied. Then again we think, "Sleep on now, and take your rest," for soon you may come, as so many sorrowful pilgrims have already come, seeking the living among the dead….[28]

War and the experience of it caused Mrs. Harris to question her religious beliefs which were the anchor of her life. After Fredericksburg [Dec. 13, 1862]: "Ought not to come to you in hours of sorrow, but I must; am so heart-weary and heart-sore. Our poor, poor country, how she bleeds at every pore…Are we to be torn, and rent, and sent adrift upon the ocean of man's reckless passions? Meet with so many difficulties here in the prosecution of my work, would have given up in utter despair, had it not been for an unwillingness to quit a field where so few are found to testify for Christ. Not a bright spot appears in our heavens."[29]

In 1863:

> We lie down tonight with the sad knowledge that not less than 1000 of our sick are exposed to this terrible storm, not even shelter tents to break its force. By tom-morrow night, we may add many thousand of wounded to this suffering, shelterless company. No adequate means to prevent freezing, should the weather continue severe, have been secured. You may form some idea of the conflict within; it is only symbolized by the storm without. And all this the Lord's doings. Are not the hairs on our head all numbered? Does He not see every throe of anguish, hear every sigh, count every groan, and know every pain? and yet He permits them all, giving a loose rein to His creatures, that they may in their madness destroy themselves….

"My letters have of late been tinged, indeed, I myself filled with sadness, and yet woes accumulate…Grimvisaged war seems more terribly hideous and repulsive than ever…*Why* hath He so dealt with us, is too often in my head."[30] "The past fortnight so full of fearful incident is ever before me; vain are all my efforts to forget the sights and wounds which have pressed upon me, extorting the bitter cry, "Is His mercy clean gone forever? How long, Lord?...[31] Mrs. Harris did find great comfort in the large prayer meetings that she organized which apparently became more and more frequent towards the latter half of the war.

Letters from the Secretary of the Philadelphia Ladies Aid Society became more condensed as the war went on. It should be noted that there was always business to be related as an agent of distributions. "All of last week was passed in looking after and distributing stores in the hospital, in the camp, and on the water…the confusion in every department here, especially that of the quartermaster, made it necessary to be ever on the alert. [She distributed]…one hundred baskets, seventy-two barrels, five bags, and five boxes of onions, eight barrels of apples, eight barrels of potatoes, three barrels of beets, three barrels of squashes, eighteen bushels of tomatoes, five barrels of pickles, one barrel of molasses, two kegs of butter, six barrels of dried rusk and crackers and eighty pounds of cheese, besides quantities of clothing, 800 shirts, 500 pairs of drawers, about 1000 handkerchiefs and towels, many pounds of soap, 62 bottles of wine, cocoa, milk, farina, &c. in large quantities."[32]

The following are three excerpts from letters that describe the conditions in Camps "Convalescent and Parole," a battlefield hospital, and a hospital transport ship. They are examples of Mrs. Harris' use of the power of the word. She made it quite clear to Northern civilians that neither the government nor the army was going to take care of their men; she called upon the people to do so and many answered her call.

> I find myself in the most melancholy and unsatisfactory, and I must add, vexatious round of duties, to which I have been called. I have told you of the inexcusable destitution of our men at Camps Convalescent and Parole, near Alexandria. I have from time to time written to "the powers that be," begging that a careful inspection of these camps might be ordered. But the axe was not laid at the root of the tree; and so it has grown and spread, until from twelve thousand to fifteen thousand of our sick have come within its deadly shade.

Camp Convalescent and Parole outside of Alexandria, Va., 1864.
(*Millers Photographic History of the Civil War*)

The attention of Congress has been called to it; and the Committee on the Conduct of the War have been required to examine these camps, and report upon them. Grave Senators have spent days in "looking around" and reports of great improvements have found their way into the public papers; but the real condition of the men there is, at this hour, beyond expression, humiliating and saddening. [She quotes written statements from surgeons to illustrate almost unbelievable conditions.] Can you wonder that men and boys grow careless of life, and lose their manhood under such treatment? I am at present exercised in mind and body to a fearful degree. Think of the cold weather of the past week, and of hundreds of our boys, many of whom we had just nursed at Bolivar and Smoketown, who came here to join their regiments, being thrown into this camp, to suffer and die. Fifteen of those in whom I was interested have died,—shall I write it?—of starvation and exposure, within three weeks, and that under the shadow of our Capitol![33]

At the field hospital:

...[T]he atmosphere full of the taint of decaying animal matter, and everything around within suggestive of the fearful curse under which we groan. The surgeons in attendance received us gladly, allowing us to pursue our work of cheering and comforting the poor sufferers...None of the sick were upon beds, a large portion of them laid upon straw in bivouacking tents...the centre being only four feet from the ground. Two occupied a tent. These being made of black cloth absorbed the sun's rays, and were fearfully hot. As we crept into the tent, between two poor fellows burning with fever, to wash their faces and necks, and lay cloths

224

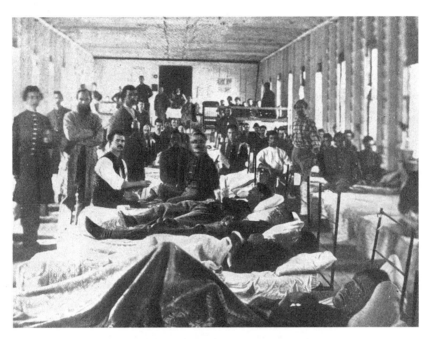

A hospital ward at Camp Convalescent.
(*Millers Photographic History of the Civil War*)

dipped in cool water and bay-rum upon their fevered brows, felt that suffocation was inevitable…[Later]…Three hours were spent in the garret of a house where lay twenty or thirty fever cases, two small windows, four panes of glass, one at each end, the only ventilation. Washed all their faces, necks, and feet with soda water…As we came from the attic, drenched in perspiration, that hottest day of the season, and thought of the pleasant mountain homes of the Pennsylvania and Michigan soldiers, all of them having comfortable, some luxurious homes, who we left there to pant for a breath of air, and long for the cooling waterbrooks, the wish that the people of the North could know the price paid by these uncomplaining soldiers…became absolutely pitiful.[34]

The transport ship *Vanderbilt:*

Imagine a steamer of immense size, crowded from stem to stern and from hold to hurricane deck with sick and wounded,—principally wounded. Passageways, staterooms, &c., &c., all more than filled; some on mattresses, some on blankets, others on straw, some in the death struggle, others nearing it, some already beyond human sympathy and help; some in their blood as they had been brought from the battle-field of the Sabbath previously, and all hungry and thirsty, not having anything to eat or drink, except hard crackers, for twenty-four hours...When we went aboard, the first cry we met was for tea and bread. "For God's sake, give us *bread*," came from many of our wounded soldiers. Others shot in the face or neck begged for liquid food. With feelings of a *mixed* character, shame, indignation, and sorrow blending, we turned away to see what resources we could muster to meet the demand...[After scouring the area for supplies]...in an incredibly short time, we were back to the poor sufferers.

When we carried in bread, hands from every quarter were outstretched, and the cry, "Give me a piece, O please! I have had nothing since Monday;" another, "Nothing but hard crackers since the fight," &c. When we had dealt out nearly all the bread, a surgeon came and, and cried, "Do please keep some for the poor fellows in the hold; they are so badly off for everything." So with the remnant we threaded our way through the suffering crowd, amid such exclamations as "Oh! please don't touch my foot," or, "For mercy's sake, don't touch my arm," another, "Please don't move the blanket; I am so terribly cut up," down to the hold, in which were not less than one hundred and fifty, nearly all sick, some very sick. It was like plunging into a vapor bath, so hot, close, and full of moisture, and then in this dismal place, we distributed [our supplies]...When I left the boat at eleven o'clock at night, I was obliged to wash all my skirts, being dabbled in the mingled blood of Federal and Confederate soldiers, which covered many portions of the floor. I was obliged to kneel between them to wash their faces. This is war....[35]

Ellen Matilda Orbison was the fifth of twelve children of William and Eleanor Elliott Orbison, born on July 19, 1816 in Huntingdon County, Pennsylvania. She married widower Dr. John Harris in 1837. After serving throughout the war, Mrs. Harris returned to Philadelphia in 1865, "her health feebler than before, suffering constantly from the effects of a sunstroke, received while laboring on the field at Savage Station."[36] In 1870 her husband was assigned U.S. Consul to Italy. "The consular residence in Venice was the meeting place of many of the most distinguished persons, Robert Browning, Whistler, and other men of art and letters were entertained by Dr. Harris and his wife."[37] Ellen's husband died in Venice on February 21, 1881. "After the death of Dr. Harris at Venice, she removed to Florence, where she has resided ever since, her health having been as such to make the voyage to the states too dangerous for her to undertake."[38] Ellen Harris died in 1902 and is buried in Florence.

Mary W. Lee

Nurse, 72nd Pennsylvania
Second Army Corps, First Division, Second Brigade

*"...[My son] told me there was a woman in the hospital by
the name of Mrs. Lee; he said you were as kind to the soldiers as a mother, and that they all loved you as a mother.
He said you were an angel..."[1]*

Mary Lee first became known to the soldiers as the leading spirit
of the Union Refreshment Saloon, which was the army's favorite institution. It had started in this way: Back in 1861 on April 23, Sherman's
battery of eight howitzers, manned by eighty very hungry and thirsty
men, passed through Philadelphia on its way to Washington. As the
troops appeared on the water front, in a shabby working-class district,
women came running out bringing the plates off their own tables, and
the saucepans and frying pans off their own stoves full of their family
dinners. Others came rushing with bottles from the pantry shelves, and
bread out of the bread box. Loiterers on the street, seeing this, hastily
bought up all the stocks of the pushcart men, who sold apples and oranges and peanuts, and added them to the food the women were assem-
bling for the soldiers. A man passed around his hat and took up a
collection which he spent buying out the nearest tobacco shop. The
soldiers departing, replete with food, drink, and smoke, gave nine cheers,
for the Union, the Constitution, and the ladies of Philadelphia.

Mrs. Mary Lee, seeing the success of the spontaneous offering of
the poor, immediately started organizing it. She set up a stove and
apparatus for making coffee in an old boathouse, and hung over it the
sign *Union Refreshment Saloon*. She organized the housewives of that
whole area, so that at any time, day or night, when the signal gun announced that soldiers were arriving by train or by boat, bands of women
appeared to serve them. Most of the women were poor. Some were so
old that they could scarcely hobble. But Mary Lee used them all. It
soon became known to weary and hungry men that, no matter how long
they had to starve, en route to a military center, there was always food
and comfort for them in Philadelphia.

Funds flowed in to the Union Refreshment Saloon from all over
the city. The Saloon outgrew its quarters in the boathouse and took

Established in April 1861, the Union Refreshment Saloon would
serve almost a million men by the end of the war.
(Library of Congress)

over one after another of the adjoining buildings as annexes…When
soldiers complained that they hadn't had a chance to wash for days,
bathing arrangements were improvised, and soon every soldier could
get a wash or a bath. Then it was found that sick or tired soldiers,
crammed for days in cattle cars, would appreciate a chance to lie down.
Soon there were dormitories and bedrooms for the transients who needed
them. Finally a hospital and medical center was established. By the
end of the Civil War…[between 800,000 and 900,000] men had been
served in this simple way, in this working class district.

Many people worked on this project, but Mary Lee was associated
with it in the soldier's mind, and wherever she went afterwards in the
army—and she seems to have been almost everywhere—she was hailed
with peculiar affection.[2]

Mary Lee's son, William, had enlisted in Co. B of the 72nd Pennsylvania in August of 1861 and by August of 1862, Mrs. Lee decided to
go to the front where her son was. When the hospital transport ship the

Spaulding unloaded its human cargo of wounded in Philadelphia, she was on its return trip. She traveled down to Harrison's Landing where she worked with the sick and wounded from the failed Peninsula Campaign [March-July, 1862].

Mrs. Lee arrived at Antietam [Sept. 17, 1862] the night before the battle in a forage wagon. During the battle she set up a station on the Sharpsburg Road where she supplied water and bread to the wounded and hungry. "Mrs. Lee was probably nearer the front than any other woman on the day of the battle, and certainly much nearer than the commander-in-chief himself."[3]

At some point after the battle:

> At one of the field hospitals where Mrs. Lee was doing the best she could for the crowd of sufferers, there was nothing found in the way of commissary supplies but a barrel of apples, and a keg of lard. To a practical housekeeper, as she is, this combination seemed to point to apple dumplings as the dish in which they could all be employed to the best advantage, and the good-natured astonishment of the poor fellows, who looked for nothing but black coffee and hard-tack, was merged in admiration for the accomplished cook who could there, almost on the battlefield, serve them with hot dumplings.[4]

This apple dumpling story became famous throughout the army. By night-fall Mary was cooking for the wounded at Sedgwick's Division Hospital and,

> was greatly annoyed by some worthless camp-followers, who would not carry food to the wounded, and when she left to carry it, they stole everything she had cooked. She went upstairs, where most of the wounded were, and asked if any one was there who had sufficient authority to detail her a guard. A pleasant voice from one of the cots, where an officer lay bleeding, said, "I believe I have. Just take the first man you can find, and put a gun in his hand." It was General John Sedgwick, and she had no more annoyance from camp thieves.
>
> In a day or two after the battle she went, with Mrs. General Barlow, in an ambulance, to see if some poor fellows had not been overlooked on the field. They found two boys in a deserted cabin, who had never had their wounds dressed, and had been living on a few crackers and water.[5]

After Arabella Barlow took charge of Sedgwick's Hospital, Mary Lee went on to Hoffman Farm's Hospital and then to the Smoketown General Hospital where she remained nearly three months. She left

Smoketown once to hasten to Harpers Ferry where an explosion of powder killed and wounded many of the men of the 72nd Pennsylvania. Her son, fortunately, was not among them.

She nursed the wounded of Fredericksburg [Dec. 13, 1862] but early in 1863 she returned home with her sick son and worked, as she did whenever on leave from the front, at the Union Refreshment Saloon. By March 1863 Mary Lee was again nursing in the II Corps Hospital at Potomac Creek and through the battle of Chancellorsville in May at the Lacy House Hospital. She was now accompanied by an invaluable aide, her daughter Amanda.

The exact date Mrs. Lee arrived at Gettysburg is unclear. There she once again served at the II Corps Hospital. "For her services in this hospital she received from the officers and men a gold medal—a trefoil, beautifully engraved, and with an appropriate inscription."[6] Mary worked in Camp Letterman, along with her son who was detailed as a nurse, for about two months. Before leaving she received this testimonial from the patients in Ward B, sixth division:

> Dear Madam: We now hasten to express to you our thanks for the numerous luxuries and kind services we have received from you, as from the hands of our own kind mothers, for which we shall ever feel grateful to you.

Mrs. Lee nursed at the Lacy House during the battle of Chancellorsville.
(MOLLUS)

While endeavoring to meet the urgent calls of our wronged country, we had the misfortune to be wounded far from home, and, as we thought, from friends. Here we have found your kind hand to care for us, and alleviate our wants as much as possible. We shall ever feel grateful to you for such motherly care as can never be forgotten; and besides the thousand thanks bestowed on you, the God of our country will ever bless you with a special blessing—if not now, surely you will receive it hereafter.[7]

In late 1863 Mary returned to Philadelphia. "Her health was impaired by her excessive labors at Gettysburg and previously in Virginia, and she remained at home for a longer time than usual...but early in February, 1864, she established herself in a new hospital of the Second Division, Second Corps at Brandy Station, Virginia. Here, soon after, her daughter joined her, and the old routine of the hospital at Potomac Creek was soon established."[8] In February another nurse wrote of Mrs. Lee: "I think Mrs. Lee is not flourishing yet until she gets a stove...there is a perfect *lot* of ladies in the army and we have so much company...Mrs. Lee's daughter is here."[9] Amanda Lee described her mother at this time: "Mother has a small stove; until this morning it has smoked very much, but it is now doing very well. The top is about half a yard square. On this she is now boiling potatoes, stewing some chicken-broth, heating a kettle of water, and has a large bread-pudding inside. She has made milk punch, lemonade, beef-tea, stewed cranberries, and I cannot think what else since breakfast."[10]

A nurse at the Second Corps Hospital wrote: "Mrs. Lee reigns supreme in the Second Division. Mrs. Lee is still flourishing. She talks and cooks as much as ever. Dr. Aiken thinks she is the best woman he ever saw in a hospital...I will say for her I do think she is one of the best women, all things considered, I ever did see...I wish I was more like Mrs. Lee, did not think about anything but my biscuit, yeast, etc. She is delighted to have my division to cook for, the more work she has to do the better she feels."[11]

From the hospital sites of Belle Plain and Fredericksburg, nursing the wounded from the Wilderness [May 5-7, 1864] and Spotsylvania [Campaign, May 7-20], Mary Lee and Cornelia Hancock traveled to White House. Miss Hancock wrote: "We left Port Royale on the Rappahannock 15 miles below Fredericksburg on the 30th of May, Mrs. Lee, Georgy Willets and I having come here from that place in an open wagon the day before. Now we are on our march for the White House—

a distance of about 45 miles…Mrs. Lee is a very pleasant travelling companion…Mrs. Lee is a very good singer. It is getting towards night and she is singing as we are wearily nearing [their destination]."[12]

The nurses were at White House but a few weeks. "Mrs. Lee has a cooking shanty up and is therefore happy…Mrs. Lee is working very hard. White House is evacuated now…Mrs. Lee got very tired of our last overland march, so went on the boats [to City Point]."[13] At this hospital Miss Hancock wrote of Mary in June of 1864: "She is here but I think played out; she has worked harder than any galley slave I ever saw…[in July] Mrs. Lee will come home soon. She was worked very hard indeed…I have six new tents added to my care now as Mrs. Lee leaves in a few days."[14]

Mary Lee went home to rest for a time. In March of 1865 Miss Hancock wrote from City Point: "Mrs. Lee wishes to return to the army, but none are allowed at the front and Dr. Parker will allow no more here, so I guess she will not get here except probably for a visit. Mrs. Lee is one of the *best* friends a soldier ever had."[15]

Mrs. Lee found work at a hospital near Fredericksburg and was there at the time of Lee's surrender. She described the reaction of the hospital:

> Such a time! The people nearly went crazy. Hospital help, ladies, wounded and all, were beside themselves. Processions were formed, kettle improvised for drums; all kinds of noises were made to manifest our joy. Bells were rung, cannon fired, steam whistle blown; men cheered and shouted themselves hoarse. President Lincoln visited the hospital while I was there. He went round to every man, and said he wanted to shake the hand of every man who had helped to gain so glorious a victory; and he had a kind word for all.[16]

Mrs. Lee stayed at the hospitals around Petersburg and Richmond until May of 1865 and then returned to Philadelphia, "participating to the very last in the closing work of the Volunteer Refreshment Saloon, where she had commenced her labors for the soldiers."[17] Mary, described as "a bouncing little Scotch-Irish woman…homely and sweet as one of her famous apple-dumplings…"[18] was 45 when she returned home from the war with her family intact.

On August 6, 1893, Mary Lee died. Her death notice in the *Public Ledger* invited "the relatives and friends of the family, committee of the late Volunteer Refreshment Saloon, Survivors Association and the Ladies Aid of the 72nd Regiment Pennsylvania Volunteers" to attend the funeral. She was buried at the Ebenezer Methodist Episcopal Church Cemetery. This church was abandoned in 1903 and part of the ground was sold to the city. The following year some remains were moved to Arlington Cemetery, Delaware County. She was reinterred to this cemetery in the Silverbrook section in early 1905, lot #163, grave #2. This was a mass grave of eight individuals with no headstone erected on the site.

In 1998, one hundred and five years later, a stone was erected on Mary Lee's grave by the people behind the Headstone Project. She was the last recipient of the five year effort to honor and remember four women of Philadelphia who gave so much to their country and its soldiers yet lay in unmarked graves.

> "Mrs. Mary W. Lee. This name will recall to the minds of ten thousands of our brave soldiers who fought in the army of the Potomac the face and the figure of a cheerful, active, efficient, yet tender-hearted woman, herself the mother of a soldier boy, who for month after month, and year after year, while the war continued, moved about the hospitals of the army a blessing, a comfort, and a hope to thousands of weary sufferers."[19]

Mary Lee's headstone was erected and dedicated in 1998.
(Author's collection)

Jane Boswell Moore

Independent Maryland Nurse

*"Worse than the hardships or exposure was the terrible strain
upon the nervous system through one's sympathies...no more
harrowing work can be imagined. To stand by men, longing for
home and loved ones, and tell them they would never see them,
to live for weeks amidst shrieks and cries of agony; to meet
wives and mothers after long journeys of agonizing expecta-
tion and longing, and have to crush out every hope because
their loved ones lay in the 'dead house or tent,' or 'the grave,'
these experiences though daily, were nevertheless awful."[1]*

Jane Boswell Moore was the child of Dr. William and Jane C. Moore,
the family residing in Baltimore in very comfortable circumstances. Her
father hailed from England while her mother was the descendant of
Revolutionary War soldiers. "My father died when I was a little child
and I had no brothers or sisters...."[2]

When the war broke out Jane was in her late teens. She began her
war work as a journalist and would continue in that occupation the rest
of her life. "After the riot in Baltimore of April 19th, 1861 I wrote
anonymous articles (signed "A Marylander') for the Balt "Daily Clip-.
per." Some of the loyal people pinned these under their flags in their
houses...I wrote series of articles called "Hospital Scenes," freely for
the loyal papers in Balt. and the North which interested the public and I
gave such things as I rec'd to the soldiers. One publication of mine
about a returned prisoner had a circulation of nearly 100,000 copies."

A few days before the 10th of June, 1861, my dear mother and I
began to visit camps and after the battle of Bull Run, the hospitals around
Baltimore (McKim's, the Camden Street, National, Stewart's,
Patterson's). "...even as we heard convalescing patients allude to the
battle-fields I fainted. But they said our sympathy cheered them, and
after a determined struggle our visits were constant. How little my
mother or self *then* thought of the scenes awaiting us!"

"During the whole war, we were never connected with any organization, Aid Society, Commission or Association whatever; never received
a dollar for our services from any quarter, nor were we employed at any

time or in any way, by the government or its agents. The government furnished us teams and we paid our own expenses on Citizen Railroads." The Moores drew many supplies from the Christian Commission and worked with them but not for them. "...we could only give ourselves and our service freely..."

Jane kept a book of her extensive travels and experiences during the war:

> The last day of Sept. 1862 or about the last we took a wagon load of stores collected by us, to Smoketown Field Hospital in the woods on the battlefield of Antietam. We gave these to the wounded and spent some days. And with a supply of stores we went again to Antietam Dec. 8th, & stayed in a tent on the field with the exception of some days, until Jan. 9th. We visited Harpers Ferry, camps and field hospitals and Locust Spring, Hagerstown, Frederick (camps A and B) afterwards; 5 weeks in all.
>
> By the light of a dimly-rising moon we rode over the burial trenches of Antietam to Smoketown Hospital, through whose scattered grove of trees the roaring of the December wind sounded like the notes of some great funeral organ. Our tent was daily visited by an ever coming and going throng of maimed and sick. How humble their thanks for paper, ink, books, and little delicacies made us! A picture of desolate grandeur was Harper's Ferry, with its rude hospitals, its dead on the hillside, whose march was over....
>
> From March 4th to 20th [1863] among hospitals in Cumberland, Clarksville, Md, Grafton, WV, Green Spring, Springfield, Romney, Martinsburg W.VA. March 19th to 31st at work in Winchester, VA, Taylor Hotel hospital among hundreds of sick.

Jane witnessed,

> ...tens of thousands of the living thronging every winding path on their way to Fredericksburg, Martinsburg, and Cumberland, in whose mill, on a wild March evening, we watched the failing breath of Dutton, a New York soldier, dying away from 'an ever-loving and almost forsaken mother'; from Grafton and Wheeling to the old ruined town of Winchester, by whose desolate churches so many of our dead are sleeping, and our little room at Taylor Hospital then (under [Major] General [Robert] Milroy) crowded with fever patients.
>
> Late at night our room in Taylor Hospital was closed, and amid the sound of nailing coffins in the next room, we sought sleep. But a constant hollow cough was heard from the opposite side, and one day a pale, consumptive boy handed us a handkerchief to hem, saying he had

bought it, and 'paid money for it.' It was *his* cough we had heard; he was the only son of a poor widow in West Virginia. When we asked him if he would not like to die at home, his sad face assumed an almost hopeless expression, as he said, 'his mother would be the proudest woman in West Virginia if she could only see her boy; but he had no hope of it.' We said nothing to raise his hopes, for we well knew the character of the surgeon of his regiment, since gone to give account for much cruelty; but we lost no time in making his case known to General Milroy, who indignation was almost as great as our own. In the evening I carried him the news, with his supper, filling his haversack with good things. He could hardly credit me, and was so weak that it seemed doubtful how he would travel the five miles from the railroad station to his home. 'Somebody will give you a lift,' I said as cheerily as I could; 'just tell them your story.' How long he lived I never knew.

On March 30, 1863 General Milroy of the 8th Army Corps, Winchester, Virginia sent a note, "My kindest regards to yourself and your mother. I would most devotedly invoke Heaven's choicest blessings upon you and all other angel ladies who come to minister to our sick and suffering soldiers."

Jane recorded, "April 1st to 21st of 1863 in Winchester, Berryville, VA. Harpers Ferry Heights, Halltown, Charlestown, WV. I frequently went home North to raise supplies which I drew largely from every available source; Ladies Aid Societies, churches, schools etc. were appealed to. About 75 or more articles, reports, appeals and descriptions of the need at the front were published (of mine) in various papers, reports, etc. to enlist sympathy for our soldiers."

The Moores next destination was Chancellorsville, Virginia [battle of May 1-4, 1863] where they delivered supplies and nursed the wounded.

There is a letter dated May 12, 1863 from General Schneck of Baltimore to the Secretary of War introducing the mother daughter team who were on their way to Acquia Creek: "Hon. E. M. Stanton... This will be handed to you by, and will introduce Miss Jane B. Moore of this city, who, desires with her mother, to visit Acquia Creek in the interest of the wounded soldiers of the Army of the Potomac. If you make any exception to the exclusion of civilians from our lines there, I pray you let these ladies pass. They carry with them from the C. Com. and of their own collection twenty boxes of supplies for the more particular comfort of the wounded and sick in the hospitals; and, you will see by the many and very strong testimonials presented by Miss Moore, that is no unaccustomed errant of mercy, but a work of benevolence and patriotism in which these ladies have been long and widely engaged."

Jane wrote,

> In the midst of spring's early blossoms we watched Siegel's march up the valley, visiting his forces just before they left Winchester, with stationery, pickles, &c., and hurried back over deserted roads, with our precious mail-bags bearing thirteen hundred letters, many of them the last messages to friends...I had the honor of carrying under my coat and dress a large Fort Flag greatly prized & this won from capture of the enemy. I safely delivered it to the Provost Marshal.
>
> May 18th to June 20th at work among some thousands of wounded from Chancellorsville in 11th Corps field Hosp, Brook Station Acquia Creek, VA...those of a single corps covering a large plain...Our tents (for store-room, kitchen, and sleeping) were in a secluded ravine, overhung with laurel. We had sad music—the bands on the hill-side with their mournful 'dead march,' by the open graves, and the plaintive cry of the whippoorwill, when our busy day was done.
>
> Among the wounded at Brook Station, were many who were mere boys. I remember the names of three from far-off states, William Lauer, Hugh McDonald, and Edward Goodman. They had lost limbs, and I shall never forget their simple, childish joy, when I put aside their coarse hospital fare, and gave them instead, on their tin plates, soft crackers, butter, and nourishing food. They were too shy to speak but little. Hugh wiped his eyes with his one remaining hand. Edward was a little German boy. On my way to a dying soldier who thought I could make him tea, and custard, such as he had at home, a nurse ran out to ask me to stop on my return at this tent, where a little boy, who had lost a leg, was anxious to see me. I went to his cot and offered him some delicacy, when he remarked, with great earnestness, 'It is not for the things you bring, though they are very nice, that I want to see you; but the sight of your face does me so much good! and here I haven't seen you in four days! A burst of laughter greeted this speech, and I was obliged to explain that my absence had been through no neglect, but from the fact that there were hundreds in that corps to whom my visits were exceedingly desirable; but from that time, whenever it was at all possible, I went in and for a few minutes let him look at me, which he always did steadily, and with an expression of sincere childish satisfaction. The last time I saw him was on the morning of that hurried abandonment of Acquia Creek, as I distributed lemons, boiled eggs, and other articles among those waiting removal. He lay on a stretcher in the sun, by the

rude freight cars, and I trembled, as I filled his canteen, for the poor maimed member, after its secondary amputation, having that rough ride in prospect.

There are three notes from June 1863 kept by Jane that exemplify the ever expanding influence and respect accorded the Moores from Baltimore:

> One dated June 16, 1863 from Provost Marshal Henry Todd in D.C.: "This is to certify that on information given me by Miss Jane B. Moore I telegraphed Lt. Col. Fish, Provost Marshal of 8th Army Corps [Baltimore] to arrest — — who was proceeding South with a large quantity of goods for —. — — was arrested and the goods seized on information given by Miss Moore." The following year Jane would learn first hand the experience of being arrested by Union authorities.

On June 17, 1863 General Hooker wrote from near Fairfax Station, Va.: "The bearer of this, Miss Moore, has been connected with the Army of the Potomac for almost a year, and has earned an enviable name for kind and devoted services to the sick and wounded during that time. She is well deserving of the kind consideration of her loyal countrymen for her philanthropic services."

On June 22, 1863, Abraham Lincoln wrote: "This morning Mrs. Moore and her daughter Miss Jane B. Moore, both noted for their philanthropic labor among our sick and wounded, have done me the honor of a call, and for which I am grateful."

Jane records that she and her mother nursed in the Second Corps hospital on the battlefield of Gettysburg from July 4th to 31st. Dr. Justin Dwinelle wrote from headquarters of that hospital: "I cheerfully testify on the field of Gettysburg that Miss Jane B. Moore has been attached to this hospital since the battle of Gettysburg, and that by her faithful and efficient services, the sufferings of the wounded have been greatly relieved and the dying made to rejoice in her ministrations of mercy." Chaplain Colins, editor of "Soldiers Messenger" Philadelphia wrote: "We met Miss Moore first at Gettysburg and there learned to love her for her work's sake. From early morn until dark, she never seemed to weary, so long as she could minister to a wounded soldier. This noble work she continued through the war. We knew her as an excellent nurse, but she has also the eye of an artist and the pen of a ready writer."

Jane wrote:

Not the least distressing sight, after a great battle, is that of friends in search of the wounded and fallen. Oft-times the claims of those suffering are so great that the dead can scarcely be thought of. One evening a poor widow, with five little children at home dependent on her earnings as a seamstress, came from Philadelphia to look for her eldest boy on the field of Gettysburg. She had heard he was dead, but could not believe it. On reaching the hospital she was told he was in one of the tents. 'O,' she said, 'how my heart beats for joy! but when I went in, they told me he was dead.' He had written to her that nothing would induce him to miss this battle, as on it depended the fate of Pennsylvania, and perhaps the whole country. During the last day's battle he raised his head from behind a stone wall to fire, and being shot through the head, was instantly killed. 'O,' said the poor mother, 'if I could only knew he was prepared!' She could be resigned to it all, she said, if her boy's body could go with her, and be buried where she could see his grave. And in perfect trust, she handed me fifteen dollars,—all she had,—and begged me to tell her what to do.

I had not a minute to spare, save early in the morning; but I made diligent inquiry, and found a comrade of her son, who described his

The Second Corps field hospital at Gettysburg. This hospital was served not only by the Moores, but by Lee, Hancock, McKay, Holstein, Jones, Souder, and a number of other forgotten women. Several ladies are visible in this image.
(GNMP)

grave. Then we went together to the man who removed and prepared bodies for transportation. It was clear her money would amount to little. I said so while I was thinking what to do, and she fearfully caught at the words, assuring me she would sew at government tents and bags, any length of time after her return, to make it up. 'Such an idea never entered my mind,' I replied; 'I was only thinking what was best to do. We will arrange it some way.' So I told her story to the grave-digger, whose wife at once gave her her board in the humble house, while her husband reduced his charges. Then we walked to Adams express office, passing a great pile of rusty muskets lately gathered from the battle-field. I could hardly get her away from these. 'I wonder if *my* boy's is there,' she said sadly; and then, as she entered the express office, where her feelings overcame her, 'It was through it,' she said, 'my boy used to send me his little bit of money!' Only the beginning, thought I, of sad memories to haunt her after-life.

Here I pleaded her case again, not doubting the result, as every facility possible had been afforded me during the war from the company. Transportation tickets to Baltimore were next procured, and I hurriedly wrote, in the office of the provost, a note to a friend who would pass her the rest of the way. Then she rode in the ambulance as far as it went on her way to search for the grave, and I promised to see her again in the evening. The excitement was then over; she found the grave, and though unable to see her boy, a lock of his hair had been cut for her, and all was ready for her to leave on the morrow, a gentleman in Philadelphia having offered her burial-room in his lot. But words failed her when she tried to express her gratitude; she could only pour out blessings."

August 11 to the 24th, 1863 found the Moores at Warrenton Junction, then Bealeton, then Rappahannock Station, VA working with men "worn out by rapid marches to Gettysburg...I had a very severe fall...near Rappahannock and I think injured my spine." Jane kept a note from General Meade dated August 20th, 1863: "I am satisfied that Miss Moore has been rendering very valuable service in attending the suffering of our sick and wounded and in consequence I recommend her to the good offices of all in authority."

"When not in the field, we were busy enlisting aid and sympathy by earnest appeals and incidents of suffering in various journals, collecting supplies and preparing them. Our parlor was turned into a store room and many a box and barrel was packed in it at midnight for the relief of those at the 'front.'"

Although not listed in Jane's dated sequence of service she mentions, "We labored a month in Taylor Hotel Hospital, Winchester, Va, among malignant fever cases" and kept two letters from that time frame. On March 2, 1864 from "HQ mid Mil. Div. to Miss Jane Moore, Winchester: Gen. Hancock acknowledges the receipt of Miss Moore's note, and books, and regrets that business affairs have prevented an earlier reply. He presents his compliments to Miss Moore, and will be ready to receive her in reference to the matter (the soldiers) suggested in her note, at her pleasure preferring the morning about 11 or 12 o'clock. He also returns the pamphlets with his thanks." And another dated April 24 from P. S. Boyd, a delegate to the Christian Commission: "In taking my rounds in the Hospital (Taylor Hotel) this morning, I found, as I had reason to apprehend, the patients quite unreconciled to the departure of Mrs. and Miss Moore who have been laboring so faithfully here and have just been compelled to bid us farewell. Their daily and kindly ministrations have been attended with great benefit to the sick and have taken captive the hearts of all to who they have ministered. The influence of their presence merely, has been most salutary, in addition to which the many delicacies dispersed and the consolation given..."

The Taylor House in Winchester, Virginia.
(MOLLUS)

The Moores were back at the front by May 1864.

Jane's diary notes "May 5th to 30th, 18th Corps Field Hospital Point of Rocks, near Port Walthall on the Appomattox, VA before Petersburg...A deserted cabin formed our next quarters at Point of Rocks...in an exposed field hospital...close to the swamps of the Appomattox..with my dear Mother...where we saw the opening bombardment of Petersburg...In the hospital at Point of Rocks...two cases were particularly distressing. One was that of a soldier...who left a mother, wife, and four little children, all very destitute. Two of his brothers had died in the army, one never having been heard from and another in the service." The soldier was dying. "In his delirium he frequently turned to his nurse, exclaiming, 'There's my wife! She came up here to see me! Why don't you let her come?' When I wished to write to his mother, 'O, no,' he said,' my mother can't bear any more trouble. She has lost so much!' He was one of the hundred days' men from Ohio, and his sorrowing family was unable even to have his remains brought home."

The second case was another hundred days' man. "About an hour before his death, as he lay on the earth, with a knapsack for a pillow, a letter, once anxiously looked for, but now, alas! powerless to give consolation, was brought in and laid by his side. It was a cheerful, happy letter, from a loving, industrious wife, telling of household straits and cares, with all the sunshine of a glad spirit, enough to give the hardest heart a pang to read it, and then look that that unconscious, dying man! In it was the first child-letter of his little daughter, Flora, 'to dear pa.'"

Jane notes "June 15th to Aug. 12th at same place first and then at the extreme front in the IX Corps field hospital, sleeping on the ground on a bit of straw and for a few days among wounded of the Mine explosion." It was at this time Jane suffered from a severe bout of malaria. "I was not convalescent from fever when we went "front" hearing that a battle was imminent and slept for weeks on a little straw on the ground to be near the wounded."

About the time of the Petersburg Mine Assault [July 30, 1864], General Meade ordered "every lady to leave the front...We were stopped and turned back while on our way thither to care for the many wounded, who lay on the ground in great agony. Being very anxious to help we appealed to General Grant [who] by a special order in his own hand gave me a pass to "stay as long as we chose to remain."

Another general added his opinion: "'Aside from the humane considerations,' stated General Smith, 'the services of these ladies are a value in the military sense, for my soldiers will fight far better when they know that out here in the field, ladies are ready to care for them braving danger to themselves in so doing.' And we did have danger for 10 wks we were in a field hospital under range of the enemy's guns, the firing upon the look out, close to us shot and shell fell in our midst. General Burnside said he did not feel at ease in seeing us at work in the extreme front as he knew the risks we ran.

"...many of the victims of the fatal mine explosion were under our care, for, by a special order from General Grant, we were allowed to remove to the 'front,' something over a mile and a half from Petersburg. Our tent, which stood in the midst of a group of pines, was shaded with boughs, and the earth strewn with a carpet of pine needles, the dull, monotonous, awful sound of continued musketry firing being ever in our ears. The soul sickens with the horror of the scenes in those woods on and after July 30. What noble letters those brave crippled colored soldiers dictated, through us, to friends they were never to see!"

"As I moved in the midst of appalling scenes on the day of the mine explosion at Petersburg, I heard many groans and prayers. One just brought from the 'table' was saying, with all the fervor of a departing soul, 'I shall never see my home again; but, Lord, don't *you* forget me.' Colored citizens of Baltimore cried to us to give them 'only one cracker,' and our hearts melted when the appeal was enforced by their directing attention to the stump of an amputated arm or leg. The distress of one poor boy was great; yet he eagerly questioned all whom he saw as to the result of the battle. No one seemed able to soothe him; he mentioned the names of the boys in his regiment and his great concern for them; then his eyes filled with tears, and he wept, unmindful of his own wound. I went to him, and told him how fearful I was that he would injure himself by excitement, which could do no good. 'Were we to give way to our feelings at such a time, what would become of us, or those around us? It is an awful day to us all; we can only trust in God. Now I want to do all I can to help these poor boys, and to do so I must be very calm; I *know* you will help me.' He smiled amid his tears, saying, 'I haven't seen a lady for months, and it does seem sweet to see one in this awful place.'"

This episode was so burned into Jane's memory that she privately wrote of her true feelings: "After one of our sad defeats...the wounded and dying being brought in constantly, I felt as if human nature could stand no more. Many of those brought from the front were mere boys and the heart rendering thought that all this butchery availed nothing, the cries of the men, and the demoniacal sights around thrilled me with inexpressible horror. Severed limbs and blood, oh! it was awful! My hand trembled so, I could hardly guide a cup to the mouth of my poor countrymen. The grief of one boy overcame all my fortitude, probably crippled for life, he was eagerly questioning me as to those of his reg't and co [company] who had fallen. I went to him and talked as soothingly as I could, though I longed to give way to my own feelings. I shall never forget how my words seemed to comfort him (he was young to have left his mother) looking lovingly up from the ground on which he lay. He exclaimed earnestly, 'Oh, I haven't seen a lady to speak to since I left my home in NY, and they cheered us on the street. And oh!' he cried in a burst of emotion, 'it does seem sweet to see one in this awful place.'"

Miss Moore must have touched hundreds with her work at this time. Her collection includes a missive dated July 28, 1864 near Petersburg from the "Soldiers of the Maryland Brigade, 1st, 4th, 7th, 8th, and also 2nd: "Among the Marylanders whose hands have worked and heart have sympathized with the lonely soldier in the field, none has ventured to seek us in the midst of our dangerous and unsightly front line. May you have the comfort that your smile has been the most cheering we have seen since we left our happy homes and may you be rewarded by the deep gratitude of thankful soldiers."

August 1, 1864 from General Grant: "The thanks of the public are one to Mrs. and Miss Moore for their unremitting kindness and attention to the sick and wounded soldiers whilst lying in hospitals, remote from kindred and friends." And on the 9th from General Burnside: "My Dear Miss Moore, You have my warmest thanks for your kindness to my soldiers and my earnest prayers for your preservation in health and happiness that you may be able to continue your good work." Also, on August 13 from Capt. Thos. McBride, Capt. Co. B, 39th US Colored Troops before Petersburg: …"I have noticed the kindness bestowed on the colored troops by Miss Moore and know that her actions will ever be held in kind remembrance."

Late in August, however, things went horribly wrong. Jane and her mother were arrested by Union military authorities. She did not keep a detailed record of the event but if she hadn't saved almost every letter, note and pass ever issued to her, the episode would not have been known.

The first mention of the event was in a letter from General Grant on August 26, 1864 when he heard of the arrest but not the investigation: "Miss Moore, Your letter enclosing a number of your contributions was duly rec'd. I laid the letter and papers on my table intending to read the letters and answer the former, but they disappeared, and I now know only your name and the city of your residence to address this. I hope however you will receive it. I must say that I was more than usually impressed with what I believe to be the Christian devotion on the part of yourself and Mother in behalf of our sick and wounded soldiers. I do not now believe that I could have been deceived and truly hope that evidence will sustain my judgment. In the mean time, no matter how innocent, from the very fact of being arrested, you must suffer. Bear it with the same fortitude you have your labors and hardships in doing good for those who needed your assistance. Deeply commiserating with you, I remain VTY"

By September 12, 1864 Lincoln was involved and wrote from the Executive Mansion: "Maj Gen Wallace please hear the complaint of these ladies Mrs. Jane C. Moore and Miss Jane B. Moore and investigate the case and report upon it." From General Wallace in Baltimore on September 28: "Miss Jane Boswell Moore, I rec'd your note last evening, and hasten to send as requested the enclosed letters, etc. explanatory of the cause of your arrest, and the mortification to which you have been subjected. The papers will doubtless satisfy you that while the authorities here and those at Fortress Monroe, were villainously imposed upon, a basis of procedure letter that [was] furnished by Mr. Thos. Johnson (see enclosed) member of the Chris. Commission, called for the prompt action of which you were the unfortunate victim. Ignorant of the many services, of the sacrifices you have made, to minister to the sick and dying in the hospitals; of the fact that your charities had followed the suffering even to the battlefield; my officers and detectives recognized you a spy and treated you doubtless with unnecessary harshness. That I sincerely regret the circumstances and have made proper effort to discover your enemy, and the cause of your arrest with a view to all possible accompanying papers. Begging your pardon and your mother's I venture to subscribe myself most heartily, Your friend very truly p.s. The President in his note calls for a report from me upon the subject. These papers are necessary for that purpose. After you have read them, therefore, it will give me pleasure to furnish you copies."

Jane's handwritten note explains a bit more: "this arrest was caused by intense jealousy on the part of others. Faithful service had won for us high favor, and we were treated with marked honor. The officers who gave us these testimonials knew well that if the humblest private soldier lay helpless on the field, and beside him, in the same condition, (had such a thing been possible) a major general, we would have cared first for the poorest and most needy, and they greatly to their credit, esteemed us for it. The Gov't gave us always a team and a driver, so that we rode to out of the way field hospitals and camps, and were able to take many supplies. On one occasion a Quartermaster who had shown us much courtesy, was indignant at my kindness to the poor colored people and sent me word that he could no longer furnish my daily team. I went to Gen. Hancock's HdQrs and stated the case. That day the quartermaster was notified that if there was any scarcity of conveyances the General's own private ambulance (Hdgr one) shall be sent daily to Mrs. and Miss Moore to carry on their work. The quartermaster of course found a wagon for us. "

"We always preferred giving out very largely, cooking and using all we had and then going home to solicit more supplies, remaining a very long time at the front and giving out slowly our limited quantities. At the time of our arrest, we were treated with much brutality, my mother and I being separated, and spoken to with course low language. Furniture and china were destroyed, for which we made no claim, the greatest injury being physical, as we were both much worn out by hard service at the front, cooking and riding in intensely hot weather."

Jane recorded: "Oct. 15th to Dec. 31st Among the wounded of Cedar Creek; at work in Sheridan's field hospital at the front. Exposed to extreme cold. Amid the booming of guns from the neighboring battlefield of Cedar Creek, on an October morning, we entered our little room on Braddock Street, Winchester. How many times were barrels and boxes of that crowded spot replenished by the Sanitary Commissions during the six long, busy months of labor among the regimental hospitals, as well as in the snowy tents of Sheridan, covering so many suffering and dying souls."

G. S. Griffith, Esq, chairman of the Christian Commission, Maryland district wrote: "Miss Moore has been one of the most active and useful ladies in our State…She is one of the most energetic spirits I ever met and deserves the thankful recognition….In the past three weeks she has distributed four thousand three hundred Testaments, besides a very large amount of reading matter, fifteen boxes of clothing, delicacies, etc. The very valuable service she has rendered has been entirely voluntary, receiving no compensation whatever, and paying her own expenses. These ladies have been the most indefatigable in their labors…We sent 20 cases of reading matter and hospital stores to them in Winchester. Many of the boxes were very valuable. "

On December 12, 1864 Dr. H. W. Brock in charge of gangrene wards, Sheridan Field Hosp, Winchester wrote: "For two months past Miss Jane B. Moore has been a daily visitor to the wards in this hospital, which have been under my charge. To say that her visits have been welcome would be but a feeble expression. They have been essential to the comfort and wellbeing of the wounded and sick soldiers to whose wants she has so kindly and faithfully administered. It has been my fortune to observe the directness and certainty with which the supplies which are placed in her hands, reach the sick and wounded, not only with this hospital but also the necessitous cases at the front, having on two occasions when visiting the front of Gen. Sheridan's army, in company with Miss Moore, marked the industry and discrimination with which she distributed her supplies to sick and needy soldiers who had been long unreminded of home comforts. There is one fact if I may be allowed to allude to it, in relation to which there can be no discrepancy of testimony, viz; that Miss Moore and her mother are of that class who can visit the armies and army hosps, with entire propriety, their true womanly bearing commanding at all times, the respect and admiration of all. Hoping they may be preserved through all the dangers incident to their noble and self sacrificing work." With the postscript: "Miss Moore, permit me to say in my own as well as in behalf of the sick and wounded to express our appreciation of your kind services, in the exercise of Woman's Rights in the truest and noblest sense of that word."

Jas. H. Meek, Co. H, 122nd Ohio wrote: "I first met Mrs. & Miss Moore in Taylor Hotel Hosp, Winchester, Va, and afterwards in Sheridan Field Hosp in 1864. It is impossible to tell what great good they did in this hosp, especially in the Gangrene Ward which Miss M visited daily striving constantly to do the soldiers good, supplying us with things which saved life and made strong in the Lord. I cannot express my gratitude for what they have done for the men under my care as nurse. May God bless them and I know He'll reward them."

In 1865, "Jan. 1st, Jan. March & April in the same in Shenandoah Valley. The last winter of the war was intensely cold in the Valley, shorn of trees and swept by icy blasts…For thirty years, we were told, Shenandoah Valley had not seen such a winter. Even in February the snow was a foot deep, and the cold was severely felt in those open tents on that bleak hill-side…It was my daily habit to visit the wounded in Sheridan's Field hospital on a bleak hill side and then ride some distance to look after the regt's sick 'front'…As I recall that piercing cold and my exposure on a night in which many of our pickets were found dead, (I was returning from collecting suitable food for men whose jaws had been fractured and mutilated in battle)."

"On one particular morning of that memorable winter, my orderly begged me not to take that usual ride, saying it was no day for anyone to be out. I had just rec'd some thick home made yarn hose, sent by some good mothers in the North and it was strongly impressed upon my mind that they ought to be given out that day. I went alone with the driver some miles to a regiment in which groups of men were crouching by open camp fires. Some were knocking their feet together; they were through some delay or neglect entirely without stockings, having only boots in that freezing air. How thankful I was that I had come!

In visiting one of the many houses in Winchester, over whose floors the wounded were strewn, the morning after they arrived from the front, I found, in a little up-stairs room, Sergeant Colby, of the thirty-fourth Massachusetts regiment, wounded in the ankle. He looked dispirited, and we brought him reading, paper and pencils, leaving him some delicacy daily. He whiled away some hours executing two beautiful drawings, now in the keeping of his bereaved mother…When I found him after his removal to the field hospital, I was startled by the frightful rapidity with which death had done his work. 'Write something cheering,' he feebly murmured, as a few lines were penciled to his mother. It was no common offering that this Christian mother laid upon the altar of her country. We can ill spare such men as James Colby. I have never read more touching letters…They breathe the fervent, earnest spirit of a devoted Christian, and a warmly affectionate and patriotic heart. "

Jane kept a letter she received from Mrs. Colby: "I cannot find words to express my gratitude to you for acts of kindness to my darling boy. Your very kind letter relieved somewhat of my agony. Your name shall be held in for remembrance while consciousness remains. After my son was wounded we waited with the most intense anxiety. One of his comrades wrote that he had heard he was dead…None can describe the feeling of utter desolation. Your kind letter came and brought with it a ray of pure light. The kind acts and words you have shown my son standing as you are in the place of kindred to him, have endeared you to me beyond all expression. But just to think I am but one of the thousands who feel just as I do toward you. The blessing of him who was ready to perish multiplied a thousand times rests upon you. From a full heart I say, may God Almighty forever bless you. Not a word came to tell us of his closing hours. Only through you, have we read any news of him since he was wounded. My mind was in such a state of agonized suspense that I felt I must have something to comfort me or die. Your letter came and brought me back to life."

That long, cold winter, with its varied and constant cares, passed away, and with tearful eyes, on a Sabbath morning in spring, we heard the church windows rattle amid the booming of great guns, and rejoiced, though in an enemy's country, that victory long delayed was ours. But the brave men who had earned it for us were weary; so we passed under Fort Drewry's now silent guns, with our stores, into Richmond, for ten weeks; labored among worn-out troops. This seemed the hardest of all our campaigns; but the end was near; we saw it when several armies passed through that city, bearing the tattered remnants of what had once been banners, intrusted [sic] to them by a redeemed people. Many were so worn out that we found it harder to cheer them than during the war…Think…of the debt we owe to those who endured for us.

" April 13th through April, May, & June at work daily among worn out, sick, & neglected soldiers in regts round Richmond VA… Directly after occupation of Richmond we spent ten weeks ministering to our sick and worn out soldiers. When the colored troops before Petersburg had been "paid off," and there was no express agent near because of their perilous condition at the "front," I received in trust, thousands of dollars from those soldiers living in Balt. and took it safely and freely to their families, a shell passing over my head while I was sealing the packages."

A missive dated April 29, 1865 from Gen. Ord in HQ of Military Gov of Richmond, Gen. Turner commanding 24th Corps: "Mrs. Moore and her daughter have a number of boxes of comforts and delicacies which they desire to distribute to the 24th Corps sick and disconsolate.

As you no doubt will appreciate the kind motives of these ladies and know how to aid them, as well as where they can be of most service, I send them to you to be duly cared for." And on June 10, 1865 from Dr. Patton, camp near Richmond: "Allow me to express the deep gratitude which the W. Va. soldiers must ever feel towards you and your mother for your unremitting kindness to them, at times too when they seemed to have been forgotten or ignored by the benevolent, perhaps because they were Virginians. May your future be as happy as your past has been useful."

"I closed my services amid the tears and blessings of our dear worn out Union soldiers In Richmond, VA July 1st, 1865."

Yet, Jane's services did not end in 1865. After the war she wrote: "The war, with its opportunities of usefulness, has indeed passed away, but the work will never be done while a maimed or crippled soldier remains in our land. *And the widow and orphan—are they not with us?*" Evidence of her efforts can be glimpsed from two letters she kept. One from General Grant with an illegible date: "Mrs. and Miss Moore are respectfully recommended to Agents of Transportation Lines, by rail and steamer, through the United States for themselves and articles taken by them for free distribution to the poor. During the war such facilities were given them by the Government and much relief was experienced in the Camp and hospital through their exertions. Now that war is at an end, they propose giving their time and services to those who have been sufferers from the effect of war." And another from December 1866, written by General O. O. Howard to the War Department: "I have advised Miss Moore to call upon you and lay before you the objects of her visits South. She wishes to carry books, etc. etc. to the soldiers. Perhaps you can renew the written permission."

In 1868 Jane married Jacob Bristor who had served as a major in the 12th W.V. The couple, along with Jane's mother, moved to Martinsburg, WV. Her husband, after serving as the State Treasurer, went into real estate and insurance. They had two sons, Charles born in 1870 and William born two years later. Decades later Jane revealed: "I left their father, my former husband now married again, and who has not seen his children since their infancy. I left him because he did not provide for us, and his treatment of me, before they were born, has injured the mind of one son. The State of Md gave me a divorce. I do not like to speak or write of these things." She returned to Baltimore when she left her husband and was once again engaged in journalistic endeavors. She continued to be an activist for temperance and women's suffrage for the rest of her life.

Jane Moore Bristor's remaining years appeared to be hard ones. Her mother's death devastated her. "…my mind is so taken up with my great sorrow. The desolation of my room tonight is dreadful…there is only an awful silence."

She lost her health. "I was for years under the care of physicians and surgeons, having rec'd severe internal injuries from constant riding over rough roads, upsets, and jars. Painful operations were performed, and I suffered intensely. Hardship, injury, poor fare and cold also brought on diabetes, bronchitis and rupture. Loss of rest occasioned by kidney and other disease, affects my sight which has been strained, not only by many articles prepared for the press but by the large number of letters written to the friends of the sick and wounded. I lost the sight of one eye and as the same disease is at work in the other, eminent oculists warn me that I may lose it at any time. If I had not been helped by members of my family, who have lost heavily, I could not have gotten on."

Her son, William, died suddenly in 1900 from a bout of pneumonia. Although she was granted a pension of $25 in 1891 based on her ill health and claim of poverty, it is difficult to reconcile that in 1910 her remaining son, Charles, had Jane declared insane as she was about to give her estate of $60,000 to a missionary board but she fought the accusation and won a reversal two months later. In 1912 she asked for an increase in her pension but it was denied. Jane Bowell Moore Bristor died April 8, 1916 and was buried in the Faith Presbyterian Church Cemetery in Baltimore.

July Fifth Through July Eighth

"Had anyone suggested any such sight as within the bounds of possibility, I would have thought it madness."[1]

n July 5th, Sallie Broadhead, a Gettysburg woman, back from nursing at the hospital in the Seminary, wrote: "What horrible sights present themselves on every side, the roads being strewn with dead horses and the bodies of some men…every step of the way giving evidence to the dreadful contest…Some weeks since I would have fainted had I seen as much blood as I have today, but I am proof now, only caring to relive suffering."[2]

When both of the armies left Gettysburg, fifty-one thousand men no longer marched with them. "General Lee has had a most bloody battle near Gettysburg. Our loss is fearful. We have heard of no casualties except in general officers…" wrote Judith McGuire. She then mourned the ones knew personally. McGuire spoke for all American women when she continued, "I dread to hear of the others. Who of our nearest kin may have ceased to live? When I think of the probabilities and possibilities, I am almost crazy."[2] From Mary Elizabeth Montfort, the 12 year old Gettysburg girl who discovered her soldier father's body at the town's railroad station,[3] to Mrs. Ora Palmer of North Carolina whose all four sons died on the field, women agonized from Maine to the Gulf of Mexico. Ten thousand men were on their way to Northern or Southern prisons. Seven thousand bodies needed to be buried. Thirty-four thousand wounded men, who were dying by the hundreds every day, needed to be saved. The second phase of a Civil War battle thus began; that of dealing with the carnage and relieving the immeasurable human suffering left behind by the armies.

"Then, from every pulpit through the North, east of the Alleghenies, was read the call to the women: 'Nurses, matrons, lady superintendents, all females qualified for usefulness in this emergency, are asked to report at once to the headquarters of their aid societies or to the headquarters of the United States Sanitary Commission, for service on the battlefield of Gettysburg.'"[4]

One parishioner recorded:

A suggestive scene was presented at Ascension Church, in Philadelphia, on the morning of the 5th of July, 1863. Two days after the
great Battle of Gettysburg had been fought. The nation knew already
that victory crowned our arms; but it stood yet on the tiptoe of expecta-
tion. As to the consequences of the rebel reverse suspense still prevailed. Hourly bulletins from the field announced the most terrible
suffering among the wounded, and appeals for help—for nurses, surgeons, and stores—rung with painful pathos over the North. The hearts
of its Christian men and women had been stirred by the sad appeal; and
here, on the Sabbath morning, with the bells beating their morning psalms
all around them, two hundred or more nimble handed women chiefly,
were assembled, busily at work preparing supplies for the field. In
place a sermon the clergyman had brought a sewing machine; instead
of Sabbath-day finery, each woman wore the more royal ornament of
plain working apparel. In every available niche a sewing machine was
shrined; even the pulpit desk was removed…Here some preparing lint,
there were others cutting shirts, drawers, bandages; while in another
place others were sizing rags—of all things on a battle-field most necessary and useful. Now and then young men staggered in under great
burdens of material contributed at the houses in the vicinity, or poured
into the treasury the gifts of friends and neighbors…By the following
noon, through the efforts of the women and young men, several tons of
stores, including garments, delicacies, and medicines, with a large money
collection had been accumulated.[5]

The shortage of medical care at Gettysburg had been brought about
by actions which had taken place long beforehand.

Early in June, Lee started for the Shenandoah Valley, with Hooker
in pursuit. Over [Jonathan] Letterman's protests Hooker cut down on
hospital tents, mess chests, medical wagons, and other essential articles.
Surgeons had great need of medical stores at Gettysburg, but the supply
train [was] parked twenty-five miles away at Westminster. The railroad
between Westminster and Baltimore was without sidings or telegraph
and took five hours to travel; still the army managed to send through
fifteen trains a day. The Sanitary Commission built up reserves in New
York, Philadelphia, Baltimore, Washington, placing Dr. [L. H.] Steiner
in charge at Frederick, Maryland. The commission stationed agents at
Harrisburg. The enemy captured Alfred Brengle, relief agent, and Dr.
Alexander McDonald, inspector, and put them into prison in Richmond.
Other sanitary agents accompanied the army on its forced march, send-

ing the empty wagons back to reload at Frederick, returning to Gettysburg either by way of Westminster or by the direct route.[6]

After the battle:

Letterman at once felt the effects of insufficient equipment in this country stripped of food and forage. Medical wagons had only a modest supply of anesthetics, dressings, drugs, and instruments. Only the XII Corps had avoided sending supply trains to the rear...Through the battle 650 medical officers worked continuously. Some thousand ambulances removed 12,000 to Union hospitals by July 4. General Meade let half the reserve medical trains approach the field on the evening of July 3. To have to care for abandoned Confederates in addition to the Union wounded strained the capacities of the Medical Bureau...furnishing attention to 20,995 did not come within the power of the Medical Bureau 'administered by the anything short of archangels in prescience and resources'; yet the bureau's preparations had been on a larger scale and were more effective than theretofore.

On July 8 one Sanitary Commission officer on the field wrote to another:

No energy you can use in forwarding by every possible chance can equal the demand here. If I were to spend a week, I could not fitly describe the horrors and suffering of our wounded men. The dead are not yet buried, hundreds are yet undressed of their wounds; thousands have not food. The country is stripped bare of ordinary supplies; there is not food for the well, and they will not sacrifice much for the sick. Indeed there is nothing to be had for love or money.

Sanitary stores reached the battlefield hours before supplies arrived from other quarters; the first arrived at Westminster by railroad on the morning of July 1. By the next morning agents had distributed them to the field hospitals. From Baltimore came tons of ice, mutton, poultry, fish, vegetables, bread, butter, eggs, clothing, hospital furniture, and many other articles. The commission spent $20,000 the first week after the battle, but the public sent in as much money. Expenditures presently mounted faster than receipts. [However] by July 23 the commission had $75,000 in its treasury [and discontinued calling for contributions].

The wounded were crowded into houses, churches, barns, and tents...Those without shelter suffered acutely from the rains. The critically wounded stayed at Gettysburg; all others went to Hanover Station in greater numbers than trains could carry them away.

The wounded were "without food, shelter, and attendants."

"Conspicuous was Sanitary help to the 6,802 Confederates wounded, suffering from a shortage of food and medicine. Houses, barns, and dilapidated tents made up their hospitals. Camp police was deplorable, but Southern surgeons were intelligent and attentive. The Sanitary Commission made every provision for the comfort of the patients, feeding those placed directly in its care. The Southern doctors in return petitioned General Lee for the release of McDonald and Brengle in Richmond."[7]

One Gettysburg woman wrote: "The merciful work of the Sanitary and Christian Commissions, aided by private contributions, was to be seen at every hospital. Without the relief they furnished, thousands must have perished miserably, and thousands more have suffered from the want of the delicacies, food, and clothing their agents distributed, before the Government could bring assistance."[8]

The first few days after the battle must have numbed the sense of reality for those who lived through it. The sights, smells, and sounds by all accounts defied description. One Gettysburg woman wrote: "The atmosphere is loaded with the horrid smell of decaying horses and the remains of slaughtered animals, and it is said, from the bodies of men imperfectly buried. I fear we shall be visited with pestilence, for every breath we draw is made ugly by the stench."[9] Another said, "I have often thought that the only thing that saved the town from an epidemic was the heavy rain that came [after the battle]."[10]

Hereafter scenes of battlefield wounded would be judged in comparison with those of Gettysburg. Before the influx of people to the battlefield from all over the country, the women of Gettysburg grappled with this overwhelming crisis. Some nursed in field hospitals, others in their own homes. No bed was empty, there were no idle hands. Nellie Aughinbaugh, age 19 in 1863, wrote: "Women and girls were evidently drafted for service as nurses and to a group of six to eight young girls there would be two older women...These patriotic women and girls gave their services wholeheartedly for many months...There was never any record made by either State or Federal government of the services given...these women, unknown and unrecognized."[11]

"When mother raised one mortally wounded by a saber cut across his face, he said, 'Angel hands,' and died."[12]

Sister Camille O'Keefe

Sister of Charity of St. Vincent de Paul,
Emmitsburg, Maryland

"I do not know just when the devoted Sisters of Charity from Emmitsburg came to the aid of the wounded in the Catholic Church...[but] Oh, how tender and welcome were their services to the poor suffering boys, to whom a gentle hand was everything in their wretchedness! They were constant in their work and devotion to the wounded."[1]

Out amidst the mountain scenery in one of the most beautiful portions of Maryland...there stands the Central House of the Sisters of Charity of Saint Vincent de Paul, about half a mile south of the village of Emmitsburg. A log home on the mountain side was the original home of this benevolent community. From here, the Sisters began their work of charity half a century before the outbreak of the Civil War. Little did Mother Seton, the foundress of this institution then realize that within that neighborhood would one day be fought [one of] the bloodiest battle[s] in history. Little, too, did she realize that the Sisters of this community were destined during the progress of the battle and afterwards to give to the world one of the grandest exemplifications of Christian heroism ever displayed on the continent.[2]

"The evening of the 27th of June the troops commenced to appear upon a small hill a little distance from St. Joseph's [where the Sisters of Charity lived]. Regiment after regiment, division after division, all advanced with artillery and cavalry, and taking possession of all the heights encamped in order of battle. The 28th, 29th, and 30th we were completely surrounded."[3] The last Union encampment on St. Joseph's grounds was on the 30th. Sister Camilla, one of the nuns in the order, wrote: "The night passed quietly. About half-past four, the whole of the Army was heard going off with their 'quick step' towards the road to Gettysburg, not a vestige of the great army was to be seen anywhere around the place. All had moved off towards the battleground. Glad we were to get rid of them!"[4]

However,

...on the morning of July 1, as the head of the One Hundred and Seventh Regiment, Pennsylvania Volunteers, Second Division, First (Reynolds) Corps was approaching St. Joseph's Academy near Emmitsburg the soldiers were greeted with a remarkable and impressive sight. A long line of young girls [some of whom were Southerners

Sister Camilla was one of the fourteen Sisters of Charity who arrived in Gettysburg on July 5.
(St. Joseph's Provincial House Archives)

unable to go home] led by several Sisters of Charity took their position along the side of the road and at a word from the Sister in charge all fell upon their knees and with upturned faces toward the vaulted skies earnestly prayed for the spiritual and physical safety of the men who were about to go into deadly battle. The sight was at once solemn and inspiring in the extreme. The roughest soldiers oft-times have the tenderest hearts, and this scene affected them more than they cared to confess. In an instant the head of every soldier in line was bowed and bared, and remained so until the prayer was finished.[5]

Sister Camilla wrote: "The great battle of Gettysburg—the most terrifying of the war. During the 30th of June the [Union] Army was making preparations for the great fight. About noon on the 1st of July, we heard very distinctly the cannonading—boom-boom—so terrible. This kept on until the afternoon of the 4th when the Confederates were defeated and retreated as fast as they could that night. They had crossed the Potomac before the Federals could reach them—too late to take prisoners."[6]

"The night of the third day the rain fell heavily, and it continued raining all the next day [July 4]."[7] Sister Camilla wrote: "On Sunday morning, the 5th of July, some poor straggling Confederates came down. How they cleared themselves was a wonder, for if the poor fellows were caught, they would have been prisoners. They got a good warm breakfast here after which they set out—for what place they did not say. They told us that the battle ended the evening before, on the 4th"[8] That same morning "...immediately after Mass, Rev. James Francis Burlando, with twelve Sisters[9] left Emmitsburg for the battlefield, taking refreshments, bandages, sponges and clothing, with the intention of doing all that was possible for the suffering soldiers...."[10]

Sister Camilla wrote:

> Father Burlando and Mother decided that some Sisters had better go up to Gettysburg, so the omnibus was made ready and baskets of things for wounded—bandages and other necessities. Father Burlando got the carriage, taking two Sisters with him; fourteen were in the omnibus and off they started. On reaching within two miles of Gettysburg, the road was blocked by some trees that had been cut and put down across the road. One the side were a group of pickets who ran toward the fence with uplifted muskets, but no sooner did they see the omnibus with the Sisters and Father in front, then they put down the muskets. Father used a white handkerchief on the end of his cane and walked up

to the pickets; this white flag represented a flag of truce. The men talked a few minutes with Father, and in a few minutes the blockade was removed and our driver beckoned to drive on. As we passed the pickets lifted their caps and bowed, showing their pleasure on seeing the Sisters going up to attend to the suffering. But on reaching the battleground—awful to see the men lying dead on the road, some by the side of their horses; it was beyond description. Hundreds of both armies lying dead almost in the tracks that the driver had to be careful not to pass over the bodies. This picture of human beings slaughtered by their fellowmen in a cruel Civil War was so terrible. The battlefield, a very extensive space on either side of the road; [the Emmitsburg Road cut through the area of Pickett's Charge] the east was Mead's [sic] stand; the west—Longstreet's. On both sides men were digging pits and putting the bodies down by the dozens. One newly made pit contained fifty bodies of Confederates…In this frightful condition we found the battleground of that fearful battle of Gettysburg.[11]

This was the condition of things that confronted the brave Sisters as they rode over the battlefield on that scorching July day. Frightful as it may seem, their carriage wheels actually rolled through blood. At times the horses could scarcely be induced to proceed on account of the ghastly objects in front of them. The sight of bodies piled two and three high caused the animals to rear up on their hind legs and kick over the traces in a most uncomfortable manner. In the midst of the sickening scenes the Sisters discovered one little group sitting about an improvised fire trying to cook some meat. The carriage was directed to this point and here again Father Burlando informed the soldiers of his errand. The officers seemed well pleased and told the Sisters to go into the town of Gettysburg, where they would find sufficient employment for their zealous charity. Every large building in Gettysburg was being filled as fast as the wounded men could be carried in.[12]

Sister Camilla remembered:

After creeping along for some time, we arrived in the town. Here all was in fearful excitement—the Federal officers sorry enough that Longstreet and his army should have escaped being their prisoners. All those officers who have been here at St. Joseph's were very glad to see Father Burlando and the Sisters. We kept on until reaching McClennnen's Hotel.[13] The parlors of the hotel were immediately given to the Sisters for their use. This was about one o'clock P.M.—so long did it take to reach there, having to go so slowly especially passing by the battleground where hundreds of men lay dead. The Sisters wanted to go to work at once. Father, accompanied by some of the officers, took us to the different places where the wounded had just been removed. One place was the Court House, then different churches. The Catholic Church had some of the worst amputated limbs; even in the sanctuary—the Blessed Sacrament having been removed to the priest's house. The public schools, houses, and in every available building there lay the wounded. Now was the time to go to work, and the Sisters truly worked in bandaging the poor wounded—some fixing drinks, etc. After visiting the different temporary hospitals where lay the wounded, we returned with our dear Father to the hotel. Father then left us for home, taking back with him two of the Sisters and leaving fourteen there. The Sisters then took possession of the parlors of the hotel as their military quarters. We took some refreshment and went again to see the wounded whom we now considered our patients of the battlefield; impossible to describe the condition of those poor wounded men. The weather was warm and very damp for some days after the battle— generally the case where so much powder was used. We didn't see a woman in the whole place that evening; they either escaped to the country or hid in cellars. But the following day they appeared in their homes— frightened and looking like ghosts—so very terrified were the poor women during the fearful battle, and no wonder!

The Sisters lay on the floor that night and did not sleep much. On the following day Mother Ann Simeon sent us beds and covering; also cooked hams, coffee, tea and whatever she thought the Sisters needed. [Father Burlando had returned with more Sisters and more provisions]…On the second day a reinforcement of Sisters came to our aid, from Baltimore.[14]

The Catholic Church in Gettysburg was filled with sick and wounded…The soldiers lay on the pew seats, under them and in every aisle. They were also in the sanctuary and in the gallery, so close together that there was scarcely room to move about. Many of them lay in their own blood and the water used for bathing their wounds, but no word of complaint escaped from their lips. Others were dying with lockjaw, making it very difficult to administer drinks and nourishment. Numbers of the men had their wounds dressed for the first time by the Sisters, surgeons at that juncture being few in number.[15]

"Four of the Sisters attended the sick in the Pennsylvania College building, which for time being was used as a prison for about six hundred Confederate soldiers."[16] The Sisters dressed their wounds as in other cases. Every morning they returned, eight or ten dead bodies lay in the entrance of the college awaiting interment."[17]

Sister Camilla wrote:

...[T]hree miles outside of that town tents and farm houses were converted into hospitals. Ambulances were provided for the Sisters to take clothing, etc. out to the wounded where many hundreds of men lay on the ground on their blankets since the battle. Straw would be given from the barns which the poor boys were glad to receive, rather than to lie on the ground. We noticed as we were going through the woods, a red flag with a board on which was marked "17,000 wounded down this way."

The driver drove on until the Sisters reached a wooded area where the wounded lay. Some were in a heart-rending state. Besides clothing and jellies to make drinks, we also took a lot of combs which were needed in the worst way—yes, for some who were in a frightful condition. The Sisters also brought plenty of the vermin along in their clothes, I shudder to think of this part of the Sisters' sufferings while they were serving in the military hospitals, especially in the field tents in Gettysburg. The weather was very warm. We noticed one large man whose leg had to be amputated; another part of his body was in such a condition that maggots were crawling on the ground on which they crept from his body. Many others almost as bad, but on the whole, many of them were crawling with lice, so that the Sisters did a great service for those poor fellows by getting combs to get their heads clear of those troublesome animals—no easy task.[18]

Around this field of blood and desolation, according to an eye witness, "the White Cornette of the Sisters fluttered like Angels' wings. At one place a Sister administering a cordial, at another, her companion, whispering the Holy Name in the ear of a man whose life was fast slipping away. Seated upon a low stump of a shattered tree, was a valiant young Nun, known in Religion as Sister Petronilla Breen, who was hurriedly preparing the compresses necessary to staunch the flow of bullet-spilt blood. To supply the shortage of bandages these 'Angels of Gettysburg' removed many of their own garments, which were quickly torn into strips and applied to the bodies of bruised and broken and bleeding men."[19]

[Sister Camilla:] It used to amuse the Sisters when they would go to the Commissary for clothing and other necessities. The persons in charge would say; "Sister, I suppose you want them for the Catholic Church Hospital?" "No," replied the Sister, "we want them for the Methodist Church Hospital." The officer would look with a kind of smile as well as surprise. Another time a Sister called at one of the stores to get some clothing for the prisoners in the Lutheran Hospital; a similar question was put to her, to which the Sister replied, "We want some articles of clothing for the prisoners in the Lutheran Seminary Hospital." The gentleman replied, "Yes, Sister, you shall have what you want for the prisoners as well as for our own. You ladies (the Sisters) come with honest faces, and you shall always get whatever you want for the suffering men whether rebels or our own." He continued speaking very kindly and finished by saying, "I sincerely hope we shall worship at the same altar one day."[20]

One of the many unusual coincidences of the battle was the story of a young nun from Emmitsburg, Thadia Klimkiewicz known as Sister Mary Serena, who volunteered to nurse at Gettysburg. While washing the blood from the face of a seriously wounded soldier she was shocked to find it was her own brother whom she had not seen in years. He was moved to the hospital to which she was attached and brought back to life with her careful nursing.[21]

In the information available on the nuns' experiences during the war, there are three consistent themes and all are present at Gettysburg through the Sisters of Charity; quality of nursing, overcoming prejudice by example, and converting non-Catholics to their beliefs. The Sisters were excellent nurses and the doctors always preferred them to any other civilian nurses. "Self-denial was a feature of their daily life, and the fact that they had taken vows of poverty, chastity and obedience peculiarly fitted them for a duty that demanded personal sacrifices almost every hour of the day and night."[22] They did anything asked of them in their own humble and gentle ways.

The manner and results of their nursing did much to advance more openmindedness towards Catholicism. One Sister wrote: "We are happy to relate that our care and kindness removed many prejudices against our religion."[23] In a country that produced the Know-Nothing party the previous decade, the Sisters occasionally faced hatred and ignorance. In some places people were not sure if they were men or women; in a hospital in the western theater a nun was actually shot at by a patient, the bullet missing her head by two inches. The most immediate hurdle for the sisters was the reaction to their unique costume. "It is not surprising that our peculiar dress was a source of amusement to many persons who had never before seen a religious. We were frequently asked why we dressed so differently from other ladies...."[24] "It took a good while, however, for the citizens and soldiers [out west] to become so accustomed to the Sisters as always to recognize them as such. One morning, as they were going processionally to Mass they met a new detachment of soldiers, who stepped aside to allow them the sidewalk. They kept a respectful silence until the Sisters had passed, when one turning to another inquired, 'Who's dead?'"[25]

The Sisters' work changed many attitudes. Sister Camilla wrote at Gettysburg:

> We will notice here a remark made by an elderly gentleman, who came into Gettysburg immediately after the battle to look for his son who was in the army and might be found either killed or living. The old gentleman with others were seated on a bench outside of the hotel. Upon seeing some of the Sisters stepping out, carrying bundles of clothing to take to the wounded in some of the hospitals, the old man exclaimed: "What! Good God! Can those Sisters be the persons whose religion we always run down?" "Yes," replied Mr. McClennan [McClellan], the hotel proprietor, "they are the very persons who are often run down by those who know nothing of their charity."[26]

Although the Sisters must have found satisfaction in healing wounded bodies and small minds, they truly rejoiced in what they believed was spiritual salvation by baptism. Sister Camilla related:

> In one of those field hospitals, three miles out, three Sisters remained there during the three weeks the wounded were there. As they became able to be moved to regular hospitals in Philadelphia, Washington, or New York, they were transferred. During that time there were sixty Confederates who were baptized; a good deal, no doubt, to the influence of Doctor Stonelate, a United States Officer who became a convert at Point Lookout and was baptized by the Jesuit Father Pecherina. This very doctor happened to step up to the hotel when the sisters were putting things into the ambulance to take out to the field hospitals that they might find. The Doctor asked for some of the Sisters who had been at Point Lookout. He was told, yes such a Sister (naming her) was in the room. He stepped in and who were there to meet him but Father Burlando and the Sister for whom the doctor inquired. We were more than glad to meet our friend. The doctor had orders from the Provost Marshal, to go out to some of the tents and farm houses where some of the prisoners were in a bad condition. So, the doctor, with the Sisters, set off and found a number of wounded prisoners in great neglect. The good doctor not only performed the duties of physician but after he had attended to them he set out to work like a carpenter. From the farmhouse he obtained a saw, an axe and nails; boards, also, and in

short time he had the men who lay on the ground raised upon a kind of frame so that the poor fellows thought they now had beds. The doctor remained there the whole time. Those wounded prisoners were mostly from Georgia and Alabama and they knew no more of religion than a Turk; no baptism nor did some of them believe in heaven and hell— only to live just as long as they could and enjoy life as it came. But God in his mercy raised up the doctor who came their way, and became converted, himself. He talked and reasoned with them, giving his own experiences, that he would never exchange for all the riches on earth. Kindness bestowed on them in their sufferings had no little effect, some would say "The Sisters are Catholics—surely they must be right anyway!" The Jesuit father visited around those localities when they could— the priest from the college also; and by the mercy of God no less than sixty embraced the Faith before leaving…to witness the change in those men was evidently the mercy of God over His redeemed creatures…Nor hereafter did those ignorant creatures of God believe in, but thanks to our merciful God they believed in the doctrine of the Holy Catholic Church before leaving their poor quarters at Gettysburg. Those who died went to our Lord, believing firmly all the sacred truths that they had been taught and with Baptism. When removed to some other military hospital, they would say to the Sisters when bidding them goodbye, "we are going to prison now, but it would be no prison if we had you along to administer to our wants of soul and body." The poor fellows were actually in tears when setting out under heavy guard.[27]

One of the reasons there were no Sisters left in Emmitsburg who could serve at Gettysburg was because so many of them were serving at other hospitals. Sister Camilla wrote: "…[I]t was difficult to get anymore [sisters] since so many were engaged in the West Philadelphia Hospital, in Washington and at Point Lookout. Only very few remained at St. Joseph's; even the Procuratrix, Sister Baptista, was down at Point Lookout with nearly twenty Sisters, where the services of these Sisters were much needed and appreciated by the government. Think of sixteen hundred wounded brought in one day, December 16, after the Battle of Fredericksburg, Virginia, where the Federals were defeated. Oh, that was a scene of terror.!"[28] "The sacrifices they made while at Point Lookout were never fully made known, not even to their superiors. Several Sisters fell victims to death and disease. One of the most conspicuous of these was Sister Consolata Conlon, who in the twentieth year of her age yielded up her spotless life while in attendance upon the sick and wounded soldiers."[29] There were several Sisters who died from disease in the western theater of the war also but the exact total lost during the war has not been ascertained. In *To Bind Up the Wounds*, Sister Mary Denis Maher cites 9 deaths within the orders during the war.

The Catholic nuns representing eleven different orders served in almost every city hospital and on every battlefield during the war. Each order is noted in the relief on the monument in Washington, D.C., that was erected to honor the service of the Sisters during the Civil War."[30] "The soldiers, like many people in civil life, made no distinction between the orders, and to them the dark-robed angels of the battlefield were all Sisters of Charity."[31]

The order from Emmitsburg was very active. "According to incomplete Civil War data, Emmitsburg's generous quota of nurses numbered two hundred and thirty-two Sisters...."[32] "The many appeals for the Sisters to repair to the war-stricken sections of the country, both North and South...widely separated the members of the Emmitsburg community....."[33]

> The Daughters of Charity of St. Vincent de Paul nursed with equal compassion, the officer and the private, the rich and poor, the native and foreign born, the Jew and Gentile, the white man and the negro, above and below the line of separation. We find them on the floating hospitals ships and transports, in the tent and field and permanent hospitals, and even in the isolated camps reserved for contagious cases, and in the military prisons...In the busy ambulances and the hospital trains they attended the men who were journeying with the army, or from one battlefield hospital to another. To the dejected in the overcrowded military prisons, who, in their dark despondency had groaned in agony and turned their faces to the wall, these Nuns seemed like angels in human form.[34]

The Sisters served both the Union and Confederacy from the very beginning of the war and long after Appomattox they worked with convalescents, prisoners of war, the white and black homeless of the South, and the sick and dying soldiers still in the hospitals. The following are a few experiences the Sisters of Charity had during the war, illustrating their devotion to duty, hardihood, sense of humanity, and, not least, their shy sense of humor.

At Harpers Ferry, "...[A] telegram was received from the authorities asking that [a] number of Sisters be detailed to serve the sick and wounded soldiers at Harper's Ferry."[35] Because of other assignments, only three were to be spared for this endeavor. On June 9th [1861], the

Sisters journeyed to Frederick, Maryland, alone, as they had missed their guide. The Sisters experienced an eerie and arduous trip. Few people were on the roads because of expectations of hostilities and the ones brave enough to move about in the divided state of Maryland were suspicious or curious. Trains were not running so stagecoach was the only available mode of travel. The heat was so intense that two horses collapsed. Finally the Sisters arrived at the Bolivar Heights Confederate military hospital where they were to serve. It was filled with all manner of sickness.

When orders came for the army to proceed to Winchester, they did so immediately. The Sisters remained with the sick at the train depot. While they waited for the returning cars they witnessed the destruction of bridges and track, and provisions thrown into the river. After the wounded left, the Sisters followed in a farm wagon during the night to Winchester.

The need there was great and they were requested to send one of the party back to Emmitsburg to get more Sisters. "One of them finally

The monument in Washington, D. C. to the Nuns of the Battlefield is on Rhode Island and M Street N.W. off of Connecticut Avenue.
(Bill Wylie)

266

started off for the mother house, going by car, then by stage, and then crossing the Potomac in a flat canoe. Then she traveled by foot as fast as possible, and after running for a mile reached the railroad car before it left the station. The evening of the next day she reached St. Joseph's, at Emmitsburg, where she was received as if from the grave. The anxious Superiors had heard nothing from or of the Sisters except what meager news was published of the movements of the two armies."[36] Four more Sisters left to join their group in Winchester. When their work was done there, they eventually journeyed to Richmond to help the Sisters in the Confederate capital who "were almost overcome with continuous duty."

At Manassas:

> After a long difficult day serving the wounded from First Manassas [July 21, 1861], the Sisters from Emmitsburg retired for the night. One remarked, "I cannot sleep; there is such an odor of death about this apartment."
>
> Nevertheless they composed themselves as best as they could. In the morning the scent of the strong odor was revealed. A pair of human limbs amputated the week before had been carelessly thrown in the adjoining room. It was a great trial for the Sister to visit that room. She covered her nose and mouth with her handkerchief and threw open the windows. Under her direction the limbs were at once interred. One of the Sisters writing in her diary at this time said: "Yesterday a man was buried with three legs."[37]

At Frederick, "On the 4th of June, 1862, a telegram was received at the Central House, in Emmitsburg, asking that ten Sisters be detailed for hospital service in Frederick City, Md. The request came from the medical authorities in charge of the hospital, and it explained the immediate and imperative need of the Sisters."[38] The Sisters were housed in the hospital of two large stone buildings [the Hessian Barracks] which served the German prisoners of the Revolutionary War. Here they nursed the sick, however, "there were continual skirmishes in the Shenandoah Valley, from whence large numbers of wounded were frequently brought to the hospital, so that in a short time it was overcrowded and the chief surgeon was obliged to occupy two or three public buildings in the city as hospitals. At the request of the doctors eight additional Sisters were sent from the Mother House at Emmitsburg, and they were divided among the various hospitals that were occupied as temporary wards until accommodations could be made at the general hospital to receive the worst cases."[39]

"There were many Germans in the barracks, and the band of Sisters who were there only spoke the English language. The Superior, however, sent a German Sister who could speak to these men and interpret for the other Sisters. At their request one of the clergymen from the Novitiate, who spoke the German language, heard the confessions of the German Catholics."[40]

In early September most of the Union wounded were evacuated from the hospitals in anticipation of the Confederate invasion. When the Confederates moved into Frederick City and the hospital was surrendered, the buildings were once again overfilled with sick.

> It was then that the Sisters witnessed a mass of human misery— young and old men, with boys who seemed like mere children, emaciated with hunger and covered with tattered rags that gave them more the appearance of dead men than of living ones. After these skeleton-like forms had been placed in their respective barracks and tents, the sick were brought in, numbering over 400. The majority of these were, however, half-dead from want of food and drink. [The Sisters were glad to relieve such an easily remedied ailment.] But, alas! a new trial awaited them. The United States surgeon called upon the Sister servant and told her that the Sisters could not at that time give any assistance to the Confederates, as they, the Sisters, were employed by the Union government to take care of their sick and wounded, but he added that the Union army was daily expected, and as soon as it would reach the city the Confederate sick would receive the same care and attention as the Union soldiers...Father Sourin, the confessor of the Sisters...deeply regretted the restrictions the Sisters were under....[41]

This position was unique to the Sisters as the other female nurses working at this site at this time nursed the Confederates with no restrictions whatsoever. Two of the Sisters obtained a pass from Lee to return to Emmitsburg and inform their superiors of the inhumane situation they were placed in. However, by the time they returned, the Confederates had marched on to Antietam, and "Frederick City was again in possession of the Union forces and the good nurses were now at liberty to exercise their duties on behalf of the sick Confederates who were prisoners at the hospital...The Sisters had to divide their services between the barracks and the tents, and even then it was impossible to do justice...General McClellan...visited the barracks and was delighted with the order that reigned throughout. Before leaving he expressed a desire to have fifty additional Sisters sent to nurse the sick and wounded, but the scarcity of Sisters made it impossible to comply with his request."[42]

Possibly the brightest example of devotion and gratitude concerning a Sister from the Emmitsburg house is one of Sister Louise and Sgt. Thomas Trahey which commenced at Frederick after the battle of Gettysburg. Sgt. Trahey of the 16th Michigan, already debilitated by wounds received the year before, fell victim to typhoid fever. The doctor…

> made a careful diagnosis of the case and said that Trahey, who was weakened from the effects of his previous wounds and suffering, could not possibly recover.
>
> It was at this juncture that Sister Louise appeared upon the scene. She inquired if careful nursing would not save the man's life. The physician said that it was one chance in a thousand, but that if anything could prolong the soldier's existence it was the patient and persistent care and watchfulness of a Sister of Charity.
>
> "Then," she exclaimed, "I will undertake the case."
>
> Sister Louise had been detailed from the Mother House at Emmitsburg, and, though young in years, had acquired considerable experience, which added to the marvelous devotedness to duty and self-forgetfulness [and] had made her phenomenally successful in the hospitals and camps…Day and night she remained at the bedside of her patient, frequently depriving herself of food and rest in order to minister to his slightest wish. Finally he recovered, only to have a relapse, which resulted in a severe case of small pox. This did not dismay the devoted nurse. She renewed her energies. For three weeks after he became convalescent the Sister fed him with a spoon.[43]

Sister Louise was ordered elsewhere and Sgt. Trahey went back to the front to be severely wounded once again. After the war and a long recovery he resolved,

> …to seek the whereabouts of the Sister in order to thank her…[H]e was willing to travel from Maine to California merely to get a glimpse of her holy face…Sergeant Trahey first wrote to the Mother House of the order, at Emmitsburg, Md, and received a reply that Sister Louise had been ordered to St. Louis soon after the war and had died there in 1867 of malignant typhoid fever, the same disease that had so nearly ended the life of the soldier…[After several pilgrimages to her grave] the soldier determined that the good Sister should have a better tomb-

stone than the modest little headpiece that occupied a place over her grave…[To do this he had to overcome many obstacles but finally] early in 1895 he was given permission to erect the stone. The simple monument of a Sister's devotion to duty and an old soldier's gratitude is in the shape of a rustic cross beautifully engraved. On it is inscribed the following: To Sister Regina La Croix, Died March 1867, in this city, Erected as a Tribute of Gratitude From an Old Soldier.[44] [Sgt. Trahey said] "…There is nothing in reason I could do to perpetuate her memory that I would not do. Her beautiful face and kind attentions have ever remained to me as one of the most precious memories of my existence. I have not the slightest doubt but that she saved my life…Every time I meet a Sister of Charity upon the street I am reminded of my ever-faithful nurse. I say, and I repeat with all reverence and fervency, God bless her.[45]

"'The Sisters,' to quote and army chaplain, 'do not have reunions or camp-fires to keep alive the memories of the most bloody lustrum in our history, but their war stories are as heroic, and far more edifying than many the veterans tell.'"[46]

The Sisters did not tell their war stories. Letters, narratives, and diaries of these women are not available; quotes from such sources are rare. There are few chronicles of their service and today their work is all but forgotten.

They have passed on to the reward they dedicated their life to attain. But while they lived on earth for the years after the Civil War, there were many grateful ones who did not forget, men like Union Sergeant Trahey and others,

"Will you allow me, ladies to speak a moment with you? I am proud to see you once more, I can never forget your kindness to the sick and wounded in our darkest days, and I know not how to testify my gratitude and respect for every member of your noble order."[47] [Jefferson Davis]

This plaque is on an exterior wall at the
Roman Catholic Church in Gettysburg.
(Author's collection)

Cornelia Hancock

Independent New Jersey Nurse

"I am black as an Indian and dirty as a pig and well as I ever was in my life."[1]

"...[A]fter the War had been a hideous reality for two years and more...[and] after my only brother and every male relative and friend that we possessed had gone to the War, I deliberately came to the conclusion that I, too, would go and serve my country. I confided this resolution to my sister's husband, Dr. Henry T. Child...who lived in Philadelphia. He promised to let me know of the first available opportunity to be of use."[2]

The summons came on the morning of July fifth, 1863...his horse and carriage...arrived in the early morning...When it was driven up in front of our house [at Hancock Bridge, N.J.], my mother threw up both of her hands and exclaimed to father: "Oh, Tom, what has happened?" I had not risen, but hearing Mother's exclamation, and surmising, I said: "Oh, nothing, Mother. Doctor has sent for me to go to war!"

It was late in the afternoon when we reached Philadelphia...Dr. Child, with a number of other physicians [and nurses], had determined to leave that night by the eleven o'clock train for Gettysburg. I was to accompany him."[3]

Cornelia's party left the night of fifth..."the darkness, the uncertainty of everything were appalling...." At Baltimore the group encountered Miss Dix. "Here Dorothea Dix appeared on the scene. She looked the nurses over and pronounced them all suitable except me. She immediately objected to my going farther on the score of my youth and rosy cheeks. I was then just twenty-three years of age...." Another nurse argued in Cornelia's favor.

The discussion waxed warm and I have no idea what conclusion they came to, for I settled the question myself by getting on the car and staying in my seat until the train pulled out of the city of Baltimore. They had not forcibly taken me from the train, so I got to Gettysburg the night of July sixth—where the need was so great that there was no further cavil about age.

Every barn, church, and building of any size in Gettysburg had been converted into a temporary hospital. We went the same evening to one of the churches, where I saw for the first time what war meant. Hundreds of desperately wounded men were stretched out on boards laid across the high-backed pews as closely as they could be packed together. The boards were covered with straw. Thus elevated, these poor sufferers' faces, white and drawn with pain, were almost on a level with my own. I seemed to stand breast-high in a sea of anguish.[4]

"Too inexperienced to nurse, I went from one pallet to another with pencil, paper, and stamps in hand, and spent the rest of that night in writing letters from soldiers to their families and friends. To many mothers, sisters, and wives I penned the last message of those who were soon to become the 'beloved dead.'"

The next morning they went out to the Third Division, Second Corps Hospital.

As we drew near our destination we began to realize that war has other horrors than the sufferings of the wounded or the desolation of the bereft. A sickening, overpowering, awful stench announced the presence of the unburied dead, on which the July sun was mercilessly shining, and at every step the air grew heavier and fouler, until it seemed to

The Hancock house circa 1890.
(Harvey Hancock Tice)

possess a palpable horrible density that could be seen and felt and cut with a knife. Not the presence of the dead bodies themselves, swollen, and disfigured as they were, and lying in heaps on every side, was as awful to the spectator as that deadly, nauseating atmosphere which robbed the battlefield of its glory, the survivors of their victory, and the wounded of what little chance of life was left to them.

As we made our way to a little woods in which we were told was the field Hospital we were seeking, the first sight that met our eyes was a collection of semi-conscious but still living human forms, all of whom had been shot through the head, and were considered hopeless. They were laid there to die and I hoped that they were indeed too near death to have consciousness. Yet many a groan came from them, and their limbs tossed and twitched.[5]

There was hardly a tent to be seen…A long table stood in this woods and around it gathered a number of surgeons and attendants. This was the operating table, and for seven days it literally ran blood…So appalling was the number of the wounded as yet unsuccored, so helpless seemed the few who were battling against demand for any kind of aid that could be given quickly, that one's senses were benumbed by the awful responsibility that fell to the living. Action of a kind hitherto unknown and unheard of was needed here and existed here only.

…[I]t was swiftly borne in upon us that nourishment was one of the pressing needs of the moment and that here we might be of service. Our party separated quickly, each intent on carrying out her own scheme of usefulness. No one paid the slightest attention to us, unusual as was the presence of half a dozen women on such a field; nor did anyone have time to give us orders or to answer questions. Wagons of bread and provisions were arriving and I helped myself to their stores. I sat down with a loaf in one hand and a jar of jelly in the other. It was not hospital diet but it was food, and a dozen poor fellows lying near me turned their eyes in piteous entreaty, anxiously watching my efforts to arrange a meal. There was not a spoon, knife, fork or plate to be had that day, and it seemed as if there was no more serious problem under Heaven than the task of dividing that too well-baked bread loaf into portions that could be swallowed by weak and dying men. I succeeded, however, in breaking it into small pieces, and spreading jelly over each with a stick. A shingle board made an excellent tray, and it was handed from one to another. I had the joy of seeing every morsel swallowed greedily by those whom I had prayed day and night I might be permitted to serve. An hour or so later, in another wagon, I found boxes of condensed mild and bottles of whiskey and brandy. It was an easy task to mix milk punches and to serve them from bottles and tin cans emptied of their former contents. I need not say that every hour brought an improvement in the situation, that trains from the North came pouring into Gettysburg laden with doctors, nurses, hospital supplies, tents, and all kinds of food and utensils, but that *first* day of my arrival, the sixth of July, and the third day after the battle, was a time that taxed the ingenuity and fortitude of the living as sorely as if we had been a party of shipwrecked mariners thrown upon a desert island.[6]

On July 7th Miss Hancock wrote: I am very tired tonight; have been on the field all day—went to the 3rd Division 2nd Army Corps. I suppose there are about five hundred wounded belonging to it. They have one patch of woods devoted to each army corps for a hospital…Mrs. Harris was in the first division of the 2nd Corps…I being interested in the 2nd, because Will (her brother) had been in it, got into one of its ambulances, and went out at eight this morning and came back at six this evening."[7] Cornelia stayed in town for only a short time. She soon had a bed in a tent on the field: "[I] have a nice bunk and tent about twelve feet square. I have a bed that is made of four crotch sticks and some sticks laid across and pine boughs laid on that with blankets on top. It is equal to any mattress ever made. The tent is open at night and sometimes I have laid in the damp all night long, and got up all right in the morning."[8]

In the days following Miss Hancock wrote:

There are no words in the English language to express the sufferings I witnessed today…I was introduced to the surgeon of the post, went anywhere through the Corps…and received nothing but the greatest politeness from even the lowest private…To give you some idea of the extent and numbers of the wounds, four surgeons, none of whom were idle fifteen minutes at a time, were busy all day amputating legs and arms. I gave to every man that had a leg or arm off a gill of wine, to every wounded in Third Division, one glass of lemonade, some bread and preserves and tobacco—as much as I am opposed to the latter, for they need it very much, they are so exhausted…I would get on first rate if they would not ask me to write to their wives; that I cannot do without crying, which is not pleasant to either party. I do not mind the sight of blood, have seen limbs taken off and was not sick at all…I feel assured I shall never feel horrified at anything that may happen to me hereafter…I could stand by and see a man's head taken off I believe—you get so used to it here…I tell you I have lost my memory almost entirely, but it is gradually returning.[9]

Cornelia appeared to thrive in her new situation:

I have the cooking all on my mind pretty much. I have torn almost all my clothes off me, and Uncle Sam has given me a new suit...I have been sick but one day since I have been here, and then I went into a tent and was waited upon like a princess. I like it here very much, am perfectly used to the suffering and the work just suits me; it is more superintending than real work, still the work is constant, I like being in the open air, sleep well and eat well...I shall not come home, unless I get sick, while this hospital lasts. I have two men detailed to wait on me, which suits of course. They are now fixing up nice little tables and all such things all around the tent. I have eight wall tents full of amputated men. The tents of the wounded I look right out on—it is a melancholy sight, but you have no idea how soon one gets used to it. Their screams of agony do not make as much impression on me now as the reading of this letter will on you. The most painful task we have to perform here, is entertaining the friends who come from home and see their friends all mangled up. I do hate to see them. Soldiers take everything as it comes, but citizens are not inured. You will think it a short time for me to get used to things, but it seems to me as if all my past life was a myth, and as if I had been away from home seventeen years. What I do here one would think would kill at home, but I am well and comfortable.[10]

Cornelia was unbending in her hard line against Southerners. "There is every opportunity for 'secesh' sympathizers to do good work among the butternuts; we have lots of them here suffering fearfully...It took nearly five days...to perform the amputations that occurred here, during which the rebels lay in a dying condition without their wounds being dressed or scarcely any food...On reading the news of the copperhead performance...[I say] Kill the copperheads...[at Camp Letterman] I have one tent of Johnnies in my ward, but I am not obliged to give them anything but whiskey."[11]

In the two remaining years of the war Cornelia met many of the nurses who devoted their time and energy to the care of the wounded. While she gave a few their due, her observations about them were sometimes tainted with a pettiness or envy. In Miss Hancock's war letters she depicts herself as being first, only, closest, etc., and she frequently recorded the opinions of others that placed her in high esteem. Women did not fare well in her letters as is evident in her Gettysburg correspondence.

Women are needed here badly, anyone who is willing to go to field hospitals but nothing short of an order from Secretary Stanton or General Halleck will let you through the lines…[It was said] I am very popular here as I am such a contrast to some of the office-seeking women who swarm around the hospitals…There have been in the corps Hospital I suppose some thirty women, and it seems I am the favored one in the lot. Several, since they have seen mine [a medal], have started a subscription for two other ladies. Most of the ladies are dead heads completely. [At Camp Letterman] I have a large hospital tent and sleep with three other ladies…We have twenty women here about, some of them are excellent, but a more willful, determined set you never saw…I look at it this way that I am doing all a woman can do to help this war along…If people take an interest in me because I am a heroine, it is a great mistake for I feel anything but a heroine. Miss Dix was in camp today and stuck her head in the tents, but she does not work at all, and her nurses are being superseded very fast. I think we have some excellent nurses; we must have at least thirty women in the whole hospital…I have no doubt that most people think I came into the army to get a husband. It is a capital place for that, as there are very nice men here, and all men are required to give great respect to women. There are many good-looking women here who galavant [*sic*] around in the evening, and have a good time. I do not trouble myself much with the common herd…Mrs. Holstein is matron-in-chief here. Mrs. Harris does not come around now. Miss Dix peeks in every week or two. There is one woman here who has the clothes department. They call her "General Duncan;" she is the terror of the whole camp. She came and blew me up sky high for having my ward so clean, said I must get more than my share of clothes. I answered very politely and held my tongue. I can get along with her if any one can.[12]

There is no doubt, however, that Miss Hancock was greatly appreciated through the war by the wounded soldiers. On Jul 21st she wrote to her mother:

I received, a few days ago, a Silver Medal worth twenty dollars. The inscription on one side is "Miss Cornelia Hancock, presented by the wounded soldiers 3rd Division 2nd Army Corps." On the other side is "Testimonial of regard for ministrations of mercy to the wounded soldiers at Gettysburg, Pa.—July 1863."…I know what thee will say— that the money could have been *better* laid out. It was very complimentary though. One of the soldiers has a sword he found on the battlefield, which he is going to give to me before I come home. If they were only where they buy I could be so loaded down with baggage, I should never be able to get home.[13]

Through the month of August Cornelia frequently wrote her family from Camp Letterman:

We have all our men moved to General Hospital. I am there, too, but the order in regard to women nurses has not yet been issued, and I do not know what my fate will be; I only know that the boys want me to stay very much, and I have been assigned to ward E. It is a great deal nicer here except that I have but fourteen of my old boys which is very trying—it is just like parting with part of one's family. I go to see the boys and some of them cry that I cannot stay. I have the first four tents abreast of the cook house, the handiest tents in the whole hospital…Our hospital is on rising ground, divided off into six avenues, and eighteen tents holding twelve men each on each avenue. We call four tents a ward and name each of them by a letter…The water is excellent and there is order about everything. I like it a great deal better than the battlefield, but the battlefield is where one does the most good. I shall go to the front if there comes another battle, if not we shall stay in this hospital until fall…Our cook-house alone is a sight; they have meals cooked for thirteen hundred men, so you may know that they have to have the pots of middling size. If you ever saw anything done on a large scale, it is done so here.[14]

I feel so good when I wake up in the morning. I received a letter announcing Sallie S's death [a family friend]. It does not appear to me as if one death is anything to me now…as surely as I live it does not seem to me as if I should ever make any account of death again. I have seen it disposed of in such a summary manner out here.

Yet Cornelia still had the capacity to be shocked. On August 17th she wrote her mother: "I saw a man die in half a minute from the effects of chloroform; there is nothing that has affected me so much since I have been here; it seems almost like deliberate murder. His friends arrived today but he had to be buried before they came. Every kind of distress comes upon the friends of soldiers."[15]

Cornelia developed a lasting distaste for military regulations which later extended to the officers implementing them.

I do think military matters are enough to aggravate a saint. We no sooner get a good physician than an order comes to remove, promote, demote or *something*. Everything seems to be done to aggravate the wounded. They do not get any butter, there is certainly a want of generalship somewhere for there is surely enough butter in the United States to feed these brave wounded. There are many hardships that soldiers have to endure that cannot be explained unless experienced.[16]

I have nothing to do in the hospital after dark which is well for me—all the skin is off my toes, marching so much. I am not tired of being here, feel so much interest in the men under my charge. The friends of men who have died seem so grateful to me for the little that it was in my power to do for them...I hope to keep well enough to stay with the men I am now with until they are all started on their way to heaven or *home*.[17]

Shortly before she left Camp Letterman on September 8, Cornelia penned a description of a hospital inspection: "We had a medical director around yesterday, had a big inspection; he was a real alive man, went with the surgeon in charge of this hospital, went into every tent, pointed to every man, asked him the point blank question 'Do you get enough to eat?' The men, of course, answered in the negative. Then in the presence of [Dr. Cyrus] Chamberlain said, 'The first thing to set your self about is feeding these men; there is nothing better, *feed them*, I say, feed them. Feed them til they can't complain.' Said *he* had been in the service twenty-five years. Said he could feed men till they would not complain. Said clean avenues and clean tents would not cure a man. Things were better today and they will be, I know. The old gentleman stuck his head in every oven, in the barrels, into everything and is still on hand."[18]

From Gettysburg Cornelia went to Philadelphia where she wrote home:

The hospital got so full of women that one had to sit down while others turned round, so I thought the patriotic one was she who took her board off of Uncle Sam until there were greater need of services. It was very pleasant living in Camp Letterman and as soon as there is another battle, I shall go again...The government paid me Nine dollars and sixty cents and passed me on the road free as a Government Nurse. So I am very little money out of pocket by this trip...It does not seem to me anything to go to war now. I look upon it so differently; nothing seems to me like a hardship. A soldier's life is very hardening; you do not care where you are so you can eat and sleep. I had a tooth drawn the other day without flinching, said to myself, if I could not have a tooth drawn after all the suffering I had seen patiently borne, it was a poor story. My nerves are in a much more healthy state....[19]

Later that year Cornelia went to D.C., which she described as "the most hellish place I ever tarried in." "Nov. 1st, 1863 [I] went to the Contraband Hospital on the northern outskirts of Washington and remained there until Feb. 15th, 1864…[then] went to Brandy Sta. to the 3rd Div. 2nd Corps Hospital, Dr. F. A. Dudley, 14th Conn Vol in charge."[20] Dr. Dudley had been wounded in the shoulder at Gettysburg and they had met there briefly. His name appears in every letter home for the rest of the war.

Cornelia was at Brandy Station two and half months and her numerous letters give vivid descriptions of the conditions and boredom of winter-quarters. By early March she had her own quarters:

My [log] house is built and I live so comfortably comparatively speaking. I am now sitting in the Steward's tent up on two boxes with my feet on a pack of back logs, a bright log-fire burns in the fireplace right in front of me. The steward is a nice looking youth and is assisted by a man by the name of Toplis who is always making all kinds of odd speeches and under these circumstances I am endeavoring to write. My stove I have at present smokes; that is the most annoying thing I have to encounter…on the walls of my log house he [a friend] has made a wreath of evergreens and put white paper for a background and in the middle is a blue club [insignia of the Third Division, II Corps] with my medal festooned in the center of that, all together a pretty thing…Between thee and me and the gatepost, that medal has done much for me in this hospital, that, and my pass from Sec. of War…[The same friend] has also made me a lounge that I defy any upholsterer to beat for shape and comfort, the back and arms are all stuffed, I am sitting in it now…He builds my fire in the morning, keeps it hot all day, does everything. I live just like a queen on her throne.[21]

Everybody swears here, if I do when I get home you need not be surprised…I do not swear *much* yet…Scarce one exception, I do not think they attached any importance to it, just from habit. I wish you could see us here. It is quite an ordeal for any woman to come here and visit however; it would be if she *knew* all the remarks made about her as well as I hear them after they leave. I think I am particularly calculated for some reason or other to get on here. I do not feel as if I was half as useful and I did in Gettysburg, but I like it much better here; here there is order and not nearly the hard labor to perform…I have easy times now…people [from the] North think it such a wonderful undertaking to visit the army. Why it is done by thousands of ladies, the army is filled with them![22]

3rd Division, 2nd Corps Hospital at Brandy Station.
Note the presence of a woman in front of the tents on the right.
(Library of Congress)

My dresses are commencing to tear…The rats have gnawed my two hoods so they cannot be worn. I am wearing now a piece of red flannel doubled, plaited behind with black strings. It looks very fantastic and is tolerable comfortable.[23]

I do not wish you to exert yourselves to send me anything more as our surgeons are so good about using the hospital fund that I do not believe we shall want long for anything. There is a system about all they do and there is not that several days interim of starvation like used to be experienced at Gettysburg.[24]

I detest war and officers, if you could know of the drunkedness [*sic*] and bearing of our Major generals down here you [would] feel indeed disgusted with military affairs. Men who have been in the Army for two years are almost demented to go home…That cry goes up from morning until night, "I want to go home, if I could only get a furlough— "…do not worry about the army. They do not intend to go to Richmond and while the ale and whisky holds out all the officers don't care, and the privates know it is a great ways farther then they wish to *march*. We don't want to go anywhere, just be let alone and be allowed to keep our men comfortable.[25]

Nothing exceeds the loneliness of a sunny Sunday in camp…I write thee while I am keeping score for our doctors while they play cards; that is the only amusement they have here and at night I sometimes get

lonesome and go over and sit with them…There are days of great rejoicing in camp that come to use once in a while, but the greatest ones
we ever know is when boxes are received or letters…I have wasted this
evening nursing a dog and keeping score for Dr. Miller and Dr. Dudley
to play cards; there is much time wasted in the Army; if it was not for
wasting my time I would learn to play cards. Sunday evening—here is
another evening almost squandered. I get so tired of the wan faces, and
"please to give me a lemon," the pots, kettles and pans, that about sundown I go into the Doctors Quarters and they order their supper, then
sit around a bright open fire and converse for an hour. Tonight a religious fit seized them, they sent for a bible and we had about six chap-
ters read aloud and explained…[The men] are singing the most mournful
tunes, some are beautiful singers here…[we] do almost anything to kill
time, play cards, chess, eat oysters….[26]

You, I have no doubt, think I speak much of myself and the Doctors. There is nothing else to speak of except the sick men and anything
you wish to know them I can tell you, for I know nearly all that goes on
in this hospital…Yesterday a man was brought in all mashed up, a heavy
wagon ran right over his leg. His leg was amputated and in an hour
after I saw one of the Drs. cut it up into three pieces for the sake of
practice. One can get used to anything. One of my favorite resorts is
our dead house, some such fine looking men die. Sometimes Dr. Dudley
embalms them, and keeps them for quite a while just to look at. Men
are put into neat coffins and buried very decently from this hospital.[27]

Cornelia had received criticism from home and swiftly dealt with it:

Sarah S—wrote me a letter expressive of great concern from
my "way of living." I wrote her a letter that she will not forget soon.
They cannot expect everyone to be satisfied to live in as small a
circle as themselves in these days of great events…The Salem [N.J.
near her home] people's concern has no effect on me whatever. You
cannot know *how* we live here unless you could be here. I cannot
explain, but there is so much distinction in different rank, and I rank
about as high as anything around…There is no danger from any thing
in the army, except an *unsophisticated* individual might possibly
have their affections trifled. But as I have long since found I had no
affections to be trifled with, I am the very one to be here…I am no
ways anxious about the future, shall do nothing rash or romantic
you may rest assured…But I think that as I have made a successful
campaign of nearly 9 months you ought to confide in my judgment
of what is best for me to do.[28]

Dr. Dudley, who visited her family while on furlough, was also criticized because he was not an abolitionist. Cornelia answered: "I do not think the salvation of one's soul depends upon your being an abolitionist. Dr. Dudley does his duty well as a soldier and has done more towards crushing this rebellion than some of the ranting abolitionists."[29]

On March 25, 1864, Cornelia wrote:

> ...[W]e received orders to send all the sick and wounded to Washington, along with the order came a snow storm, along with snow storm came an orderly countermanding the previous order, along with him came a splendid morning, along with it, came another orderly ordering to move on Thursday; and at 8 o'clock we had them all loaded on stretchers, and proceed with the long train from the three hospitals to Brandy station. There the platform was strewed full of helpless men wounded at Morton's Ford. How like Gettysburg it seemed to me. I had all our worst cases put in a pile, took a whisky bottle, and sat down and helped all the poor souls to live while they were loaded. Two mortal hours we sat in the sun and heard the locomotive hiss, the cars back and go ahead, then back, etc., etc., etc., just what always happens at the depots. One of our nice wounded wanted to give me some greenbacks right in the hubbub. There were two women who stay at the station with hot tea, etc. They supplied all hands and retired. There I sat, I supposed five hundred men staring at me, but Dr. Miller and our own steward and hospital boys were with me and I did not care. By dint of great perseverance a hospital car was provided for the worst cases and I went in and saw them lying comfortable upon the stretchers, saw the cars trudge off with their groaning load, and think I to myself, the idea of making a *business of maiming men* is not one worthy of a civilized nation. By the time I got home over the corduroy had a headache of the first water, went to bed and there could lay, as my occupation is nearly gone now.[30]

The Third Division of the Second Corps was broken up; part going to the First Division, part to the Second Division. The medical personnel were unhappy with the change, including Cornelia: "I am very much grieved that Gen. Grant should deem it necessary to break up the third Division as I had got to be well known there and got on first rate. Now I shall have a new set soon to learn."[31]

By the end of March, Cornelia looked ahead to the inevitable summer campaign. "When the artillery practice it makes me feel just as the first week at Gettysburg, it is awful; sometimes it booms for the whole day and we know not whether it is a battle or not. I do not know whether

I want to see a battle or not. I suppose my seeing it would make it no worse, but it is terrible. Every one dreads the summer campaign...I want to come home. I dread a battle awfully...."[32]

"When General Grant took command of the Army of the Potomac all civilians were ordered to leave the Army. I returned to Philadelphia, but remained only a short time..." The battle of the Wilderness was fought and Cornelia and Dr. Child went to Fredericksburg where "...there is suffering [for food] equal to any thing anyone ever saw, almost as a bad as Gettysburg...have worked harder than I ever did in my life..." Although Cornelia was much grieved by the many deaths among her friends in the army, she was able to write from Fredericksburg "I never was better in my life; certain I am in the right place."[33]

On May 31, 1864, the New York *Tribune* carried a description of Cornelia at Fredericksburg: "...[I]f success attended the efforts to ameliorate the sufferings it was in so small degree owning to her indefatigable labors...Let me rise ever so early, she had already preceded me at work; and during the many long hours of the day she never seemed to weary or flag...One can but feebly portray the ministration of such a person. She belonged to no association, and had no compensation. She commanded respect, for she was lady-like and well educated; so quiet and undemonstrative that her presence was scarcely noticed except by the smiling faces of the wounded as she passed...."[34]

Cornelia wrote:

> From Fredericksburg we went to Port Royal. Had the base of operations there for a short time only when all moved to White House...[On June 1] Our train this morning is 15 miles long and more is expected to catch up...If I ever get through this march safely I shall feel thankful. If not, I shall never regret having made the attempt for I am no better to suffer than the thousands who die.[35]
>
> There [at White House] the wounded were brought from the fight upon the North Anna River and it was another dreadful scene. I joined the train which had been three days coming from the field having had no attention except what could be given to them lying in the ambulances. All expected to be relieved from their unpleasant situation; but when we got to the Pamunkey River the bridge was destroyed so we could not cross and soon we saw that another day of trial was before the wounded. I was with the San. Com. train and in the wagon were stores plenty...I took water from the river and washed the face and hands of all in our Div. train. To wash one's face and hands when on duty is

considered a luxury at any time, but no one can know the relief one feels in using water after a three days' march...

There has been no day's work that I have done since this campaign that gave such extreme relief as cleansing those poor fellows' faces. All were cases of severe wounds. At dark night while it was raining the long rain moved over a newly constructed bridge and loaded the men in transports. In the second Corps hospital the wounded continued rapidly to arrive until they laid out in the open field without any shelter. Here I dressed more wounds than in all my experience before...They mostly arrived at night when all the ladies would fill their stores and feed them as they came in...Such tired, agonized expression no pen can describe. By the time one set of men were got in and got comfortable another set would arrive, and so it continued night and day for about two weeks.[36]

Here Cornelia remarked: "There are lots of women; but I seem to be still in favour in the 2nd Corps and certainly please the wounded men."[37]

"At that time there was a very good opportunity to make a visit to the hospital up at the extreme front. There I stayed for a week, the men were then in the rifle-pits and if they moved out to get a drink of water were shot in the action. I saw them as soon as they were wounded but the custom here is to operate upon the wounded and immediately send them to the rear. So there is very little opportunity for a lady to be of much service.[38]

Cornelia damned the officers: "He [Grant] has ordered all the poor little drummer boys to shoulder muskets and go into the Rifle pits. He has no more right to order them in than to order any other *attache* of the Army. I told Genl. Barlow today it was unjust." And she praised the foot soldier. "God bless them, I say, when I see a soldier faithfully plodding through the dust protecting me. I feel more insignificant than words can express. Who would not help a soldier? Everything within me does honor to them."[39]

When the Hospt. was ordered to move I came back to White House and found all wounded moved and the place ready to be evacuated. I remained behind to go thru with the Sanitary Com. train, thinking to get to the James River ahead of those going round in transports, but was very much mistaken in that. As we were dependent upon Sheridan's cavalry for an escort they were detained fighting for one week. And a long, tiresome week of waiting was before us. But the monotony was broken upon the 20th of June by the Rebels planting a battery upon a hill and shelling our train for six hours, in which time it behooved all to make the best of the situation and keep out of the shells as best we could. One shell struck in the rear of the carriage I was in and one rifled cannon came between Mrs. Husband and myself while we were walking on the beach…After the shelling commenced the train passed to the south side of the Pamunkey River and there remained until Sheridan and his cavalry returned and then started for City Point…

…[W]herever the 1st Div. 2nd Corps Hopsital was, I was…I arrived [at City Point] June 26th, 1864 and was in the 1st Div. 2nd Corps Field Depot Hosp. until the close of the war.[40]

Cornelia hung on for the duration of the Siege of Petersburg nursing in a "corner field" outside City Point "where she made practical use of her knowledge and abilities as a first-class army nurse as well as exemplifying her devotion to the comfort and well being of every sick and suffering soldier"[41]

The letters home at this time sounded weary:

I would like this cruel war to get over, then I could come home…the dust here is just like ashes, 6 inches deep…It is really awful here. The cannons boom along the line almost all the while,

The dead at City Point.
(MOLLUS)

286

the heat is intense and the day of the explosion it seemed like what we read about hell. Our ladies in camp are being reduced considerably by sickness and indisposition to stay. I pray for health. I can stand all other hardships but sickness...Some of the ladies remain here during a spell of sickness. It is terrible to be sick here for a lady...I was sick but one day and I might as well have been in an arcade for all the privacy that is possible for me.[42]

Miss Hancock recorded one bright spot on July 10th, 1864: "The first Div. band are playing beautiful music. The leader serenaded me...He has a piece called the Hancock Gallop, which is beautiful."[43]

Time wore slowly for the Army of the Potomac. "All suffer this campaign. I have lost all interest in political affairs, have no eyes, ears, for anything but the sufferings of the soldiery...It has been just one sea of misery here all summer...any person who says a word against a soldier who has endured this campaign will have a black line marked against them thru all eternity."[44]

Dr. Dudley was captured at Hatcher's Run [Dec. 8-9, 1864] and other friends were killed or died in her hospital. "If I look as if I was ninety when I get home you need not be surprised, for something has happened to almost all I ever knew."[45]

It wasn't until a month after Lee surrendered that Cornelia left City Point for home.

Cornelia, one of four children, was born in 1840 in Hancock Bridge, New Jersey to Thomas and Rachel Hancock. She would return to this small quiet village for visits only after the war. She had "seen the el-

Hancock Bridge, New Jersey, remembers their famous daughter.

287

ephant" and would enjoy a long, active and productive life. In 1866 she went to Mt. Pleasant, South Carolina to open a school for free black children. She worked there until 1875.

Cornelia and others started the Society for Organizing Charity in 1878 in Philadelphia and she worked with the poor as superintendent of the Sixth Ward. In 1882 she helped to found the Children's Aid Society and was a paid worker until her resignation in 1895. Cornelia applied for and received a pension that same year.

In 1884 she became the agent and co-worker of Edith Wright in Wrightsville, Pennsylvania, where she successfully experimented in a unique housing program. She worked with the people in this area until 1914 which by that time every tenant had become his own landlord.

"She never married. There is room, perhaps, for speculation over a bundle of letters which were left, at her death, 'to be burned without reading.' Her real interest in Dr. Frederick Dudley with whom she worked in the Hospital at Brandy Station is apparent, as is also his friendship for her."[46] She must have had some contact with Dr. Dudley as he wrote a deposition for her pension submission thirty years after the end of the war.

Miss Hancock sits second from the left in this photo taken at a reunion in Gettysburg.
(Harvey Hancock Tice)

288

In 1866 Miss Hancock wrote her mother: "Men, as the generality of them appear in public life, have few charms for me, and if thee has any lingering hopes of yet in my advancing years committing matrimony, thee must keep thy anticipation in good check...."[47]

Cornelia Hancock died in Atlantic City in 1927. She is buried a few miles from where she was born in Harmesville, New Jersey.

Cornelia Hancock later in life.
(Harvey Hancock Tice)

Charlotte Elizabeth Johnson McKay

Independent Massachusetts Nurse

"...[W]e say that it was a stupendous struggle, which gave to every man, woman, and child in the country something to do and something to suffer, calling on each to renounce some pleasure and take up some burden..."[1]

Charlotte McKay was in Washington during the battle of Gettysburg but on July 4th she traveled to Baltimore and then Hanover Junction. At this place there was no train, no horses or wagons available and heavy rains had turned the roads into a quagmire. Charlotte managed to join a group of relief agents from Indiana and they...

...found ourselves seated, or rather reclining, on bags of forage, very near the canvas covering of a huge Government wagon, one of the train going to the front—a conveyance which we thought ourselves fortunate to obtain. When the train halted for the night, we found lodgings at a farmhouse, and the next day I found my division hospital near the battle-field, five miles from Gettysburg. [By the time of her arrival this site must have been on the Jacob Schwartz farm near Rock Creek.] There, lying along a little stream, and spread out over the adjacent fields and hills, were our wounded men, their sufferings increased by want of food and clothing. Agents of the Sanitary and Christian Commissions, men and women who had come for the emergency, medical officers and soldiers detailed for hospital duty, were all hard at work.[2]

Mrs. McKay explained her regimen at this field hospital:

My programme for a day at Gettysburg was to rise as early as possible in the morning, and send out everything that was available in the way of food to the wounded. An item for one morning was a barrel of eggs, and as it was impossible to cook them all, they were distributed raw, the men who had the use of their hands making little fires in front of their tents and boiling them in tin cups, for themselves and their disabled comrades. Breakfast being over, I would ride to the town, and gather up everything in the way of sanitary supplies that I could get, from the Sanitary and Christian Commissions, the large and generously filled storehouse of Adams Express Co., or any quarter where they could

**The Distributing Store House (Fahenstock building) of the
U.S. Sanitary Commission in Gettysburg, July 1863.**
(Library of Congress)

be obtained. I would take butter, eggs, and crackers by the barrel, dried
fish by the half kettle, and fresh meat in any quantity and, having seen
them loaded on an army wagon, would return in my ambulance, which
was well filled with lighter articles, in time to give some of such stimulants as eggnog and milk punch,—which would be prepared in large
buckets, and served to the patients in little tin-cups,—or supplying them
with clothing, pocket-handkerchiefs, cologne, bay rum, anything that
could be had to alleviate their sufferings.

Thus passed nearly six weeks at Gettysburg, with little variation in
the daily routine, save that which came from urgent claims of special
cases of suffering, which, indeed, were many. Men with both hands
amputated or disabled, who would eat nothing unless I gave the food
with my own hands; men discouraged and desponding from loss of limbs,
and painfulness of wounds, to whom a few cheerful or playful words
would do good like a medicine; men dying, to whom a few words of
sympathy and encouragement as to the future were so precious.[3]

Charlotte related an incident which is another example of how the
presence of women influenced the soldiers and the deference shown to

almost all females serving with the armies. Mrs. Mckay's book, as in may other nurses' narratives, along with doctors' and soldiers,' stress the positive effect women had on the soldiers' conduct.

A soldier, greatly excited, rushed, one day, into my tent, and begged me to come a little distance down a hillside, and stop a fight between two men, where, if something of the kind was not quickly done, there was likely to be a murder. Without a moment's thought I ran to the spot, where was the humiliating spectacle of two of our men, their faces already bloody and swollen, grappling and fisty-cuffing each other with the fury of wild beasts, while a dozen or more of their comrades, standing around, were urging on the fight. No sooner had I lad my hand on one, and uttered a few words of surprise and shame at their unsoldierly conduct, then they drew off one another, and relinquished the fight, though not without muttering of future vengeance; and I afterwards heard that one of them deprecated the interference of *the woman*, which prevented the full punishment he was intending. I attribute the success of this effort solely to the fact of my being a woman, and believe that it was not so much my personal presence as the suggestion of some mother, wife, or sister, far away, that tamed their ferocity, and shamed them out of their bloody purpose.

My chief embarrassment at Gettysburg was the want of a stove, and all suitable means of cooking. My only resort in that line, with the exception of a chafing-dish, heated with a spirit-lamp, that I have brought from Washington, was to fire in the open air on the hillside, over which were stretched long poles, resting at the ends on upright stakes. On the poles were suspended great camp-kettles and cauldrons, where we cooked rations for from a thousand to fifteen-hundred men. In my distress at seeing so many wants in the way of special diet that could not be met, I went to the town, and having found that a nice stove could be purchased there, I made application to the quartermaster of the post, and received from him a promise to buy the stove, and furnish for it immediate transportation, provided I would send him a requisition to that effect from the surgeon-in-chief of the division, approved by the chief medical officer of the corps hospital. This was easily done, and I was rejoicing in the hope of the valuable acquisition, when, to my dismay, the requisition was returned disapproved by the medical director of the post. I then went to this officer, represented our great need, and begged him to approve the requisition. But I might as well have appealed to a rock. He was going, he said, to receive some stoves from Baltimore for the general hospital, which was to be established at Gettysburg, and he would loan me one of them; but when the stoves came they were not adapted to our use, and so time and opportunity slipped by, while scores of our men were dying daily, and my tent filled with supplies, which could not be suitably cooked. (Another effort to purchase a stove from our hospital fund was frustrated in the same manner.) Our men were also suffering for want of sheets, the coarse army blankets being their only defense against the flies, and those were terrible on their wounds in hot weather. I have seen men, with both hands disabled, crying in helpless agony from the tortures of these merciless little insects. When I entreated the medical officer to furnish us some sheets from the Government stores, he put me off with the excuse that he would need them all for the new hospital which was to be; and not a sheet could be obtained for our division hospital save a few that I begged from the Sanitary and Christian Commission.

I do not mention this conduct of the chief medical officer at Gettysburg as an illustration of the way in which our efforts to alleviate the sufferings of our wounded soldiers were generally seconded by surgeons and other officers, for the majority, so far as my observation extended, were kind-hearted and sympathizing, appreciated the difficulties we had to encounter, and aiding us as they could,—but it does illustrate a phase of difficulties to which women working in our military hospitals were *liable*.[4]

Charlotte McKay "had early in the war been bereaved of her husband and only child, not by the vicissitude of the battle-field but by sickness at home, and her heart worn with grief, sought relief, where it was most likely to find it, in ministering to the sufferings of others."[5] Charlotte had married William P. McKay in South Reading, Massachusetts on August 16, 1854, and he died there on April 10, 1856. Her only child, Julia Sargent, was born on May 14, 1855 but died there also on February 1, 1861. Barely a month later, Charlotte was off for the front. "Mrs. McKay...sought oblivion, and at the same time usefulness, in the Army of the Potomac."[6] Although committed to her decision, Mrs. McKay found the first step difficult.

> ...[T]he contemplated journey offered nothing inviting to my anticipations. I was leaving behind me all that I held pleasant in social life. My own home, it was true, stood desolate and uninviting, with no tear for my departure, and no smile to welcome my return; but many other homes, "Homes not alien, though not mine," still warm and bright with the light of hope and love, stood open to me, and it was something to turn away from these. My journey would lead me among strangers and away from any human protection to which I might lay claim. The

rushing rail-car, the creaking, flying steamboat would bear me swiftly where all was strange and terrible to my apprehension.[7]

In the end Mrs. McKay would serve "...forty months' service in our military hospitals, during the period intervening between the early part of March, 1862 and July, 1865"[8] and long afterward working with the Freedmen.

Charlotte first went to the Camden Hospital in Baltimore which at that time did not need more nurses. While there, a request for same was received from the hospital in Frederick, Maryland, so she proceeded there. "The hospital at Frederick City consisted of two large stone buildings, erected as far back as the time of Washington [these were the Hessian Barracks built for German prisoners-of-war of the Revolutionary War], but well preserved, and to these were added from time to time, as the number of patients increased, long wooden barracks, each of which would accommodate about a hundred beds; a row of fifty on each side, with a sufficiently wide walk between."[9] Charlotte had "lodgings just outside the hospital grounds...[a] sleeping room which was on the ground floor."[10] This hospital received wounded from the battle of Winchester [May 1862] and from the Bull Run Campaign [June-September 1862]. In early September the Confederates came through Frederick during the Antietam Campaign and the hospital where she worked was surrendered.

"Then the surrender was made, protection promised, and guards placed at the door of every ward."[11] She nursed the Confederates dur-

The Hessian Barracks in Frederick, Maryland.
(MOLLUS)

ing the occupation and remarked on their conduct: "...so ragged were they, so filthy and squalid in appearance. Yet the events of the last few weeks had borne honorable testimony to their fighting abilities, and closer acquaintance proved that they were by no means ruffians...many of them I found to be good, intelligent, thoughtful men, having implicit faith in their cause, in God as their especial leader, and next to Him in Stonewall Jackson."[12]

As soon as the Confederates left town, the leading units of the Army of the Potomac came through. The Frederick hospital then had a great number of both Union and Confederate sick. Also, this hospital received wounded from Antietam [September 17, 1862]. During her stay at this hospital Charlotte repeatedly commented on the low morale of the soldiers, but said: "But for the sufferers in the Frederick City hospitals there was one source of comfort which they can never forget—the visits of the warm-hearted, loyal, generous women who came daily in bands, bringing, and distributing through the wards their gifts of delicacies to tempt the appetite, reading matter, paper and envelopes, always with such words of cheer, comfort, praise, and gratitude, that fainting hearts were reassured, and to die for one's country seemed, in their presence, 'sweet and decorous.'"[13]

Mrs. McKay worked in the hospitals, some of which were government offices, in D.C., in December 1862 and January 1863, nursing wounded from Fredericksburg [Dec. 13, 1862]. "Who saw the Patent Office at that time will ever forget its great halls and corridors filled with rows of pale-faced sufferers, while there again the gloom was relieved by the presence of faithful, true-hearted women."[14]

Charlotte finally succeeded in her requests to go to the front. "My pass, from the War Department, was dated January 12th, 1863, and gave me permission to go to the Army of the Potomac with supplies for the sick and wounded[15] and thus began her service as nurse in field hospitals and at the front.

She arrived in Falmouth, Virginia, on the Rappahannock River. "All along the river for miles stretched the white camps of our army, in their winter-quarters; but among them all I sought out those of the First Division, Third Corps, then the Third Brigade, and Seventeenth Maine regiment, because in the latter were a brother [Lt. Dudley Johnson] and several other friends, by whose request I had come to this new field of labor."[16]

Mrs. McKay explained the concept of field hospitals:

Hitherto the sick and wounded of the army of the Potomac had been sent to Washington hospitals, but the experiment of field-hospitals was now to be tried, and that of the First Division, Third Corps—General D. B. Birney's—was just being established. The establishment of a field-hospital consisted of pitching a number of tents in a row or rows, according to the number of patients, bringing the latter from their own more narrow quarters in their little shelter tents, and laying them on the army blankets, which had been spread on the ground. Then men from the ranks were detailed as attendants, and for such nursing as soldiers could give.

A favorable position had been chosen for our division hospital. It was on high ground, and near a house which furnished lodgings for medical officers and lay nurses...General Lee's army was encamped on hills around Fredericksburg. The river being narrow, the soldiers of the two armies, picketed along the opposite banks, could easily exchange words, and sometimes in riding along the river in my ambulance, I would stop and listen to their questions and replies.

On our first visit to the hospital, we found men in burning fevers, or with rheumatism, dysentery, or frozen limbs, lying on the ground, with no nourishment but the common soldier's ration of hardtack and coffee, or as a special luxury, beans baked with pork. Here, indeed, was need enough of work and supplies. The hospital could afford us nothing in the way of cooking utensils. We were welcome, however, to the use of the large kitchen fire-place in the house where we lodged, and an obliging colored woman...kindly lent for our use a little iron boiler. In this, with the help of a few simple utensils we had brought from Washington, and the tin cans which had contained preserved fruit and meats, we were soon able to prepare puddings of corn-starch and farina, gruel, tea, chocolate, soup, beef-tea, and wine jelly, which, with good bread and butter, and our canned fruit, were a great help to our sick soldiers. By degrees our hospital improved, and assumed a comfortable, even cheerful appearance. The doctors were pleased with our efforts, and gave us every facility in their power. General Birney, at our request, sent large details of men into the woods to cut poles for bunks, until all our patients were raised from the ground, and placed on beds of straw, covered with blankets. This was indeed a step in the right direction, and none who were at the time inmates of our hospital, can ever forget Mrs. Birney's visits, and her untiring efforts for the comfort of the men, and the cheer and encouragement that her sweet presence and generous gifts afforded. It was also through General Birney's kindness that I was after a while furnished with a nice cooking-stove, which was brought up from Aquia Creek, and installed in its place with great rejoicing, Mrs. Birney assisting at the important ceremony. Large quantities of supplies were furnished by the Sanitary Commission, valuable boxes were sent from friends at the North, and also from friends of the Birneys, in Philadelphia, and our special diet table soon showed an extensive variety.

In the spring the army was re-organized, camps were changed, and our division, with its hospital, was removed to Potomac Creek, four or five miles from Falmouth.[17]

As the battle of Chancellorsville commenced on May 3, 1863, Charlotte left the hospital (about 10 miles away) for the front.

At an early hour on Sunday morning, May 3rd, I left the hospital and went out towards the battle-field, my ambulance well loaded with sanitary supplies, and a young soldier for an assistant. Never can I forget this morning. The fearful roar of artillery, which had scarcely been interrupted since daylight; the clear shining of the sun in the lovely spring morning; our way, partly through deserted camps—those rude homes whence so many noble souls had just gone out, even then many of them lying dead on the battle-field; long trains of army wagons moving slowly toward the front; couriers rushing back and forth.

Just before we reached the river was a small house, that had been taken for a hospital. Horses were picketed around it in all directions; quartermaster's wagons, with their tents near by; a throng of soldiers coming and going.

Finding many wounded men lying in and around the house, I immediately commenced the distribution of stimulants and nourishments. Milk punch and crackers were given to all who could take them. Tea, chocolate, coffee, and beef-soup were prepared and given, not only to the wounded, but to others, officers and privates, many of whom had had nothing but a bit of hard-tack for the day…and so passed the time till late in the night, when Dr. Dexter, corps inspector, came to me and said that he had been ordered to take charge of the wounded of our corps on the south side of the river, and asked if I would go over. [She requested and received a pass to Chancellorsville]…and in a few moments I was in my ambulance, leaving one scene of suffering for another still more terrible.

The way was difficult at night. Now we were entangled in a thicket, and again blockaded by heavy army wagons. In going down a steep hill, my driver lost his balance, and was thrown from his seat…He recovered his seat, but lost control of the horses, and they were brought up by a train of wagons. It was nearly midnight when we got to the pontoon bridge across the Rappahannock, lying so smooth and white in the clear moonlight. At length, about three miles from the river, we found the large brick house to which the wounded of the Third Corps were brought from the Battle-field. As we approached we saw that wounded men were lying all along the fences, all through the grounds, some under little white tents, but more under the open heaven. They were on the piazza, under the piazza, in the cellar, through the halls, in all the rooms above and below, while cries and groans broke out where the agony was too great to be repressed. Some stimulants were given out, and a closet, not large enough for a man to stretch himself in, answered for my store-room and dormitory. Early in the morning the work of administering food and stimulants began, and went on as rapidly as possible all day.

We were within three miles of the front line of battle, and could see artillery posted in various directions.[18]

Here an officer asked Charlotte:

'Is not Lieutenant Johnson, of the 17th Maine, your brother?'
'Yes, have you seen him?'
'I fear you have to hear bad news of him.'
I felt myself growing faint, but asked, 'Is he wounded?'
'Wounded, but not brought in.'
This was equivalent to saying he was dead or taken prisoner; yet I could not at once receive the terrible truth, for his parting kiss seemed still warm on my lips, but before night I knew that he was dead... [Johnson left a widow and an eight month old daughter.][19]

"Efforts were made to recover the body but he fell, shot through the heart, as the division was falling back, and the ground was in possession of the enemy. 'We hope to recover the ground to-morrow,' said the commanding general, in answer to a request to a flag of truce, 'and then every effort shall be made to recover the body of Lieutenant Johnson.' But the ground was never recovered and his dust mingles with that of thousands who lie in nameless graves on that fatal field."[20]

An order came to send off the wounded men, which, we supposed was preparatory to fresh arrivals from the coming battle. I was just giving directions for having the floors cleansed from stains and pools of blood, when Dr. Harris, of the Sanitary Commission, came in, calling me aside, told me that I had better be in readiness to move at a moment's notice, as the artillery was changing position, and there was a probability that the house where we were might be shelled. I immediately began to pack up my remnants of supplies, when I heard Dr. Dexter call for my ambulance driver, and order him to "load up and be off with me as fast as possible, for the house would be riddled with shells in fifteen minutes." So my ambulance was reloaded, with the addition of two of our wounded boys, the pontoon bridge re-crossed, the hospital on the northern side regained....[21]

Charlotte's ambulance plodded through the night and a merciless rain storm. Progress was blocked by wagon trains and swollen creeks, and bridges swept away. Charlotte stopped whenever possible to provide hot drinks and crackers to the wounded on this endless, grueling journey back to the hospital at Fredericksburg where: "Our hospital had been greatly enlarged since we left. The hills around were covered with the white tents of our Third Corps hospital, while those of the Sixth, Seventh, and Eleventh were with an area of five or six miles."[22]

The hospitals were broken up in June 1863 and the wounded moved to Washington when the Army of the Potomac marched north to follow the Army of Northern Virginia into Pennsylvania.

September 1863 found Mrs. McKay at Sulphur Springs, Virginia. There she rode in her ambulance between "Rowdy Hall," a building used for a hospital, and the tented regimental hospitals, nursing the sick and wounded. She also rode 14 to 18 miles a day to obtain any kind of supplies for the men. Since supplies were so scarce, Charlotte was vexed with a common occurrence in the army, but at this time seemed especially cruel:

> In Washington a large box had been packed for me, containing some useful cooking utensils, articles of special diet, clothing, stimulants, etc. Having obtained transportation for it, I saw it placed on the same train of cars which I took passage. At Bealton, the nearest station to Sulphur Springs, I inquired for my box, and was told that the baggage train had stopped several miles back, at Warrenton Junction, but that it would come the next day, and my box would be forwarded without delay. I went directly to General Birney's head-quarters at Sulphur Springs, nine miles from Bealton, and found in the regimental hospitals of our division many cases where articles of special diet were greatly needed. But what could I do without my box? In that was a complete outfit for the present emergency, but without it I was quite powerless. The need was pressing, so much so, that one of our doctors rode one day twelve miles for a paper of cornstarch, and I made a journey of fourteen miles for half a bottle of brandy. Every morning an order was

sent by the quartermaster to Bealton to have the box brought upon an army wagon, and every evening the wagons returned without it, until at length, being furnished with an ambulance and a mounted orderly, I set out with the determination to find it, if it was to be found. Leaving our headquarters at six o'clock in the morning, I went first to Germantown, where General Meade, who then commanded the Army of the Potomac, had his head-quarters, to inquire for tidings of it of Surgeon-General Letterman, to whose care it was consigned. Not finding it there, I next went to Bealton Station, where I learned it had been sent to Warrenton Junction, and to that place I next went in pursuit of it. There, after much unnecessary delay on the part of officials, I found it, and taking it in the ambulance returned to head-quarters by way of Warrenton, having ridden thirty-five miles.

Being too weary to open it that night, I sent it to a place of safety, and early in the morning requested the services of one of our men for that purpose, when, to my grief and dismay, I found that all my useful and much desired articles had been taken out, and the box filled with rusty chains, old halters, bits of harness and leather, carefully packed in, and covered with a filthy, old horse-blanket! The fraud had undoubtedly been committed by the teamsters at the station, who, having taken out the original contents, had filled it with refuse articles, pertaining to their vocation. Such is army life![23]

She followed the armies to Rappahannock Station after they Sulphur Springs and hoped to go on to Washington. She related her experience trying to get to the Capitol from Rappahannock Station.

Here, as my occupation was, for the present, gone, I left the ambulances, intending to take the next train to Washington, with which there was then railroad communication. This, however, did not start for several hours, and while I waited, an intelligent young civilian, who had charge of a telegraph station, offered me the hospitality of his home, which was nothing more nor less that a railroad car. Here I sat until the welcome whistle sounded along the road, and, as the train stopped, was assisted to climb into the great box with sliding doors, dignified with the name of car. But here a new difficulty arose. There was no officer at Rappahannock Station who had authority to give me a pass, and without one the conductor refused to take me, even a few miles, to the next station, where, I assured him, I could get one. In vain I explained my position and urged the necessities of the case. In vain, a kind-hearted staff officer, wearing the badge of the Sixth Corps, interceded for me. The inexorable conductor, rudely pulled me out of the car, threw out my valise, gave the accustomed signal, and the train whisked off, leaving me standing astounded and alone by the roadside. My friend of the telegraph, seeing that something had gone wrong, came to the rescue, took up my valise, and assured me that I should be safe in his car till he could telegraph for a pass to General Howard, whose head-quarters were nine miles away. So, remounting the car, a telegram was sent, to which there was an instant response, with an order to the commander of the post to give me a pass to Washington. But there would be no train until the next day, and I was thrown upon the hospitality of my new friend for the night. Fortunately for me, their kindness was equal to the emergency. Several of "our boys in blue" dropped in during the evening, and seeing my dilemma, a council of war was held in one corner of the car, the result of which was a tent pitched alongside, its top being about even with the floor of the car. In this, when I retired for the night, I found that, by the skillful arrangement of boxes, blankets, and rubber cloths, a comfortable bed had been improvised, where I passed the night without anxiety…[After breakfast the next day] armed with my pass, which no rude conductor dare gainsay or resist, I was kindly assisted to mount the morning train of huge boxes bound to Washington.[24]

Col. Chamberlain, a brigade commander in the Fifth Corps, suggested to Mrs. McKay that her services were needed in his regimental hospitals. She left Washington in October 1863 and spent several weary days and nights searching for the camp of the Fifth Corps which was in constant movement. She finally caught up with it and traveled with them for a few days. It was during this march that she vividly recalled a sight as it struck a personal chord in her heart.

Just off to the right, a short distance over the brown plain, was a soldier's grave, newly made, and, ranged along, side by side, bowed on reversed muskets over the grave of their comrade, four soldiers, apparently engaged in prayer. They had turned aside from the weary march, and there…with heads bowed low, and solemn countenances, gave a few moment to communion with heaven, and a few tears to the sleeper below…Did they think, in those moments, of breaking hearts far away, yearning with vain desire to kneel by that lonely grave?…Yes, this was a solitary grave, but on many hillsides and in many valleys of Virginia you may find them…There sleep our brothers and our sons, the best we had to give, the costliest sacrifice we could offer on the alter of our country.[25]

When learning that "the re-establishment of field-hospitals was postponed to an indefinite future," Charlotte returned to Washington.

Charlotte was in the Army of the Potomac's winter-quarters at Brandy Station during the winter of 1864-65, nursing the sick. Here she stayed until the spring, and then back to Washington due to one of General Grant's "women" orders, only to return to her hospital then located at Fredericksburg after the battle of the Wilderness [May 5-7, 1864]. From there the hospital was moved to Port Royal and then to White House Landing to receive the wounded from the battle of Cold Harbor [June 3, 1864], with Mrs. McKay's descriptions of the suffering echoing the other nurses' narratives. At this time the units that she served with from the Third Corps were consolidated into another and she fulfilled a request for her services at the Cavalry Corps hospital where she remained until March of 1865.

Soldier's prayer-meetings were held outside in good weather and Mrs. McKay described one held on October 24, 1864: "The meetings are conducted by hospital attendants and convalescents, and they have one nearly every evening, changing from one ward to another."

> Last evening, when we entered, the services had commenced. The beds were so arranged as to leave a small vacant space in the centre of the ward, which consists of three hospital tents. On one side of this little square was a small table covered with rubber cloth; on the opposite side, a box covered with newspapers—reserved seats for the ladies; while the men were seated through out the ward on the beds. A large Bible was open on the table; two candles threw their light on its yellow pages, and the leader of the prayer meeting was just beginning to read. Those sacred words of life and peace were not less precious that the sound of the reader's voice mingled with the roar of cannon a few miles distant, reminding us that the cruel strife is going on. The above mentioned Bible possesses for us something of unusual interest. I had often noticed that it was quite difficult for the men to read in their little Testaments by candle-light, and one day had asked at the headquarters of the Christian commission if the entire Bible, and one of large print, could be obtained. They gave me this, the only one to be had, looking, at its old-fashioned calf binding, and antiquated lettering, as if it might have done service in the War of the Revolution, or been a passenger on the May-Flower. Yet, notwithstanding its advanced age, it was well preserved, with the exception of a few leaves missing at the beginning, and at the end, and had made its rounds from ward to ward a most welcome visitor, the source whence many a dying soldiers had derived help and comfort.[26]

After the reading, individuals who were moved to speak, did so, and hymns would be sung.

Mrs. McKay felt that the Cavalry Corps Hospital at City Point was a cheerful place as many of the men were well enough to decorate the walls with framed pictures from magazines and the ceilings with chandeliers of colored tissue paper. The men spent the days carving wood, bone or cigar boxes; rehashing battles or talking of their families. "The greeting a woman coming into the hospital receives is sometimes affecting," wrote Charlotte.

> "It seems so good to see a woman 'round; you look so much like my wife, my sister, or my mother." "How soft your hand feels on my forehead." "How shall I ever pay you for what you have done for me?" "That looks like the light of other days," are frequent expressions, and leave the person addressed nothing to regret but that she can do so little for men to whom a little is worth so much. Yet it is difficult for many of them to understand the motive which prompts a lady to undergo the hardships and privations of life in a field-hospital; and one of the most frequent questions is, "How much pay do you get?" When I tell them that I do not wish or receive pay but that of the satisfaction of doing something to make their situation more tolerable, they cannot comprehend it, and ask if I have a husband or brother in the service.[27]

Charlotte's diary at this hospital is full of descriptions. Descriptions of desolation and ruin in the area, rides to signal posts to witness artillery duels or observe activities going on in the Confederate works, her joy or grief at individual soldiers' recovery or death, meeting with General and Mrs. Grant, and the steady influx of wounded, from a few to a hundred. Singularly, Mrs. McKay praises the work of the male nurses:

> Indeed, the patience and fidelity with which these men discharge their duties, often affords me a matter of sincere admiration. It is a chapter in the history of the war which can never be fully written about. Watching their patients day and night with the kindness and solicitude of brothers,—even when their wounds have arrived at such a stage that it is impossible to breathe the same atmosphere without risk to health, if not to life,—and when all efforts are unavailing, and it becomes certain the no human power can ward off from the poor sufferer the grasp of death, with what grief do they witness his departure, and with what tenderness perform for his mortal remains the last offices of affection.[28]

She cites one patient who lay for three weeks with "a man sitting by his side, and with his thumb compressing the femoral artery just about the extremity of the stump; thus holding the life current until the artery

The trains at City Point brought the wounded from the
battlefield, where they were taken to the hospital or to
transports at the wharf.
(MOLLUS)

could close up and form for itself a ligature." And another patient who, "received from the first moment of his entering the hospital, the most unremitting and faithful attentions from his comrades on duty as nurses."[29]

Mrs. McKay described the last months of the war at her hospital at City Point.

> From the moment when, at early dawn on the 25th of March [1865], we had heard heavy cannonading at Fort Steadman, [sic] which, though at the time we were ignorant of its meaning, proved to be the reveille of the spring campaign...
>
> Day by day there had been heavy firing, sometimes near, sometimes more distant. Day by day, we had seen but one phase of its results, in exhausted, lacerated forms—many of them friends and old acquaintances—laid along on straw in the crowded box-cars, as they came in train after train from the battlefield, and thence borne to the hospitals, or the transports lying at the wharf.
>
> The gun-boats and all the transports having been within a few days withdrawn from City Point, which had more than nine months been the base of army operations, the great hospitals with their long lines of tents and barracks, and thousands of wounded men, as well as the vast quantities of government stores,—supplies for the grand army,—were left without military protection; and as we were totally ignorant of how things were going at the front, we were not without anxiety lest the rebels should break through and make a raid on us. There was indeed such an attempt on the evening of the 29th of March, when at half-past ten we were electrified by a sudden outburst of musketry and artillery, which continued, in a prolonged deafening roar, without a moment's letting down, for one hour, then with slight intervals for an hour or two more; while in the direction of Petersburg, shells were continuously flying up and swooping over like rockets, and the sky all aglow with those death-dealing pyrotechnics. Then came on a pouring rain, the sounds ceased, and we could breathe freely again.
>
> Then in early dawn of April 3d, we were startled from our beds by terrific explosions in the direction of Richmond—concussion breaking on concussion, roar upon roar, louder than the loudest thunder; the earth trembling as if affrighted, and the sky lighted with an angry flare. It was then that the confederate iron-clads and bridges on the James River were blown up, and Richmond fired by its defenders. But the end of these fearful catastrophes was a hand. Before another sunset, tidings came for which we had long waited and prayed, but scarcely dared hope—Petersburg and Richmond are evacuated by the rebel army and occupied by our troops!

The fourth of July, unlike many of its predecessors, dawned peacefully and brightly at City Point, Virginia....[30]

Along with many other curious people, Mrs. McKay traveled in an ambulance into Petersburg. Passing massive amounts of battle debris, thousands of prisoners, and fresh cemeteries, she rode the nine miles into the city. There window shades were drawn and women, both black and white, wandered the streets with empty baskets on their arms looking for food. She remembered one particular woman. "One elderly lady, richly dressed, walked slowly along, with her white handkerchief held closely to her eyes, as if she could not bear to witness the overthrow of her beloved city, or perhaps her heart was breaking for sons or brothers slain in battle."[31]

Lee's surrender [April 9] was celebrated at City Point by bonfires, rejoicing, and a visit from President Lincoln. But less that a week later they were plunged into gloom by Lincoln's assassination.

After the surrender Charlotte worked at Cavalry Camp for a couple of days, went back to City Point, and then took over the special diet kitchen in a hospital in Petersburg, where she said, "...my strength gave out, and I was obliged, with great regret, to relinquish the work, and leave the men who need the care I would gladly have continued to give."[32] By this time Charlotte had received a gift from the men of a gold medal and chain which she would wear along with the Kearny Cross presented to her by the officers of the Seventeenth Maine. Mrs. McKay stayed in Virginia through the winter of 1865-66, where she distributed supplies sent down from the North for the freed blacks both in Poplar Springs and in Petersburg.

Mrs. McKay had some interesting thoughts on Divine intervention in the form of angels which she wrote about in her book *Stories of Hospital and Camp* after the war. For her, it served as an explanation for part of her experience during those years:

> ...[H]uman helpers are our true angels. That when one comes to me in my want, my sorrow, or distress, bearing relief, that is my angel. For, granting there are spiritual beings around me, witnesses of my anguish, they, not being endowed with physical forms and members, cannot furnish with material aid, which is what I need.
>
> Often and often, when I have looked around on the ghastly relics of the battle-field, and heard from every quarter cries for help! help! help! have I wondered if there were indeed pitying angels who beheld the sight, and, if so, must they not long for human hands and human feet,

that they might run quickly with relief. And then with their superior wisdom and skill, how efficient would be their aid—for slow and inadequate as was the relief we could bring with human hands, it was often received as a heavenly ministration.[33]

Born August 2, 1818 in Waterford, Maine, Charlotte lived in various places in that state; Sullivan, Cherryfield, Brewer, and Presque Isle. Charlotte was one of seven children of Julia Sargent and Dr. Abner Johnson. Her father was a physician who "was the originator and manufacturer of a popular liniment called 'Johnson's Anondyne Liniment' which he compounded in a small building in Sullivan Harbor [in 1834]."[34] Charlotte was a teacher in a private high school.

Little is known about Charlotte's life after her work with the Freedmen. She wrote her book in Wakefield, Massachusetts in 1876. In 1893 she swore out a deposition in her sister-in-law's [Dudley's widow] behalf for an increase in pension. At that time she lived in San Diego, California and was 75 years old. She did not file for a pension and never remarried. Charlotte Johnson McKay died in San Diego on April 10, 1894, 38 years to the day of her husband's death. She was buried in Olivewood Cemetery in Riverside, California, Section F, Division 3, Lot 2, Space 4.

For God and native land,
In hospital and camp.

Charlotte McKay's headstone carries the inscription
"For God and native land, In hospital and camp, 1861-1865."
(Author's collection)

307

Anna Morris Holstein

Pennsylvania Nurse

"As I passed through the first hospitals of wounded men I ever saw, there flashed the thought—this is the work God has given me to do in this war…It seemed a long time before I felt that I could be of any use…until the choking sobs and blinding tears were stayed; then gradually the stern lesson of calmness, under all circumstances, was learned."[1]

After the stories her husband brought home from the Antietam battlefield [Sept. 17, 1862], Anna Morris Holstein turned from collecting stores for aid societies to nursing. Almost always accompanied by Mr. Holstein, her first experiences were the general hospitals at Sharpsburg and Frederick, Maryland. When the couple commenced their work, Anna was 37 and William was 46.

They served at the Second Corps hospital near Falmouth after Fredericksburg [Dec. 13, 1862]:

> Army life taught, perhaps *all* who were in it, many useful lessons. I never knew before how much could be done, in the way of cooking, with so few utensils…a little "camp stove," very little larger than a lady's band-box, fell to our lot, upon which…seventy men were daily supplied…We still depended entirely upon home-supplies for our own use; frequently, during that winter, our bread was *four* or *five weeks* old; we never called it stale even then…at length, at the request of the surgeon in charge, we drew army rations, and were spared much trouble. Our dwelling was a little "Sibley" tent, whose only floor was the fragrant branches of the pines…[T]here, while fully occupied, the winter slowly wore away. The deep mud, and impassable roads, cut by the army, precluded travel; no chaplain, that I ever saw, came to our camp until the roads were in good order; men sickened and died, with no other religious services, save the simple Scripture reading, and prayers, which I was in the daily practice of using for them….[2]

The couple went home a week before Chancellorsville [May 3, 1863], but came back to nurse at the hospital near Potomac Creek. Mrs. Holstein gave an interesting description of this hospital and its evacuation for the march to Gettysburg:

...And now that milder days gave promise of the coming spring, the "surgeon in charge" commenced the work of beautifying the grounds; soon the sloping hillsides were covered with a neatly planted garden, containing a large variety of vegetables. Flowers, roots, and seeds were sent to us; and as if by magic, beds of flowers were scattered everywhere; many springing into beauty in the form of the *corps badge*— needing but a few weeks' sunshine and showers to perfect the red color of the Division [red is the color of the 1st Division of each corps]. Rustic work of the most artistic order graced the grounds; all this was done for a twofold reason—to give employment to the convalescents, and amusement to the patients. In front of our tent was a rustic arbor, so complete that any of our country homes would prize it for its beauty.

Work went on, and everything made apparently as lasting as though we expected to spend the summer within sight and sound of rebel batteries...Things continued in the way until Saturday, the 13th of June, 1863; while at dinner, the order was received to break up the hospital; quietly and rapidly it was obeyed; the ambulances were in readiness to take all who could not walk, and in two hours the seven hundred men were on their way to the station. It was surprising to see how quickly crutches were thrown aside, and all who could, were willing to start for the cars—exulting in the prospect of going that much nearer home. When the order to "break up" was given, the gardener was putting the finishing touches to some ornamental rustic work about our tent: instantly hammer and hatchet were thrown aside, flowers remained unplanted, and, with a hurried "good-by," he fell into line with his comrades. The remainder of the day was a busy scene of destruction and confusion; but the night found us all occupying our tent, though nearly all the others, except for a few of the officers' quarters had been "Struck."

Almost the first object which the early morning revealed to us was the Army of the Potomac in motion. Looking down upon the plain beneath, far as the eye could reach, was a moving mass of men, horses, and artillery, with the heavy army wagons and trains of ambulances; gleaming through and above it all, in the bright sunlight, were the bayonets—upheld by that heroic column, which the future record proved to be firm and enduring as their trust steel. It was a grand sight, never to be forgotten; in one continued stream this mighty army poured along. At six in the evening, our hospital train of empty ambulances was in readiness; and then the torch was applied to all that remained of so much beauty about our camp. We sat, quietly watched the flames as they curled and flashed from one arbor to another, encircling in a wall of fire the evergreen screens which had so pleasantly shielded us from heat and dust, and crumbling into ashes in a few moments the work of months. All hospital and army property which could not be transported was thus consumed, two officers remaining to see that work of destruction was complete; what could not be burned, the axe rendered useless. As the flames lessened, we took our places and moved on with the train...To lookers-on, if any could be found in that desolate region, it must have presented the appearance of an almost unending torch-light procession; as from nearly every ambulance and wagon was suspended a lantern, to point out the danger of an unknown road...This day's march brought us to Dumfries, and camped in its vicinity at 11 p.m., the occupants of our ambulance most thoroughly used up, all but myself...After three hours of rest, the order was given, quietly, to move quickly as possible, but cautiously, as we were in sight of rebel camp fires. Here, as elsewhere in this hurried journey, whenever such orders were given, some of the soldiers ran with our ambulance, steadying it, as the wretched roads required.

The morning of the 16th of June was cool and delightful, but the mid-day heat was intense; the soldiers feeling it painfully, but bearing it cheerfully. From this place onward, our course could be traced by the blankets, coats, and knapsacks thrown aside by the foot-sore and weary men; broken, abandoned wagons and disabled horses, seen all along the route. The difficulty of procuring water was greater than any previous time; number of wells by the roadside were observed filled with stones; the water was always muddy and bad, and could be had only at long distance from the road. This day found both men and horses needing a full night's rest; quite early in the evening we halted at the edge of a beautiful wood in Fairfax county, and in its shade our little tent was pitched; with the dawn we were astir, deeply thankful for our safe, refreshing rest and shelter during the night. Of course, in all this journey, our bed was a soldier's couch—the ground, with gum-blanket, and satchel for a pillow, we could at any time or hour sleep soundly.

[They crossed the Occoquan and]...Here, on June 15th, 1863, we heard the first tidings that the rebels were in Pennsylvania; the excitement the news created was intense. The day's heat told sadly upon the men; despite their eagerness to reach Pennsylvania, they could not bear up, and many fell by the wayside from exhaustion; in one division, one hundred and twenty reported with sunstroke. During the hurried march, numbers of cavalry horses had been abandoned by their riders, who only required a few days' rest to recoup, and again they were ready for duty. They were to be seen all along our route, undisturbed by the passing column, except when caught by some of the foot soldiers. It was amusing to observe the ingenious arrangements made to answer for the horses' trappings; a piece of old tent-canvas was soon converted into an admirable bridle; another piece of the same shelter kept the saddle (a blanket) in its place; thus mounted, he would be delighted; and day by day added to the number of this escort. There were constantly exciting incidents; sometimes we were in a dangerous position, from our driver losing his place in line; then the crossing of infantry through the train, the frequent breaking down of bridges, and the delay caused by disabled wagons constantly impeded our progress.

Near "Union Mills," our troops camped for the night in "line of battle;" our little tent was pitched upon the banks of a stream, in rear of *our* army...Here the order was given to reduce officers' baggage to twenty pounds, forward the surplus to Washington or destroy it. Many officers and men came with the request that we would take charge of money and valuables for them. It was a touching sight, upon the eve of a battle, as it was thought—to see keepsakes, from loved ones at home, instructed to comparative strangers, hoping thus to save them in case of attack...I wore under my coat a belt, and carried the costly sword belonging to it under my dress. A civilian, as my husband was, could not do so without danger of arrest, while I would pass unnoticed. The large amount of money and valuables in our possession were brought safely to Philadelphia, the former soon restored to its rightful owners; a sword with some other articles were unclaimed until near the close of the war.

As a battle was anticipated, and we were now accessible to railroad, near Sangter's [*sic*] Station, it was thought advisable to proceed without delay to Alexandria and Washington, from whence we could easily return if our services were needed. After remaining some days in Washington, Mr. H. was threatened with an attack of malaria fever—warning us to proceed homeward without delay. We came to it, worn out and wearied as we were, as to a haven of *rest*.[3]

While waiting for her husband to recuperate, the battle was fought but the Holsteins arrived in Gettysburg:

...within one week after it...reaching the town late in the evening, spent the night upon the parlor floor of one of the hotels; with a satchel for a pillow, slept soundly. In the morning we went to the Field Hospital, where we were most warmly welcome by our old friends of the second corps. The wounded, at that time, lay just where they had been placed when carried from the battle—friend and foe resting together...

We soon found where and how to resume work, which we had so lately left off; a tent was promptly prepared for our use; it was not many hours until the "diet kitchen" was in full operation...in a wonderfully smooth efficient manner.

The scenes around Gettysburg were horrible in the extreme; the green sod everywhere stained with the life-blood of dying men; the course of the fearful struggle marked by the "ridges" which furrowed the ground until one *great* hillock would be pointed out where *hundreds*, perhaps, had sternly fought and bravely fallen. To persons unfamiliar with such things, as sad a sight as any are the heaps of bloodstained clothing, the shattered muskets, the discarded knapsacks, disabled cannon and caissons, and the innumerable heaps of slain horses which literally cover the hard fought field.

For a few weeks, the events daily occurring in the hospitals were most painful; they might be summed up, briefly, to be: fearfully wounded men; nurses watching for the hour when suffering would cease, and the soldier be at *rest*; parents and friends crowding to the hospital hoping for the best, yet fearing the worst; strong men praying that they might live *just long enough* to see, but *once* more, wife, or child, or mother.

After this battle relief came promptly…All of home luxuries that *could* be carried, were lavished with an unsparing hand by a now deeply grateful people…The government, fully equipped for the contest, had medical and hospital stores abundantly supplied. With the perfectly organized system and immense resources of the "United States Sanitary Commission," ever ready and anxious to fill up all the demands which the government *could not,*—aided by the Christian Commission and large volunteer assistance,—there was no long-continued suffering, as in the early battles of the war…

I recall a burial where three were at one time taken to the little spot we called a cemetery. One sultry afternoon in July the stretcher-bearers came tramping wearily, bearing three bodies of those who had given their lives for *freedom*; as the last reached the place, the men dropped with a rough, jolting motion the army couch whereon he rested. The impatient effort to be rid of their burden was probably the means of saving a precious life; for the man—*dead,* as the supposed—raising his head, called in a clear voice: "Boys, what are you doing?" The response was prompt: "We came to bury you, Whitey." His calm reply was "I don't see it, boys, give me a drink of water, and carry me back." And then glancing into the open grave: "I won't be buried with this raw recruit!" The raw recruit was a lieutenant of his own regiment. Not many stand so near the "dark valley" that they look into their own graves, and *live*. The "boys" did carry him back, and with the greatest care, his life *was* saved….[4]

While the hospitals remained in the *woods*, the number of deaths daily was very large; as soon as the removal to the clover-field was accomplished, the night after, only two deaths occurred….

Detail from a group photograph of medical personnel at Gettysburg after the battle. Anna Holstein is standing in the center next to Dr. Henry May, a surgeon from New York.
(MOLLUS)

Mrs. Holstein did not like the Confederate wounded: "Large number of rebel wounded, numbering thousands, were left in our corps hospital; and though attended by their own surgeons, they neglected them so shamefully that it was an act of common humanity to provide better treatment for men helpless and suffering,—prisoners as they were. One of our surgeons volunteered to undertake the duty of attending them, and others were detailed for that purpose. Their condition when captured was so filthy that the task of waiting upon them was a revolting one…" Mrs. Holstein detailed some instances of Union men refusing to have Confederate wounded in their tent, quoting angry oaths and threats that seemed to have been close to her own feelings. "About one third of the camp were rebels; this proportion was almost uniformly kept up; rebel ladies from Baltimore and other places were permitted to come and wait upon their own wounded; as matron, it was part of my duties to attend to the distribution of delicacies, etc. I have waited upon them hour after hour, as kindly as I ever did upon our own loyal men…The orders were imperative in the hospital; no difference was permitted in the treatment of the two…" Mrs. Holstein related examples of Confederate prisoners who were really Union men and suffered terribly at the hands of the Confederates and implied that the Southern wounded were complaining and impatient. She is among the few women who nursed at Gettysburg who did not grasp the larger picture. With Mrs. Holstein there was no natural compassion for all sufferers; there were still enemies to be fought.

"All of our wounded that could bear transportation were forwarded, as rapidly as it could be done, to hospitals in Pennsylvania and Maryland. By the 7th of August there still remained *three thousand*, who were moved into tents at the United States General Hospital on the York Turnpike; when our corps hospital was merged into this, we removed there; I remained as its matron until the close."[5]

Dr. Henry May, surgeon of the 145th New York, remembered Mrs. Holstein at this time: "…[I]n August of 1863 while on duty at Camp Letterman Hospital at Gettysburg, Pa., I met Mr. and Mrs. Holstein…who were devoting their whole time gratuitously to the cause of the sick and wounded soldier. Mrs. Holstein was placed in charge of the 'Low diet Kitchen' of that large Hospital and from its organization to its close in November 1863, she did most faithful, efficient, and acceptable service. Her work extended from the early hours of each day to its close; and a host of grateful men were ever loud in her praise for many kind words and offices rendered aside from that of preparing their food."[6]

One of her patients, Capt. John Hilton of Co. K, 145th Pennsylvania, wrote of Mrs. Holstein: "Mrs. Holstein's work at Gettysburg in Camp Letterman General Hospital can hardly be described by those who were wounded and helpless at the time. All we know is that Mrs. H. had full charge of the diet kitchen and all of the many delicacies we received were from her hands, and in addition to this she constantly visited the wounded to ascertain what would be good for them and to encourage them, and give them a motherly care. Such care a woman only can give, such delicacies a woman only can serve. The lives of badly wounded men depended more from nourishing food than medicine. Having been one of the doubtful cases, I know had it not been for such care I received from Mrs. Holstein, I never could have recovered."[7]

The kitchen, Camp Letterman Hospital, Gettysburg.
(GNMP)

Nurse Cornelia Hancock mentioned Mrs. Holstein in a letter written from "Camp Letterman, Gen. Hospital near Gettysburg, Pa., Aug. 31st, 1863: I like Mrs. Holstein real well. I am almost too smart for her. I *will* get the things for the men without orders and she is a great respector of order."[8]

In September, while the hospital was still crowded with patients; a festival was given for their amusement. The surgeon in charge, with the other officers, entered heartily into the plan. The Christian Commission took an active part in completing the arrangements, soliciting and obtaining abundant supplies of fruit and delicacies from friends in Philadelphia; to this were added contributions from the town and adjoining counties, making a grand feast of good things. The day selected, proving bright and balmy, tempted men, who had not yet ventured outside their tents, into the open air, hoping they might be able to participate in the promised enjoyments. The streets and tents of the hospital had been decorated with evergreens, and everything on this gala day had a corresponding cheerful look. Hospital life, with its strict military rule, is so wearisome and monotonous, that what would be the most trivial pleasure at other times and places, is *here* magnified into a matter of great importance.

When the hour came for the good dinner, which was known would be provided, hundreds moved upon crutches with feeble, tottering steps

315

to the table, looking with unmistakable delight upon the display of luxuries. Bands of music enlivened the scene. All the variety of army amusements were permitted and encouraged, followed in the evening by an entertainment of *negro* minstrels,—the performers being all *white* soldiers in the hospital. This last, the soldiers thought the crowning pleasure of the day. At an early hour the large crowds who had enjoyed it all, with the patients, quietly dispersed.

Our long residence at the hospital gave us the opportunity of understanding fully all the prominent points of interest in the battle-field, which was constantly before us...Among the few valued friends who regularly met in our tent, when the fatiguing duties of the day were over, was frequently discussed the propriety of placing upon some part of the field a flag, to manifest our sympathy and esteem for those who "here fought and won this great battle for our liberties." Some intimation of the plan reached our friends at home, and directly we heard that a flag would be sent by persons residing in our immediate vicinity. To two of the ladies most active in procuring it, was given the pleasure of conveying it to Gettysburg. Many of the wounded knew when it arrived, and the arrangements being made to receive it; at their request, the flag (twenty-five feet in length) was carried through the streets of the hospital, then taken to "Round Top." All who could leave the hospital — officers, ladies, and soldiers — joined the procession.... Appropriate and eloquent addresses were delivered.... The ceremonies ended, we came back to the sad routine of hospital life and suffering, brightened, however, with the pleasant remembrance of the events in which we had been participating.

The work of reducing the number of patients was now commenced in earnest. Sixty were at one time sent in the cars, who had each but one arm apiece; the next train took the same number with one leg apiece, and one little cavalry boy who had lost both at the knee.

The sights have always been to me the saddest, most painful of any. Amid scenes like these we were constantly occupied until the breaking up of the hospital, and the dedication of the National Cemetery. That had to *us* a deeper interest than to many of the lookers-on; many of the quiet sleepers, by whom we were surrounded, we had known, and waited upon until care was no longer needed.

During the ceremonies of that day, we were so fortunate as to have a place directly in front and within a few feet of our now martyred President, and there heard distinctly every word he uttered of that memorable speech...There was now, November, 1863, nothing more to be done at Gettysburg, and we gladly turned our faces homeward....[9]

Mrs. Holstein spent the rest of 1863 speaking at the request of the Sanitary Commission across the state to solicit support from civilians. Anna Holstein did not return to the front until May 1864, although "The inaction and feeling of doing nothing for the wounded was unbearable, and a constant source of anxiety and trouble."[10] She was at Belle Plain and Port Royal and White House where her reactions to Southern civilians and wounded Confederates began to take the abusive stance of an arrogant invader; even to the point of suggesting like actions to the Union soldiers. At these sites Mrs. Holstein worked in her diet kitchen, and when needed, as a nurse.

At White House she related an interesting story not as uncommon in the Civil War as one may think:

> The 5th of June, Mr. Schall came, bringing the body of his brother, Col. Edwin Schall, to be embalmed. He fell at Cold Harbor on the 3rd of June, shot through the neck. Connected with this gallant officer's death is an incident so singular that it is worthy of record: …in the officer's Hospital in Georgetown [D.C.], my niece was sitting by her husband's bedside, watching the passing away of life now near its close. As the things of earth receded, and another world dawned upon his gaze, the lamp of life flickered and flashed in this closing scene. Suddenly rousing up, his voice which had previously been faint and feeble, rang out in a clear, loud tone; "Lieutenant, lieutenant!" A wounded lieutenant lying near him answered; "What is it captain?" He replied; "I'm not calling you, it is Lieut.-Col. Schall; I saw him fall, and thought the way he was lying perhaps he was dead." His wife soothed him, telling him "the colonel was all right;" and he sank exhausted on his pillow. But in a few moments called in the same tone; "Lieutenant, lieutenant!" repeating again the same words, that "he had seen him fall, etc." Again he was soothed to quietness. Fully conscious that death was near, the brave soldier…commending his soul to God, and committing [his] wife and children to the same loving care, in two hours peacefully passed…When Mrs. B [Bisbing] returned with her husband's body to their home, she then first learned that the colonel had fallen— as the captain described—two days previously. His body was also brought home for burial, and interred the day preceding the captain's funeral.[11]

By mid June 1864 Mrs. Holstein was at City Point. "Nothing before us all day but wounded; wounded men every step you take." She also complained of the dust: "Clouds of dust fill the air; and though the hospital is some distance from the traveled road to the front, yet by four o'clock the rows of tents which stand but a few yards from us are obscured, and the river, about one square distant, is invisible...wounded were constantly sent in; and old scenes were again and again repeated."[12] Mrs. Holstein described the explosion that paralyzed Elmina Spencer:

> ...[A] terrible explosion occurred on board the ordnance barge at City Point; at the moment, I was occupied in the arbor in front of our tent, and so had an unobstructed view; with the first shock stooped to the earth, as though struck upon the head; the tent quivered as though it *must* fall...There now rose to a great height a dense column of smoke, spreading out at the top in form of an umbrella, and from it fell a shower of death-dealing missiles; it literally *rained* muskets; shells flew in all directions; some passing over us, exploded beyond the hospital. The scene upon the bluff near the landing was sickening; dismembered bodies were strewn about the ground, and the dead and dying side by side; the wounded were soon gathered up and brought to the hospital...A large amount of government property was destroyed and many buildings.[13]

In November of 1864 the couple again returned home because of Mr. Holstein's health. Anna spent the remainder of the war on speaking tours and working with returning prisoners-of-war at Annapolis.

Written in 1867, Mrs. Holstein's book, *Three Years in Field Hospitals of the Army of the Potomac*, detailed events still fairly recent so her descriptions are vivid and provide an excellent primary source. Her dates and general geography are sometimes incorrect and her stern prejudice against anything Southern gets in the way of objectivity but her book is written spontaneously and with an emotion that related experiences that changed her life forever.

Anna applied for and received a pension of $12 per month in 1892 by a special act of Congress. In her submission were letters and depositions from Harriet Dada, Mary Morris Husband, various officers, enlisted men, and Pennsylvania Civil War Governor Andrew Curtain.

Late in the nineteenth century Mrs. Holstein was spending her energy "to arouse public sentiment and appreciation for the great historical importance of the hills of Valley Forge, where Washington's army was encamped during that terrible winter of 1777-1778. She was made regent of the Valley Forge Centennial and Memorial Association at its organization and held this office until her death. She labored untiringly that the association might purchase Washington's headquarters at Valley Forge and restore it 'as a memorial for all time to come.'"[14]

Anna Morris Holstein died on December 31, 1900 at her home in Upper Merion, Pennsylvania, where she had spent all her married life. She was buried at Swedes Church cemetery, Swedesburg, Pennsylvania. Both she and her husband have modest headstones with the unique feature of the signature inscribed on the top of the stone.

Mrs. Holstein later in life.
(MOLLUS)

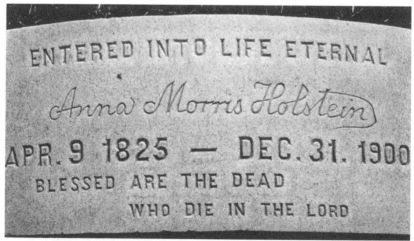

Mrs. Holstein's gravestone carries her signature.
(Author's collection)

Harriet Dada and Susan Hall

Government Nurses

*"It was a strange expression a poor fellow made the other
day, 'You are the God-blessedest woman I ever saw.' He
lived only a few days after being brought to the hospital."[1]*

Harriet Dada and Susan Hall were both from the state of New York;
Dada from Oswego County and Hall from Tompkins County. Before
the Civil War they had worked together out west with the Choctaw Indians for The American Board of Commissioners for Foreign Missions."[2]

Both offered themselves to the Women's Central Association of
Relief, New York, immediately on the formation of that useful organization for any service, or in any capacity, where their aid could be made
available. Both had formerly been employed by one of the Missionary
Societies, in mission labors among the Indians of the Southwest, and
were eminently fitted for any sphere of usefulness which the existing
condition of our country could present to women.

They were received by the Association, and requested to join the
class of women who, with similar motives and intentions, were attending the series of lectures and surgical instructions which was to prepare
them for the duties of nurses in the army hospitals.

Harriet Dada
(MOLLUS)

At noon, on Monday, the 22nd [July 1861, the day after the battle of First Manassas] Miss Dada and Miss Hall received instructions to prepare for their journey to the scene of their future labors; and at six p.m. they took the train for Washington, with orders to report to Miss Dix. Tuesday morning found them amidst all the terrible excitement which reigned in that city. The only question Miss Dix asked was, "Are you ready to work?" and added, "You are needed in Alexandria."

And toward Alexandria they were shortly proceeding. There were apprehensions that the enemy might pursue our retreating troops, of whom they met many as they crossed the Long Bridge, and passed the fortifications all filled with soldiers watching for the coming foe who might then so easily have invaded the Federal City.

In some cabins by the road-side they first saw some wounded men, to whom they paused to administer words of cheer, and a "cup of cold water." They were in great apprehension that the road might not be safe, and a trip to Richmond, in the capacity of prisoners was by no means to be desired.

At last they reached Alexandria, and in a dark stone building on Washington Street, formerly a seminary, found their hospital. They were denied admittance by the sentinel, but the surgeon in charge was called, and welcomed them to their new duties.

There they lay, the wounded, some on beds, many on mattresses spread upon the floor, covered with the blood from their wounds, and the dust of that burning summer battle-field, many of them still in their uniforms. The retreat was so unexpected, the wounded so numerous, and the helpers so few, that all were at once extremely busy in bringing order and comfort to that scene of suffering.

Susan Hall
(MOLLUS)

Their labors were extremely arduous. No soldiers were detailed as attendants for the first few weeks, and even the most menial duties fell upon these ladies. Sometimes a contraband was assigned them as assistant, but he soon tired of steady employment and left. They had little sleep and food that was neither tempting nor sufficient. So busy were they that two weeks elapsed before Miss Dada, whose letters furnish most of the material for this sketch, found time to write home, and inform her anxious friends, "where she was."

They worked there a month. Many of the convalescents were sent home and as the winter came on typhoid broke out among the troops and they nursed these men.[3]

About the beginning of April, 1862, soon after the battle of Winchester, Miss Dada and Miss Hall were ordered thither to care for the wounded. Here, they were transferred from one hospital to another, without time to become more than vaguely interested in the individual welfare of their patients. At length at the third, the Court-House Hospital, they were permitted to remain for several weeks. Here many of the interesting cases were found, and they became much attached to some of the sufferers under their care, and found great pleasure in their duties.

On the 22nd of May they were ordered to Strasburg, and preceded thither to the care of several hundred sick, entirely unsuspicious of personal danger, not dreaming that it could be met with beside the headquarters of [Major] General [Nathaniel] Banks. But on the following day troops were observed leaving the town on the Front Royal road, and the same night the memorable retreat was ordered.

It was indeed a sad sight which met their eyes in the gray of early dawn. Ambulances and army wagons filled the streets. Soldiers from the hospitals, scarcely able to walk, crawled slowly and painfully along, while the sick were crowded into the overfilled ambulances.

Pressing forward they arrived at Winchester at noon, but the ambulances did not arrive till many hours later, with their dismal freight. The fright and suffering had overpowered many, and many died as they were carried into the hospitals. A little later the wounded began to come in, and the faithful, hard-working surgeons and nurses had their hands full. The retreating Union forces came pouring through the town, the rebels in close pursuit....[4]

Soon the rebels had possession of town, and the ladies found themselves prisoners with a rebel guard placed about their hospital.

Their supplies were now quite reduced, and it was not until personal application had been made by the nurses to the rebel authorities, that suitable food was furnished.

When the army left Winchester, enough men were ordered to remain to guard the hospitals, and an order was read to all the inmates, that any of them seen in the streets would be shot.

Miss Dada and her friend [Susan Hall] remained at this place until the months of June and July were passed. In August they were assigned to Armory Square Hospital, Washington....[5]

The month of November [1862] found Miss Dada at Harper's Ferry. Miss Hall had been at Antietam, but the friends had decided to no longer be separated.[6]

May and June, 1863, Miss Dada and Miss Hall spent at Acquia Creek, in care of the wounded from the battle of Chancellorsville, and the 8th of July found them at Gettysburg—Miss Dada at the hospital of the Twelfth Army Corps at a little distance from the town, and Miss Hall at that of the First Army Corps, which was within the town.[7] The hospital of the Twelfth Army Corps was at a farm-house. The house and barns were filled with wounded, and tents were all around, crowded with sufferers among whom were many wounded rebel prisoners…Miss Hall and Miss Dada remained there as long as their services could be made available.[8]

The Armory Square Hospital in Washington, D.C.
Miss Dada and Miss Hall were assigned here in August 1862
and stayed until the battle of Antietam.
(Library of Congress)

Another view of Armory Square. Note the Capitol Building.
(Library of Congress)

There is an order from Dorothea Dix dated October 14, 1863 for Susan Hall that read: "You are ordered to proceed direct from the city of Washington to the city of Nashville, Tenn., there to report immediately to the medical director for assignment and service in any general hospital where your abilities and experience will be most available."[9]

[By] December, 1863, they were ordered to Murfreesboro, Tennessee, once a flourishing town, but showing everywhere the devastations of war. Two Seminaries, and a College, large blocks of stores, and a hotel had been taken for hospitals, and were now filled with sick and wounded men. A year had passed since the awful battle of Stone River [Stones River, Dec. 1, 1864 to January 2, 1865]—the field of which, now a wide waste lay near the town—but the hospitals had never been empty.

When they arrived they reported to the medical director, who "did not care whether they stayed or not," but "if they remained wished them to attend exclusively to the preparation of the Special Diet." They received only discouraging words from all they met. They found shelter for the night at the house of a rebel woman, and were next day assigned—Miss Hall to No. 1 Hospital, Miss Dada to No. 3

When they reported, the surgeon of No. 1 Hospital, for their encouragement, informed them that the chaplain thought they had better not remain. Miss Dada also was coldly received, and it was evident that the Surgeons and chaplains were very comfortable, and desired no

324

outside interference. They believed, however, that there was work for them to do, and decided to remain.

Miss Dada found in the wards more than one familiar face from the Twelfth Army Corps, and the glad enthusiasm of her welcome by the patients, contrasted with the chilling reception of the officers.

Most of these men had been wounded at Lookout Mountain [Nov. 24, 1863], a few days before, but many others had been suffering ever since the bloody battle of Chickamauga [Sept. 19-20, 1863].

Miss Hall was able to commence her work at once, but Miss Dada was often exhorted to patience, while waiting three long weeks for a stove, before she could do more than, by the favor of the head cook of the full diet kitchen, occasionally prepare at his stove, some small dishes for the worst cases.

Here the winter wore away. Many a sad tale of the desolations of war was poured into their ears, by the suffering Union women who had lost their husbands, fathers, sons, in the wild warfare of the country in which they lived. And many a scene of sorrow and suffering they witnessed.

In January, they had a pleasant call from Dr. M——, one of the friends they had known at Gettysburg. This gentleman, in conversation with the medical director, told him he knew two of the ladies there. The reply illustrates the peculiar position in which they were placed. "Ladies," he answered with a sneer, "We have no ladies here! A hospital is no place for a lady. We have women here, who are cooks!"[10]

In the latter part of the ensuing May, they went to Chattanooga. They were most kindly received by the surgeons, and found much to be done. Car-loads of wounded were daily coming from the front, all who could bear removal were sent further north, and only the worst cases remained in Chattanooga.

Miss Dada, often rejoiced, while here, in the kindness of her friends at home, which enabled her to procure for the sick those small, but at that place, costly luxuries which their condition demanded.

As the season advanced to glowing summer, the mortality became dreadful. In her hospital alone, not a large one, and containing but seven hundred beds, there were two hundred and sixty-one deaths in the month of June, and there were from five to twenty daily. These were costly sacrifices, often the best, noblest, most promising,—for Miss Dada's records—"Daily I see devoted Christian youths dying on the altar of their country."

With the beginning of November came busy times, as the cars daily came laden with their freight of suffering from Atlanta. On the 26th, Miss Dada records, "One year to-day since Hooker's men fought above the clouds

325

on Lookout. To-day as I look upon the grand old mountain the sun shines brightly on the graves of those who fell there, and all is quiet."

Again, after the gloomy winter had passed, she writes, in March, 1865, "Many cases of measles are being brought in, mostly new soldiers, many conscripts, and so down-spirited if they get sick."[11]

The following request is part of Susan Hall's pension records:

Office United States Army General Hospital No. 1
Chattanooga, Tnn., May 22, 1865

Miss Susan E. Hall has been on duty as nurse at this hospital since June 12, 1864, and has discharged her duties in a most satisfactory manner. The war being over, she is desirous to return to Washington, D.C., whence she came. She has therefore been relieved from duty, and I request in her behalf that quartermasters furnish the necessary transportation to the above named place.

John H. Phillips
Surgeon United States Volunteers
In Charge General Hospital No. —, Chattanooga, Tenn.

Patients were in May being mustered out of the service, and the hospitals thinning. Miss Dada and Miss Hall thought they could be spared, and started eastward. But when in Illinois, word reached them that all the ladies but one had left, and help was needed, and Miss Dada returned to Chattanooga. Here she was soon busy, for, though the war was over, there were still many sick, and death often claimed a victim.

Miss Dada remained till the middle of September, engaged in her duties, when, having given more than four years to the service of her country, she at last took her leave of hospital-life....[12]

In May of 1866 Harriet Dada was present at Susan Hall's marriage to Robert Barry. The war couldn't separate the friends, but marriage did. Susan wrote:

I first saw Robert Barry of the Chicago Board of Trade Battery at Murfreesboro, Tenn. in 1863 and early part of '64, where I was acting U. S. Army nurse in said hospital...[He] remained in the hospital three months before he was sufficiently strong to rejoin his command...He was not in my ward but I saw him a few times afterward while drug clerk at the hospital I saw more of him...I did not become very well acquainted with him but I [wrote] him a number of letters and after he left for his battery we began corresponding and continued to do so until our marriage. A year after the close of the war in May 1866 I was married to

326

Robert Barry at Homer, N.Y...He supposed he was able for business at the close of the war and showed great perseverance and energy but his nervous system was shattered. We came directly to California....[13]

Susan moved out to California and remained there the rest of her life. The Barrys would have no children. Her rather sad life was reflected in the affidavits given in Robert Barry's pension records. Mr. Barry was an alcoholic and was in a sanitarium in 1868. In 1875 he had a stroke. In 1887 Susan received a pension of $12 per month. In 1890 Robert received the same. Requesting an increase in 1899, the same year Susan became his guardian, Mrs. Barry said: "I suppose his sprees have lasted longer than a week sometimes...He doesn't remember when he's sober...He acted like an imbecile." Witnesses testified that "he was always fond of his whiskey, when by a possible chance he could get any...He was kind of a lay preacher and would go off to preach on Sundays...."[14] Mr. Barry was accepted and expelled from a number of Soldiers Homes and finally died at the Pacific Branch National Home for Disabled Volunteer Soldiers in 1905. Susan lived in Pasadena, California, for many years and was active in the Stanton [Women's] Relief Corps in Los Angeles. Susan Hall died on March 15, 1912, and was buried in Rosedale Cemetery in Los Angeles.

Harriet Dada, like some of the other Civil War nurses, went on to become a doctor. She graduated from the Women's Medical College in New York in 1868. On May 6, 1869, the *Journal* of Syracuse contained the following article:

"Homeopathic Physician and Accoucheur"
We call the attention of our readers to the card in another column of Harriet A. Dada, M.D., Homeopathic and Hygienic Physician and Accoucheur, who has taken up her residence in our city, and entered upon the practice of her profession. It is with no ordinary testimonials that Miss Dada comes to us, having not only a diploma as a graduate of the New York Medical College for women, but the experience of five years active service in the field, camp and hospital during the rebellion, where her name stood high among those who service have endeared them to thousands of maimed heroes. Miss Dada was attached to the 12th Corps Hospital in the east and the 20th Corps Hospital at the west, and has the testimony of many a soldier of the "White Star" Division, and of our veteran 149th Regiment, whose life is due to her assiduous care and self-sacrificing devotion. From the bloody field of the first Bull Run, through the sanguinary contests of Chancellorsville,

Susan Hall Barry moved to California in 1866 and spent the rest of her rather sad life there.
(MOLLUS)

Dr. Harriet Dada Emens continued to lead a productive life in the service of medicine.
(MOLLUS)

Gettysburg, and Chattanooga, and in the hospitals at Alexandria, Harper's Ferry and Murfreesboro, until long after the close of the war in 1865, her labors were untiring and unremitting. With such a practical basis to work upon, Miss Dada entered upon the theoretical study of medicine, and has now for more than a year been prepared for the more extended work to which her life is devoted. Previous to the war, her knowledge of medicine was not inconsiderable, having in the capacity of a missionary of the American Board, among the Choctaw Indians in the Indian Territory, necessarily made the study of the healing art a part of her labor. These facts, of which we are peculiarly cognizant, lead us to cordially commend Miss Dada to the patronage of those of our citizens who may have occasion for her services.

An ad followed with her office hours and it was noted that "Especial attention paid to diseases of women and children."

In 1873 Harried married the Reverend Peter W. Emens, a widower of six months. He had three children at that time: Walter, age 14; Homer, age 11; and Laesa, age 6. Reverend Emens became a doctor in 1876. In that same year on November 28, the *Journal* carried another piece on Harriet:

"Free Lecture to Women"

This Evening, at Association Hall, Mrs. Dr. Dada Emens will give another lecture, to women only, for the benefit of those who were not able from any cause, to attend the lecture give by her last Friday afternoon. The subject of the lecture is inviting—"The Structure of the Body, and how to Promote Health, Strength, and Beauty." We assure those interested that the lecture will be thoroughly practical, deeply interesting, and based upon the most enlightened medical knowledge. It will be illustrated by the employment of a French manikin. Mrs. Dr. Emens has long been a resident of Syracuse, and is everywhere recognized by physicians as a lady of remarkable culture in the profession. The lecture is particularly designed for working women, who will be kind to themselves in attending it.

By 1898 the Emens had apparently separated. They both lived and worked at different sites.

On January 21, 1908, the *Herald* ran an amusing story of a reunion between the former nurse and a former patient. Most likely many such stories were written in newspapers all over the country for decades after the war.

When Dr. Harriet Dada Emens of No. 360 Westcott street heard a ring at her doorbell one afternoon last week and started down the stairs to answer it, she was stopped before she reached the bottom of the flight by a rubicund, white haired man carrying a long paper box under his arm.

"Is that something for us?" asked the doctor, stretching out her hand for the package and taking the bearer for a delivery man.

"Yes, it is something for you," was the reply; as the stranger laid the box in her arms and piled on top of it another large parcel tied with a red ribbon and bearing the label of a well-known candy manufacturer. "And so is this. They both come from an old sweetheart of yours and he told me that I should collect a kiss from you before I give up the packages."

Dr. Emens is 76 years old and not very tall, but she drew herself to her full height and squelched the intruder in the sternest tones she could command.

"Sir, you must be insane!" she declared. "I have no old sweetheart and I am not in the habit of kissing anyone."

The intruder burst into a hearty laugh.

"Well," he exclaimed, "I'll prove to you that I'm one of your old sweethearts if you will let me come inside a minute."

The doctor acquiesced, still doubtfully. But when the visitor entered her parlor, and stood before her in the light of day, she dropped the packages in her excitement and held out both hands.

"Why, Charlie Sherwood!" she cried. "It can't be possible that this is you!"

And this the manner of meeting of those two old friends who had not seen each other in nearly forty-seven years.

It was at Camp Franklin, Va., that the first meeting took place when pretty Hattie Dada of Fulton was an army nurse and Charles K. Sherwood was orderly sergeant of Company F, Fifth Maine Volunteers. The young sergeant was taken ill with typhoid fever and for a few weeks it was touch and go whether he should live or die, but the tender care of his nurse saved his life and both doctors and patient felt that the debt owing to her was one that could not easily be repaid.

When young Sherwood was finally transferred, he asked his nurse for her home address, promising that he would to Fulton [New York, where she grew up] and look her up after the war was over. But that was on the day after Christmas 1861, and the war lasted for nearly four years after and in the meantime many things had come to both nurse and patient, and although neither forgot the other, their meeting was deferred far longer than either expected it would be.

Recently, Mr. Sherwood, who had become a large pickle manufacturer in New York city, was drawn to Oneida by his business interests, and, the other day while looking over some old papers, he came upon the address of his former nurse. Spurred on by grateful memories, he lost no time in looking up his benefactress. Search at Canastota of which place he had heard her speak, failed to produce any trace of her and for a time, his search at Fulton was fruitless, but at length, after much difficulty, he discovered a clue which led him to Syracuse where he learned that his old friend had married and was living at No. 360 Westcott street in this city.

Wishing to surprise her, Mr. Sherwood armed himself with a box of flowers and another of candy and started off to renew the old acquaintance which took up a pleasant afternoon for the two. Mr. Sherwood is married and has a family. His wife having been an invalid for many years. When the two friends separated, it was with the assurance that they would not lose sight of each other in the future and Dr. Dada has received a hearty invitation to go to New York and visit her old patient's family.

Born in Hannibal, New York, in 1835, Harried Dada Emens died in Syracuse on September 1, 1909, and was buried in Oakwood Cemtery.

Remainder of July

*"God mercifully veiled the future from my eyes and gave me
needed strength from day to day...."[1]*

ithin just two weeks or so after the Battle of Gettysburg,
it became obvious to the Medical Department that something had to be done to consolidate the thousands of
wounded left behind by the two armies. Henry Janes, a
U.S. volunteer surgeon...reported that in early July he was placed in
command of "all field hospitals" around Gettysburg and had "under my
charge some 60 different hospitals with over 20,000 Union and Rebel
wounded needing prompt attention." Of these numbers, he stated that
5,456 were Confederates in twenty-four of those hospital camps.

When the medical director of the Army of the Potomac, Jonathan
Letterman, left with the army on July 6, he ordered 106 surgeons to
remain behind with these wounded. Shortly afterwards, the army dispatched a few more doctors to assist those left at Gettysburg. Very
slowly, these injured men were either sent away to permanent military
hospitals in cities along the east coast, or moved to Camp Letterman
[the George Wolf farm] which was established on July 20. By July 25,
16,125 wounded had been sent away from Gettysburg and approximately
4,217 remained because they were unfit to travel.

There were good reasons to position a "general hospital" near the
battlefield. The most important reason was that there were the thousands of severely injured men who could not go anywhere else, and had
to remain behind for a while to recuperate. As it turned out, the hospital
did not actually close until November 20, one day after Lincoln's visit.
Also, it was a very difficult task to supply so many outlying field hospitals, where conditions were becoming even more unhealthy as time
passed.

The site chosen...was about one mile east of town, along the York
Pike. This location was a good one for other reasons. At that time, it
was on high, mostly well-drained ground, in a large grove, which provided both shade and free movement of fresh air...the camp area was
drained and the tents were pitched...The railroad was only thirty rods
away, which permitted litters to be walked to the cars. A good spring on

the property, along with several wells that were later dug, provided a neverending supply of clean, fresh water.

...After a while, the general hospital, became the very model of a clean, efficient and well-run medical facility, one of the first of its kind on a battlefield anywhere...At its peak, the hospital had more than four hundred tents, set up in six double rows, about ten feet apart. Each tent held up to ten patients, and was heated (in the fall) with a Sibley stove. Every medical officer had charge of from forty to seventy patients, which totaled 1,600 on August 30, but dropped to about three hundred in late October, and ran as low as one hundred on November 10.[2]

One woman, who had twenty-six wounded men in her house, wrote:

No small disturbance was occasioned by the removal of our wounded to the hospital. We had but short notice of the intention, and though we pleaded hard to have them remain, it was of no use. So many have been removed by death and recovery, that there was room; and the surgeon having general care over all, ordered the patients from private houses to the General Hospital. A weight of care, which we took upon us for duty's sake, and which we had all learned to like and would have gladly borne, until relieved by the complete recovery of our men, has been lifted off our shoulders, and again we have our house to ourselves.[3]

During the last weeks of July many more women would come to Gettysburg to help with the wounded. The women were not there to serve the vast war machine of the North or South; they came to serve humanity. With few exceptions they were just as willing to relive the suffering of both the enemy as their own men. To a woman, they were sickened by the insanity of the war. Yet, they were part of the war, part of the history that was made during those four agonizing years.

In 1869 a citizen wrote:

It is said that republics are ungrateful, but in the progress of events, when the claims of the common soldier have been more fully considered, then will these noble women, who saved thousands of common soldiers to fight again for freedom, find *their* names also inscribed on the long Roll of Honor? American can well afford to be grateful to every class of her defenders, when from pure patriotism of her striving millions she draws the life blood which makes her a power amongst the nations of the earth.[4]

332

Jane Eliza Newton Woolsey and Georgeanna Muirson Woolsey

New York Nurses

"It was a satisfaction to be in Gettysburg, though I confess to a longing to shut out the sight of it all, sometimes."[1]

The entire Woolsey family of New York was dedicated to the Union. At Gettysburg it was represented by three of its members: Mrs. Jane Woolsey, the mother, Georgeanna or "Georgy," one of the seven girls of the family who had been serving as an army nurse since 1862, and the youngest child and only son, Charles, who was on Meade's staff. Georgy would later write a booklet at the request of the Sanitary Commission entitled *Three Weeks at Gettysburg*. It is from this tract and private letters that the two women's experience at Gettysburg is told.

"We at home knew that Charley was in the thick of it, and were most anxious and ready to believe the worst, when a telegram to me (G.) [Georgy] came from our old commander, Mr. F. L. Olmstead [of the Sanitary Commission], saying, 'If you are going to Gettysburg let me know." We jumped at the conclusion that *he* knew of bad news for us from Charley, and Mother and I started at once to go to him...."[2]

Twenty-four hours we were in making the journey between Baltimore [where they learned Charley was safe] and Gettysburg, places only four hours apart in ordinary running time; and this will give you some idea of the difficulty there was of bringing up supplies when the fighting was over, and delays in transporting wounded. Coming towards the town at this crawling rate, we passed some fields where fences were down, and the ground slightly tossed up. "That's where Kilpatrick's cavalrymen fought the rebels," someone said; "and close by that barn a rebel soldier was found, day before yesterday, sitting dead;" no one to help, poor soul, "near the whole city full." The railroad bridge, broken up by the enemy, [the] government had not rebuilt as yet, and we stopped two miles from the town, to find that, as usual, just where the government had left off, the Commission had come in. There stood their temporary lodge and kitchen, and here, hobbling out of the tents, came the wounded men who made their way down from the corps hospital, expecting to leave at once in the return cars.[3]

...[B]eing on hand, [we] were fastened upon by Mr. Olmstead, to take charge of a feeding station, and lodge for the wounded men. So there we were, looking after other people's boys, since our own was safe, for three weeks, coming as near the actual battle field as I should ever wish to. You know all about that fighting, how desperate it was on both sides; what loss, and what misery; the communications cut, no supplies on hand, no surgeons, or so few that they were driven to despair from the sight of the wretchedness they could not help,—20,000 badly wounded soldiers and only one miserable, unsafe line of railroad to being supplies and carry men away.[4]

...[We] gladly fell in with the proposition to do what we could at the Sanitary Commission Lodge after the battle. There were, of course, the agents of the Commissions, already on the field, distributing supplies to the hospitals, and working night and day among the wounded. I cannot pretend to tell you what was done by all the big wheels of the concern, but only how two of the smallest ones went round, and what turned up in the going.

This is the way the thing was managed at first: The surgeons, left in care of the wounded three or four miles out from town, went up and down among the men in the morning and said, "Any of you boys who can make your way to the cars, can go to Baltimore." So off start all who think they feel well enough, anything being better than the "hospitals," so called, for the first few days after the battle. Once the men have the surgeon's permission to go, they are off; and there may be an interval of a day, or two days, should any of them be too weak to reach the train in time, during which these poor fellows belong to no one, the hospital at one end, the railroad at the other, with far more than chance falling through between the two. The Sanitary Commission knew this would be so of necessity, and, coming in, made a connecting link between these two ends.

The first few days the worst cases only came down in ambulances from the hospitals; hundreds of fellows hobbled along as best they could, in heat and dust, for hours, slowly toiling, and many hired farmers' wagons, as hard as the farmers' fists themselves, and were jolted down to the railroad and three or four dollars the man.[5] ...If at any time you would like to swear, call your enemy a Dutch farmer—nothing can be worse, or if he is a man of decency, make him feel more indignant. The D— farmers of Gettysburg have made themselves a name and a fame to the latest day, by charging our poor men, who crawled out of barns and woods, where they hid themselves after they were wounded, three and four dollars each for bringing all that was left of their poor bodies, after defending the contemptible D— firesides, down to the railroad. We found this out, and had a detail from the Provost Marshal to arrest the next farmer who did it, and oblige him to refund or go to prison.[6]

Georgeanna "Georgy" Woolsey
(MOLLUS)

Think of the disappointment of a soldier, sick, body and heart, to find, at the end of this miserable journey, that his effort to get away, into which he had put all his remaining stock of strength, was useless; that "the cars had gone," or "the cars were full;" that while he was coming others had stepped down before him, and that he must turn all the weary way back again, or sleep on the roadside till the next train "tom-morrow." Think what this would have been, and you are ready to appreciate the relief and comfort that was. No men were turned back. You fed and you sheltered them just when no one else could have done so; and out of the boxes and barrels of good and nourishing things, which you, people at home, had supplied, we took all that was needed. Some of you sent a stove (that is, the money to get it), some of you the beef-stock, some of you the milk and fresh bread; and all of you would have been thankful that you had done so, could you have seen the refreshment and comfort received through these things.

As soon as the men hobbled up to the tents, good hot soup was given all round; and that over, their wounds were dressed,—for the gentlemen of the commission and cooks or surgeons, as occasion demands,—and finally, with their blankets spread over the straw, the men stretched themselves out, and were happy and contented till morning, and the next train.

On the day that the railroad bridge was repaired we moved up to the depot, close by the town, and had things in perfect order; a first-rate camping ground, in a large field directly by the track, with unlimited supply of delicious, cool water. Here we set up two stoves, with four large boilers, always kept full of soup and coffee, watched by four or five black men, who did the cooking under our direction, and sang (not under our direction) at the tops of their voices all day…

Then we had three large hospital tents, holding about thirty-five each, a large camp-meeting supply tent, where barrels of goods were stored, and our own smaller tent fitted up with tables, where jelly-pots and bottles of all kinds of good syrups, blackberry and black currant, stood in rows. Barrels were ranged round the tent walls; shirts, drawers, dressing-gowns, socks, and slippers (I wish we had more of the latter), rags and bandages, each in its own place on one side; on the other, boxes of tea, coffee, soft crackers, tamarinds, cherry brandy, &c. Over the kitchen, and over this small supply tent, we women reigned, and filled up our wants by requisitions on the Commission's depot. By this time there had arrived a "delegation" of just the right kind from Canandaigua, New York, with surgeon dressers and attendants, bringing a first-rate supply of necessities and comforts for the wounded, which they handed over to the Commission.

Twice a day the trains left for Baltimore or Harrisburg, and twice a day we fed all the wounded who arrived for them. Things were systematized now, and the men came down in long ambulance trains to the cars; Baggage cars they were, fitted with straw for the wounded to lie on, and broken open at either end to let in the air. A government surgeon was always present to attend to the careful lifting of the soldiers from ambulance to car. Many of the men could get along very nicely, holding one foot up, and taking great jumps on their crutches. The latter were a great comfort, we had a nice supply at the lodge, and they travelled up and down from the tents to the cars daily. Only occasionally did we dare let a pair go with some very lame soldier, who begged for them; we needed them to help the new arrivals each day, and trusted to the men being supplied at the hospitals at the journey's end. Pads and crutches were a standing want—pads particularly. We manufactured them out of the rags we had, stuffed with sawdust from brandy boxes; and with half a sheet, and some soft straw, Mrs. — [Woolsey] made a poor dying boy as easy as his sufferings would permit. Poor young fellow! he was so grateful to her for washing and feeding and comforting him! He was too ill to bear the journey, and went from our tent to the church hospital, and from the church to his grave….the quartermaster's department was overtaxed, and for many days our dead were simply wrapped in their blankets and put into the earth. It is a soldierly way, after all—lying wrapped in the old war-torn blanket, the little dust returned to dust.

When the surgeons had the wounded all placed, with as much comfort as seemed possible under the circumstances, on board the train, our detail of men would go from car to car, with soup made of beef-stock or fresh meat, full of potatoes, turnips, cabbage, and rice, with fresh bread and

336

coffee, and, when stimulants were needed, with ale, milk punch, or brandy. Water pails were in great demand for use in the cars on the journey, and also empty bottles, to take the place of canteens. All our whiskey and brandy bottles were washed and filled up at the spring, and the boys went off, carefully hugging their extemporized canteens, from which they would wet their wounds, or refresh themselves, till the journey ended. I do not think that a man of the sixteen thousand, who were transported during our stay, went from Gettysburg without a good meal; rebels and Unionists together, they all had it, and were pleased and satisfied. "Have you friends in the army, madam?" a rebel soldier, lying on the floor of the car, said to me, as I gave him some milk. "Yes; my brother is on——'s [Meade] staff." "I thought so, ma'am. You can always tell; when people are good to soldiers they are sure to have friends in the army."…It was strange to see the good brotherly feeling come over the soldiers—our own and the rebel—when side by side they lay in our tents. "Hallo, boys! This is the pleasantest way to meet—isn't it? We are better friends when we are as close as this, than a little farther off." And then they would go over the battles together—"We were here" and "You were there," in the friendliest way.

After each train of cars, daily, for the three weeks we were in Gettysburg, trains of ambulances arrived too late—men who must spend the day with us until the five P.M. cars went, and men too late for the five P.M. train, who must spend the night till the 10 A.M. cars went. All the men who came, in this way, under our own immediate and particular attention, were given the best we had of care and food. The surgeon in charge of our camp, with his most faithful dresser and attendants, looked after all their wounds, which were often in a most shocking state, particularly among the rebels. Every evening and morning they were dressed. Often the men would say, "That feels good. I haven't had my wound so well dressed since I was hurt." Something cool to drink is the first thing asked for, after the long, dusty drive, and pailfuls of tamarinds and water—"a beautiful drink," the men used to say—disappeared rapidly among them.

After the men's wounds were attended to, we went round giving them clean clothes; had basins, and soap, and towels; and followed these with socks, slippers, shirts, drawers, and those coveted dressing gowns…How lucky we felt ourselves in having the immense satisfaction of distributing these things, which all of you, hard at work in villages and cities, were getting ready and sending off, in faith.[7]

I saw very few who were *slightly* hurt among the wounded…So brave as they were too, and so pleased with all that was done for them—even the rebels. We had our station with tents for a hundred, with kitchen, surgeon and "delegation" right on the railroad line between Gettysburg and Baltimore. We had the full storehouse of the Commission to draw upon…

[This was Mrs. Woolsey's first battlefield experience.] Mother put great spirit into it all, listened to all their stories, petted them, fed them, and distributed clothes, including handkerchiefs with cologne, and got herself called "Mother,"—This way, Mother." "Here's the bucket, Mother," and "Isn't she a glorious old woman?"—while the most that *I* ever heard was, "*She* knows how; why, it would have taken our steward two hours to get round; but then she's used to it, you see;" which, when you consider that I was distributing hot grog, and must have been taken for a barmaid, was not so complimentary![8]

One of the Woolsey daughters wrote: "Just imagine Mother in a straw flat and heavy *Gettsyburg* boots, standing cooking soup for 200 men at a time, and distributing it in tin cups; or giving clean shirts to ragged rebels; or sitting on a pile of grocer's boxes, under the shadow of a string of codfish, scribbling her notes to us."[9]

The Gettysburg women were kind and faithful to the wounded and their friends, and the town was full to overflowing of both. The first day, when Mrs. — [Woolsey] and I reached the place, we literally begged our bread from door to door, but the kind woman who at last gave us dinner, would take no pay for it. "No, ma'am, I shouldn't wish to have that sin on my soul when the war is over." She, as well as others, had fed the strangers flocking into town daily; sometimes over fifty of them for each meal, and all for love, and nothing of reward; and one night we forced a reluctant confession from our hostess that she was meaning to sleep on the floor that we might have a bed—her whole house being full. Of course we couldn't allow this self-sacrifice, and hunted up some other place to stay in. We did her no good, however, for afterwards found that the bed was given up that night to some other stranger who arrived late and tired; "An old lady, you know, and I couldn't let an old lady sleep on the floor." Such acts of kindness and self-denial were almost entirely confined to the women.

One woman we saw…whose pluck helped to redeem the other sex. She lived in a little house close up by the field where the hardest fighting was done—a red-cheeked, strong, country girl. "Were you frightened when the shells began flying?" "Well, no; you see we was all baking bread round here for the soldiers, and had our dough a-rising. The neighbors they ran into their cellars, but I couldn't leave my bread…" And here she stood…while great holes, which we saw, were made by shot and shell through the room in which she was working.[10]

The streets of Gettysburg were filled with the battle. People thought and talked of nothing else…Hundreds of old muskets were piled on the pavements…The private houses of the town were, many of them, hospitals; the little red flags hung from upper windows.[11] It will be a long time before Gettysburg will forget the Army of the Potomac. Their houses are battered, some of them with great holes through and through them. Their streets are filled with old caps, pieces of muskets, haversacks, scraps of war everywhere, and even the children fling stones across the street, and call to each other, "Here, you rebel, don't you hear that shell?" and one babe of four years I found sitting on the pavement with a hammer peacefully cracking percussion caps from the little cupful he had.[12]

Besides our own men at the lodge, we all had soldiers scattered about whom we could help from our supplies…a great treat to the men condemned by their wounds to stay in Gettysburg, and obliged to live on what the empty town could provide. There was a colonel in a shoe shop, a captain just up the street, and a private round the corner (whose young sister had possessed herself of him, overcoming the military rules in some way, and carrying him off to a little room, all by himself, where I found her doing her best with very little). She came afterwards to our tent, and got for him clean clothes and good food, and all he wanted, and was perfectly happy in being his cook, washerwoman, medical cadet, and nurse. Besides such as these, we occasionally carried from our supplies something to the churches, which were filled with sick and wounded, and where men were dying,—men whose strong patience it was very hard to bear,—dying with thoughts of the old home far away, saying, as last words for the women watching there, and waiting with a patience equal in its strength, "Tell her I love her!"[13]

Then those rebels too, miserable fellows; we hated them so much when they were away from us, and couldn't help being so good to them when they were in our hands…They had just as much good hot soup, when our procession of cans and cups and soft brad and general refreshment went round from car to car, as they wanted; and I even filled the silver papcup [*sic*] that a pretty boy from North Carolina had round his neck, though he was an officer and showed no intention to become a Unionist. "Yes, it was his baby-cup," and "his mother gave it to him;" and he lay on the floor of the baggage car, wounded, with this most domestic and peaceful of all little relics tied round his neck. We had lovely things for the men to eat—as many potatoes and turnips as they wanted, and almost "*too* much cabbages;" and custard pudding, and codfish hash, and jelly an inch high on their bread, and their bread *buttered*—"buttered on *both* sides," as the men discovered, greatly to

339

their amusement one night, considering that the final touch had been given when *this* followed the clean clothes and cologne,—"cologne worth a penny a sniff." "I smell it up here," a soldier called to me, poking his head out of the second story window, while I and my bottle stood at the door of his hospital.[14]

Late one afternoon—too late for the cars—a train of ambulances arrived at our lodge with over one hundred wounded rebels to be cared for through the night. Only one among them seemed too weak and faint to take anything. He was badly hurt and failing. I went to him after his wound was dressed, and found him lying on his blanket, stretched over the straw, a fair-haired, blue-eyed young lieutenant…I could not think of him as a rebel. He was too near heaven for that. He wanted nothing—had not been willing to eat for days, his comrades said; but I coaxed him to try a little milk gruel, flavored nicely with lemon and brandy; and one of the satisfactions of our three weeks is the remembrance of the empty cup I took away afterwards and his perfect enjoyment of that supper….[15]

This was Lt. Henry Rauch, of the 14th South Carolina. When Georgy learned that the lieutenant's brother was also wounded and in the cars, she had him found and carried to the tent where Henry was. The brother was put next to him, where he lay until Henry died. The brother was "by his side on the straw, and for the rest of the day lay in a sort of apathy, without speaking, except to assure himself that he could stay with his brother without the risk of being separated from his fellow-prisoners.

And there the brothers lay, and there we, strangers, sat watching…at sunset I put my hand on the lieutenant's heart to find it still!"

All night the brother lay close against the coffin, and in the morning he went with his comrades, leaving us to bury Henry, having "confidence," but first thanking us for what we had done, and giving us all that he had to show his gratitude—the palmetto ornament from his brother's cap, and a button from his coat.

…[A] number of colored freedmen, working for the government on the railroad, had their camp [in a field nearby] and every night they took their recreation, after the heavy work of the day was over, in prayer meetings. [Georgy and Mrs. Woolsey went at night to hear them.]…Very little care was taken of these poor men. Those who were ill during our stay were looked after by one of the officers of the Commission. [Mrs. Woolsey sewed handkerchiefs and distributed them to the workers.] One man came over to our tent next day to say, "Missus, was it you who sent me that present? I never had anything so beautiful in all my life before…"

Among our wounded soldiers, one night, came an elderly man, sick, wounded, and crazy, singing and talking about home. We did what we could for him...The next morning he was sent from the Lodge, and that evening two tired women came into our camp—his wife and sister, who hurried on from their home to meet him, arriving just too late...It seemed about hopeless for two lone women, who had never been out of their own little town, to succeed in finding a soldier among so many, sent in so many different directions, but we helped them as we could, and started them on their journey the next morning...[The Woolseys found out later that the two women found the man and took him home.]

The same night we had in our tents two fathers, with their wounded sons, and a nice old German mother with her boy. She had come in from Wisconsin, and brought with her a patch-work bed quilt for her son, thinking he might have lost his blanket; and there he lay, all covered up with his quilt, looking so home-like, and feeling so too, no doubt, with his good old mother close at his side. She seemed bright and happy—had three sons in the army—one had been killed, this one wounded—yet she was so pleased with the tents, and the care she saw taken there of the soldiers, that while taking her tea from the barrel-head as table, she said, "Indeed, if she was a man, she'd be a soldier too, right off."[16]

The day before we came away a sleepy-looking, utterly stupid Dutchman walked into camp, having heard we had "some rebels." He lived five miles from the city and had "never seen one," and came mooning in to stare at them, and stood with his mouth open, while the rebels and ourselves were shouting with laughter, he "pledgin his word" that "he never saw a rebel afore." "And why didn't you take your gun and help drive them out of your town?" Mother said. "Why, a fellow might a got hit;" at which the rebels, lying in double rows in the tent, shook themselves almost to pieces.[17]

...We had, on an average, sixty of such men each night, for three weeks, under our care; sometimes one hundred, sometimes only thirty; and with the "delegation," and the help of other gentlemen volunteers, who all worked devotedly for the men, the whole thing was a great success; and you, and all of us, can't help being thankful that we had a share, however small, in making it so. Sixteen thousand good meals were given, hundreds of men kept through the day, and twelve hundred sheltered at night, their wounds dressed, their supper and breakfast secured, rebels and all. You will not, I am sure, regret that these most wretched men, these "enemies," "sick and in prison," were helped and cared for through your supplies, though certainly they were not in your minds when you packed your barrels and boxes. The clothing we reserved for our own men, except, now and then, when a shivering rebel needed it; but in feeding them we could make no distinction. It was curious to see, among our workers at the Lodge, the disgust and horror felt for rebels giving place to the kindest feeling for wounded men.

Our three weeks were coming to an end; the work of transporting the wounded was nearly over; twice daily we had filled and emptied our tents, and twice fed the trains before the long journey. The men came in slowly at the last, a lieutenant, all the way from Oregon, being among the very latest. He came down from the corps hospitals (now greatly improved), having lost one foot, poor fellow, dressed in a full suit of the Commission's cotton clothes, just as bright and as cheerful as the first man, and all the men that we received, had been. We never heard a complaint. "Would he like a little nice soup?" "Well, no, thank you, ma'am," he hesitating and polite. "You have a long ride before you, and had better take a little; I'll just bring it and you can try." So the good thick soup came. He took a very little in the spoon to please me, and afterwards the whole cupful to please himself. He "did not think it was this kind of soup I meant. He had some in camp, and did not think he cared for any more; his "cook" was a very small boy though, who had just put some meat in a little water, and stirred it round." "Would you like a handkerchief?" and I produced our last one, with a hem and cologne too. "O, yes, that is what I need; I have lost mine, and was just borrowing this gentleman's." So the lieutenant, the last man, was made comfortable, thanks to all of you, though he had but one foot to carry him on his long journey home.

Four thousand soldiers, too badly hurt to be moved, were still left in Gettysburg, cared for kindly and well at the large, new government hospital, with a Sanitary commission attachment.[18]

Before the Woolsey women left, they received a farewell:

...to give the Baltimore fireman his due, who, being one of our friends at Gettysburg, secured two bands before we came away and marched them down to camp to serenade us, which they did standing at the mouth of the long tent and refreshing themselves afterwards with gingerbread and punch, unmindful of the fact that the jolly Canandaigua "delegation," finding its fingers inconvenienced by the sugar on them, just dipped their hands in the claret and water without saying anything![19]

"Our work was over, our tents were struck, and we came away, after a flourish of trumpets from two military bands, who filed down to our door and gave us a farewell,—Red, white, and blue."[20]

"I, [Georgy] being urged, wrote later a little pamphlet giving Mother's and my experience at the front, and called 'Three Weeks at Gettysburg.' It was meant to 'fire the hearts' of the sewing circles, which, all over the country, were keeping up the Sanitary Commission supplies. The Commission ordered 10,000 copies for distribution, and I went off to Point Lookout Hospital, leaving Abby [a sister] all the work of getting it printed."[21]

Jane Eliza Newton and Charles Woolsey had eight children: Abby, Jane, Georgeanna, Mary, Eliza, Harriet, Caroline, and Charles. They had lived in Boston until Mr. Woolsey's death in 1840 when they moved to New York City. The Woolseys were an affluent, influential family with many highly place connections. They were all abolitionists, including Mrs. Woolsey who was from a slave holding family in Alexandria, Virginia.

Georgy explained the early war efforts in New York City:

> On April 25th, 1861, the first steps were taken by fifty or sixty New York women towards organizing systematic work for the sick and wounded.

Central Office of the U.S. Sanitary Commission, 244 F Street, Washington, D.C.
(MOLLUS)

From this "Woman's Central Association of Relief" together with Boards of Physicians and Surgeons proposing to furnish hospital supplies in aid of the army, came the first suggestion to the Department of War at Washington that a "mixed commission of civilians, medical men and military officer" be appointed, charged with the duty of organizing and directing the benevolence of the people towards the army.

As the result of this petition the great United States Sanitary Commission, was, on the 13th of June, 1861, duly appointed by Simon Cameron Secretary of War, with the signature and approval of President Lincoln.

While retaining its independence, the Woman's Central Association became at its own instance an auxiliary branch of the commission, and other branches sprung up all over the northern states.

The headquarters of the commission were in Washington, where also was stationed Mr. Frederick Law Olmstead, its life and soul. With its work we, as a family, were associated from the beginning.[22]

As part of their excellent work, the Woman's Central Relief Association organized a nursing staff for the army, selecting one hundred women and sending them to the various hospitals in New York City for such drill as could be secured in a few weeks, through the kindness of the attending staff. The Sanitary Commission undertook to secure recognition for these women from the War Department with the pay of privates; and they were sent on to the army hospitals on requisition from Miss Dix and others, as needed.[23]

All the family members worked at home sewing clothes, making lint and bandages, or collecting supplies, all for the Sanitary Commission. "We women regretfully 'sit at home with ease' and only appease ourselves by doing the little we can with sewing machines and patent bandage-rollers. Georgy, Miss Sarah Woolsey [a cousin] and half a dozen other friends earnestly wish to join the Nurse Corps, but are under the required age. The rules are stringent, no doubt wisely so, and society just now presents the unprecedented spectacle of many women trying to make it believed that they are over thirty!"[24]

But Georgy overcame opposition from the Nursing Corps and from her family. A sister wrote: "Georgy had fairly begun at the hospital—the City Hospital on Broadway—but as she has requested me not to 'discuss her' with anybody I had better leave her to tell her own story. She and Mrs. Trotter go daily at twelve o'clock, and yesterday, Mother tells me, they went before breakfast beside, at 6 a.m. Thinks this, with her other activities, are too much for Georgy."[25]

Georgy explained:

It was hard work getting myself acceptable and accepted. What with people at home, saying "Goodness me! a nurse!" "All nonsense!" "Such a fly-away!" and what with the requisites insisted upon by the grave committees, I came near losing my opportunity.

First, one must be just so old, and no older, have eyes and nose and mouth expressing just such traits, and no others; must be willing to scrub floors, if necessary, etc. etc. finally, however, by dint of taking the flowers out of my bonnet and the flounce off my dress; by toning down, or toning up, according to the emergency, I succeeded in getting myself looked upon with mitigated disapprobation, and was at last sat upon by the committee and passed over to the Examining Board. The Board was good to me. It has to decide upon my physical qualifications; and so, having asked me who my grandfather was, and whether I had had the measles, it blandly put my name down, leaving a blank, inadvertently, where the age should have been, and I was launched, with about twenty other neophytes, into a career of philanthropy more or less confused.

Then began the serious business. Armed with a blue ticket, [an authorization] I presented myself with the others at the door of the hospital and was admitted for instruction. "Follow me," said our guide,

Nurses destined for service with the Army visiting the New York city hospital in August 1861.
(*Frank Leslie's Illustrated Newspaper*)

345

and we followed in procession. "This will be your ward; you will remain here under so and so, and learn what you can; and this, yours; and this, *yours*." That was *mine*! I shall never forget the hopeless state of my mind at this exact point. To be left standing in the middle of a long ward, full of beds, full of sick men—it was appalling! I seized another nurse, and refused to be abandoned. So they took pity, and we two remained, to use our eyes and time to the advantage of the Army of the Potomac which was-to-be. We took off our bonnets and went to work. Such a month as we had of it, walking round from room to room, learning what we could—really learning something in the end, till finally, what with writing down everything we saw, and making elaborate sketches of all kinds of bandages and the ways of applying them and what with bandaging everybody we met for practice, we at last made our "reverses" without a wrinkle; and at the end of the month were competent to any very small emergency, or very simple fracture.

In looking over my little note book of those first days at the New York Hospital I find it full of extracts from the lectures…at the bedside of the patients, and with sketches of four-tailed, six-tailed and many tailed bandages. I remember it gave me a little shock that first day in the ward to hear the young "house" say peremptorily "Nurse, basin!" I presented the basin promptly, and as promptly tumbled over in a faint at seeing a probe used for the first time. I came out from this ignominy to find that my associate-nurse was dashing my face with water from a tumbler which she dipped her fingers before offering it to me to drink from."[26]

Mrs. Woolsey wrote: Georgy is more earnest than ever about being a nurse for the soldiers. *I shall never consent* to this arrangement unless some of her own family go with her." One of the Woolsey daughters wrote: "She [Georgy] comes home ragged-looking but determined to 'stick it out…' It will not surprise us if by and by Georgy starts for the wars."[27]

Her mother's attitude prompted Georgy to write her sister Eliza in May of 1861. Eliza's husband, Joseph Howland, had joined the 16th New York.

…I hope you will take into serious consideration the small plan I suggested to you about being a nurse…Not that we have any idea of really going south now, no one will till the fall…Then if there is really a necessity for more nurses we shall send substitutes agreeing to pay their expenses,—unless the opposition in the family has come to an end, in which case, having tested our strength and endurance a little in this training, we shall be very glad to carry out our plan and go…don't say a word to anybody about our being at the Hospital; I don't want to have to fight my way all through the course, and be badgered by the connection generally, besides giving a strict account of myself at home.[28]

By June Georgy and her sister Eliza prepared to leave for Washington, D.C. Georgy fixed up what she believed would suit as a hospital nurse's costume. "I have *two* grey cottonish cross-grained shirts, and a Zouave jacket giving free motion to the arms—so the skirts can be, one of them, always in the wash…Four white aprons with waists and large pockets; two stick-out and washable petticoats to take the place of a hoop, and a nice long flannel dressing-gown, which one may put on in a hurry and fly out in, if the city is bombarded, or 'anything else.'" She also made up a trunk of things for the sick and obtained a "small camp cooking affair."[29]

In Washington the sisters went to a reception at the White House and shook Lincoln's hand plus Secretary of State William Seward who "gave us welcome with the remark that 'the fewer women there were the better.'"[30]

Eliza Woolsey Howland, Goergy's sister, had a husband in the army. The sisters went off to war together adhering to the wishes of the family that none of the family go alone.

(MOLLUS)

The sisters reported to Miss Dix:

> Miss Dix received us kindly and gave us a good deal of information about the hospitals, and this morning we went out to the Georgetown Hospital to see for ourselves.[31] [The Woolseys were attached to a tent hospital in Alexandria, which was on part of their Southern ancestors' land. Both Mrs. Woolsey and Georgy commented on the irony in their letters:] ...[H]ow strange to me that poor Old Alexandria, where all my eleven brothers and sisters were born, and where my father and mother and relatives lie buried, should be the scene of such warfare—the camping ground of my children under such circumstance! You must have been very near the graves of your grandparents....[32] It was such a pretty spot, our camp in a valley in Virginia—the hillside, covered with white tents, sloping to a green meadow and a clear bright little river. The meadow was part of my great-great-aunt's farm years ago, and in the magnolia-bordered stream my grandfather's children had fished and paddled. Now, we, two generations afterwards, had come back and pitched our tents in the old wheat fields, and made ready for war, and there were no magnolia blossoms any more.[33]

Here Georgy and Eliza found sick men in a shanty behind their "headquarters." "There we found them, one day, wretched and neglected, and 'most improperly' at once adopted them as our own. We asked no one's permission, but went to work; had the house cleaned from top to bottom; shelves put up and sacks filled with straw; then we prescribed the diet and fed them just as we pleased. All this was a shocking breach of propriety, and I have no doubt the surgeon of the regiment was somewhere behind a fence, white with rage."[34]

The nurses were required to take an oath of allegiance and to secure passes at all times. Georgy met with hostility from all corners. She wrote:

> No one knows, who did not watch the thing from the beginning, how much opposition, how much ill-will, how much unfeeling want of thought, these women nurses endured. Hardly a surgeon whom I can think of, received or treated them with even common courtesy. Government had decided that women would be employed, and that the army surgeons—unable, therefore, to close the hospitals against them—determined to make their lives, so unbearable that they should be forced in self-defense to leave. It seemed a matter of cool calculation, just how much ill-mannered opposition would be requisite to break up the system...These annoyances could not have been endured by the nurses but for the knowledge that they were pioneers, who were, if possible, to

gain standing ground for others,—who must create the position they wished to occupy. This, and the infinite satisfaction of seeing from day to day sick and dying men comforted in their weary and dark hours, comforted as they never would have been but for these brave women, was enough to carry them through all and even more than they endured...At last, the wall against which they were to break, began to totter....[35]

After the First Bull Run [July 21, 1861] Georgy was ordered by a surgeon and Miss Dix out of a hospital, never to return for the sin of fanning a man without permission. "We have had an encounter with Miss Dix—that is rather the way to express it. Splendid as her career has been, she would succeed better with more graciousness of manner. However, we brought her to terms, and shall get along better."[36]

One sister at home wrote this advice, which could well have been the Woolsey family motto: "Whatever you do, go in and win. Outflank the Dix by any and every means in your power..."[37] It was this attitude that eventually brought about the mandate that Chaplains be assigned posts in all military hospitals. Many nurses had complained about this lack, but none louder than the influential Woolseys.

Georgy and Eliza nursed around D.C. and Alexandria until April 1862 when they were asked to join "the floating hospital service" and take the *Daniel Webster* down to the Peninsula under the auspices of the Sanitary Commission. Charley accepted a clerkship, then purser, on the *Webster* at this time. Their family worried about them: "...it seems to me a very trying position for you; you will work yourselves sick..."[38] "...it is rather a perilous position for the girls. It is no longer *visiting*, but *living*, in an atmosphere of infection, day and night, typhoid, rubeola [*sic*], gangrene, and what not. They will be in for anything going...[but] what an excellent thing to have these boats systematically provided, and to have *ladies* on board. It will go far to humanize the horrid vehicles. Heavy reproaches belong *somewhere* for the want of foresight and humanity in the government arrangements of the kind..."[39]

After the battle of Fair Oaks [May 31, 1862], they established a shore kitchen at White House Landing. Georgy described this base on the Pamunkey: "...a modern cottage if ever 'white' now drabbed over, standing where the early home of Mrs. Washington stood...an unpretending place, with old trees shading the cottage, a green lawn sloping to the river, and an old-time garden full of roses. The house has been quite emptied, but there are pieces of quaint furniture, brass fire-dogs etc.; and just inside the door this notice is posted: 'Northern soldiers who profess to reverence the name of Washington, forbear to desecrate the home of his early married life, the property of his wife, and now the home of his descendants. (Signed) A granddaughter of Mrs. Washington.'"[40] Later, expecting an attack: "All night the wood choppers were at work cutting down the woods at the White House to give the gunboats a chance to command the land beyond, and just now as we passed, the banks were shorn and the pretty little place laid bare."[41] Though later there was no attack, White House was abandoned and the stores burned. Later during the war the house itself was burned down.

The Woolseys worked in the White House kitchen and on the transport boats getting men ready to be shipped north. Like many of the other nurses who worked on the transports, Georgy was appalled at the quality of care provided by the government for the wounded. "Without exception, the Government boats so far have been inadequately provisioned, wretchedly officered, and in a general state of confusion...Our government boat, which had been lying here waiting for wounded for a fortnight, would have left this morning, crowded with suffering men, without food (except hardtack), but for the commission; without a cup, or a basin, or a lemon, or a particle of lint, or bandages, or old linen, without clear water for bathing, without an ounce of beef, though their official report had been to the Commission that they were 'all ready'...We fed from our kitchen 600 men for two days on two of these Government 'all ready' boats."[42]

It was during this summer that the well-known nurse's garment, the "Agnew" came into being. Eliza explained: "The red flannel shirts of the Garibaldian troops used to be called the Garibaldis when adopted as part of a lady's outfit, after the Italian battles. When Dr. C.R. Agnew came down to the front in a delightful black and white flannel shirt, the eye of the shabby-looking G. [Georgy] was fastened upon it, and she made bold, cut off from all supplies as she was, to say to the departing doctor, '*Please* give me your shirt for my own wear.' He did, and from that time we wore 'Agnews.'"[43]

Eliza left the service that summer when her husband was wounded. Charley and Georgy came home about mid July. From there, Georgy, sister Jane, and cousin Sarah went to work at the Portsmouth Grove Hospital in Newport, Rhode Island at the request of the head nurse: "I want to point out to you that no ladies have ever *been allowed* to come to a *U.S. General Hospital* in this way—much less warmly requested, and thanked, and confided in, as *we are*…it is General Hammond's first cordial reception and experiment of ladies in hospital, and is in consequence, as he told me, of the grateful sense he had of what we did at White House…"[44]

They were at Portsmouth for five months until small pox broke out and their families ordered them home. The next time the Woolseys served was not until Gettysburg. After Mrs. Woolsey returned to New York and Georgy to the hospitals at Fairfax, they were contacted to return to Gettysburg. Georgy wrote her future husband: "The authorities want us to go back again, and look after the special diet in the new and fine General Hospital for 3000 men, too sick to be moved. We can't do so, as Jane and I have promised to spend the winter at Point Lookout in the Hammond Hospital. Look with respect upon your correspondent; she is at the head of the Protestant half of the women's department of that hospital. The Sisters run half the wards, and I expect to have fun with their Lady Superior and to wheedle her out of all her secrets, and get myself invited out to tea. Why shouldn't she and I compare notes on the proper way to make soup? I will call her 'Sister,' and agree to eat oysters on Friday,—(they are particularly fine on the Maryland shore.)"[45]

Mrs. Woolsey wanted very much to return to Gettysburg. She had kept a notebook of her patients which she treasured. One daughter wrote of her: "She has many a memento of that strange battle—one, of a rebel lieutenant who died in her care; and a score of palmetto buttons from rebel coats—dirty but grateful, poor wretches…"[46] When Georgy and Jane left for Point Lookout, Georgy consoled her mother in a letter that contained the last comment on any objections to nursing soldiers. "No wonder you regret Gettysburg. You will be gladder all the time that you went there and did what you did; and you will be ready to give me great praise, I hope, when I tell you that I have given up all idea of going back there, and have accepted in place of it Mrs. Gibbons' offer of the position she is giving up at Point Lookout Hospital…After the intense satisfaction you have experienced at Gettysburg, you cannot, my dear and patriotic Mamma, be otherwise than delighted at the prospect before us, while you must regret that I cannot also pull the special diet of Gettysburg through."[47]

Mrs. Woolsey contented herself with visiting a military hospital while she and other family members retired to Brattleboro, Vermont for a rest. One of her daughters remembered her there: "The Brattleboro

Hammond Hospital at Point Lookout, Maryland.
(Library of Congress)

Hospital was full of returned soldiers, and Mother, who was longing for Gettysburg, took a little consolation in visits there." Here she met a former patient from Gettysburg. "One man was almost convulsed at seeing Mother, and, with tears, would hardly let her hand go, 'I knew you, ma'am, the minute you came in. You were at Gettysburg, and were the first one that dressed my arm.' And there the poor arm still lay, useless and swollen, and constant streams of cold water necessary to keep down inflammation."[48]

Georgy did not stay long at Point Lookout. "Women were only recognized, in connection with the *regular army* service, as washerwomen, and were so entered on the payrolls, and detailed to the nursing department when needed. As Point Lookout was a regular army hospital, we were obliged by army regulations to be mustered in, and paid $12.00 a month. [The Woolseys donated their pay to the hospital fund.] But we were hardly well established and in good working condition, when the following general orders were received and issued by the Surgeon-in-charge. The Point became a camp for rebel prisoners, and our connection with it ceased. [The order was dated Sept. 26th that] 'seven hundred wounded prisoners from Chester, Pa.' were coming. 'Upon arrival you will discharge the female nurses (both of Miss Dix's and Miss Gibbons' selection) reserving only one suitable person in low-diet kitchen and one in linen room.'"[49]

From Point Lookout Georgy and Jane went to nurse at the Fairfax Theological Seminary hospital grounds in Virginia. Here they nursed Charley who had since joined the 164th New York and had the opportunity of being a staff officer for the successive commanding generals of the Army of the Potomac. He had developed inflammatory rheumatism. Georgy brought him home to New York. He returned to the army as soon as possible and served the rest of the war.

Georgy wrote: "It was an understood thing with the Sanitary Commission and myself (G.) that I was to be called on at any time for hospital service at the front; and immediately after these late battles (May 12th [1864]) the summons came—a courier arriving at the Fairfax Seminary Hospital to summon me. I left at once via boat down the Potomac for Fredericksburg."[50] This experience was worse than anything she had seen before. In one hurried letter she scribbled: "Hard work, dirt and death everywhere."[51]

In a letter from Fredericksburg dated May 15: "Mrs. Barlow and I at Fredericksburg-town full of badly wounded...This a.m. we have started a diet-kitchen...The hospitals are delighted to have ladies come right in and feed the sick; we can go in any where...We are required to show reason for being here, or go to the guard house. I have a pass from the Surgeon General as 'volunteer nurse.'"[52]

Georgy and Jane were called home in late May when their sister Mary died. Georgy stayed home until the late summer when she answered the request to nurse at the new military hospital in Beverly, New Jersey, where conditions were very bad. "Their experience has been new and very trying—more wearing, Georgy says than anything she has gone through before, because of the mental anxiety to provide for so many wounded men without the means to do it, and without authority to *compel* the means from the hands of dishonest stewards and indifferent doctors."[53]

Georgy wrote in September of 1864: "This set of regulations was promulgated this morning regarding 'female nurses'; 'All deliberations, discussions, and remarks having the object of expressing comparative praise, or censure, of the medical officers of this hospital, or their individual course or conduct, are positively prohibited!' The provision against our 'praise' is truly judicious...We cannot keep our men alive; eleven of them have died in three days."[54]

"We had a good natured laugh over a visit from Miss Dix, who, poor old lady, kept up the fiction of appointing all the army nurses. She descended upon Beverly for this purpose, when, finding us already established without consultation with her, she served this printed assignment to duty—not on me only, but on [another nurse] whom she had never spoken to and knew nothing about!"[55]

"The Beverly Hospital was perhaps the worst one claiming to be a Regular Army establishment that I ever went into, and the conditions exasperating, because it was in the midst of a land of plenty."[56] This would be Georgy's last assignment.

Right after the war the Woolseys traveled to Richmond to visit the conquered city and then on to D.C. for the grand reviews. For the first time since the war started Georgy became ill of an unspecified ailment. "I think the last four years is the matter with her. It would not be human that she could endure, without some ill effects, the constant exposure and trials of that time..."[57]

Members of the Woolsey family turned to philanthropic endeavors after the war. On June 7, 1866, Georgy married Dr. Francis Bacon, whom she had known and corresponded with during the war. He was a professor of surgery at Yale Medical School. They moved to New Haven, and the couple were the principle founders of the Connecticut Training School for Nurses. Georgy wrote the *Hand Book of Nursing for Family and General Use* in 1879 and spent the rest of her life working through various agencies for people on the lowest rungs of society; children, mentally ill, and prisoners. She died in 1906 and is buried in the Grove Street Cemetery in New Haven. Mrs. Woolsey died in 1874 and is believed to have been buried in the family plot near Glen Cove, Long Island.

Clarissa F. Jones

Independent Pennsylvania Nurse

"...in receiving my services, during the Civil War, voluntarily given to my country and without egotism I say it was as good as service and as readily given as that of any other women in the employ of the government...." [1]

The Christian Commission in Phila. sent no females to the Battlefields, when I applied to Mr. Geo. H. Stuart for a Pass as Nurse to go to Gettysburg, he directed me to Mr. G. S. Griffith [Chairman of the Christian Commission] in Baltimore...so furnished with letters to that gentleman I went with my baggage consisting of 8 barrels of the finest Drugs from the druggists of Phila., my trunk and a large basket. Arriving early in the morning I was most cordially received and started for Gettysburg...Mr. Griffith very promptly accepted my services and directly obtained transportation for me, sending me to the Second Army Corps Hospital with a letter to Mrs. and Miss Moore of Baltimore who were already at work.

My barrels arrived the next morning, were seized by the Court Martial [*sic*] and contents distributed. The people had carelessly read Miss C. F. Jones the name of a noted rebel woman *Mrs. C. F. Jones* instead of Miss C. F. Jones. I got across the Street quickly, sat down upon my trunk which a black man was about to get into with a hatchet. I still sat there and he finally report[ed] me to the C.M.[2] who came down and I explained to him that this was my trunk. I told him those empty barrels were also mine. He examined and found the mistake apologized etc.

[Clarissa arrived at the Second Corps Hospital.]...I worked among those wounded men. Most of them our boys and the rest of Picketts Brigade [Division]. When the wheat field of 14 acres was garnered the Gov. with all speed rushed cots and tents and the men were carried across the creek (Rock) and the blues on the right and the greys on the left. There were plenty of nurses but when all the Blues were furnished with nurses the rest fled to Gettysburg and upon a call for volunteers

Clarissa Jones
USAMHI

355

A Christian Commission nurse on the field.
(Virginia State Library)

I was the only one to offer myself...Dr. Dwinell Sur-in-chg asked me to take charge of the Rebel wounded, whose tents were on one side of the fourteen acre field.

I never heard one word out of the way...I was a woman alone, and I appealed to them. I[t] would not have been safe for any man to say a rough word to me. I will never forget my first case. He was a young fellow, lying on a rock, and suffering intensely from lockjaw. Beside him was his brother, nursing and caring for him. The anxious brother did not even have a handkerchief; he was bathing the boy's wounds with a piece of paper. I was burdened with handkerchiefs at the time, so I gave the rebel a few, and my, he was so glad to get them. I stayed with him some time, bandaged his wounds and did what I could for him, and his brother told me his story. Their name was Presgraves[3] and they lived on the James River. He said that he had two other brothers in the battle, and he feared they had both been killed. When he saw his brother fall, he allowed himself to be taken prisoner, purposely, so that he could be with him. When he told this much of the story, he looked up at me with his big tear-filled eyes, for he knew his brother was going to die. "How am I going back to my father and tell him of this, and that, in all probability, his other two boys have been killed in this same battle? I am afraid that I am the only one left. My poor father! He was more like a big brother to us and you don't know how much we loved him." The tears came to my own eyes. I did everything I possibly could do for that poor boy. He was affectionate to his brother and waited on him night and day. Four days later the poor young fellow died. His brother asked if he could not go into Gettysburg and buy a pine coffin, for he intended to come back after the war and bring the body home. He was given permission and, instead of being buried in a blanket, as was the case with the great majority, this one boy had a pine coffin. Major Holstein and his wife read the burial service each day over the long stretch of dead, and Mrs. Moore and I always accompanied them. But at this particular time, Major Holstein did not have his glasses with him, and could not read without them. They were preparing to bury the boy without any service. As soon as the brother realized this, he sat on a log and cried as though his heart would break. Finally he regained his composure and, looking up, said; "Is there not somebody who will say a word over my brother? Must I go home and say that he was buried like a dog, without even a prayer for him?" Miss Moore and I could not resist this appeal. Major Holstein let us have his book, and we read the burial service. We all felt intensely sorry for this poor boy, he was so much affected by his loss. He told us that he was going to escape—told us how he was going to do it and how he was going back to his father. We all knew about it, but we said nothing. We let him go. So, of course, we were not surprised when we heard that he was missing; but no one told on the poor fellow or what course he had taken.

We had a nephew of Jefferson Davis in our camp. Poor fellow, he suffered terribly. A special chair was rigged up for him because his back was injured; but he begged so hard to be taken out of it that the doctor finally consented. But no matter in what position he was placed, he was not satisfied. When the orders came to take the men who were not dying to Camp Letterman, the Union men had considerable trouble in lifting him into the wagon, he suffered so intensely. Finally, one gruff soldier said, "That's what you get for fighting against us." But the poor fellow answered in a kindly tone of voice, "I fought you only once, and I'll never fight again. And remember, my dear man, the Lord says that you must forgive, if they fight seventy times seven." That was the last we ever saw or heard of him.

After the wounded were moved to the wheatfield, four men from the Sanitary Commission went among the 600 men every night, singing their favorite hymns. I always went with them and led the singing...For the Union men we sang "Sweet Hour of Prayer." But the Confederates wanted the old plantation hymn. Every night, when we asked, "What will it be tonight, boys?" the answer always was "Oh, Sing to Me of Heaven." It was a beautiful hymn and the first stanza began, "Oh, sing to me of heaven, when I am called to die." The chorus went: "There'll be no more sorrow there, in Heaven above where all is love, there'll be no more sorrow there."

The Union men could not understand my devotion to the Confederates, and finally I noticed among them a coldness to me. I asked them what was the trouble, and one of them said: "Miss Jones, where are you from?" I told them

I was from Philadelphia. "Are you a rebel sympathizer?" another asked. I answered most decidedly no. And then I had a heart to heart talk with them, and told them of the sufferings of the rebels and how desperately they needed the affectionate care of a woman, just as much as they did. The boys soon saw the other side, and agreed with me. "That's right, Miss Jones, you do all you can for those Johnnies; they're not such a bad sort, after all." We became better friends after that.

I did not realize at the time what a dreadful thing this battle was, for when one is busy trying to abate a fire she hasn't time to think what the consequences will be. It is those who are in the distance who can see better. When the fire is over everything comes to us. So it was with the Gettysburg battle. I was too much occupied caring for those poor fellows to think how terrible it really was, and how much the men had suffered. When the trouble was over everything came to me.[4]

...[We] remained there till the Camp Hospitals were consolidated....

Clarissa Jones was 28 years old when the war broke out. She taught at the Rittenhouse Grammar School in Germantown, Pennsylvania and was the sole support of her widowed mother. Clarissa nursed during the summers and on school vacations.

I did not register as a nurse, because being the breadwinner of the family I could not give my entire time to Hospital work. From the beginning to the close of the war I gave my best energies to the service of my country...I never received pay in any form for services rendered thru the war.

In 1861 I was a member of a class of women receiving instruction from a Professor who was coaching Students for their exam, as doctors. The Professor agreed to extend to a class of women who desired to become nurses a like benefit, so I was better fitted to go to the field than most women...[In 1861 she] Served as volunteer in Philadelphia Hospitals till December when in company with Miss Maria McClelland I visited the camps around Washington, notably Camp Pierrepont, distributing stores, instructing the soldier nurses in the care of the sick, preparing food for them and finding the actual needs of the Camp Hospital. I had previously forwarded supplies to Dr. Read surgeon-in-charge.

[In 1862]...[I] served as volunteer in Phila. Hospital till July when I was received on board [the] Steamer State of Maine. First trip we carried exchanged Rebel prisoners to Aiken Landing and carried back our own soldiers who had been exchanged.

Then transporting sick from Camps to Northern Hospitals. Remained on board till the Steamer went out of commission as a Hospital boat.

At this time Dr. H.L.W. Burrett, Surgeon in Charge wrote:

Miss Clara F. Jones has been acting as volunteer nurse on board our steamer for the last month and I am happy to say has satisfied me in every respect of eminent capacity for that position.

Miss Jones is a lady of cultivated and refined deportment as well as great force of character. Her tender care and humanity toward the sick and suffering and her constant attention to them is remembered by all and will not soon be forgotten.

[In August she] hastened to Phila. for supplies awaiting me, then to Washington to the Surgoen Genls office and...I went to the War Dept., presented my credentials and asked for a pass to go to Alexandria, Va. There I learned that Miss Dix had been appointed to take the responsibility of choosing the nurses. I was directed by the Sec. of the War Department to come back if Miss Dix refused me. Miss Dix had no use for me...[she] objected to me on accounts of my not being able to engage in Hospital work for an indefinite time...and I went back to the War Dept. The gentleman was writing me the desired document when Miss Dix came in, she immediately entered into a conversation and the gentleman told her she was wrong in ignoring a letter written by the Mayor of Phila. and the credentials I had. She finally accepted me. [I] passed...by Gov. boat to Alex. Sept. 6th. While in Phila. I had obtained leave of absence [from her teaching job] till Oct. 1st, which was afterward extended to Nov. 1st.

On board the boat to Alexandria I was introduced to Mr. Stephen Shinn the President of the Union League of Alex. who said that any one living in Alex. on Friday night (this was Saturday) would never forget it. All night long the wounded men who had lain upon the ground of the battlefields of Bull Run [Aug. 29 & 30, 1862] and Chantilly [Sept. 1] were dragged thru the streets and their groans were fearful! Dr. Leon Hammond had charge of the Baptist Church Hospital and the Lyceum that were on opposite sides of the same St. Dr. Somers had charge of a Division. He visited us almost daily. I had been at the Lyceum for about a week and [he] complimented me in my management of the work I had undertaken, the good sanitary conditions and the satisfactory deposition of my patients. He said, "You have not registered." I replied, "No, Doctor." He continued, "Why you will get no pay unless you do." I told him I was the only support of my mother and she was a widow. I could not fulfill the conditions required to become a contract nurse, that I was willing and anxious to serve my country to the best of my ability. I gave the whole of my vacations to nurse the sick and wounded and spent every hour of my time not required by my school duties...My

The Steamer *State of Maine*.
(MOLLUS)

bed while at the Lyceum was on the bare floor in a passage leading from the floor of the assembly room to the platform…I left Lyceum Military Hospital Oct. 15th 1862 having served 6 wks, after being accepted by Miss Dix. I was so ill [fever] that the Surgeon in charge at Alexandria would have sent me to a private Hospital, but I insisted upon going home. I soon became convalescent and went to my school. At Thanksgiving I went back to Lyceum with a dinner sent to the boys I had nursed by the parents of the girls in my school. It was a sumptuous repast; I divided my supplies among three (3) Hospitals.

Miss Jones returned to her school that year and in the summer of 1863 did hospital work in Germantown until July when she left for Gettysburg.

…After leaving Gettysburg, Mrs. Moore, her daughter and I went to Baltimore and Washington to replenish our stock, then commenced the hardest task of getting a Pass to the Front. This I achieved and we went on to Rappahannock Station where our army was resting. We remained there until Sept. 1st when my school duties called me home.

Again in 1863 Winter Quarters at Rappahannock Station and Brandy Station I carried supplies, medical and comfort. At Rap—I could not stop to unload because, while my barrels and boxes were on the floor of the car, they were covered by coffins that were to be delivered at Brandy Station from the platform of my car, I told the boys of the situation and promised to return as soon as possible. Arriving at B. Station I was

The Lyceum Hall Hospital had a capacity of 80 beds.
(Miller's *Photographic History of the Civil War*)

most cordially entertained in an almost empty house, and next morning hunted up our boys one of whom got a wagon and drove me to the car and took all the parcels that were for their regiments. And in the evening I started for Bristow Station where I was to be met by the 1st Pa. Reserves.

By mistake of the Engineer of the train I was carried a mile past it and I was left standing on the elevated track alone—After many trains passed I was able to make myself known to the man attending the watering tank over Broad Run and he helped me across the ice covered sleeper [crosstie] to safety…

My journey to and from was an eventful one. I went entirely alone, walked miles to find the Camps. The night of my arrival the mud was so deep that I could hardly pull my feet out of the mud which was nearly knee deep. I wore high boots. The next morning everything was frozen. I was awakened by hearing the noise of chopping ice from around the mules whose legs were imbedded in solid ice.

After leaving the stores and xmas cheer there I returned to Rappahannock Station and distributed the rest.

Miss Jones' field duties ended abruptly: "My sister, dying in 1864, my trips to the front were discontinued, as She left me her family of three small children whose welfare prevented me leaving home.[5] I however continued collecting and forwarding hospital stores till the close of the war."

In December of 1872 Clarissa married John H. Dye, a widower with four children thus she was the mother to seven children. John Dye had served for a short time in the army as a lieutenant in Co. G, 33rd Pennsylvania. Ironically, though Clarissa Jones Dye was the Chairman of the Pension Committee for the Association of Army Nurses of the Civil War, she submitted several times for a nurse's pension but was consistently denied. The 1920 census shows Clarissa at age 87, John having died decades before. Her sister's children remained living with her into their sixties. Clarissa Jones Dye is believed to be buried in Mt. Moriah cemetery, Philadelphia. The cemetery has been abandoned and the records are unavailable.

The shell of the Rittenhouse School. Clarissa taught at the Rittenhouse Grammar School in Germantown, nursing during the summers and on school vacations.
(Author's collection)

Annie Bell

Pennsylvania Nurse

"I was not old enough to go at first under Miss Dix, but she knew me well and gave me the hospital reference to assist me in my work at Nashville…through my writings I collected large stores for the soldiers—both east and west."[1]

Very little of Annie Bell's life or war experiences can be told except for the vital statistics. She was born on April 9, 1839 at Elizabeth Furnace in Blair County, Pennsylvania. Her father was an ironmaster there. Her parents, Martin and Eliza, had four daughters as of 1860: Anna (Annie) age 21, Clarra age 14, Margaret age 12, and Elizabeth age 8.

Annie enrolled at Harpers Ferry on December 8, 1862 and "served about one year volunteer as a nurse in U.S. Hospitals at Harpers Ferry, Acgnia [*sic*] Creek, 12th Corp hospital after Chancellorsville and Gettysburg—& Nashville."[2] The Bureau of Pensions stated she enlisted as a nurse on May 27, 1863, making her a volunteer for about six months. At enlistment her complexion was fair, eyes gray, and hair light.

Did she march up with the army to witness the battle at Gettysburg? Was she one of the nurses who accompanied the wounded to Washington and then came on to the battlefield, or did she arrive from another place such as her home or military hospital? There is no record that specifies her movements. Perhaps she knew some of the men in the 5th U.S. Artillery, Battery K, in the XII Corps, some of whom were from Blair County.

Miss Bell could have been at Gettysburg for a very short time or as long as two months. Perhaps she left as many of the other ladies did when the men were moved to Camp Letterman in the beginning of August.

The 12th Corps hospital was on the George Bushman farm west of Rock Creek and today is visible from Hospital Road. It was described as "a farm house and large barn…occupied by wounded, but the great body of them were under hospital tents."[3] It may have been in one of these tents that Annie's photograph was taken. The photograph is com-

Nurse Annie Bell during the war.
(MOLLUS)

monly called upon as an example of a nurse in action and was used in the late 20th century as a stamp although she was misidentified.

In September of 1863 Annie Bell was present at Hospital No. 1 in Nashville and later in Hospital No. 8, serving in both as Chief Matron. At Nashville Annie met George Stubbs, a doctor from Maine, who was a contract surgeon in the hospitals at Nashville. Miss Bell was honorably discharged in 1865 [no date] and married Dr. Stubbs at her father's house on September 14, 1865. George, however, was not discharged until November 1865. Through their married life the couple lived in Cincinnati, Philadelphia, and finally settled in Merion, Pennsylvania. They had four children: Martin Bell in 1866, Julia Eastman in 1870, Claribel in 1872 and Ethel in 1880.

In 1893 Annie applied for and received a nurse's pension of $12 per month. George applied for a pension in 1904 but did not receive it until 1907. He also was awarded $12 a month. In 1909 Dr. Stubbs died and was buried in Northwood Cemetery in Philadelphia. Annie Bell Stubbs died on January 26, 1916 and is buried in lot 473, the Rockland Section of West Laurel Hill Cemetery, Lower Merion Township, Pennsylvania. Her grave had no marker until 1996 when she became the second woman so honored by the Headstone Project.

Mrs. Annie Bell Stubbs
later in life.
(MOLLUS)

Annie Bell Stubb's headstone.
(Author's collection)

The color guard at the dedication of Annie Bell's new headstone.
(Author's collection)

Emily Bliss Souder

Independent Pennsylvania Nurse

*"As the days passed on we received continued accounts of
the suffering and distress among our noble soldiers and with
three other ladies, [I] decided to visit Gettysburg to aid in
the great work there."[1]*

Emily Souder's book, *Leaves from the Battlefield of Gettysburg*,
consists of letters she had sent home while nursing on the field. She
arrived the night of July 14th. Her description of the journey to
Gettysburg showed that even after 11 days, confusion reigned and want
of food and supplies was still very much present. Emily arrived at
Gettysburg via Baltimore. She wrote from Hanover Junction [PA] the
afternoon of the 14th:

> We left Baltimore at half-past seven this morning and have been
> waiting here till we are almost *cooked*,—the only word that gives an
> idea of our discomfort. We understand that we are to leave at six o'clock.
> The immense amount of government supplies and hospital stores which
> are being sent forward and the trains of wounded soldiers coming from
> Gettysburg, make the transportation of passengers inconvenient and
> uncomfortable to the last degree. Two or three days ago, an open freight
> car was the only accommodation and in this the ladies slept, with the
> sky above them. A train of wounded soldiers passed down about an
> hour ago.[2]
>
> A car is stationed here, close to the railroad track, where four la-
> dies from Baltimore prepare lemonade, bread and butter, to refresh the
> men, beside pies, farina, etc.—"The Christian Commission Car." They
> have three stations on the way. We made a visit to this car and saw the
> ladies at work. Presently, a young man, a member of the Commission,
> came in with a market basket, filled with loaves of bread, which he had
> procured from farm-houses not very far distant. I bought a barrel of
> bread from a baker in Baltimore and could hardly restrain from adding
> this to the their store; but the accounts which we have received of the
> great necessity for bread in Gettysburg induced me to retain it, as the
> distance to this point is more easily passed over.
>
> A kind-hearted woman, by the wayside, has been baking sixty pies
> per day, the materials being furnished to her, —not a trifling service,
> with the thermometer at ninety degrees or more.

Wartime view of Hanover Junction.
(Library of Congress)

A gentleman belonging to the Sanitary Commission came next, with an anxious face, to inquire if the ladies "had any way to cook some meat?" The ice in the "provision car" had melted and he feared that the fresh meat would spoil, the heat was so great and there was so much delay on the road.

We see, at every step, the need for effort. Persons coming and going all agree that there is a great deal to be done…Boxes are piled up at this point, marked for the "Sisters of Charity." Adams Express seems the only reliable way of sending. If you can come yourself, you must keep your eyes on what you have in charge…It is in a manner impossible to get anyone to handle these things and on this account ladies who are alone have much trouble. I have a supply of paper and envelopes and can write letters without boxes and this also is much needed. A surgeon from Ohio, who is waiting for the Harrisburg train, says he…started from his home immediately after receiving tidings of the battle and walked twelve miles across the county to reach a railroad train, that he might arrive at Gettysburg as early as possible.

We were all disgusted with a young surgeon in the cars yesterday, who was ordered to report to Gettysburg without delay. He was thoroughly indifferent; said "he was not going to kill himself hunting transportation, he would go to Barnum's [hotel] and take it easy and go in the morning."[3]

367

We waited at the station [Hanover Junction] from eleven o'clock a.m. till two or three in the afternoon, the sun beaming down upon us with withering power, when we took our seats in the cars, thinking that we would not feel the heat more and would probably be more comfortable. We waited till past seven, the car crowded to suffocation; six Sisters of Charity with a priest, just opposite to us, going to nurse the sick; people looking for their dead, or hoping to find their wounded still living.[4]

[While Emily was waiting for the cars, she observed a squad of soldiers guarding a nearby road.] As we sat waiting in the car, hour after hour, several of them were sitting on the embankment, cleaning their muskets and singing "Who will care for mother now?" That picture will always rise up before my mental vision whenever I hear that song.[5]

...[W]e had scarcely started from thence, when the rain began to fall in torrents. Darkness came on. We seemed to have scarcely breathing space in the single car, closely packed with passengers, where there was no arrangement for light, except indeed an empty lantern which hung on one side of the car. Happily for us, I had put two or three candles in my carpet-bag, and the cheerful ray of light was gladly hailed. Long before we reached the town, the odors of the battle-field were plainly perceptible.[6]

The distance to Gettysburg from the Junction is but thirty miles but it was nearly eleven o'clock when we reached the hotel, to learn that there was no possible place for us, unless we would sit up in a parlor, where some forty men were to sleep in the adjoining room, separated by folding doors, each with a carpet-bag on the floor for a pillow.[7]

Mrs. Souder and her party found lodgings in a house in town, coincidentally next door and across the street from other Philadelphia women who she knew. The next morning Emily began the work she had left her husband and seven children to do.[8] "We were aroused from sleep very early by the sound of ambulances driving past on their way to the camps for the wounded, and also by the perpetually passing of wagons loaded with coffins, either going empty to the battle-fields, or returning with their sad freight...While we were waiting, as the ambulances passed on their way to the depot, we handed the poor soldiers a drink from the doorstep and when the boxes [their stores had just arrived] were safely housed, we got into an ambulance and rode to the hospital tents of the Second Corps."[9]

Long before the camps were reached, which lie some distance [about four and half miles] beyond the town, we see abounding evidence of the conflict, which was raging only two weeks ago…In Chambersburg Street [where Mary McAllister lived] still lie wrecked caisson and wagonwheels. The broken windows, the marks of bullets and cannon-balls…The churches are filled, and almost every house has one or more wounded in it…We were driven by a pleasant fellow from Vermont who told us interesting things about the battle-ground, which we crossed. We saw the rifle-pits, the dead horses, the shattered windows and the stone walls, all scattered and many soldiers' graves. But who shall describe the horrible atmosphere which meets us almost continually? Chloride of lime has been freely used in the broad streets of the town and to-day the hospital was much improved by the same means; but it is needful to close the eyes on the sights of horror and to shut the ears against sounds of anguish and to extinguish, as far as possible, the sense of smelling.[10]

The atmosphere is truly horrible, and camphor and cologne or smell-ing salts are prime necessities for most persons, certainly for the ladies. We think that diminutive bags of camphor, say an inch square, would be a great comfort to the soldiers, relieving them in some measure from the ever-present odors.[11]

The aspect of the camp hospital of the Second Army Corps is quite sufficient to fill the stoutest heart with dismay; long ranges of tents, in each one six to eight or ten men, who almost without exception have suffered amputation. It is the office of the ladies to prepare nourishing and stimulating food for these unfortunate brothers…We dispensed buckets of milk and brandy, besides sundry cups of tea, an unwonted luxury and broth made of beef jelly condensed, with many other ser-vices and a little chat occasionally with some poor fellow. I found a great many Maine boys; many from Wisconsin and Minnesota; scarcely one who had not lost an arm or a leg.[12]

[On her first day] we had scarcely entered the field of labor when some one came and begged me to see a young Mississippi lieutenant. A momentary conflict arose in my mind. "He is a rebel," I said, "and I had not felt as if I could do anything for a rebel." "I think he is a fine young man," was the answer, "and he is going to die." I could hesitate no longer, but signified my willingness to go. Lying on the ground in front of one of the large hospital tents, was a young man, whose face, as I looked at him, seemed that of one of my own kindred, the same blue eyes, brown hair, and light complexion…He was groaning in spirit, and suffering greatly, having been wounded in five places, and had also suffered amputation....[13] [Four days later when Lt. Seal of the 42nd Mississippi died, it was Emily who wrote his farewell letter to his wife.]

The sights and sounds are beyond description. There are hundreds of men who will never leave the battle-field alive and hundreds more who have "fought their last battle." Dead men are being carried out to be buried every hour of the day. They are laid to rest under a tree, the spot marked by a small strip or board or the lid of a box, with the name rudely cut with a pocket-knife or marked with a pencil by some kind-hearted comrade. Wrapped in a blanket, they are put in the ground till some relation or friend comes....A constant procession of coffins meets the eye; groups of men, standing in the fields, searching for the name of some friend or brother. The town has been filled with people on these mournful errands.[14]

The poor nurses were quite worn out with their wearisome days and wearisome nights, and many of the surgeons looked very much worn in the hard service they had performed. We were told, however, that the aspect of things was much improved from what it had been. The ladies did not get fairly to work in the way of cooking till the afternoon of our arrival, when their tents were set up a little aside from the camp and their stoves and stores arranged. We were very near to the

An amputation scene at Gettysburg.
(MOLLUS)

Christian Commission tent, and their supplies were always at our service, if anything was wanting which we had not…The amputation-table is plainly in view from our tents. I never trust myself to look toward it.[15] How grateful our soldiers are to the ladies for their labors of love, you can hardly imagine. You can see their eyes brighten, when we pause at the door of a tent to inquire how they are thriving…Almost every hour has its own experience to tell.[16]

…[A]ll day long we found the Union soldiers side by side with the rebels…The Union soldiers and the rebels, so long at variance, are here quite friendly. They have fought their last battle…how sorely stricken and wounded our noble soldiers are, and how grievously these rebel wounded are suffering and both lying side by side, like brothers.[17]

Death is very busy with these poor fellows on both sides. It seems hard for no kind voice to speak a word of cheer to the parting spirit and yet there are many laborers in the vineyard; but the work is great…the necessity of more help is terrible. The men dying all around us and there is no time to say more than a friendly word, as one is called from tent to tent and request to prepare "milk punch for eight men," or "cornstarch," or "tea," "a portion for seven and also for eight." What can we do, when these poor souls, who have just undergone amputation, require nourishing and stimulating food to keep the life in them at all? We cannot stop to talk with them. We can only labor assiduously with our hands…I provided myself before leaving home wit a large quantity of paper, stamps, etc. expecting to write many letters for the soldiers, but thus far, have not found time and many that were alive yesterday are gone to-day and several that we saw to-day, I fear we shall see no more forever.[18]

Two desperately wounded men begged for *ice*, with an earnestness of agonized entreaty which could brook no denial. I promised, if possible, to obtain it; but found that the surgeon had absolutely forbidden that the ice should be touched, as the lives of many men depended upon their having it. You may judge how painful it was to carry this message in lieu of the cooling morsel of which I hoped to be the bearer.[19]

The groans, the cries, the shrieks of anguish, are awful indeed to hear. We heard them all day in the field, and last night I buried my head in my pillow to shut out the sounds which reached us, from a church quite near, where the wounded are lying. We could only try to hear as though we heard not, for it requires strong effort to be able to attend to the various calls for aid…Few persons are able to remain here more than a week. The water has been very bad; the atmosphere shocking. I only wonder how we have born [*sic*] it; but the last few days it has been much more endurable.[20]

On July 18, Mrs. Souder wrote:

We are very busy, from seven in the morning till seven in the evening. Twelve poor souls passed yesterday to their final account, six Union soldiers and six rebels. We sleep in town, riding out in the morning and returning at night. Both going and returning, we pass the [National] Cemetery which must henceforth be so interesting to all loyal Americans, but we have not allowed ourselves time to enter the gateway...[Yesterday we allowed] ourselves a little space for taking an observation of a portion of our surroundings, walked a few yards from the border of the encampment, and visited the slaty [sic] ridge where our Union soldiers belonging to this corps are buried. We read the names with sad interest....We have not yet found time to visit any other corps hospital, we are so constantly engaged.... A perpetual procession of coffins is constantly passing to and fro, and so it has been ever since we have been here; strangers looking for their dead on every farm and under every tree. I have said to several who proposed the removal, "The Cemetery at Gettysburg is the most honorable burying place a soldier can have. Like Mount Vernon, it will be a place of pilgrimage for the nation."[21]

This is the first day [July 18] without rain since we came here. The camp ground is so wet and muddy that we can scarcely get on, even with the India rubbers. The cool wet weather has been extremely favorable, both for the men, who have almost all suffered amputation, and for the citizens also, as it washed off the ground and relieves the surface by absorption. There has been a great change since we came in this respect. This morning the ride to the camp was quite comfortable by comparison, except when we were passing those places where the dead horses poison the atmosphere. It seems strange that they are not destroyed, but by degrees they are being consumed by fire....[22]

On Thursday [July 23] the camp was changed to another location known as "the clover field," a change which was very needful on every account. The moving was a very serious matter. It was necessary to carry every man on a stretcher, about a third of a mile. The tents were taken down and moved beforehand. It was pitiful to see the faces of many of these men, who feared and dreaded to be moved, and yet exhibited a degree of fortitude which was truly wonderful....The hospital is now located on a beautiful ridge, open to sun and air, and forms a hollow square. The ladies tents are in a little hollow, among the trees. It is a lovely spot. A bright stream flows close to the encampment, and the water is good. The former encampment was shaded with forest trees, which prevented the sun and wind from exerting their purifying influences.[23]

On Tuesday, the 28th, Mrs. Souder recorded: "I have not been well enough for two or three days to go to the field. On Sunday, I was really sick all day and the greater part of yesterday. This morning I thought I would ride to the Seminary hospital and see what was wanted there…Some *ladies* from Baltimore made themselves a name and a fame, a few days since, by furnishing citizens' clothes for some rebels to flee in. They stole several horses, and made their escape, but most of them were retaken…It should be understood that there are many Southern sympathizers here…After leaving the Seminary, I paid a visit to the Sanitary Commission tent, near the railroad."[24]

On July 27th: "We learn this evening that the ambulances are all ordered to join the regiments to which they belong. At all events, the Second Corps is being moved to the General Hospital with all convenient dispatch. Dr. Duinelle said that the surgeons were wanted with their regiments, which made concentration necessary…The sick have been removed from several of the churches, and the process of purifying is going on very energetically. The third and Fifth Corps are being brought into the General Hospital, which is near the railroad. The twelfth corps is entirely removed; the Eleventh nearly so. The ambulances and litters are constantly passing through the town."[25]

Emily Bliss Souder served at Gettysburg for a little over two weeks and she was determined to return for the dedication of the National Cemetery in November: "I had felt as if I *must* be in Gettysburg whenever the ceremonies did take place."[26] On her trip she encountered great crowds of people of the same mind. The day after she arrived she toured the battlefield and visited the site of Camp Letterman which was "now occupied as a camping ground for the soldiers who have come hither to take part of the ceremonies."[27] Emily was glad to see a few familiar faces there.

That evening, November 18th, Mrs. Souder walked through the town. She described the excitement:

> The tranquility of the little town was, if not before, completely broken up…The churches were lighted and warmed for the reception of those who could not find quarters elsewhere. The streets were filled with crowds of people. A band was playing the national airs in front of the house where Mr. Lincoln was staying, and eager calls were made for "the President," who finally stood a few minutes on the doorstep, and in response to the wishes of the people, made a few characteristic remarks, promising to speak at some length the next day. Mr. Seward

The crowd at the dedication of the National Cemetery at
Gettysburg. Notice the Evergreen Cemetery gatehouse.
(MOLLUS)

"It was a magnificent sight. The long line of infantry with their
bayonets gleaming in the sunlight, the artillery, the distinguished
guests, the great multitude."
(GNMP)

was next called upon for a speech, and we were so near that we heard his remarks quite distinctly, as well as those of some of the other speakers. It was quite a new experience, you may be sure, and the whole time and circumstances were unlike anything we had known before.

Thursday, the 19th of November, dawned dull and cloudy, and a storm seemed threatening, but the shadows passed over, and the day proved fine. Before it was quite light, the perpetual tramp of foot passengers gave token of the anticipated solemnities. The crowds continually augmented by fresh arrivals, coming in every direction, and by every avenue of approach, on foot, in carriages, and on horseback...

As the hour approached, heavy guns were fired at intervals, pealing like a solemn anthem on the air. The sadness of recent bereavement seemed to rest upon every heart. Soon we heard the sounds of funeral marches, and the long line of military passed through Baltimore Street toward the Cemetery. Then came the President, easily distinguished from all others. He seemed as chief mourner. With him were the members of the Cabinet, the governor [Curtin] of Pennsylvania, and Governors and delegates from nearly all the loyal States, marshals with batons and badges on horseback, a large cavalcade, and then citizens on foot, men, women, and children—a great multitude. We joined the company and proceeded to the Cemetery. Mr. Everett, the orator of the day, and the Rev. Mr. Stockton rode in a barouche. A beautiful flag floated over the platform, which was arranged with seats for the distinguished guests, but there was no place for the ladies. The crowd was excessive...The sight was truly imposing. Among the many banners was one which touched every heart with its mute lamentation, a white flag, shrouded with black, bearing the inscription, "We mourn our fallen comrades" and on the reverse, "The Army of the Potomac." I gathered in the Cemetery many little sprays and green leaves, to send friends at a distance, who might value such mementos of the day and hour....

It was long past noon when the procession returned. It was a magnificent sight. The long line of infantry with their bayonets in the sunlight, the artillery, the distinguished guests, the great multitude. As the president passed, every head was uncovered, and three hearty cheers were given for him. The same compliment was paid to our Governor Curtin. The solemn pageant was over.

At five in the afternoon, the citizens were introduced to the President, and we did ourselves the honor of paying our respects to him and to the Governor. In the evening various meetings were held, and many speeches were made in the open air, some of which were greeted with hearty applause by citizens and soldiers. It seemed difficult to settle down to quietness.[28]

Mrs. Souder stepped onto the pages of history for but a moment. The slim book she compiled reflected her feelings and experiences, offering a glimpse of two momentous events. And then, like so many women, she is gone.

Emily Bliss Souder died on December 22, 1886, at age 72. She is buried in Section F, grave 348-349, of Woodlands Cemetery, Philadelphia. At one time there was a headstone and footstone that marked her grave in the family plot. As of the first printing of this volume both stones were gone.

Emily Souder was the first recipient of the Headstone Project. In 1995 a stone was dedicated at her grave. A collateral descendent of Emily's, Kevin Souder, attended the ceremony and unveiled the newly-placed stone.

Emily Souder later in life.
(Courtesy Kevin Souder)

The dedication of Emily Bliss Souder's new headstone, the first woman so honored in the Headstone Project. To the right of the Celtic Cross is Andy Waskie and kneeling in front of the cross is Jane Peters Estes. They were the energy behind the project.
(Author's collection)

Kevin Souder and son at the ceremony honoring their ancestor.
(Author's collection)

Mary Alice Smith

Independent Pennsylvania Nurse

"When Lee's army passed through Greencastle [PA] en route for Gettysburg, my sister Sadie and I waved the American flag in front of them, and were heartily cheered by the 'boys in gray.'"[1]

Mary Alice Smith is an example of the thousands of American women in the North and most especially in the South. Though she did not travel with the army and labor at the front, she was not content to stay at home and sew or otherwise work for a local aid society. She mostly nursed at local hospitals and in her case at the two large battlefields within traveling distance. She was one of the many women who worked at hospitals with the soldiers, be it reading to them, writing home, visiting, washing them, dressing wounds, or anything else they were called upon to do. When asked to write of her nursing experiences for a book published in 1895 [*Our Army Nurses*], her narrative is modestly short yet she was an active participant in the history that was being made.

When the war broke out I was living in a little town called Greencastle, about eleven miles from Chambersburg, Penn. My father was a great Union man, and threw our house open as headquarters for the officers. The generals quartered there were [James Jackson or Napoleon Jackson] Dana, [William "Baldy"] Smith, [?] Fitshugh, and they had their staffs. We did all we could for the comfort of the soldiers, and when the call came for nurses, I was one to volunteer. I served three years; first in the hospital at Hagerstown, Md., then at Greencastle.

During my hospital service I was on the battlefields of Antietam and Gettysburg, after the fight, helping the wounded and caring for the dying. Many of the injured men were carried to our little town of Greencastle, and we sisters did what we could for them, picking lint, knitting socks, etc. I was then Mary Alice Smith, and but eighteen years of age.[2] I served under Gen. David Detrich, in Greencastle, but do not remember who was the surgeon in charge at Hagerstown. When I was not engaged in the hospitals, I was out with an ambulance, gathering provisions for the soldiers. My father had a large warehouse, and we fed them there.... I left [nursing] to become the wife of Sergt. M. I. Frush, of Company B, 6th [West] Virginia.[3]

Marquis Frush was born at South Mountain, Washington County, Maryland but enlisted in West Virginia units. He was always on detached duty as Provost Guard and perhaps it was on his travels that he met Mary. He was mustered out in August 1864 and they were married at Greencastle on December 20 of that year and settled in the area. They had five children; Eva May, born and died in 1866, Charles Alfred, born in 1867, William R. Lee, born in 1869, Anna Lucretia, born in 1871, all in the Greencastle area. After they moved to Youngstown, Ohio, they had Wynette Virginia, born in 1875 and died in 1877.

Mary wrote: "Upon my marriage...I left the service, but was not discharged, so I have no papers." When she applied to a pension in 1893 she was rejected. "...as to her service as a nurse, she states that her name never was recorded as such & she was not commissioned by anyone & worked voluntarily & is of course not entitled."[4] This situation would have applied to thousands of women.

Mary Alice Smith Frush died December 24, 1901 in Youngstown, Ohio. She is buried in Oak Hill Cemetery, Lot 946.

Mary Alice Smith Frush after the war.
(*Our Army Nurses*)

Mary Brady

Independent Pennsylvania Nurse

*"'Don't you know me, Mrs. Brady?'...said the soldier, his
eyes now filling with tears; 'don't you remember the day you
held my hand while the doctors took my arm off? You told
me to put my trust in God, and that I should get well over it.
You said I was sure to recover; and here I am, dear Madam,
thank God!'"[1]*

...[S]o, among the heroines, some followed their husbands, and
were ready to dare everything and suffer everything for them and their
cause; others sought the field out of a generous rivalry not to be out-
done in the sacrifices by the sterner sex; others were incited by pure
patriotism; while a few moved and acted from motives rarer and purer,
perhaps, then all these—a simple and unmixed desire to alleviate human suffering, a philanthropic kindness of soul, and the swelling of a
large hearted charity, that was willing to labor anywhere, and in any
manner, to relieve the wants of those who were suffering pain and privations in a worthy cause...Prominent among this numerous class must
be placed the record of [Mrs. Mary Brady]...She had no son, or brother,
or husband in the war.

What demand of mere patriotism could have made it her duty, as
an American citizen merely, to forego all the comforts of her home in
Philadelphia, leave a family of five little children,[2] push her way through
all embarrassments and delays, through all the army lines, and sometimes in spite of general orders, to the very front, or to those hospitals
where men were brought in with clothing red with the fresh-flowing
gore of battle, and spend days and weeks at the field hospitals just in
the rear of the great battle-fields, and return home only to restore her
wasted energies, and start out again on her errands of tireless philanthropy? Yet such is the outline of Mrs. Brady's life...

It was on the 28th of July, 1862, that Mrs. Brady and a few others
met at her husband's law office, to take into consideration the condition
of the soldiers who had been brought from James River, and were then
languishing in various hospitals in and around Philadelphia, but principally at the Satterlee Hospital, in West Philadelphia, not far from Mrs.
Brady's home.[3]

"The Soldiers' Aid Association," was organized on the 28th of July, 1862, mainly through the efforts of Mrs. Mary A. Brady, a lady of West Philadelphia, herself a native of Ireland, but the wife of an English lawyer, who made his home in Philadelphia, in 1849. Mrs. Brady was elected President of the Association, and the labors of herself and her associates were expended on the Satterlee Hospital, one of those vast institutions created by the Medical Department of the Government, which had over three thousand beds, each during those dark and dreary days occupied by some poor sufferer. In this great hospital these ladies found, for a time, full employment for the hearts and hands of the Committees who, on their designated days of the week, ministered to those thousands of sick and wounded men, and from the depot of supplies which the Association had established at the hospitals, prepared and distributed fruits, food skillfully prepared, and articles of hospital clothing, of which the men were greatly in need. Those cheering conversations, reading and singing to the men, writing letters for them, and the dressing and applying of cooling lotions to the hot and inflamed wounds were not forgotten by these tender and kind-hearted women.

But Mrs. Brady looked forward to work in other fields, and the exertion of a wider influence, and though for months, she and her associates felt that the present duty must first be done, she desired to go to the front, and there minister to the wounded before they had endured all the agony of the long journey to the hospital in the city. The patients of the Satterlee Hospital were provided with an ample dinner of the day of the National Thanksgiving [Mary had the soldiers in the guard house released for the day], by the Association and as they were now diminishing in numbers, and the Auxiliary Societies, which had spring up throughout the State, had poured in abundant supplies, Mrs. Brady felt that the time had come when she could consistently enter upon the work nearest her heart.

In the winter of 1863, she visited Washington, and the hospitals and camps which were scattered around the city, at distances of from five to twenty miles. Here she found multitudes of sick and wounded, all suffering from cold, from hunger, or from inattention. "Camp Misery," with its twelve thousand convalescents, in a condition of intense wretchedness moved her sympathies, and led her to do what she could for them.[4] ...she penetrated to the extreme front...Here she took a four-mule wagon, and went through the army, stopping wherever a little red flag indicated a sick tent.[5]

She returned home at the beginning of April, and her preparations for another journey were hardly made, before the battles of Chancellorsville [May 3, 1863] and its vicinity occurred. Here at the great field hospital of Sedgwick's (Sixth) Corps, she commenced in earnest her labors in the care of the wounded from the field.[6]

With a view to immediate and practical efficiency, she took two cooking stoves, and proceeded at once to the great field hospital of the sixth corps, where she soon had a tent pitched, her boxes piled around for a wall, her stoves up…but her labors were not confined to her little extemporized kitchen. At night she could hardly sleep for the groans from the tents where the worst cases lay, and she often passed several hours, moving softly through those tents of pain, going to those who seemed to suffer most, and soothing them by words, and by little acts of kindness; fitting a fresher or softer pad under some throbbing stump, talking with some poor fellow whose brain was full of fever…moistening lips, stroking clammy foreheads, and helping another soldier to find his plug of tobacco….[7] For five weeks she worked with an energy and zeal which were the admiration of all who saw her, and then as Lee advanced toward Pennsylvania, she returned home for a few days of rest.[8]

Mary left again for the field after Gettysburg.

Operating in her usual homely but effective and most practical manner, she at once sought a camping ground near a great field hospital, reported for duty to the division surgeon, and had a squad of convalescents assigned to assist her. Her tents were erected, the empty boxes piled so as to wall her in on three sides, and the stoves set up and fuel prepared; so that in two or three hours after reaching Gettysburg, the brigade and division surgeons were pouring in the "requisitions," and the nurses were soon passing from her tent with tubs of lemonade, milk punch, green tea by the bucketful, chocolate, milk toast, arrowroot, rice puddings, and beef tea,—all of which were systematically dispensed in strict obedience to the instructions of the medical men. Whenever during the day she could, for a short time only, be relieved from these self-imposed kitchen duties, and for many hours after nightfall, she was sure to be among the cots, beside the weakest and those who suffered most. Her frequent visits to the army had made her face familiar to a great number of the soldiers, so that she was often addressed by name, and warmly greeted by the brave fellows.

Speaking of her first days at these hospitals, Mrs. Brady says, "We shortly found ourselves rubbing away the pain from mutilated limbs, and bathing the feet of others, speaking cheerful words to them all, which later we believed to do good like a medicine. In the daytime we cook and fill requisitions for all sorts of things, and personally distribute our miscellaneous stores to the men with our own hands, conversing cheerfully with the patients. Thus we spend our days as well as our nights.[9]

These labors continued till August, when the field hospitals at Gettysburg were mostly broken up.[10] More than month was spent in these labors, and at their close Mrs. Brady returned to her work in the Hospitals at Philadelphia, and to preparation for the autumn and winter campaigns.[11] [Mary spent the winter collecting supplies and money for the soldiers on the field and much of the latter for the widows and families.]

Early in the year 1864, when Meade, in command, was maneuvering unsuccessfully against Lee for the occupation of the south bank of Rapidan, in what was known as the Mine Run Campaign [Nov. 26 to Dec. 1, 1863], Mrs. Brady made her fifth and last visit to the front. She was now so well and so favorably known, that every facility was afforded her in the transportation of her boxes, and she penetrated to the front, and made herself useful in the primary field hospital that was established in consequence of the action at Morton's Ford on the 6th of February. Her ministrations were of the same nature described above, except that here she saw the wounded just as they were brought from the field, and shared in the deep excitements and agitations of battle. She was just in the rear of an engagement that threatened at one time to become general and bloody. Most of time she secured no better bed than a bundle of wet straw. As a natural consequence of such hardships and exposures, we find her reaching home on the 15th of February, "completely worn out." An examination of her condition by the physicians revealed the grave fact that rest and quiet alone could never restore her. An affection of the heart, which had existed for some time, but which, on account of her strong health and fine powers of constitution, had never before caused any uneasiness, had been rapidly developed by the last few weeks of uncommon excitement and fatigue.[12]

On May 27, 1864, Mary Brady died. "Died in Christ on Friday the 27th instant from disease of the heart, contracted by her voluntary efforts on behalf of the sick and wounded soldiers on the battlefields of the army of the Potomac."[13] She was 42 years old. Her funeral was largely attended and tributes were received by the family from soldiers and officers away in the army. She was buried in Mt. Moriah Cemetery in Philadelphia. At the time of publication of the first edition of this volume her grave site was unmarked. But in 1998 the Headstone Project stepped forward in their last effort. Mary Brady now has a headstone. Unfortunately, Mt. Moriah Cemetery, which had most currently been privately owned, has been abandoned and is in a disgraceful state. As well as Civil War nurses, there are a number of Union dead buried there.

Mary Brady was a casualty of the war. As was Laura Wesson, a seventeen year old nurse in South Carolina who died while nursing Confederate soldiers with small pox. As was Margaret Breckenridge from Kentucky who had been warned, "You must hold back, you are going beyond your strength; you will die if you are not more prudent,"[14] and who literally laid down and died when she went home for a funeral of a family soldier. As was Mrs. William Kirby, who was arrested for smuggling and died in a prison in Louisiana. As was Fanny Warriner, a hospital transport nurse, who died in Louisville, Kentucky on her way home. And as was Arabella Barlow, the woman in Pickett's Charge and Jennie Wade.

"I Yield Him Unto His Country and His God."
This is a relief on a monument in Devil's Den recognizing women's sacrifice.

The staggering figure of 620,000 casualties from the Civil War does not tell the whole story. Primary sources of nurses' work during the war reveal dozens of women's deaths. The actual number of Americans who lost their lives from our Civil War is far beyond battle casualty figures and can only be guessed at. The number of women who died in the war while serving their country and countrymen has yet to be investigated.

> And the great harvest of souls shall appear,
> And the reapers shall garner the grain,
> And the angels shall shout "Resurrection!"
> For those who died and were slain.
> A million brave women who fought the same fight
> Will ascend through the blossoming sod
> And go up through the lilies that bloomed o'er them here
> To live on as lilies of God.[15]

The final dedication of the Headstone Project was for Mary Brady at Mt. Moriah Cemetery. Directly behind the stone is Jane Peters Estes and the right, second row is Andy Waskie.
(Author's collection)

Sophronia Bucklin

Government Nurse

"Because we could not don the uniform of the soldier, and follow the beat of the stirring drums, we chose our silent journeys into hospitals and camps, and there waited for the wounded sufferer."[1]

Four years after the war Miss Sophronia Bucklin published her experiences as a Government nurse in a book entitled *In Hospital and Camp*. She wrote: "When, in the complexity of national affairs, it became necessary for armed men to assemble in multitudes, to become exposed to the hardships and privations of camps and the deadly peril of battle fields, there arose the same necessity for woman to lend her helping hand to bind up the wounds of the shattered soldier, and smooth the hard pillow of the dying hero...From the day on which the boom of the first cannon rolled over the startled waters in Charleston harbor, it was my constant study how I could with credit to myself get into the military service of the Union."[2]

Miss Bucklin was sponsored by the Board of Managers for the Soldiers Aid Society of Auburn, New York. Accepted by Dorothea Dix, Superintendent of Army Nurses, she began work at Judiciary Square Hospital in D.C. in September, 1862, right after the battle of Antietam [Sept. 17]. It would be three years before Sophronia would return home.

Almost immediately after arriving at Judiciary Square Hospital, she visited the dead house with the head nurse and looked into the future. "I did not think when, shudderingly, I first looked into the dead-house, and saw the three icy corpses, that these feet would ever stumble over stiff mortal clay, and hardly pause to not what lay within their path."[3]

The Dix, or Government nurses, were supposedly the only "authorized" nurses for the armies. Sanitary and Christian Commission nurses, state agents, regimental nurses, independent nurses, etc. were also acceptable as the need was so great. There is apparent hostility in war era writings towards Government nurses. Perhaps it was indirectly aimed at Miss Dix, who was once described as "a self sealing can of horror tied up with red tape," or perhaps at the Government itself. At one field hospital when Sophronia and her sister Government nurses had not eaten for two days, they were told "not one mouthful" of food would be given them from the Sanitary Commission. At another field hospital where she often begged food from the Commission for the men under her care, she wrote: "Although I felt rather indignant, yet I could not blame the Commission for withholding that which it was the business of the Government to provide."[4] Many women who were rejected by Miss Dix found great fault with the lady, but Miss Bucklin not only feared but admired her. Sophronia was the recipient of fairness, support, and gen-

Sophronia Bucklin with an unidentified soldier.
(*Our Army Nurses*)

erosity from Miss Dix. All nurses were annoyed to varying degrees by surgeons and officers, but for the Dix nurses, these men were the bane of their existence. Miss Bucklin complained of their actions in all the hospitals in which she worked.

"Officers now and then threw out hints that women were a nuisance in war...No man of generous heart wished women shut out from the doors of either field or city hospitals...It was only the ruffians who feared the just censure of compassionate women, who wished to exclude these from performing the labors, which kept our feet on the ground from early morn to the setting of the sun. Such were not the fair exponents, however, of manliness in the army, while thousands of brave men, who aided us in the duties devolving upon our heads, cheered us with appreciative words."[5]

From Judiciary Square Hospital Miss Bucklin went to the Point Lookout Hospital in Maryland where she learned a lesson in abusive power. "It was in his [ward surgeon] power to make our paths smooth, or to throw disagreeable things in the way which would make our positions extremely unpleasant, and subject us to no ordinary annoyance. Yet no murmur or complaint dared pass the lips of a hospital nurse, for disgrace and dismissal only awaited the beck of his authorative hand...The buffetings, and rude jarring against the sharp rock of military law were new to me then. I hardly thought I should grow so callous as to fling back word for word, and almost dare a blow for a blow."[6]

Miss Dix sent Sophronia out of the frying pan into the fire, which was the Wolfe Street Hospital in Alexandria, Virginia. The nurses and enlisted men received such poor food that Sophronia became weakened. Those in charge, however, feasted. She wrote about conditions at that time: "If we went into the city, a soldier was every moment at our heels, and no one was allowed, by purchasing an article of food, to cast an imputation upon the hospital—which, from its beauty, and the desirableness of the buildings, had acquired the reputation of a 'model hospital.' If visitors questioned, and complaints were made, the culprit was punished with extra diet. This was done with three soldiers who were thrust into the attic where no man could stand upright, and there forced, under a guard, to eat each three full rations at a meal."[7]

"The steward often stood in the pantry adjoining the dining-room, to listen, and report in case we made complaint about our miserable food. Thus a course of espionage, unworthy of the dignity of the hospital officials, was kept up among us all, and the weapon of relief from duty kept constantly suspended over our heads…Many surgeons, at this date of the war, were determined, by a systematic course of ill-treatment toward women nurses, to drive them from the service. To this class the surgeons in Wolf-street Hospital belonged, without any shadow of doubt."[8]

"*We* [the nurses] were not cowered from any fear of corporeal punishment being inflicted; no thought of bearing a load of wood on our backs, and being marched around by a guard for hours, deterred us from speaking of the wrongs we endured; but rather thought of usefulness cut off, of the disgrace of dismissal, of being shut out where our hands could not minister unto the brave wounded—those considerations argued against all complaints, and kept sentinel over our tongues to their every utterance."[9]

Sophronia was dismissed from the Wolfe Street Hospital for the transgression of baking biscuits. She waited in Alexandria for a new assignment, completely frustrated when after the battle of Chancellorsville [May 3, 1863] she was deemed too young by Dorothea Dix for field duty. After the battle of Gettysburg was fought her inactivity was almost unbearable and finally she got her chance.

The Wolfe Street Hospital in Alexandria, Virginia.
(Miller's *Photographic History of the Civil War*)

Two weeks had gone by, and, one day, Mr. Knapp, of the Sanitary Commission, said to me, as I was tarrying in my restlessness…"Miss Buckin, will you go to Gettysburg and help distribute stores?"

I replied that I wished to go; more than that, it was in my heart to hasten there but I have been positively forbidden to go, by the woman whom I acknowledged as my director.

"Go with Mrs. Caldwell [wife of a doctor]," he said, "and I will stand between you and all blame."

"I will go," I said, and twenty minutes remained in which to gather up a little bundle of clothes, and roll them in a newspaper, to eat my supper, and go on board the train.

Friday afternoon we left Washington, and arrived at Baltimore in the evening, when the first person who met me in the hotel parlor where I stopped was Miss Dix, on her return from Gettysburg.

"Where are you going, child," she said, looking into my face with keen searching glances.

"To Gettysburg, madam," I replied.

"And did I not forbid you—why do you disobey my orders?"

Mrs. Caldwell related the persuasion which had been brought to bear upon me, and the kind superintendent, with no chiding, forgave me, and said, "Report to the Seminary Hospital for duty."[10]

On Saturday [July 18] we entered the battle town. Everywhere were evidences of mortal combat, everywhere wounded men were lying in the streets on heaps of blood-stained straw, everywhere there was hurry and confusion, while soldiers were groaning and suffering…I was told, when asking to be directed to the Seminary Hospital, that I was not needed there, but that urgent necessity for a woman's work existed in the field, and I must consent to go there for duty. Also that the patients from the Seminary were soon to be brought to the field and that the hospital was to be broken up. So on the following morning—a lovely dawning of the Sabbath—we took our way up to the hospital ground [Camp Letterman], where five hundred tents had already been erected.[11]

A line of stretchers, a mile and half in length, each bearing a hero, who had fought nigh to death, told us where lay our work, and we commenced it at once. I washed agonized faces, combed out matted hair, bandaged slight wounds, and administered drinks of raspberry vinegar and lemon syrup....

The hospital lay in the rear of a deep wood, in a large open field, a mile and a half from Gettysburg, and overlooking it, the single line of rail which connected the battletown with the outer world sweeping it on one side, and winding through the woods. In this open field our supplies were landed from Washington....

We were the first women on the ground, but the number soon increased to forty, including seven Government nurses.[12]

The hospital tents were set in rows—five hundred of them—seeming like great fluttering pairs of white wings, brooding peacefully over those wounded men, as though to shelter them from further evil. Walks were thrown up between these rows, in order that they might dry quickly after the summer rains. The ground, now sodded—soon to be hardened by many feet—was the only floor in the wards, or in our quarters. The latter, with those of the surgeons, were set at the edge of the woods....[13]

There was an abundant supply of water which came from "the uncovered wells, which had been dug on the verge of the timber to supply the hospital with water" and were, at night, "a great terror."[14]

Camp Letterman was "placed in charge of Dr. Chamberlain. The original five hundred tents, spread in the rear of the old wood, soon increased to many more; and each nurse was assigned her position, and went forward with a will."[15] Sophronia was assigned Ward B in the Third Division. "As fast as one bed was vacated, another wounded man seemed to spring up in the place, and we were always full to our utmost capacity. Whence they came we could not tell; but doubtless, from the farm houses and the town, where they had been taken direct from the bloody field."[16]

My tent contained an iron bedstead, on which for a while I slept with the bare slats beneath, and covered with sheets and blanket. I afterwards obtained a tick and pillow, from the Sanitary Commission, and filled them with straw, sleeping in comparative comfort. I soon found, however, that the wounded needed these more than I, and back I went to the hard slats again, this time without sheets, which were given for the purpose of changing a patient's blood-saturated bed.

As time passed, and the heavy rains fell, sending muddy rivulets through our tents, we were often obliged in the morning to use our parasol handles to fish up our shoes from the water before we could dress ourselves. A tent cloth was afterwards put down for a carpet, and a Sibly stove set up to dry our clothing. These were ofttimes so damp, that it was barely possible to draw on the sleeves of our dresses. By and by I had the additional comfort of two splint-bottomed rocking chairs, which were given me by convalescent patients, who had brought them to the hospital for their own use, and on departing left them a legacy to me. With these a stand was added to my furniture. I here learned how few are nature's *real* wants. I learned how much, which at home we call necessary, can be lopped off, and we still be satisfied....[17]

Camp Letterman with the town of Gettysburg in the distant right.
(GNMP)

"For several days our duties had been general. I did whatever my hands found to do, drawing stores in food, bandages, and cooling drinks from the Sanitary Commission—administered alike to friend and foe— writing letters to rebel mothers and union wives, finding my heart and soul engaged in the cause of bleeding humanity to an extent which banished personal discomfort from my mind, for the time, altogether."[18]

Like the other nurses and patients, Sophronia felt the effect of lack of food at Gettysyburg.

> Hunger gnawed at my vitals; swollen feet almost refused to support me; wearied limbs found but little rest upon the bare slats of my bedstead through the short summer nights…Hunger only made eatable the wretched food which was spoiled in its long heated journey over the dusty road from Washington. It was with much interest that we watched the progress of the new kitchen, the advent of the monster stoves, the filing of the huge caldrons....[19]

> The Christian Commission established itself on the ground, and did its work nobly. Both Sanitary and Christian Commission tents were located on the edge of the woods, convenient proximity to our quarters. One woman, employed by the Christian Commission, daily took a team and scoured the country round for the solid things which only farmers usually possess in plenty. From her we obtained generous gifts of fowls, eggs, milk, and butter.[20]

Nurses darted in and out with the bedraggled skirts and shaker bonnets, hither and thither from Christian to Sanitary commission, and then to the general cook-house, each one eager to secure for her patients the greatest amount of luxuries.[21]

Citizens remembered us in the way of brimming pails of milk, of rolls of golden-hued butter, of luscious fruit…One [Gettysburg] woman, came to us, and pitched her tent with the nurses—and for four months worked for the wounded soldiers of her country. Many a pail of butter, and rich jug of milk she brought back from her home, after brief visits, and they were dispensed with a willing hand.[22]

The regular routine of hospital life was the methodical operations of a thorough housekeeper…As only wounded men were in this field hospital, our duties were varied from what they had been at other points. The first round in the morning was to give the stimulants, and to attend to the distribution of the extra diet. After the thorough organization of the plan had been completed, we were not called upon to dress wounds, unless by special request, wound dressers being assigned to each section of the ward; but for a time, that duty had come next after the distribution of the extra diet.

Beef tea was passed three times a day, stimulants three times, and extra diet three times—making nine visits which each woman nurse made a day to each of the two hundred men under her charge. This was done besides washing the faces and combing the hair of those who were still unable to perform these services for themselves, preparing the extra drinks ordered by the surgeons, and seeing that the bedding and clothing of every man was kept clean by the men nurses. We were not however responsible for any other neglect in the ward.[23]

Surgeons were not immune to frustration in the care for the wounded. Sophronia related two incidents at Gettysburg concerning food and pads for amputees.

While the extra diet kitchen had been under the control of Mrs. Holstein, we had been forbidden the privilege of preparing extra food ourselves, and were not even allowed to go inside of the kitchen—she deeming it necessary to keep a guard, with fixed bayonet, at the entrance. Often she refused to fill the orders from our surgeon, remarking that he was the most unreasonable man she ever saw. When I reported back to him, after failing to receive what I had been refused, he often went to the kitchen himself, and, with his own hands cooked the food, saying that what was the rightful property of the patients, that they should have.[24]

The making of these pads and pillows took away many a moment of mine, for I fancied I could fit them better than those who had never worked among the wounded. But I drew upon my devoted head, by thus doing, the severe displeasure of the overseer of the linen room [aka General Duncan], who reported me for taking *hospital pillows*, with which to stuff my pads. The surgeon in reprimanding me said, "Miss Bucklin, use all the pillows you want—you know they cost three dollars a pair, and that is more than a soldier's life is rated here"—and I obeyed him to the letter.[25]

Sophronia met more than a few drunk, incompetent, or cruel surgeons and she abhorred them. "Often we felt it was an insult to our womanhood to be constrained to give an outward show of respect when within there was nothing but loathing and detestation." She witnessed several in the amputating room who "paused for awhile to have their photographs taken, the suffering patient lying in this critical condition. My blood boiled at the cruelty of the scene, but I could not avert the torture for a moment."[26]

Sophronia had both Confederate and Union men in her ward. "It was quite a study to see and ponder upon the contrast between the men of the two sections…more than half of the wounded men in the hospital were rebel soldiers, grim, gaunt, ragged men—long-haired, hollow-eyed and sallow-cheeked. It was universally shown here, as elsewhere, that these bore their sufferings with far less fortitude than our brave soldiers."

"With the same care from attendants, and the same surgical skill, many more rebels died than of our own men—whether from the nature of their wounds, which seemed generally more frightful, or because they lacked the courage to bear up under them or whether the wild irregular lives which they had been leading had rendered the system less able to resist pain, will always remain a mystery to me. The truth of the assertion however is corroborated by army nurses all over the land.

"Of the twenty-two rebels who were brought into my ward at one time, thirteen died, after receiving the same care that was given to our men."[27]

"The rebels who were prisoners of war, as yet had no reason to sink under the generous fare and kindly nursing they received; and the bare fact of capture could hardly have wrought any disadvantage in their condition."[28]

In spite of their dying too easily and their "hydrophobic fear of water," Sophonia developed a high regard for the Southern character.

Soldiers in blue, who had been in Southern prisons, told of the perfect discipline of the Confederate troops....They endured hard fare without a murmur, and toilsome marches through midnights, when the steady tramp of the brigades roused the Union prisoners who were huddled together in the open air to sleep, and almost awed them into silence respect for the ragged soldiers of the rebellion.[29]

The spirit which held them through all the only years of deadly peril seemed as enthusiastic as the spirit which fired a few of our troops, who in the first flush of enthusiasm went down to "whip them out in three months at most." Bitter complaints against Government, when Government was not responsible for their hardships; loud murmurs against long marches and stinted rations were seldom heard from the grey-clad soldiers, who silently endured on and almost depended upon their leaders for their thoughts.

Had the Confederate troops possessed the same spirit as our own, the rebellion would never have outlived its infancy. But instead, all through the South, the full tide of patriotism swelled high, and women gave all they had to the cause, and made every sacrifice with heroic fortitude. When prisoners returned to us it was with a duller confidence in the ultimate success of our arms, in view of this seeming united state of the South....

The strictest military rule could not utterly drive demoralization from our ranks. There was no complaint of this among Southern leaders, and no signs of its working among those whom we held as prisoners of war.[30]

A commendable spirit of devotion, generally unknown amongst our soldiers, pervaded the rebels, and while our men were singing and joking, morning and evening prayers were being said, and Old Hundred chanted by their lips.

Notwithstanding their hostility to us Northerners, I had much respect for them, and felt, when I watched their intense sufferings, that only an honest feeling could have driven them into such a conflict.

...That some appreciated the kindness done them I know, for I often received looks of thanks, and words of sincere gratitude.[31]

Miss Bucklin recorded the gore of the battlefield:

I visited the battle ground on several occasions—the first time soon after the conflict, when the evidences of the horrid carnage which had ranged over it, lay on every hand in fearful sights...everything that ingenuity could devise for the crushing out of human life seemed scattered promiscuously about...

Battered canteens, cartridge-boxes, torn knapsacks, muskets twisted by cannon shot and shell, rusted tin cups, pieces of rent uniform, caps, belts perforated with shot, and heaps of death's leaden hail, marked the spots where men were stricken down in solid ranks. Earlier in life it would have been almost impossible for me to walk over such a field of horror, but I had grown familiar with death in every shape. Yet, when right about my head, at one place, so close that it touched me, hung a sleeve of faded army blue—a dead hand protruding from the worn and blackened cuff—I could not but feel a momentary shudder.

Boots, with a foot and leg putrefying within, lay beside the pathway, and ghastly heads, too—over the exposed skulls of which insects crawled—while great worms bored through the rotting eyeballs. Astride a tree sat a bloody horror, with head and limbs severed by shells, the birds having banqueted on it, while the tattered uniform, stained with gore, fluttered dismally in the summer air.

Whole bodies were flattened against the rocks, smashed into a shapeless mass, as though thrown there by a giant hand, an awful sight in their battered and decaying condition. The freshly turned earth on every hand denoted the pits, from many of which legs were thrust above the scant covering, and arms and hands were lifted up as though pleading to be assigned enough earth to keep them from the glare of day.

I could scarcely lay my hand upon tree trunks but it touched an indentation made by a Minnie ball—so thick they had rained down among the products of these hills...Round Top, Little Round Top, and Culp's Hill....[32]

Every advantageous position was marked with torn turf, lopped tree boughs, and the graves of the slain. Indeed, our whole way was lined with the narrow strips of earth...It was heart-sickening to think of the deep agony which those few dreadful days spread abroad among the little groups at the firesides of fond homes all over the land. In fancy I saw the long procession of widows, and orphans, and kindred, who mourned for the slaughtered heroes. Every grave has its history, and thousands were there.[33]

Many of Miss Bucklin's memories from Gettysburg were of the people who came to the hospital for their loved ones.

"Many scenes transpired which drew tears from our eyes and filled our souls with pity for those who were still to live on after those they loved had gone...In the ward assigned to me, after the first days of disjointed effort were over, there were three wives and two mothers..."[34] who were nursing their men in her ward.

One mother watched as a surgeon took 26 pieces of shattered bone from her son, another mother's son had suffered five bullet wounds. She "...was busy in the ward caring for his comfort. In cases of this kind, many eyes were attracted to the boy thus fortunate in having a mother's care, and many hearts longed to be where a fond mother's thoughts and prayers went up constantly for them.

"We witnessed a happy meeting one day, when a father, who was also a soldier, came in to the ward, met his wife, sitting at the bedside of their son. Many tears were shed around them, which they knew not of, nor could have regarded in the full thankfulness of their hearts that the life of the dear boy had been spared to them."[35]

One soldier, in the presence of his wife, was striving to endure with calmness the pain of a fractured thigh and an amputated arm. No hand but hers could smooth his pillow, no other give him the nourishment to support his life; no fingers were as tender as hers over the throbbing wounds, where worms were feeding upon the living, human flesh. But his life was spared, and the brave and anxious wife cared little for hardships, so long as his life could be saved to her, and she could look into his eyes, and know that she was a comfort to him in this victorious conflict with death.

Another wife, clasping to her bosom a little child of eighteen months, sat for hours with bowed head, leaning over the prostrate form of her husband, whose frightful wound [he was gut shot] made it necessary to keep him stupefied with morphine, so that his unearthly groans should not keep the whole tent in undue excitement.

...He lay in this unconscious stupor, and the stricken wife waited in vain for some signs of recognition. A humane heart lay in the bosom of our surgeon, and he allowed the drug to exhaust itself, and the consciousness to return, that he might recognize his wife and child before he died.

Slowly it passed away, and his mangled body was racked with intense suffering. He lay on his face, with his eyes turned toward her, that when his senses revived, she might be the first to meet his gaze. After a while he looked up—the wild glare of pain in his eyes—and said, as he saw whose face bent over him, "Oh! Mary, are *you* here?" His groans were terrible to hear, and in mercy he was again given the opiate, and slept his life out....

How our hearts were pained for that wife, sitting motionless beside the body, holding in her lap the little boy who was so soon to be fatherless, tearless in her great agony, stricken as by the withering stroke of palsy—yet breathing and living.

"A widow, whose husband lay somewhere in his gory shroud of blue under the battle clods, tried to minister to the wants of the patients in the hospital, but the sense of bereavement, and the shock it bore to her heart, so wrought upon her that her heart was steeled against those who lay prostrate in grey uniforms, and she refused to give food or drink or aid of any kind to them…That instinct, which in the highest brute creation resents an injury to itself or its loved, was blindly rampant in her chilled heart…She was necessarily discharged."[36]

"One woman worked with us through the whole period of four months, after she had taken the body of her soldier son from the trench in which it was buried, and carried it home to sleep with kindred dust. She had sought him out from the dreadful pit, and lifted him up with her own hands, her motherly heart yearning over the dead boy with an unutterable anguish, nerving her to endure the horrible contact with the putrid corpses of the slain. Now, other mother's sons were stricken down, who with care might be restored to those who loved them, and her brave unselfish heart could work for that end."[37]

One soldier died before his father arrived. "I collected together the few articles belonging to him, consisting of a comb and brush, a razor and strap, a looking glass, a cigar, and a roll of bandages with which his limb had been dressed, and as he took them, he said, tremulously, 'Oh! how much his poor mother will think of these things!' 'Surely,' I thought, 'they will be a sorry comfort to the heart aching for the darling boy, who would never sit by their hearth again.'"[38]

Sophronia took over another ward where two men lay dying:

> These soldiers were of the first who were buried in the new National Cemetery at Gettysburg, and they were laid to sleep under that dewy sod with military honors. At their burial the coffins draped with the flag preceded, the ambulances containing the women nurses followed, and then came the convalescents marching with reversed muskets to the plots of ground set apart for the dead of that particular State to which the deceased belonged.
>
> The bodies of our men, who had been buried the hospital cemetery, were afterwards exhumed, and each laid within the plat appropriate for the dead of his own state. But nearly two-thirds of the twelve hundred graves, which had been made there, were filled with rebel dead…
>
> Thus they perished; but the terrible weight of woe did not fall on any one soul, else it had crushed it into the depths of the grave. We sorrowed, but not as those who held those departed ones so dear to the

heart; and the days came and went, carrying other separations in their train, and leaving their saddening influences.[39]

The hospital was at last broken up...and we saw car load after car load depart...All were gone—my occupation was gone; the strain of months was suddenly let go, and I found how much the strength of my hands depended on keeping them steadily employed.

The hospital tents were removed—each bare and dust-trampled space marking where corpses had lain after the death-agony was passed, and where the wounded had groaned in pain. Tears filled my eyes when I looked on that great field...So many of them I had seen depart to the silent lands; so many I had learned to respect and my thought followed them to other hospitals, and to the fresh battle fields, which would receive them, when health was fully restored.

The dedication of the new National Cemetery was to take place immediately...The crowds began to arrive...Gettysburg was full to its capacity, and again the while tents were spread on the hospital ground, to accommodate the crowds of people....[40]

On the 19th of November the dedication took place. It was a clear autumn day, and the last leaves of summer were fluttering down upon the newly broken sod, and over the dense crowds of thousands, who seemed packed like fishes in a barrel. We stood, almost suffocated, for an hour and three-quarters, listening to the masterly oration of the lamented [Edward] Everett.

The calm, honest face of the President at once exhibited the pride of country, and an affection for her fallen sons unusual among those high in authority. His soul was unconscious that he himself, ere the consummation of the great sacrifice, should be given up to the death by which martyred soldiers die.[41]

We felt sorrowful when we left. Those hills had become familiar to our eyes, and as they receded from our view many parting tears were shed in memory of the dead who died upon them.[42]

Sophronia served at the Seminary Hospital in Washington, D.C. after Gettysburg, then visited Camp Stoneman, a cavalry hospital six miles outside Washington. She requested to be assigned there. Miss Dix not only gave consent, but since there were no monies provided at post hospitals, Miss Dix paid her out of her own pocket. "So, trusting that our generous Government would reimburse Miss Dix, I accepted an appointment at Camp Stoneman."[43]

In the winter of 1863-64 Miss Bucklin contracted first measles, then typhoid fever from which she was not expected to recover. "A council

An unidentified group at the entrance to the Seminary Hospital in
Washington, D.C. Miss Bucklin nursed here after Gettysburg.
(Miller's *Photographic History of the Civil War*)

Miss Bucklin requested to nurse at Camp Stoneman Cavalry Hospital.
(MOLLUS)

400

of the hospital surgeons said I would die; no hope remained for me. They little comprehended the amount of endurance my constitution was capable of, and how, in a close contest, the love of life had its hidden advantages over death...."[44] That endurance and the commissary sergeant's nursing saved her life.

Letters from New York urged her to come home. "Though a humble nurse in the hospital service of the Government, I had just patriotism enough to feel myself proud in my position as a queen could be on a throne. There may be those who not regard a feeling of this kind in a woman proper, in view of her relation to man and the requirements of modesty (?); but there are also those who have an abundance of it, and are strong enough to lead a correct life in the full employment of it. Go home! Not while strength lasted...."[45]

Sophronia's release from Camp Stoneman was brought through an incident of sexual harassment perpetrated by a surgeon on a civilian. Miss Bucklin described the situation:

> During my illness, a soldier, from Syracuse, New York, named George Bolier, was brought in, slowly dying of consumption. His wife was sent for, at his request, when it was made known to him that he had but a few more days to live. She came, leaving two sick children at home, hoping by her presence to cheer her dying husband as he entered the dark valley, and with her heart nigh broken by this accumulation of sorrows. She saw him, and remained by his side for days, comforting and soothing him, when a fiendish spirit tempted the surgeon in charge to insult her with infamous proposals.
>
> She turned upon him with the most scornful indignation, as he told her that her husband should be sent home on furlough, and herself allowed the freedom of the hospital, and nobly said, "If my husband died, he shall go knowing that I am true to him."
>
> She was forbidden to enter the ward; every annoyance was put within her pathway, and the poor creature, torn with suspense for her children, and distracted with sorrow for her dying husband, had no resort but to return home and suffer on. Unaccustomed to journeying alone, she had employed a neighbor to come to Washington with her, but the man having an opportunity to get Government employment, had concluded to do so, and she became quite nervous with fear.
>
> I took the stage for Washington with her—brought her a ticket, checked her baggage through, and saw her comfortable on her way home. By some chance the surgeon learned that I had been absent, whereupon he questioned me in regard to alleged disobedience of orders. "If you

were a man I would put you in the guard-house," he said in suppressed passion. I replied that he could do so as it was, if he saw fit, but I rather thought he would stand in some danger of losing his other eye (he had lost one), for I had some friends at Camp Stoneman yet—friends, who were well aware of the disgraceful proceedings which had lately been enacted, and who were eager for the opportunity this would afford.

The tiger was roused in the man—the brute passions were in the ascendant, and, although he had hitherto been kind and considerate to me, I feared him almost as much as an enraged beast.[46]

Sophronia went to Miss Dix, who told her to return to the hospital, and then immediately issued orders by mail that all her nurses were to leave Camp Stoneman. The soldiers gave a farewell party for the nurses. Miss Bucklin went to see George Bolier before she left.

[He] was failing rapidly, and a dispatch was sent to his wife, praying for her immediate return. He pleaded with me to remain until she should arrive…But the worn-out body gave up the spirit while she was speeding her way to the hospital hoping to stand beside him when the last struggle should come. The surgeon was beside himself when he died, and when no signs of life remained, said, heartlessly, "She can have him now."

Was there no compunction in his narrow soul for the terrible offence he had committed? For the sorrow he had heaped upon the stricken widow, who journeyed twice over the long route, only to take home, at the last, the emaciated clay, without even one parting word to reconcile her to the almost insupportable loss? Her grief was heartrending, and every one experienced a sense of mortification at the conduct of the brute, whose beastliness sought to stand between her and the death-bed of him she loved…It was little satisfaction, afterwards, to learn that the surgeon was safe in old Capital Prison, with several charges preferred against him. He was court-martialed, his pay withheld, and himself disgraced and dismissed from the service.[47]

Miss Bucklin was next assigned to White House Landing. "…White House, on the Pamunky River. It had been the home of Gen. Fitz Hugh Lee, son of the rebel commander and under its roof Gen. Washington was married—therefore much interest was associated with it in my mind. All that remained of it now were two stacks of blackened chimneys, and a row of negro huts made of hewn logs, standing on the brink of the river."[48]

She arrived right after the battle of Cold Harbor [June 3, 1864] had been fought. "Such dreadful suffering I hope never to witness again.

The remains of White House Landing in 1864.
(MOLLUS)

The field was one vast plain of intense mortal agony, tortured by the sun and chilled by the night dews...Everywhere were groans and cries for help; everywhere were the pleading and glassy eyes of dying men who were speechless in the delirium of death. It was a scene to appall the stoutest hearts, but the excitement nerved us to shut our sense to everything but the task of relieving them as fast as possible. The dead lay by the living; the dying groaned by the dead, and still one hundred ambulances poured the awful tide upon us...Day and night they were dying during each lagging hour."[49]

Here she saw a fourteen year old die calling for his mother. "Often the look of that boyish face haunts my recollection, and I wonder if the mother, on whom he called in the last extremity, ever knew how her boy suffered before death released him. No sight of manhood's agony ever moved me like these scenes of youthful distress. It seemed like the tearing up of a plant which was just putting out its buds with the promise of a fair summer nestling deep in its heart...."[50]

"It was a time of intense excitement, when we could scarcely wait for the night-shadows to pass away, before we began a new day's duties. Scenes of fresh horror rose up before us each day. Tales of suffering were told, which elsewhere would have well nigh frozen the blood with horror."[51]

Other nurses spoke of immense thirst on the field, as does Sophronia. "So tortured were we all, in fact, by this thirst, which could not be allayed, that even now [1869], when I lift to my lips a drink of pure, cold water, I cannot swallow it without thanking God for the priceless gift."[52]

As she steamed away from White House she looked across its fields. "The souls which had gone up thence!—who could number them, or who, could measure the extent of agony which made that field henceforth a place of sorrow! I at times imagined, as I looked upon these grounds, that the spirits of brave men would ever move along the tall grass, and whisperingly commune over the little knolls of earth on which they breathed out their lives; that, with the small mounds for their pillow and the sod for their beds, they would yet wear their heaviness of soul, and, with the wailing of the wind, sigh for the loved mother, or wife, or sister whose presence they longed for when their eyes closed to earth."[53]

It took about a week to arrive at her next destination which was City Point, where she was one of fourteen Government nurses. "I have often, since those days, thought how strange it was that no feeling of home-sickness ever came over me whilst in the midst of these trying circumstances. I scarcely ever even stopped to think that if I had remained at home I should have been spared these privations. I seemed to be sustained by an almost unnatural courage, and strengthened to a remarkable degree."[54]

At City Point she wrote: "I was not rested by the longest night of sleep during those months of hospital service, and my feet and fingers were always stiff and lame, until warmed up with my work in the morning—yet I complained not, while so many noble examples of patience and endurance were continually set by the brave sufferers around me."

She was present for the ammunition boat explosion. "We were startled one day by a near explosion, the sudden shock of which sent one of my attendants from the bed on which he was lying, straight to the door of the ward. For several seconds report followed report, during which a grape-shot raked across my tent corner, marking the canvas, and ploughing [sic] over the ground till its force was spent and it lay buried a little distance under the surface. I dug it out of its hiding place, and it lies to-day amongst my relics of battle-fields."[55]

Sophronia incurred the disfavor of yet another surgeon for cooking extra food in her tent for her men. This resulted in her being relieved from the City Point hospital in late October, 1864. She then went to Point of Rocks hospital.

"Point of Rocks Hospital was located on a large plantation belonging to Rev. Jack Strong who was formerly a Baptist minister. It over-looked the Appomattox river, and had been deserted by its owner as he beheld the first long lines of glistening guns and bayonets advancing from the pontoon bridges, just crossed, and steadily nearing his residence."[56]

At this site were nine Government nurses and the New Hampshire State Agent, Harriet Dame. "Everything seemed as favorable to nurses and patients at Point of Rocks as it was possible for them to be in a field hospital, and, in point of civilization, it went far beyond any other in which I had ever labored."[57]

"A regimental dog in our hospital became an object of no little interest to all. He was a noble-looking fellow, of the Newfoundland species, and was possessed of a remarkable intelligence. His master had been detailed to work in the cook house, whence he would carry a basket of meat as faithfully as a man and with astonishing quickness and

Point of Rocks field hospital.
(Library of Congress)

fidelity. He seemed to prefer the active service to hospital life, and he again and again ran away to the front, and joined the regiment, in which he seemed to be as well drilled as any of the soldiers. He enjoyed the crack of the rifle, and boom of the cannon, and had been thus far through the war without receiving injury."[58]

Sophronia remained at Point of Rocks until after Lee's surrender and visited Petersburg and Richmond before she left for Washington to report to Miss Dix. She was dismissed from service May 30, 1865.

"You will have some pleasant as well as sad remembrances of your military life!" [said] Miss Dix, as I left her residence, for the depot, on my homeward way.

I arrived at Auburn, New York, just in time to meet with an old friend, and hear the salutation, 'Well, I suppose you have fought, bled and died for your country,' when, in wildest excitement, several ladies rushed in and exclaimed, 'They have come!' and without giving me time to effect a change of clothing, I was marched off to assist in welcoming the remnant of the war-worn One Hundredth and Eleventh Regiment back to its native city.

Sick, weary with travel, dusty, and ragged, many were taken into the clean rooms of the hotel, and laid on the white counterpanes, while I, who was supposed to know how, went about my old work of washing begrimed faces and combing tangled hair. *This time the heroes were not blood-stained.*

Later Sophronia would write: "Among the sad memories of these years in hospital and camp, of some fast friendships formed when the dead lay around us, with the suffering and groaning on every hand, there remain some pleasant ones—the cherished of my life. In the silent watches of the night and the peaceful hours of the day they come to me as ministering angels to soothe my soul, when troubled with life's many little perplexities, and awaken in me a charitable view of earthly affairs."[59]

Miss Bucklin never married, a situation shared by Harriet Dame, Cornelia Hancock, and many other American women at that time. After the war with so many men having died, and women used to activity outside the house, the single working woman was accepted in society. The war opened the door to alternatives to marriage for women.

Sophronia was granted a pension of $12 in 1892. She died in Ithaca, New York, on November 29, 1902, at the age of 74. She is buried in Lakeview Cemetery.

Euphemia Mary Goldsborough

Independent Maryland Nurse

"Then call us rebels if you will.
We glory in the name.
For bending under unjust laws,
And swearing faith to an unjust cause,
We count a greater shame."[1]

A number of Southern women from Maryland and the occupied areas of northern Virginia mobilized in Baltimore after the battle of Gettysburg with the intention of attending the wounded Confederates on that field.

When this volume was first published one could say that these forgotten Confederate women were part of "history from under," a phrase coined for the historical abandonment of the ones who were conquered. Now, decades later, we suffer under the additional curses of a variety of "isms." Figures and events in history are maligned and presented through a web of bias. Examination of history using today's social standards produces nothing of value nor does dumbing down complicated issues to foolish simplicity. Protecting these "isms" are the academics, collectively citing each other in an endless loop almost to the exclusion of other sources. In the fog of "isms" most things Confederate, or even Southern, are not well received.

Regardless, Southern women exhibited courage, endurance, and supreme sacrifice, but because of historical neglect, their worth has been ignored, their voices have been silenced. Miss Euphemia Goldsborough was one of these women.

Miss Effie arrived in Gettysburg sometime around the 12th of July to nurse first at the College Hospital and then at Camp Letterman. A wounded North Carolinian described the Confederate prisoner's hospital at the Gettysburg College building:

> ...It was to the College Hospital I was carried [July 7]...In this hospital, there were six hundred of our wounded men, and about five of our surgeons remained with them...As a consequence of the small number of surgeons left with us our men in the hospital suffered much. Unless

A portrait of Miss Euphemia Goldsborough before the war.
(Goldsborough Collection)

it was a case of amputation needed immediately or the stopping of hemor-
rhage, they had not time to attend to anyone. Thus for the first two weeks
there were no nurses, no medicines, no kinds of food proper for men in our
condition…and for men who were reduced to mere skeletons from severe
wounds and loss of blood, the floor was a hard bed with only a blanket on
it…Day after day passed by with no difference, the same hard floor, the
same hard crackers, the same want of attention, and it had its effect of the
men, as is always the case. We each day became weaker and thinner…
   …And in that hospital,—those weary days,—those restless nights, ah,
mothers, sisters, wives, at home, your presence was the sunshine needed in
those gloomy hours, it was the heart yearning for you, that showed itself
on quivering lips and moistened eyes. Yet we were not wholly forsaken.
One day as I lay waiting, I heard a lady's voice, it was sweet music to my
ears. A few moments afterwards, two ladies from Baltimore came into our

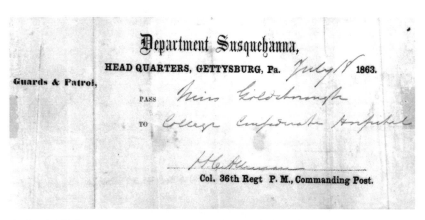

Department Susquehanna,

HEAD QUARTERS, GETTYSBURG, Pa. _July 18_ 1863.

Guards & Patrol,

PASS _Miss Goldsborough_

TO _College Confederate Hospital_

H C Alleman

Col. 36th Regt P. M., Commanding Post.

Miss Effie's pass to nurse at the "College Confederate Hospital."
(Goldsborough Collection)

room. To speak a few kind words, to ask us what was our principal wants, to promise to come soon again…next day, more came and then more, until every hospital had two or more of "our angels," as we used to call them, doing their works of mercy. And what they did, and what they told us, and what they passed through for us, what tongue can tell?

But the ladies of Baltimore were preeminently the persons, to who we were indebted for everything that made our situation bearable. For weeks, they had been preparing for the entry of Lee into Maryland,—into Baltimore, and comforts, clothing, delicacies of every description, they had hoarded up, hoping soon to be able to distribute them, with their own fair hands, among the men, who were fighting for the cause they loved; and when the dreadful news of our repulse reached them, their first thought was to visit our hospitals and supply our wants. What if passports to leave the city on the railroad were denied to all except those who would take "the oath;" did they not take their carriages and ride through the country? What if the bridges were guarded, did they not ford or ferry the stream? And when the hotel keepers in Gettysburg were ordered not to receive them in their houses; did they not go the houses of private citizens,[2] stay in barns and outhouses, or remain with us day and night in the hospital, reclining in a chair or resting on the floor, in a room of the building we vacated for them, when sleep would overcome them? What if large trunks full of comforts for us were seized on their arrival; did they not go back to Baltimore and return with dresses that had pockets as large as haversacks and almost numberless? And, finally, when every plan to thwart them had failed, and the yankees hoped by personal hardship inflicted upon them, and by insults directly given, to drive them away; did they not tell the yankees to their

409

Gettysburg College Dorm is the large building on the right where wounded Confederate prisoners were housed after the battle.
(MOLLUS)

faces they had come prepared to bear insults and wrongs for the men they loved? Or as I heard one put it in very strong language (speaking to an officer who had the politeness to apologise [sic] for a false accusation made against her, which caused her arrest) "I want no apology, we came here expecting and prepared for this, we can bear it for the cause; to *us* contact with such as you is synonymous with insult, *there is the door*." And when we were in prison, and until we were prevented from receiving supplies from friends; did they not do all in their power to clothe and feed us?

The last few days I was in Gettysburg, I was able to walk out in the grove surrounding the building, owing to attention bestowed upon me by our indefatigable nurses…One of the most villainous acts of our keepers, while at the College Hospital—besides the insults offered the ladies—was this: when our men were brought to the building, all of them being wounded, were more or less covered with blood and dirt, and the ladies from Baltimore made arrangements with a sympathizer, who lived near, to have all the washing done that would be needed at the hospital, and they would pay for it. As soon as the yankees found out this was being done, the stopped it, making many of them who were unable to obtain a change of underclothing, lie for weeks in clothing covered with a mass of putrid blood. After our friends came, the majority of us got at least part of a change of clothing…[3]

When the guns at Gettysburg had ceased to volley and thunder many of the ladies of Baltimore offered their services to nurse in the hospitals there. Among these ladies, Miss Euphemia Goldsborough, who was one

410

of the most active spirits of the Southern Cause in Baltimore hurried with...many others to the scene where they were assigned to duty as hospital nurses and to other departments of usefulness.[4]

Immediately after the battle of Gettysburg she offered her services as a hospital, or field, nurse and with other Baltimore ladies was assigned to duty in the College Hospital at first and the Camp Hospital later on, having fifty Federal soldiers and fifty Confederates in her ward. The U.S. soldiers were placed there to insure her discharge of duty without treason to the government.

Miss Goldsborough recognized the importance of showing no partiality, and many of both armies owed their lives to her good nursing, common sense and justice, while she gladly forgot party spirit for the time and saw the necessity of sacrificing herself to the good of the Southern wounded, dying soldiers of the Confederate Army. She remained there nine weeks, working incessantly, forgetting the world and self, living only to comfort and support the suffering and dying. Finally exhausted nature demanded rest and she returned to Baltimore.[5]

Miss Goldsborough was first put to work in the College Hospital. The North was a new field for active operations and the fight at Gettysburg found the people of the town unprepared for the emergency thrust upon them by the "Rebels." The College was the only suitable place they could make use of and was bare of all necessary comforts.

While the confusion was greatest and heroes were lying without pillows on the bare floor of the ward legless and armless, waiting for their time to come for attention, Miss Goldsborough found it her privilege to support, in his last moments, the gallant Col. Patton, a Virginian [7th VA], whose bravery has since been the theme of many tongues.

The surgeons in charge decided that is was imperative to place Col. Patton in practically a sitting posture to prevent suffocation. Being shot through the lungs, and unconscious, it was impossible to save his life unless he could be propped up, and there was absolutely nothing to be had to prop him with. Seeing the difficulty Miss Goldsborough decided to offer herself as the necessary agent. Accordingly she seated herself on the bare floor, feet extended, the surgeons tenderly placed the dying officer against her back [and] secured him there. She sat there, still as a wooden image never daring to move lest the slightest motion should bring on a hemmorrage [sic] and death insue [sic].

I have heard her describe the numbness that stole over her as she sat the night through, holding up the fast dying officer. It was said by a veteran afterwards, that of all the touching sights in his memory, the recollection of that picture would stand before him. "Midnight, a brave soldier, for whom the last taps were sounding, a young frail woman [Miss Effie weighed 98 lbs.] sitting by the light of the flickering candle supporting the dying hero of many hard fought battles, surrounded by the dead and dying and some 'grown old in war.'"

All efforts to save Col. Patton were futile, he died soon afterwards...

An amusing incident occurred while in the Camp Hospital. There were one hundred men assigned to Miss Goldsborough's ward, fifty Federal and fifty Confederate soldiers, some officers and some private soldiers. Among them was great need for suitable clothing and, for some reason known only to men in authority, it was against the rules to provide these men with new boots and clothes, but Miss Goldsborough was determined that one at least whose needs were especially great should not be sent to a northern or western prison destitute as he was. She feigned an excuse to go to town, secured a permit and started off in an army ambulance that was going there that morning. After securing the longed for treasures and what articles she could find, she happened upon a friendly spirit...They tied the boots securely under the immense hoop-skirt Miss Goldsborough rejoiced in and all the other traps that could be fastened on and then started off bravely to camp. But on reaching the official place to meet the ambulance, to her dismay, there stood the dreaded Yankee officer instead of just a teamster. The officer officiously insisted upon assisting her to get in the ambulance, her fears of detection were something appalling. She was sure the boots would bump against the side of the ambulance as soon as she attempted to get in it. However, she made a desperate effort and got in safely. Neither of the boots dropped down or bumped against each other. The camp was reached safely. The officious Yankee assisted her out and [she] reached her tent in safety. Then, when the opportunity presented itself, she smuggled in the effects to the rejoiced "Reb" and went on her way tending the wounded and dying. Her entire time was passed, nursing day and night except such time as sleep was absolutely desired, for fully nine weeks.[6]

One of Miss Effie's treasures was a book compiled at the time of her nursing at Gettysburg. It contains letters and signatures of almost a hundred men. The letters reflect much gratitude and heartfelt thanks. One mentions the fact of the sacrifice she hade to humble her "proud spirit" to nurse in spite of "those whose conduct in the war have shown them to be enemies of 'Woman,' oppressors of woman and destitute of manliness and true honor." Another, the hope that "Maryland, your own state, shall be relieved of her own yoke and shall occupy a proud place in the Southern Confederacy."

The letters range from the formally eloquent: "After being so long with us and being thy majestic self in meekness to meet the wants of the wounded while at the College and here [Camp Letterman]—I could not write my autograph without an appreciation of your kindness and benevolence. Such a being is too lovely for earth, and Heaven's reward can only reward, can only repay thee. I hope we may meet again after the hush of war way down south where beautiful rills, streams, and rivers wind their majestic course to the mighty deep."[7]

To the simply sincere: "Well, Miss Euphemia, I am no hand for writing poetry or pretty mementos in albums but I can leave you my name and say that when Genl. Lee again crosses the Potomac I will strike my third blow for Maryland provided God our father, 'the God of battles' will have by that time put strength in my wounded limb. For Right and Liberty, Maryland and Miss Euphemia, I will ever fight."[8]

There was one special soldier, Sam Watson, in Miss Effie's care. If she did not actually fall in love with him, she was deeply moved by his plight. On August 22, 1863, his cousin, T.J. Sneed, also a prisoner, wrote at the General Hospital:

> In behalf of my cousin, my thanks are due to Miss Goldsborough for her kindness to (S.H.W.) my cousin. An exile from home, and debarred from pleasures in which he was wont to indulge, arising from social delights, we can keenly appreciate this manifestation of kindness from a daughter of Maryland. In his behalf I therefore tender my heartfelt thanks.

The glass Miss Effie used as a nurse in Gettysburg.
(Goldsborough Collection)

With all the hardships and dangers of a soldier's life, there are no pleasures like those which are associated with the memories of home, and the daughters of the South, whom in former days we were wont to love. The mere thought, the suggestion, of a woman's love awakens memories of the past.

The joys of a mother's tenderness and affection seem as of yesterday—as when I look up through the blue silence of the sky, fresh stars shine out where at first none could be seen. Wherever I have wandered since this war began, I have found the women of the South were ever the same, developing next excellences of character which I had thought peculiar to the sex of my own home in the West.

Fresh memories and half-forgotten tones of those I have loved are awakened by the kind words and kind attention of the Lady of Baltimore to my little cousin. An affectionate mother, a kind and loving sister will bless thee, Miss Goldsborough, for the kind attention given to an absent son and brother.

Will you now accept my thanks?

Euphemia wrote in her hospital book:

Samuel Watson, 5th Texas Regt. Lost his right arm. One of the most attractive boys I ever saw. Very ill. But little hope of his recovery but hope for the best. Better today, decidedly. Again, poor fellow.

9th. Much better today. Strong hope of his recovery. Sacred.

Died Sept. 13th, Sundown Sunday afternoon, 1863. Buried in grave No. 3 commencing at the right. 8th Section.

My poor lost darling. Would to God I could have died to save you, but all is over, worldly sufferings are ended. If tears or love could have availed, I had not been left to weep by his graveside.

Miss Effie must have left Gettysburg almost immediately after the burial of Sam Watson. Her sister told of her homecoming: "She returned to us the most dilapidated young girl that tongue or pen could describe. During the nine weeks of camp life and hard work at nursing she had worn out all supplies taken there and sent to her by her family and the traveling garments she wore up to Gettysburg were things of the past. The hornets had built a nest in her bonnet and so it was necessary for her to return to Baltimore in her nurse's attire."

We did not know her at first. It was the [middle] of September, 1863, a warm afternoon. Our mother was lying down taking an afternoon nap as usual; the writer was sitting near her. Suddenly a vague consciousness of another presence was felt and looking up a figure stand-

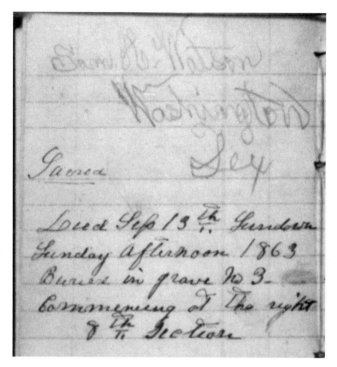

"Sam H. Watson, Washington, Tex."
(Goldsborough Collection)

ing in the doorway explained the sensation. At first we scarcely knew her, so worn and changed, so utterly exhausted with the sights of the battlefield and death bed scenes in the hospitals. The awful sights of those days, the anguish and suffering, witnessing the operations in the hospitals where legs and arms were sawed off like those of cats and dogs, and where the blood poured in streams from the operating tables, where she stood beside the poor boys in grey and heard their last messages and prayers. Little wonder to us of mature years that the life and youth in this frail woman's body was almost exhausted, for in truth she was never the same joyous girl again. Such things leave red letter marks that time never effaces.

We mingled our tears with hers as we listened to descriptions of the closing scenes of young lives sacrificed to duty and honor and country. Some were mere boys in years but brave and "counting it gain" to die in such a cause while far away from home and friends with only a stranger's hand to close the eyes that would never again behold the dear home faces or respond to other eyes that would watch in vain for the soldier's return.[9]

From Baltimore on September 22, 1863, Euphemia wrote to Sam Watson's mother:

Mrs. Harriet Watson,

I suppose you have already received intelligence of your son, Sam H. Watson being wounded at the battle of Gettysburg. His right arm was amputated and for a time he seemed to be getting on nicely, but unfortunately for himself, and those who loved him, an abscess formed under his arm, which, with sorrow be it said, terminated his young life. It was my privilege to nurse him six weeks, during which time I looked to his comfort as I would my own *only brother* and learned to love him *just the same.* He died in my arms, Sunday evening, Sept. 13, *just at sunset* his precious brown eyes fixed on mine, without a struggle, and his last fleeting breath I caught upon his lips. He spoke of you and his sister during the day and asked his cousin, Thomas Sneed of Texas, to return to you two plain gold rings that each had given him. Also a likeness of himself taken about four months back to say "he had come for a solider, *done his duty* and died for his country. I know every word I am writing will carry *grief to your heart*, and yet, judging you by myself, I feel that you would like to know all. I had him buried with my own, the Episcopal Church service, and marked his grave. Mrs. Watson, you *must not* feel that your son died in an enemy's country with *none* to *love* or care for him. His whole brigade loved him as did all who came in contact with him, *even those* who were opposed to the glorious cause for which so many brave and noble have already been sacrificed, and many were the bitter tears shed over his untimely grave. If this should ever reach you, may I ask that you will answer it. I hope that we may meet after this unhappy war is ended and that I may be able to give you back your *darling son's* dying kiss. Hoping I may hear from you and with a heart full of sympathy and sorrow for your loss, with profound respect I remain,

Your friend
E. M. Goldsborough

Direct to Miss Euphemia M. Goldsborough
No. 49 Courtland St., Balto. Md.

Enclose it to Jackson Douglas, 1st Auditor's Office, Richmond, Va. and she [*sic*] will send it through *under ground* to me. Excuse a faulty letter. I have no control over my feelings while writing or thinking of this subject.

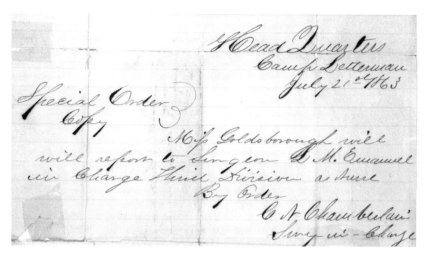

The order for Miss Effie to report to the surgeon of the
Third Division, Camp Letterman.
(Goldsborough Collection)

Euphemia Mary Goldsborough was born June 5, 1836 on Boston
Plantation in Talbot County, Maryland. The family moved to 49
Courtland Street in Baltimore in the 1850s. By 1860 the household
consisted of Martin and Ann Goldsborough whose children were: Ann
age 27, Emily age 25, Louisa age 23, Elizabeth age 21, Caroline age 19,
J. Randolph age 16, Laura age 15, and Mona age 11. Euphemia was
most likely in Florida at her uncle's school when this census was taken.
Miss Effie, or Pheme, was intelligent, creative, and adventurous, all
attributes that would be tested to their limit in the impending war. She
most likely enjoyed the social and cultural activities of the day. Apparently she was quite popular and had several beaus at one time; all of
whom had the bad timing to show up simultaneously at her house one
Sunday. Miss Effie "begged to be excused" from this one confrontation
she chose not to face.

The Goldsboroughs, like many other Marylanders, were ardent
Southern sympathizers in a no win situation. Baltimore and Annapolis
were under martial law. Unable to secede due to the arrest of the state
legislators, Confederate Marylanders may still have been excluded from
the Confederate States of America even if the South had won the war.
They had everything to lose and nothing to gain by adhering to their
political beliefs which must have been strong indeed to risk all as they

did. Marylanders were looked upon with suspicion by both sides and the Confederate soldier from Maryland suffered uniquely. A nurse in the Chimborazo Hospital in Richmond wrote of this. She claimed prejudice against Marylanders and the difficulties of Maryland soldiers who usually remained as privates and did not rise up in the ranks: "Luxuries received from other states for their soldiers, which though trifling in themselves were so gratifying to their recipients could not come to them, the furlough, that El Dorado to the sick soldier, was the gold that could not be grasped, for there was no home that could be reached. Even letters, those electric conductors from heart to heart, came sparingly after long detention, often telling of the loss of the beloved at home, months after the grave had closed upon them."[10]

[Euphemia Goldsborough]…was one of the central and most active figures in the late war, so far as Maryland was interested. She devoted her youth to the Southern Cause, was almost unequaled in her successful efforts in sending supplies, and sometimes arms, to the officers and men of the Maryland line.

Into every Federal prison in the United States where Confederate soldiers were confined went articles of comfort, both of food and raiment, to the suffering prisoners, while she worked day and night to procure funds to further that purpose.

Boston Plantation in Talbot County where Euphemia was born.
(Goldsborough Collection)

After the battle of Antietam, Miss Goldsborough went at once to Frederick City where the wounded had been conveyed and gave the Confederate soldiers assigned to her ward unremitting care.[11]

A ticket has survived for a tableaux given at the Goldsborough home for Tuesday, Oct. 21st, 1862 at 8 o'clock, admission 50 cents. On the back is a note to some recipient of Effie's endeavors: "God bless you my dear, dear friends, keep you from harm and bring you safely back to home and friends when all is over. I will see you in the morning as you go. Truly, Pheme."

…[We hid] Maryland boys who came and stayed with us in the face of all danger, Rebel boys home to see family and sweethearts found plenty of their rebel friends here ready to hide them away for weeks at a time and take chances of discovery and all the punishment the government sat fit to deal out to us. There are some living today who can recall just such cases as I describe. If the old Courtland house could speak it could tell some curious tales of refugees from Fort Delaware and Camp Chase; of the Baltimore boys who wore the grey and slipped home sometimes the underground route, as blockade running was called; of piles of clothing stacked up to be sent down South as soon as the opportunity presented itself; of hundreds and hundreds of letters destined to be sent to the Army by the Confederate blockade runners, but in one instance a few were destroyed and that was after the war was over. Our little "Reb" did not come for them in time and so, we had to destroy them. Among the articles sent [via] our house to be forwarded South were some boxes marked quinine. They were received under the assurance that it was to go South to be used for the soldiers in Richmond hospitals. After the surrender, the Confederate mail, which was buried in our cellar together with these boxes, was dug up; the letters burned, but the boxes were opened to find a clue, perhaps to the owner so as to notify him to get them. Imagine the astonishment of everyone when instead of quinine there lay snugly packed in rows hundreds of false teeth. Afterwards it was discovered that the man who brought them to us, to risk our liberty in sending, was sending his partner in Richmond these false teeth to make money and not as he said to relieve the sick in the hospitals. He must have been born north of the Mason Dixon line![12]

For Euphemia the axe fell a few months after Gettysburg.[13] Her sister told of the events that began the night of November 23, 1863.

…[A]t midnight Col. Fish [Provost Marshal VIII Corps], who was then in charge of this department sent three officers and a number of guards to arrest Miss Goldsborough for treason. The soldiers surrounded the house…[in] a neighborhood well known and popular as a residence locality.

The Yankees filed into the house and took up formidable attitudes, while some stood guard outside. They had enuf [*sic*] powder and shot along to kill a company, but the idea in those days was to over-power wherever they could. This was not such an easy matter as they sometimes found out to their loss, Southern women are not cowards and some of the besieged families were frightened, though of course excited, for the arrest was made at a serious time. There were hampers packed and waiting to be smuggled into Fort McHenry that very night, and it was almost impossible to get them unpacked and hustled out of sight without attracting the attention of the guards. The family was large, however, seven daughters, all with their wits about them and a father and mother especially on the alert. The unpacking was accomplished while the searching party was upstairs looking all over the house, in bureau drawers, in old closets, wardrobes, and every empty and occupied room being looked over for evidence of treason;[14] this little pleasantness, had been vouchsafed before, when the Yankees reported finding a wagon load of guns secreted. In reality, not a gun had been in our house for the past twenty years, at least.

A detective made the arrest first, and then after asking Miss Goldsborough if she had nursed at Gettysburg and she had told him "yes," he put his hand on her shoulder and said, "You are my prisoner, consider yourself under arrest." Then my Lord Cardinal called in his gallant officers and guards with their little swords and guns and all rushed upstairs and spread over the house like the darkness that spread over Egypt.

Before leaving the hall where all this took place a very knightly officer told the guard that if Miss Goldsborough attempted to move to shoot her down. She quietly remarked, "I'm not coward enough to run." After an hour spent in ransacking desks for papers, they departed, actually telling us they were tired and sleepy; but only the officers left, and the guards locked up the prisoner in a cold room; and took position on the outside of the door. They had strict orders not to allow any members of her family to speak to her, but they did. Each one as he went on duty said if we would not tell the next guard he would let us see and speak to our sister and one kind hearted soldier, when he found she was in a room with no fire, and the weather bitterly cold, even went so far as to assist us in getting a stove into the room, and each guard kept up the fire as he came on duty during the time she was locked in that particular room.

The news of the arrest spread on the wings of the wind. Friends and strangers in sympathy with the South full of interest and genuine feeling. There were no idle curiosity seekers abroad in these war times. About

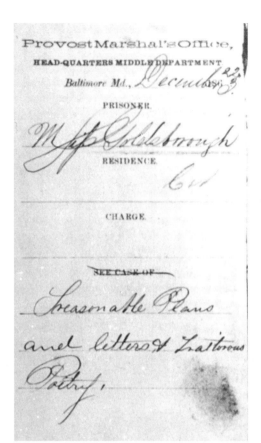

The cover of Euphemia's Provost Marshal File containing "Treasonable Plans and letters & Traitorous Poetry."

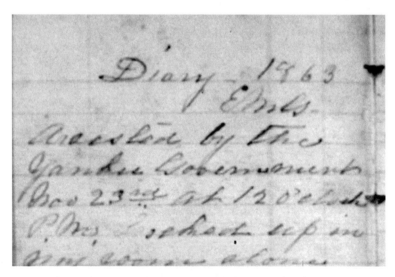

"Arrested by Yankee Government...."
(Goldsborough Collection)

eleven o'clock the following morning a detective came to escort Miss Goldsborough before the great Col. Fish of pestilential memory. She said unless he brought a carriage he would have to see Col. Fish alone as she had no intention of walking through the public streets with him to Col. Fish's office. He insisted and she steadfastly refused so he had to go and bring a carriage though as a matter of course he could have forced her to go on foot.

Our father was greatly grieved but he accompanied his daughter to the Provost Marshal Office and there heard them pronounce the sentence of banishment for the war. She was given permission to carry two trunks and just exactly $225 in federal money, and not another cent and was told if she tried to come back before the close of the war she would be tried for her life and shot as a spy. But in the face of this, when the war suddenly closed, she was arranging to run the blockade to visit us, and she would have come too and we would have hidden her away...

...She was sent South after about five days, under escort. She left the house about three o'clock in the afternoon. The streets, doorsteps, windows and every available spot was packed with an eager, sympathetic crowd to see her leave under such painful circumstances. Not a sound disturbed the peace! All seemed to feel it a funeral instead of a military banishment. She faced the crowd bravely but fell forward like a dead woman as soon as she was seated in the carriage. She was determined to show no signs of fear or distress before any possible enemy in that dense crowd, so she threw off our father's assisting arm and with erect head passed down the steps to the carriage alone, followed by the gentlemen and friends of our family, and the high official who was there to see his orders carried out.[15]

No sympathy was shown this heroic Southern girl by Gen. [Benjamin] Butler.[16] No regard for her tender sex or youth, but he sternly demanded to know what she had been sent to him for. Her reply was, "For feeding the hungry and clothing the naked." She refused to reply to another question or shaft of bitterness, but calmly awaited the decision. Though subject to the most rigorous search personally, her trunks upset on the floor and examined, she nevertheless carried through to Richmond certain dispatches and delivered them safely to headquarters. This, in the face of a Northern prison—even death itself—she ventured and accomplished.[17]

Miss Effie carried with her a lap desk that had a secret compartment. In the front of the desk were three small drawers with a long space underneath that could hold objects or thick documents. The smuggled dispatches were hidden in that compartment.

"Belonging to an old colonial family, she was widely known and friends and some relatives used every effort to secure official influence, and succeed in getting her removed for a time from the damp, cold cellar where General Butler had her confined while waiting the flag of truce boat to convey her to City Point."[18]

Miss Effie began a diary beginning with her arrest:

Arrested by the Yankee government Nov. 23rd at 12 o'clock p.m. Locked up in my rooms alone until the next day, Nov. 24th 11 a.m. Through a hard rain taken before the military authorities under guard. Sentenced to banishment during the war. Allowed to remain at home until Nov. 28th under strong guard day and night. Saturday afternoon, Nov. 28th at 4 p.m. put on board the steamer Adelaid (in a fainting condition) for Fortress Monroe with military escort. Reached the Fortress at daybreak Sunday morning, Nov. 19th, raining fearfully. Taken to Beast Butler about sunrise the same morning. Found the Beast not up. Wet and cold sat shivering in his office until a fire was made. Finally he came (this dreaded monster) I was turned over into his hands by the guards and evidence handed in, strong enough, the Beast said to cost me my head "under any other government than the mild and glorious stars and stripes." Again banished for the war with orders if I attempted to return, to be shot. But what was sentence of death and banishment at the hands of these cruel tyrants that I hated then and now with all the intensity and fervor of my passionate nature. Freedom to breathe for a brief time the pure breath of our glorious Confederate nation.

Held a prisoner until Wednesday night, 8 p.m. Dec. 2nd. Put on board the U.S. Truce Steamer, New York. Before starting was stripped of all my clothing, minutely examined by two Yankee women, open doors with all around Yankee soldiers laughing and jesting at my expense. If I live for half a century I can never forget the humiliation of that hour. My blood seems turning to fire even now when I write of it…Alone save for a guard reached the steamer by way of a tug-about 10 o'clock p.m. Lay at anchor all night in the Roads. Introduced to Maj. (now Gen.) Mulford. More of a gentleman than any I ever knew in Yankee blue. He also was most kindly. My heart swells with grateful emotions at the remembrance of the same. I was so desolate, alone, that a kind word fell like oil upon troubled waters.[19]

The next morning, Dec. 3rd, we were to have started up the James by daylight but the boat got aground and it was sunrise before we got off—passing the wrecks of the Congress and the Cumberland off Newport News, and indeed many other points of interest. Indeed every foot

The U. S. Truce Steamer, *New York.*
(Miller's *Photographic History of the Civil War*)

of the ground along that noble river has been rendered historical by the great struggle for independence on its banks. The evening of the 3rd we anchored at City Point about an hour before sunset. There was a French frigate anchored in the stream. Our own (the Confederate) truce boat had not arrived. I have never been up the James River before. The country is picturesque and beautiful and the night clean and faultlessly lovely. I passed an hour on the yards of the boat looking for the Shortly, watching the signals from a station on the top of a hill hard by. And the stars as they came out one by one like sentinels guarding their posts. Had a visit from one of the officers of the French Crown—invited me to breakfast the next morning which I was obliged to decline being still a prisoner.

Her sister elaborated about this event. "While waiting off at some point of the route a French Frigate of War was recognized lying near them. Soon a boat was launched and manned. An officer descended and took his seat then and the seaman rowed rapidly to the Exchange boat, pulled up and the officer came on deck. Bowing and smiling he said he called to pay his respects to the Miss Confederate whom he was told was on board. He was dressed in full uniform, low cut shoes and silk stockings, evidently arrayed to make a call of ceremony. Miss

Goldsborough was presented, the officer paid her all the compliments his limited command of the language allowed, placed his hand over his heart, bowed and returned to his ship."[20]

Miss Effie continued:

When I awoke in the morning, Dec. 4th, our boat had arrived and with a light and bounding heart I bid goodbye to Yankee rule and tyranny. And for the first time, found myself seated on our little boat with the starry-bars—the flag of the free—waving over me. I forgot to say that horrid woman Bell[e] Boyd, was sent up on the same truce boat with me, but enough of her. I reached Richmond about night-fall the same evening, Dec. 4th. Was escorted up to the Spottswood Hotel by Gen. G Smith. The evening was dark and the lights not lighted. The hotel was dark and cheerless-the parlor shadowy, with gay groups sitting around laughing and chatting. Officers and ladies, all strangers to me, alone, the General having gone to order my room. My very heart died within me and I felt truly that I was alone "a stranger in a strange land." After supper [she saw] the first familiar face…I retired early, tired and dispirited.

Dec. 5th went down to breakfast; found [two friends] waiting for me, took breakfast with me. Had no sooner reached the parlors than [more people arrived]…all old friends. Before 12 o'clock I had some fifteen friends and the feeling of loneliness was wearing away.

Mona remarked: "Upon arriving in Richmond, Miss Goldsborough was welcomed right royally, feasted—not as they could have done before the war—but generously and proud. Many doors were opened to her and many hearts…Col. Patton's family sought her out, having heard of her efforts to save his life, and insisted she should make her home with them during the war. Though appreciated, this kind invitation was not accepted."[21]

Miss Effie's diary continued:

Dec. 6th Sunday. Went to St. Paul's Church in company with [friends]. They know everyone and pointed them out to me, our grand people. For the first time I saw our grand and glorious president, Mr. Davis—knew him from his strong resemblance to his photograph.

Remained at the Spottswood until Wednesday, Dec. 9th, seeing many friends and making many new ones. Went to Mrs. M. T. Southall's—on the corner of Grace and T Streets—on the 9th to board. A pleasant household…Heard from home for the first time since banishment. [A friend] brought me the letter via underground, per the hand of a K-a brave and faithful man. The letter was from my dear mother. Did not read it until after retiring to my room. Cried all night. Received an appointment in the Commanding General's office...The same day went before the examining board, Dec. 15th. Passed.

Christmas Day was lonely and miserable. Went to church in the morning...

"On her arrival in Richmond President Davis appointed her to a position which she successfully filled until the surrender."[22]

"Mr. Davis instructed General Northrope to offer Miss Goldsborough a position in the Treasury Department, which was then filled to overflowing. When informed there was no vacant position for Miss Goldsborough, he said, "Well then make one!"

"The Maryland Line sent a formal invitation to Richmond for her to dine with them in camp and far and near came letters from the wives and mothers of officers and men who had been nursed at Gettysburg. On one occasion when the Maryland troops were in Richmond and were passing through the streets, Miss Goldsborough was recognized in the crowds of Department ladies, who were eagerly watching the troops."[23]

The Confederate Treasury Department was housed in the old U. S. Customs building in Richmond. It was one of the buildings that survived the war. Many of the employees in this department were refugees or exiles like Miss Effie.
(Virginia State Library and Archives)

"The word passed rapidly along the line and Maryland's bravest sons paid tribute to her, exiled daughter, and while cheering, the entire regiment passed her with hats off—a compliment to her personally."[24]

Miss Effie worked at the Treasury Department in the mornings and spent her afternoons at the city hospitals. Her diary for 1864 contained brief and sporadic entries:

> Entered upon my duties at the Department 1st of January, 1864. How different from others I had passed with the friends of youth gathered around. Jan. 9th left Mrs. Southall's to board in a private family on Main Street near 3rd from no fault but that of reducing expenses. Found a pleasant home with Mrs. Judge Nichols. Staid with her until her son was married. Roomed with a sweet, lovely girl from Clarksville, Tenn. Went back to Mrs. Southall's on May 9th. Roomed with Mrs. Seldon from Norfolk—found a dear friend in her. Battles raging all around—sound of cannon ringing in my ears day and night. Days or sorrow with our bravest and best being brought back to us dying, or dead.
>
> Left Richmond July 18, 1864 to visit Rockbridge, Va. Capt. Houston met me in Lexington.[25] Brought me to his home, a sweet lovely spot with the beautiful blue mountains piling up one above the other on every side. His family, God bless them, I can never forget their kindness to the homeless exile. Returned to my Post Sept. 14th, reaching Lynchburg that night in company with Capt. A. Houston who escorted me to Barkville Junction. Reached Richmond Sept. 15th…with a head cold. Sick several days. Many Marylanders and friends wounded in the hospital. My time divided. Department in the morning, hospital in the afternoon, until entirely broken down.
>
> Mrs. Southall's board raised to $50 a day, five extra. Obliged to move on that account. Nov. 15th went to board with Maj. Young, corner 6th and Leigh. A fine and most extravagant home, rich with grandeur. Nearly all the while throat much congested and but for the kindness of outside friends should have suffered for everything. Got up for the first time Christmas Day. A large dinner party. Was present at the table but ate nothing. Sick in bed nearly all week after, [the] Dr…attending me twice a day.

Miss Goldsborough's diary for 1865 begins:

> Jan. 1st left on the Danville train to visit Dr. Martin's family. Had known Col. M at Gettysburg.[26] Went in a box car, the only lady on the train, escorted by Maj. Wood. Fine transportation. Reached D[anville],

10 o'clock a.m. Found Col. M. waiting for me at the depot. Started to Tunstal House, got in about 2:00 p.m. Next morning, Jan. 2nd, started for the Colonel's house. A most uncomfortable day—besides being sick rode twenty miles in a snow storm. Found his kindness to the weary wanderer. I staid with them, making many new and pleasant acquaintances until Feb. 16th...

That night reached Danville about 8 p.m. Started at 10 p.m. on the train for Richmond, meeting all the refugees from Columbia, S.C., old and young drinking and smoking, "fleeing from the wrath to same"—Lay on the road broken down the greater part of the next day—violently sick several hours—the same day. Reached Richmond at 12:00 that night.

Feb. 14th went to board with Cousin Em Garnett—corner Grace and Jefferson. A week passed pleasantly enough (Early I was on walks in the balmy sunshine, dreaming of the happy hours away). A month of weariness—hard work at the office, doubts for success of our beloved cause, the safety of our capital, headaches and heartaches. Then came sunshine for when did not sympathy and kindness make glad and bright the heart.

March 22nd. Our prisoners from Johnson Island returned.[27] Brave soldiers and gentlemen. Know my heart warmed toward all of their kind.

Thursday, March 23rd. Had a perfect reception...of officers and friends I had known upon the bloody field of Gettysburg when it had been my happy privilege to nurse and attend them.

March 26th, Sunday morning. I left Richmond in company with Capt. T. D. Houston to visit his dear home again, little dreaming the terrible fate of our glorious capital in a week's time...We reached Lynchburg that night and found the canal boat not running. Left Lynchburg Tuesday morning, March 28th in an ambulance and pair of condemned mules to journey over the mountains, a distance of forty miles (with Capt. Houston and McCullough) which we were two days accomplishing. The first night we stopped in the mountains at the home of a stranger and asked for lodgings. With true Virginia (all honor to the brave old state) hospitality we were received by the owner whose ancestral name and blood had its heading in the veins of Cavaliers. Mr. Minor and his family were indeed a charming family in whom beauty of both soul and mind shone forth. Early the next morning we started, reaching the home of Capt. Mack [McCullough] about 4 p.m. where we were most cordially greeted, he having returned from imprisonment of two years.

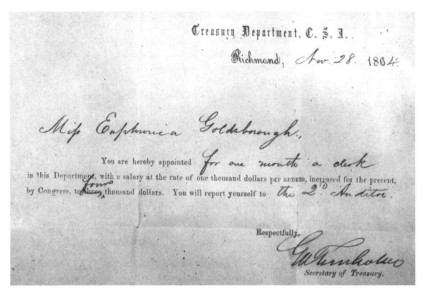

**Miss Effie's appointment to a position as clerk at the
C.S. Treasury Department dated November 1864.**
(Goldsborough Collection)

In deep sorrow and humiliation I must record the evacuation of our much-loved city, Richmond, April 2nd, 1865. April 5th I came to Dr. Houston's and here the news of Gen. Lee's surrender, April 9th reached us on Monday afternoon. I could not believe it at first but in a few hours our weary, worn, crushed, and bleeding soldiers began to come returning through the mountains. Our army disbanded, their muskets stacked, our people scattered to the four winds. Oh! days and weeks of agony, fears, with no word of comfort, of hope or of home.

June 19th my dear Father came for me. Left Rockbridge June 27th. Reached home July 2nd, Sunday morning before breakfast, 1865.

Miss Effie's diary of the next three years related excursions to Virginia's sites of natural beauty and visits to friends of that state.[28] The latter part of 1868 revealed Pheme involved in an intense relationship with a Mr. Douglas, a man she treated with both caution and passion. There is some mystery connected with the romance and her diary ends abruptly on a euphoric note.

It was not Mr. Douglas, however, who won Effie's hand. Charles Perry Willson was the widower of a close friend of Miss Effie. He was a veteran of the Laurel Brigade and a man with a delightful sense of humor. They married in Cambridge, Maryland on June 29, 1874. Effie's hair which showed streaks of gray after her incarceration by the Union military was, by the time of her marriage at age 38, almost completely white. Upon her marriage, Pheme became the mother of five children. She and Charles would have three more; Martin, Sam and Ann.

> When the war closed she came back to Baltimore, married a Marylander of Frederick County, Mr. Charles Perry Willson, an ex-Confederate soldier. They removed to Summit Point, Jefferson County, West Virginia, where their hospitality was soon acknowledged and will be long remembered. Twenty years ago it was a real privilege to meet there in winter and all gather round the blazing fire, when host and hostess and many guests would recall their war experiences. Sometimes the guests would be snowed in and we would have a house party for days of the bachelor veterans of the war and there we would sit hour after hour in the old Southern home, the soldiers with their favorite dogs that followed them everywhere, stretched at full length before the huge fire of logs that burned away only to be replaced while first one battle scene and then another was repeated by some who were in the fight. This would go on for days and never get tiresome. Finally Mrs. Willson devoted the same energy to church work that she had given to the Confederate cause and the beautiful stone church standing now at Summit Point is largely due to her efforts.[29]

In Summit Point Charles would farm, run a mercantile establishment and a boarding house. Their home and the boarding house still stand. Remaining also is the Episcopal Church of the Holy Spirit. Effie was one the moving forces behind its erection even soliciting a donation from the Queen of England.

Sons Martin and Sam would die the same week in November 1880. Charles died in 1893. Miss Effie buried her family in one of the first family plots in Green Hill Cemetery, outside Berryville, Virginia, on a small knoll, according to Charles' wishes that he be buried where he could see the sun rise. Euphemia Mary Goldsborough Willson died of cancer in Baltimore on March 10, 1896.

"In 1896 this earnest, active, self-sacrificing Southern lady with the spirit of Joan of Arc quietly joined the great army of martyrs and laid down the cross in the shadow of the Rock and was laid to rest in Virginia, the State she dearly loved, near the little town of Berryville in Clark County, beside her husband and children."[30]

Miss Effie, left, and friend in Virginia shortly after the war.
(Goldsborough Collection)

A photo taken a year after Miss Effie married Charles Willson.
(Goldsborough Collection)

Martin Willson, one of Miss Effie and Charles' sons.
(Goldsborough Collection)

Ann Willson, daughter and only surviving child of Miss Effie.
(Goldsborough Collection)

The Willson's house in Summit Point, West Virginia.
(Author's collection)

The boarding house in Summit Point owned by the Willsons was next to their home.
(Author's collection)

The Episcopal Church of the Holy Spirit in Summit Point.
(Author's collection)

"Acknowledged as a genius with pronounced intellect, she was urged to write reminiscences of the war for Southern History—but falling into ill health she never complied with the wishes of her many friends.

And so a varied life has closed and shut up the treasury house of a brilliant memory. Like many for whom she risked life and liberty, she has passed—fully prepared tho' untrumpeted to a glorious reward. Thus with tears for her loss, regret for her sorrows, we lay with reverence the laurel wreath upon her grave."[31]

Miss Effie's legacy has survived through her descendants who are in possession of her many war mementos. These mementos tell only a tantalizing part of the story of a woman who helped shape history and who touched many lives with her resolution, courage and kindness, all at great risk to herself. Miss Effie's life was a treasure rich with history, honor and sacrifice—the ingredients of a legend.

Much has transpired to honor Pheme's efforts since this volume was published. Through Mrs. Elizabeth Crim, Miss Effie's granddaughter who rejoiced in her ancestor's story, I was allowed free access to the Goldsborough collection. In 1998, *Exile to Sweet Dixie* was released after years of researching the names and events in the documents, letters, hospital books and diary. In 1999 the Order of Southern Gray, a

Miss Effie's lap desk with secret compartment and drawers.
(Goldsborough Collection)

ladies organization, named the newly formed chapter in the Berryville area after Pheme Goldsborough. That same year a dedication ceremony was held on November 20th when a plaque commemorating her service to the Confederacy was laid on the grave. One of the participants was a young woman who had begun to portray Pheme in the living history programs of the Gettysburg National Military Park, the only Confederate woman then recognized.

I nominated Euphemia Goldsborough for the Maryland Women's Hall of Fame and she was inducted in March 1995. The night of the award ceremony was unforgettable. The first three rows of the auditorium were filled with Goldsborough descendants from West Virginia, Louisiana, North Carolina and Utah as they watched Pheme's granddaughter, great granddaughter and great grandson receive the recognition from the Governor. Miss Elizabeth, who had suffered a stoke the year before, told me if she died that night she would die happy. My

Stephanie Wortz, portraying Euphemia Goldsborough, stands at
Effie's gravesite during a wreath laying ceremony preceding
Goldsborough's induction into the Maryland Women's Hall of Fame.
(Author's collection)

Dedication of the plaque commemorating Effie's war service.
(Author's collection)

435

heart still swells at that memory and the time I was allowed with that wonderful lady before she passed.

Defeat is not dishonor,
No, of honor not bereft,
We should thank God that in our breast,
This priceless boom is left.

Oh, should we reach that glorious place
Where waits the sparkling crown
For everyone who for the right
His soldier life lay down.

God grant to us the privilege
Upon that happy day,
Of clasping hands with those who fell
'A wearing of the gray.'

The Maryland Women's Hall of Fame induction ceremony in Annapolis. Seated is Elizabeth Crim, granddaughter. Standing (l to r) are, Gov. Parris Glendening, Stuart Crim, great-grandson, Betsy Stagner, great-granddaughter, and Phyllis Trickett, chairwoman of the Maryland Commission for Women.
(Author's collection)

Maryland's monument to Confederate Women was unveiled in Baltimore in 1918.
(Museum of the Confederacy)

Conclusion

he war would drag on for two more years. In the summer of 1863 no one knew how many more battles would be fought and how many thousands of lives were yet to be lost. It was Abraham Lincoln who defined the democratic principles for which he believed men should fight and die in his Gettysburg Address delivered November 19, 1863. Ironically, Southerners believed in those same American principles, though in an irreconcilably different way. It was the Southern soldier, Robert E. Lee, who showed courage and intelligence when he put an end to the killing and surrendered to U.S. Grant at Appomattox on April 9, 1865.

Knowing, now, these women who served at Gettysburg, one may be more sensitive to women's rightful place in history. Perhaps there will be some new thoughts and images when considering the battle. Will our mind's eye see Annie Etheridge galloping from the Trostle farm into the line of fire or the female Confederate soldier dying in agony on the field in front of the angle? Will we think of Elizabeth Thorn digging graves, or Clarissa Jones turning a blind eye towards a prisoner's escape, or Effie Goldsborough sitting on the floor with a dying soldier tied to her back? Woolsey's intelligence, Dame's humor, Harris' faith, Brady's sacrifice, and Gilson's love all contribute to the rich legacy left by our American foremothers.

When Arabella Barlow died, a friend wrote: "All of us are the poorer for her loss, but our history has been enriched by her death. Let it always be remembered as one of those details which, like single pearls, make up the precious string of history and which a patriot rejoices to contemplate and to transmit like inherited jewels to the rising generations.

Here is one strand of pearls. The history these women made at Gettysburg is a gift for us and for our children.

Endnotes

POEM

1. Sybil, a well know war era poet, was the pen name of Miss Anna Platt. This poem was found in one of the photograph albums at the U.S. Army War College in Carlisle, PA.

PREFACE

2. Frederick Phister, *New York in the War of the Rebellion 1861-1865*, Vol. I (Albany: D.E. Lyns Co., 1912) 142
3. William H. Tunnard, *A Southern Record-the History of the Third Regiment Louisiana Infantry* (Baton Rouge, LA, 1866) 345
4. United Daughters of the Confederacy, South Caroline Division, *South Carolina Women in the Confederacy* (Columbia, SC: The State Company, 1903-07) Vol. I

THE CAMPAIGN

5. Charlotte McKay, *Stories of Hospital and Camp* (Philadelphia: Clayton, Tensen, & Hoffelfinger, 1876) 50
6. McKay, 86-88
7. Alice Powers, *Gettysburg Compiler*, "Dark Days of the Battle Week," July 1, 1902.
8. See "Jennie Wade."
9. Belle Boyd, *Belle Boyd in Camp and Prison*, ed. Carroll Curtis Davis (Cranbury, NJ; Thomas Yoseloff, 1968) 215-216
   Belle Boyd was a Confederate spy which was the reason for her incarcerations. Boyd's early war experience serves to illustrate how Southern women's status as the "weaker sex" protected them only in the beginning of the war. In July 1861 Belle shot and killed a Union soldier who tried to raise the U.S. flag over her house. Because the soldier had been drunk and offensive, the Union commander excused her behavior with the judgment she "had done perfectly right." Compare this to the establishment of women's prisons such as the St. Louis Prison for Southern Women in 1863 and to Mary Surratt's death by hanging after the Lincoln conspiracy trial.
10. Judith McGuire, *Diary of a Southern Refugee* (New York: E.J. Hale, 1867) 224-225
11. McGuire, 226
12. M.E. Massey, *Bonnet Brigades* (New York: Knopf, 1966) 223: a quote from Margaret Junkin Preston. A Confederate soldier wrote that the Northern women "were in no danger themselves. There was no Milroy, no Butler, no Hunter, no Sheridan, no Sherman, to taunt and upbraid them, to strip them of their most precious mementos, to steal or scatter their scanty store of provisions and burn their homes over their head." [Capt. Francis Dawson, *Our Women of the War*, (Charleston, SC: Walker, Evans, & Cogswell Co., 1887) 1.] The above named Union generals were infamous for the burning and looting of Southern homes and institutions, destruction of crops and stock, and abuse and sometimes torture and murder of civilians.

JULY FIRST

1. *Gettysburg Compiler*, unidentified Gettysburg lady, July 4, 1906
2. Jennry McCreary, GNMP Civilian Folder
3. Sally Broadhead, *Diary of a Lady of Gettysburg, Pennsylvania*: preface states it was not published, but "printed" for friends, relatives, and the Sanitary Commission, no date, 13
4. *Gettysburg Compiler*, Mrs. Joseph Bayly's Story of the Battle," pp 1 & 2, GNMP scrapbook.
5. It was the 6th Wisconsin who bagged these Confederates. It is said that is was this regiment whose impression on Julia Ward Howe sparked her lyrics to the "Battle Hymn of the Republic," a much loved war song of the North. Howe, a prolific writer, wrote the Battle Hymn in early 1862. Five years after the Civil War, Mrs. Howe had a change of attitude toward war. Sickened by the Franco-Prussian War she wrote in 1870 an "Appeal to Womanhood throughout the World" in which was the following poem. Her call was to all women through all time.

Arise then, women of this day!
Arise all women who have hearts,
Whether your baptism be that of water or of tears!
Say firmly:
"We will not have great questions decided by irrelevant agencies,
Our husbands shall not come to us, reeking with carnage,
For caresses and applause.
Our sons shall not be taken from us to unlearn
All that we have been able to teach them
Of charity, mercy, and patience.
We women of one country
Will be too tender of those of another country
To allow our sons to be trained to injure theirs"
From the bosom of the devastated earth a voice goes up
With our own. It says, "Disarm! Disarm!"

6. General John B. Gordon, *Reminiscences of the Civil War* (New York: Charles Scribner and Sons, 1903) pp.151-152
7. Mrs. Jacob A. Clutz, *Personal Recollections of the Battle of Gettysburg*, GNMP civilian files.
8. Broadhead, 14

PLANK

1. This was told to the Plank family by a medical orderly as they entered the house with wounded. Lizzie Plank's entire narrative is taken from the transcription of an interview housed in the Blake Collection, Civilian Accounts, at the U.S. Army War College, Carlisle, Pennsylvania.
2. For an excellent work on the hospitals at Gettysburg, see Gregory A. Coco's *A Vast Sea of Misery* (Gettysburg, PA: Thomas Publications 1988)

BARLOW

1. Brockett & Vaughn, *Women's Work in the Civil War* (Boston: R.H. Curran, 1867) 228
2. Francis Channing Barlow Civil War letters, 1861-1865, Massachusetts Historical Society, not published.
3. "An Echo of the Battle," Gettysburg *Star and Sentinel* 2 July 1913, p. 1, cols. 6-8: this article contains excerpts from Miss Jane Smith's war diary.
4. Skelley narrative, GNMP Civilian folder
5. Letters. Barlow's correspondence to his relatives does not mention General Gordon's kindness. He does mention, however, the destruction of letters, one being an offer of the position of Superintendent of Freedman, a letter which Barlow thought disadvantageous to the opportunity of parole. There were only two houses in the area around the Almshouse complex, that of Josiah Benner and a large white house locally known as the Crawford house. The latter house was most likely where Mrs. Jane Smith resided. Both houses still stand today.
6. Brockett & Vaughn 227
7. *The Sanitary Commission Bulletin*, Vol. I, 616
8. Don Richard Lauter, "Once Upon a Time in the East…Arabella Wharton Griffith Barlow,"*The Journal of Women's Civil War History,* Vol. I (Gettysburg, PA: Thomas Publications 2001) 9,14. Arabella was acquainted with a remarkable number of well known social, political and artistic people and can be found mentioned in surprising places. Though her life was cut short, it was a rich and interesting one that deserves its own published biography and there is only one man I know who could do her justice.
9. Letters
10. Letters, Dec. 14, 1861
11. Letters
12. Letters, June 2, 1862
13. Letters
14. *Bulletin*, 614
15. Letters

16. Letters
17. Letters
18. Lauter 21
19. Ibid.
20. Letters
21. Brockett & Vaughn 228-229
22. *Bulletin* 615
23. Cornelia Hancock, *South After Gettysburg*, ed. Henrietta Jacquette (StrattonCowell Co., 1937) 106
24. W. W. Potter, *Reminiscences of Field Hospital Service with the Army of the Potomac*, "Buffalo Medical & Surgical Journal," (New York, October and November 1889) 23
25. Letters
26. Letters
27. Brockett & Vaughn 232-233; excerpted from DR. W. H. Reed's *Hospital Life in the Army of the Potomac.*
28. Mrs. P. M. Clapp, *Old and New*, "Helen L. Gilson: A Memorial," (April & May 1872) 570

GORDON

1. Fanny Gordon letters, Georgia Department of Archives and History
2. *Confederate Veteran*, Vol. 39, pp 234-235
3. John Gordon papers, Hargrett Rare Book and Manuscript Library, University of Georgia Libraries, Athens, Georgia
4. Papers
5. Papers. This last letter could hold its own with any other written declaration of love, any where, any time.
6. Papers
7. *United Daughters of the Confederacy Magazine*, May 1952: 10
8. Gordon 3-4
9. Letters
10. Gordon 49
11. Gordon 52
12. Gordon 59
13. Letters
14. Gordon 91
15. Ibid.
16. Letters
17. Gordon 320-321
18. Gordon 322-323
19. Gordon 379
20. Gordon 406
21. *Confederate Veteran*, Vol. V: 23
22. Gordon 423
23. *Confederate Veteran*, Vol. V: 23
24. *Holland's Magazine*, February 1938
25. Papers
26. Augusta *Herald*, Sunday, 30 July 1930
27. Gordon 454
28. Holland's
29. Gordon xviii
30. Holland's
31. *Confederate Veteran*, Vol. XL: 34
32. Augusta *Chronicle*, 28 April 1931
33. The Atlanta *Journal,* no date, Gordon papers

HORNE

1. John A. Chapman, *History of Edgefield County from the Earliest Settlements to 1897* (Spartanburg, SC: The Reprint Co.) 490; statement by Pvt. Rufus Harling of Co. K who was wounded the first day of the battle of Gettysburg and also at the Wilderness.

2. J.F.J. Caldwell, *The History of a Brigade of South Carolinians known first as Gregg's and subsequently as "McGowan's Brigade"* (Philadelphia: King & Baird, 1866) 94
3. Chapman 482
4. Chapman 488
5. South Carolina Historical Society paper
6. S.C.H.S. paper
7. Chapman 489-490
8. Clarence Poe, *True Tales of the South at War; How the Soldiers Fought and Families lived 1861-1865* (Chapel Hill: The University of North Carolina Press, 1961) 35
9. Chapman 483
10. O.V. Burton, *In My Father's House Are Many Mansions, Family and Community in Edgefield County, S.C.* (Chapel Hill: The University of North Carolina Press, 1985) 107
11. Chapman 490
12. Chapman 22
13. Papers sent from the War Memorial Building Museum in Columbia, SC.
14. Chapman 490
15. Chapman 491
16. Chapman 490
17. Chapman 490
18. *Confederate Veteran* 183
19. S.C.H.S. paper
20. Chapman

MCALLISTER

1. McAllister's entire narrative comes from the Philadelphia *Inquirer*, June 26-29, 1938 housed in the Civilian folders at GNMP.
2. Brigadier General James J. Archer was a Confederate officer captured the morning of the first day near McPherson's Ridge. Although Dailey had nothing to do with the capture, he took the prize of the General's sword. One can speculate the priority put upon this military souvenir by a terrified woman whose home was filled with wounded men and surround by enemy soldiers and gunfire.
3. A parole is a pledge of honor under which a prisoner of war is released with the understanding that he will not again bear arms until exchanged.
4. The fear of being fed poisoned food by "enemy women" was not uncommon during the war. This researcher has not yet found a verified account of any instance.
5. The evening of July 3 the Confederates got off their wounded and withdrew to consolidate their line along Seminary Ridge.

GARLACH

1. All quotations are from the papers in the Garlach family folder in the GNMP files on civilians.

SPENCER

1. Seventeenth Publication of the Oswego County Historical Society, 1954 (Oswego, NY: Palladium Times, Inc.) 42
2. RG 233, Records of the U.S. House of Representatives, 48th Congress, H.R. 7262, pension for Elmina Spencer. Quotations are from depositions by veterans.
3. Oswego 41
4. Pension
5. Oswego 42
6. Pension
7. Pension
8. Brockett & Vaughn 408
9. Pension
10. Brockett & Vaughn 408
11. Pension
12. Pension
13. Pension
14. Pension

15. Pension
16. Oswego 43-44
17. Pension
18. Oswego 44-45
19. Sophronia Bucklin, *In Hospital and Camp*, (Philadelphia: John E. Potter & Co., 1869) 258, 271
20. Oswego 44-45
21. Bucklin 323-324
22. Oswego 42
23. Oswego 45
24. Bucklin 317

JULY SECOND
1. Harriet Bayly, *Gettysburg Compiler*, 30 October 1939, GNMP Civilian File
2. Susan Leigh Blackford, compiler, *Letters from Lee's Army* (New York: Charles Scribner's and Sons, 1947) 4.
3. Simpkins and Patton, *The Women of the Confederacy* (Richmond and NY: Garrett & Massie, Inc., 1936) 206
4. *Confederate Veteran*, Vol. 39: 235

DAME
1. U.S. Army War College, quotation written in her own hand found in photography collection.
2. Report attached to HR 3307, 48th Congress, pension for Harriet Dame, 7.
3. Martin A. Haynes, *A History of the Second Regiment, New Hampshire, Volunteer Infantry in the War of the Rebellion, Co. I*, (Lakeport, NH, 1896), 167.
4. Haynes, 301
5. Haynes, 183
6. Major Otis F. K. Waite, *New Hampshire in the Rebellion*, (Claremont, NH: Tracy, Chase, & Co., 1870) 125
7. Pension, 4
8. Pension, 4
9. Haynes, 297
10. Haynes, 297
11. Pension, 4, 5
12. Haynes, 97
13. Haynes, 297-299
14. Pension, 5
15. Poem by Enoch George Adams

> *Harriet Dame and Stonewall*
>
> Give her a niche in the Temple of Fame—
> Our hospital matron, Harriet Dame!
> She left her home in the Granite State,
> To share with the soldier his lot and fate;
> Wherever the Second New Hampshire was called,
> There was our matron, unappalled.
> She followed us close to the battle's brink,
> And never was known to flee or shrink;
>
> Mid danger and death, mid sickness and pain,
> We never looked for her face in vain.
> To visit and comfort, to cheer and bless,
> To sorrow appease, and relieve distress,
> This her ambition and soul's desire,
> That burned in her breast like a vestal fire.
>
> After the terrible fight was done
> At the second battle of Bull Run,
> Our wounded were left in the rebel lines,

And she was there, mid the stunted pines,
In the midst of the bloodiest field accurst,
Bearing water to quench the thirst
Of the wounded men, in delirium wild,
With the blood and dust of war defiled.

Stonewall Jackson, he found her there,
And was filled with respect for her noble air;
He said to his surgeons, "Pitch her a tent,
This kindly woman of grand intent,
In safety her mission to fulfill;
Give her protection—it is my will."

Then the rebel soldiers, first and last,
Blessed her and bowed when'er she passed;
A guard 'round her tent at night they stood,
In the kindly feeling of brotherhood.
"If such are Yankee women," they said,
"No wonder we do not get ahead!"

And when an armistice was arranged,
And the wounded men were interchanged,
As off the field the last ambulance rolled,
And the dead were buried beneath the mold,
Stonewall Jackson said to his men,
"Convey the lady home again."

Rebels before, and rebels behind,
Were a guard of honor, as he designed.
Such a shout of joy was our boys upsent,
When she rested at home in her own snug tent,
Never was heard by the welkin blue.
I have told the story; and what say you?

From Waite 335-336. Almost a complete fabrication of the actual event, it was gratifying that Jackson was not accused of threatening to shoot Harriet's "old gray head" off.

16. Pension, 5
17. Pension, 2
18. Pension, 5
19. Pension, 6
20. Pension, 6
21. Pension, 6 & 7
22. Pension, 7
23. Pension, 7
24. Waite, 126
25. Pension, 7
26. Waite, 126
27. Pension, 7
28. Pension, 8
29. Pension, 8
30. Haynes, 296

FARNHAM

1. Mary A. Gardner Holland, *Our Army Nurses*, "Amanda M. Felch," by Marshall P. Felch, (Boston: B. Wilkins & Co., 1895) 290. Dorothea Dix to Amanda Farnham.
2. HR 8388, 51st Congress, Amanda Farnham pension
3. Holland, 287-88
4. Pension
5. Holland, 288
6. Pension

7. Holland, 288-89. There is no concrete evidence where the well incident took place. A probable guess would be the Jacob Schwartz farm which was at the junction of Rock Creek and White Run. This was the site of the III Corps hospital but it also held VI Corps wounded.
8. Pension
9. Holland, 289
10. Holland, 283
11. Pension
12. Holland, 283.
13. Pension
14. Holland, 284-85
15. Pension
16. Holland 286
17. Pension, Andrew W. Brazel, late Major 48th N.Y.V. & Provost Marshal, Second Div., VI Corps
18. Pension
19. Holland, 286
20. Pension
21. Holland, 287
22. Pension
23. Holland, 287
24. Holland, 285-287
25. Pension
26. Pension, Brazel
27. Pension
28. Holland, 290
29. Pension
30. According to Henry Colburn's war records he was wounded May 6, 1864, and was sent to a U.S. General Hospital in Brattleboro, Vermont, and mustered out July 27, 1864, as his term of service expired.
31. Pension
32. Pension, Brazel
33. M.P. Felch 1890 pension submission
34. Felch pension
35. Felch pension
36. Articles were written on Marshall Felch's work in the *Canon City Register*, available through the Canon City Historical Society. Marshall Felch committed suicide in 1902.

PIERCE

1. Tillie Pierce Alleman, *At Gettysburg or What a Girl Saw and Heard of the Battle* (New York: W. Lake Borland, 1889) 47.
2. Alleman 43-44
3. Alleman 49-50
4. Alleman 51-52
5. Not everyone in the group reached the destination. For some reason in this panic stricken exodus from the frying pan into the fire, Mrs. Weikert suddenly remembered she had left a new petticoat in her house and insisted her husband return for it. And he did! The group met him on the front steps of the Weikert house carrying the treasure when they returned.
6. Alleman 53-56
7. Alleman 58
8. Alleman 61-64
9. Alleman 72
10. Alleman 74
11. Alleman 82-83
12. Alleman 84
13. Alleman 117

ETHERIDGE

1. Etheridge Pension, RG 46, S 2884, 49th Congress

2. Pension, Exhibit B
3. Pension, Exhibit B
4. Pension, Exhibit O
5. Pension, Exhibit B
6. Agatha Young, *Women and the Crisis* (New York: McDowell, Oblensky, 1958) 125
7. Pension, Exhibit U
8. Pension, Exhibit B
9. Young, 125
10. Pension
11. Edwin B Houghton, *The Campaigns of the 17th Maine* (Portland, ME: Short & Loring, 1866) 62
12. Pension, Exhibit P
13. Houghton 63
14. Houghton 64
15. Brockett & Vaughn 749
16. Pension, Exhibit B
17. Pension
18. Colonel S. B. Hayman, Pension, Exhibit L
19. Houghton 63
20. Brockett & Vaughn 749
21. Robert G. Carter, *Four Brothers in Blue* (Austin & London: University of Texas Press) 215
22. Carter 248
23. Pension, Exhibit O
24. Pension, Exhibit U
25. Pension, Exhibit C. "[Gen.] D. B. Birney, who succeeded Kearny, directed on 13 Mar. '63 that a 'cross of valor' be awarded to enlisted men who had distinguished themselves in battle. This was a bronze cross pattee with 'Kearny Cross' on the front and 'Birney's Division' on the back…Among the first to receive the award were two women, Ann Etheridge and Marie Tebe [*sic*]" (Boatner 449)
26. Houghton 70
27. Pension, Exhibit B
28. Pension, Exhibit B
29. Pension, Exhibit S
30. Pension, Exhibit U
31. Brevet Major General Clair A. Mulholland, *The Story of the 116th Regiment Pennsylvania Infantry* (Phildelphia: F. McManus, Jr. & Co) no date, 135
32. Daniel G. Crotty, *Four Years Campaigning with the Army of the Potomac* (Grand Rapids, MI: Dysart Bros. & Co., 1874) 107
33. Pension
34. Pension, Exhibit B
35. Brockett & Vaughn
36. Hancock 113
37. Hancock 131
38. Hancock 156. Hancock didn't like any nurse to be more well known or admired than she.
39. Pension, Exhibit U
40. Pension
41. One of these poems was printed in *Women of the War*, page 517

> *To Miss Anna Etheridge*
> *The Heroine of the War*
>
> Hail, heroine of the battle-field!
> Sweet angel of a zeal divine!
> Hail, Maiden, whose device and shield,
> Sculptured in tears and prayers, will shine,
> On Love's eternal column reared
> In memory of the martyred dead,
> To be, through coming time, revered,

And sacred to the pilgrim's tread!

Hail, dauntless maid! whose shadowy form,
Borne like a sunbeam on the air.
Swept by amid the battle-storm,
Cheering the helpless sufferers there,
Amid the cannon's smoke and flame,
The earthquake roar of shot and shell,
Winning, by deeds of love, a name
Immortal as the brave who fell.

Hail, angel! whose diviner spell
Charmed dying heroes with her prayer,
Stanching their wounds amid the knell
Of death, destruction, and despair.
Thy name my memory shall be wreathed
Round many desolate hearts in prayer;
By orphan lips it shall be breathed,
And float in songs upon the air.

And History's pages shall embalm
The heroine's deed in lines of fire;
Her life shall prove a hallowed charm,
And every loyal heart inspire.
Press on, press on! in glory move!
Unfading laurels shall be thine
To gem the victor-crown of Love,
And sparkle in the realms divine!

42. Brockett & Vaughn 752
43. Hancock 175
44. Crotty 171
45. Pension
46. Crotty 204
47. Two sources list the date as 1844 which would make Annie barely 17 years of age at enlistment. Since she was already twice married by 1861, this birth year is highly unlikely. Annie's tombstone is unreadable and Arlington National Cemetery does not keep a record of stone inscriptions. Her death certificate, the next best source, place her birth at 1839.
48. This seems the most probably circumstance. There are some sources that claim Annie was supporting her father after the war in D.C. but there is no evidence to support this; just as there is not evidence to support that her father died when she was a child.
49. Two Michigan men by the name of James Etheridge were found. One served in Co. C, 2nd Michigan, enlisting May 10, 1861, for 3 years. He was discharged for disability at Baltimore, MD on Sept. 30, 1862. The other James Etheridge was in Co. I, 7th MI Cav., which one source states definitely as her husband. He received $25 for enlisting on Feb. 19, 1863, and deserted sometime after Aug. 1863. He was mustered out from Ft. Leavenworth on Dec. 15, 1865. Whether either of these men was her husband or some other James Etheridge, it appears the only thing Annie kept from this marriage was the name.
50. Pension, Exhibit M
51. Annie lived in her veteran comrade's memories. They rallied by her side in her times of need and never abandoned her; history was left to forget her. One wonders how the men of the Army of the Potomac would feel about that. "And History's pages shall embalm The heroine's deeds in line of fire..."
52. Pension

TEPE

1. *Military Images,* July-August 1983, 14
2. Carter 281-82
3. Carter 282
4. Carter 282

5. Frank Rauscher, *Music on the March 1862-1865 with the Army of the Potomac* (Philadelphia: Press of Wm. F. Fell & Co., 1892) 24
6. Rauscher 34
7. Carter 282
8. McKay 40
9. Rauscher 68. Coincidentally, at the same time, the Army of Northern Virginia considered medals for their soldiers, which effected much the same reaction. "An effort was made, during this period, to introduce the system of conferring medals as rewards and incentives of gallantry. One was offered to each company, to be given to the soldier whom the majority of his company should select as the most distinguished for gallantry in the battle of Chancellorsville. But it excited no competition, no enthusiasm. It was most commonly conferred on men killed in that battle, partly from the inability of the men to select the most gallant of the company, partly to afford the families of the dead some consolation in their bereavement. The system failed after this, entirely. Some attributed it to a culpable indifference to reputation, others to a high, stern patriotism which felt the cause far above baubles of metal. I believe both causes combined to produce the result...(Caldwell 89)
10. Carter 281
11. Rauscher 93-95
12. Rauscher 139-140
13. *Military Images*, March-April 1983, 18
14. *Pittsburgh Dispatch,* 14 May 1901
15. *Military Images*, March-April 14

ROONEY

1. Fannie A. Beers, *Memories* (Philadelphia: J. B. Lippencott Co., 1888) 217-218
2. Terry L. Jones, *Lee's Tigers* (Baton Rouge: Louisiana State Univ. Press, 1985) 253-254
3. Jones 13
4. Collection #55V, Bound Volume 10, Louisiana Historical Association Confederate Records Collection, Special Collections (commonly known as Historical Memoranda), Howard-Tilton Memorial Library, Tulane University, New Orleans
5. "Although the Peninsula [Campaign] was where the Tiger's reputation was largely born, it was near Manassas and Centreville, Virginia that the term 'Louisiana Tigers' came into being. It was while stationed near these towns that Wheat's Battalion earned it *nom de guerre* because of its fierce fighting at the First Battle of Manassas and subsequent career of unbridled lawlessness. The title was most probably taken from the Zouave company, Tiger Rifles, because its members were the most conspicuous and proved to be the wildest of the battalion. The term was widely used by the autumn of 1861, and soon because the deeds of the Peninsula Louisianans received such great publicity, was applied to all of the state's soldiers in Virginia." Terry L. Jones, *Louisiana History,* "Wharf Rats, Cutthroats and Thieves: The Louisiana Tigers, 1861-1862" Spring, Volume 27, #2, 158
6. *Louisiana History* 152
7. Historical Memoranda
8. Historical Memoranda
9. Beers 218
10. Beers 218
11. Beers 218-220
12. Beers 220
13. *Daily Picayune*, 5 February 1893, col. 4: 17
14. *Daily Picayune*, 1 March 1895, col. 7: 4

MYERS

All quotes in this narrative came from *The Care of the Wounded after the Battle of Gettysburg—July to November 1863* from the GNMP Civilian file.

JULY THIRD

1. Gettysburg *Star and Sentinel*, 2 July 1913, cols. 6-8: 1.
2. Broadhead 17-18

WADE

1. J.W. Johnston, *The True Story of "Jennie" Wade* (With the endorsement of her sister, Georgia Wade McClellan) [Rochester, NY: J. W. Johsnton] no date, 21. This was the last thing Georgia heard Jennie say.
2. Johnston 7, 11
3. Johnston 9
4. Johnston 13
5. Johnston 17, 15
6. Johnston 19
7. Johnston 23
8. Johnston 25
9. Johnston 27
10. Johnston 27
11. Johnston 27
12. The following is a letter from "Jack" Skelley to his mother. Punctuation and capitalization have been added for clarity, but the spelling is original.

Winchester, April 7/63

Dear Mother,

We received your wecom letter on the first. It found us both well and sorry to hear that you had a sore finger and that Anna was sick again. She has had a Pretty hard time of it this winter. You need not trouble yourself about being such a heavy charge on us boys for it (?) more pleasure to know what our money is doing some good when I sent it home than if I was to keep it and spend it foolishly. I always keep as much as I think ought to do me till I get Paid off again but the Pay Master has been so long that we are getting tired waiting on him. But I don't care for myself as long as I know that you are not in want. Their is seven Months pay due us now I suppose we will get six months pay when we get it. We expect it this week but Blessed are they that do not expect for they will not be deceived. About that affair with Jennie. I wrote to her and she denies keeping comp so late but she don't deny that she had some company and she wrote for my Arthur and I wrot to her telling who it was but I told her I did not know you author it was before you wrote. And I hope this will be the last of it till I get hom anny way then I will settle it. You should of said something to me when I first commenced their if you did not like it. Their has somebody being trying to raise a fuss between us is my honest belief but their is know use of trying wile I am away. I don't want you to think that I blame you at all for writing about it but it is all over for the present and I hope for the future. We received the box on Saterdy with the boots and things in and I would like to know what you sent them drawers pattern for. I don't need anything of the kind. Danny talked of coming out to see us. I wish he would come before he goes to West Point. I supose John had a great talk about our mess when he got home. I think he enjoyed himself when he was here. He did not care much about ging home but he did not say anything. I was on picket the morning he started so I did not get to see him. How is Georg getting along. Can he bawl as much as he did when we came home? Nothing more. I remain as every your affectionate sons,

Johnston H. Skelley

13. There were several poems written about Jennie Wade housed in the GNMP Cyclorama library. One was chosen as an example that read the best and with the least amount of misinformation. There is no evidence that any Union soldier tried to extradite Jennie or her brother from the McClellan house.

The Union Soldier

"What, Jenny Wade! Are you still here?
Against the table idly leaning
With naught on earth, you or your house
From the hot bullets' pathway screening.
The cannon-balls! You hear their hissing!
The youngster here, with terror shiv'ring.

He feels the earth beneath him quiv'ring."
"Come, fly!" the Union soldier said,
"For shot and shell fly o'er your head.
Nay, Jenny! Look not at your bread,
But hasten through won dusty tract,
Nor turn, like Lot's wife, to look back.
You and the boy must hurry on;
For all from Gettysburg have gone.
My horse stands at the door,
I only stepped this threshold o'er
To see if 'twere you or your ghost,
Here still, like sentry, at your post.
Our reinforcements swift come on;
I must be back here by the dawn.
God grant, not at our own hearth-stone,
Like cowards, we lie down to feel
Upon our necks th' invaders heel.
Oh, Jenny! Old John Burns is where
Thickest the fight, brightest the glare;
Had Pennsylvania's sons stood up
Like him, we need not of this cup
Of shame, have drunk the dregs. But haste!
Not yet these precious moments waste;
Come, Harry! Come! Spring up behind,
I will for you a refuge find.
Jenny! Tread thou where yon hill-side
Will thee from rebel bullet hide.
Follow its path, 'twill lead thee down
Where many, from our poor old town,
Are trembling like the birds that hear,
In forest aisles, the hunter near."

Then Jenny said, "I know not fear;
Shield thou the boy! Give him to those
Who'll guard him safe, until our foes
Are from our grieving valley thrust;
For drive out they'll be – they must!
Farewell, and God be with thee, Harry!"

"Jenny, I must away! Why tarry?"
The Union soldier said, perplexed.
And Jenny cried, "Oh! Be not vexed;
Go on thy errand, for, indeed,
Our fate may hang upon they speed.
Here I must stay!"

Away he reels;
The dust flies round his horse's heels;
Jenny hears not his steed's loud tramp,
Tears her eyes dim, her lashes damp.
The horseman round the steep path whirls;
She sees no more the golden curls
That, floating like eve's parting light,
Look brighter as they pass from sight.
The child she loved so well—Oh! Who
Will say that ever to her view
Will come again those eyes of blue,
That seemed oft from the grave's decay

To toll the heavy stone away,
And show from out the shadowed air
The angel-mother waiting there?

Soon Jenny's eyes forgot to weep,
For troops of horsemen by her sweep,
And, like the sunbeams on the river,
She sees their gleaming sabres quiver;
She hears the bullet whirring by;
She hears the trumpet's blast defy
Far hill and vale deep ravine
That sleep Wyoming's groves between,—
That, lulled by songs of peace, awake
When war's hoarse shout their slumbers break,
Like those affrighted from their rest
By footsteps of unwelcome guest.

Still, Still the noisy conflict raves,—
Still, still the rebel standard waves.
Not long that cliff will dare to hold
In heaven's sight that ensign bold.
On! gallant soldiers! Thrust aside
Th' escutcheon of the invader's pride,
That a purpose God will serve,
The shrinking, trembling heart to nerve,
The dauntless soul to make more sure
Freedom's great triumph to secure.

MILLER

1. *The North American Review*, General Slocum, February 1891, 141-42
2. *The North American Review*, 141-42
3. W. C. Storrick, *Gettysburg, The Place, The Battle, the Outcome* (Harrisburg, PA, 1932) 59-60
4. *The Press*, Philadelphia, 4 July 1888, col. 3: 1
5. GNMP Civilian Files

UNKNOWN

1. *The War of the Rebellion Official Records of the Union and Confederate Armies,* Series I, Vol. 27, Part I, 378. This was a notation at the bottom of General William Hays' report of the burial of Confederate dead by his command.
2. Mary Livermore, *My Story of the War*, p. 119-20.
3. DeAnne Blanton and Lauren Cook, *They Fought Like Demons* (Baton Rouge, LA: Louisiana State Press, 2002)
4. Blanton, 50
5. Blanton, 57
6. Blanton, 114
7. Blanton, 16
8. Blanton, 96
9. Blanton, 16

DEAVERS

1. Moore 535. A quote credited to Deavers at the battle of Fair Oaks [and Seven Pines, May 31 to June 1] during the Peninsula Campaign.
2. Moore 109
3. Brockett & Vaughn 771
4. This is almost surely due to misspelling of her name. During the time of mass immigration Irish women were generally referred to as Bridget or Biddy and Irish men called Patty. The various spellings of her name that were used have all been checked against the records. Even the Gaelic spellings which would be pronounced as Deavers or Divers when Angli-

cized, i.e., Ni'Dhuibhir, O'Duibhir, and O'Dwyer depending on what part of Ireland she was from or whether she was indeed married, have been checked. Since she was most likely unable to read or write, any information on her would be written as the individual scribe would deem correct. She, among many others of the "laboring class," have been lost in the usual historical research sources.

5. Livermore 116-7
6. Moore 110,111
7. Brockett & Vaughn 771
8. Brockett & Vaughn 535
9. Hancock 140, 144, 151, 162-32, 173
10. Moore 111
11. Moore 111
12. Mckay 124-26. "Moseby" was Lt. Col. John Singleton Mosby, a famous Confederate Partisan Ranger who operated in the eastern theater.
13. Moore 533
14. Brockett & Vaughn 772-73. Narrative by Mary Morris Husband "who knew her well."
15. Moore 461
16. Moore 535
17. McKay 139

GILSON

1. Clapp 459
2. Holland 535
3. Clapp 560-561
4. Brockett & Vaughn 137
5. Marjorie Barstow Greenbie, *Lincoln's Daughters of Mercy* (New York: G. P. Putnam & Sons, 1944) 182
6. Brockett & Vaughn 134
7. Brockett & Vaughn 134-35
8. Clapp 457
9. Greenbie 132, 184
10. Clapp 460-61
11. Clapp 461
12. Holland 535
13. Clapp 571
14. Clapp 463
15. Brockett & Vaughn 135
16. Greenbie 132
17. Brockett & Vaughn 136
18. Brockett & Vaughn 138
19. Clapp 462
20. Clapp 462
21. Clapp 463
22. Clapp 463-65
23. Brockett & Vaughn 136
24. Clapp 561-62
25. William Howell Reed, *Hospital Life in the Army of the Potomac* (Boston, 1866) 39, 40
26. Clapp 564
27. Clapp 567
28. Holland 539
29. Clapp 567
30. Clapp 567
31. Greenbie 132
32. Reed 81
33. Greenbie 132
34. Brockett & Vaughn 139-40
35. Greenbie 132

36. Reed 81-83. Dr. Reed was greatly impressed with Miss Gilson's menus: "I took down her diet list for one dinner and give it here with a note,* to show the variety of the articles, and her careful consideration of the condition of separate men. *List of rations in the Colored Hospital at City Point, being a dinner on Wednesday, April 25, 1865:

Roast beef – Shad – Veal Broth – Stewed Oysters – Beef Tea – Mashed Potatoes – Lemonade – Apple Jelly – Farina Pudding – Tomatoes - Tea – Coffee- Toast – Gruel – Scalded Milk – Crackers and Sherry Cobbler – Roast Apple

Let it not be supposed that this was an ordinary hospital diet. Although such a list was furnished at this time, yet it was only possible while the hospital had an ample base, like City Point. The armies, operating at a distance, could give but two or three articles and in active campaign these were furnished with great irregularity."

37. William Quentin Maxwell, *Lincoln's Fifth Wheel*, (New York: Longmans, Green & Co. 1956) 258
38. Clapp 569, 570
39. Maxwell, 132, 181
40. Brockett & Vaughn 147
41. Maxwell 132
42. Clapp 570, 571
43. Clapp 565
44. Clapp 565, 567
45. Maxwell 282
46. Brockett & Vaughn 147
47. Reed 83
48. Brockett & Vaughn 147, 148
49. Holland 544
50. Clapp 571
51. Clapp 572. A memory of Reverend W. H. Channing

JULY FOURTH
1. Broadhead 19
2. As told by Henry Jacobs, GNMP Civilian File

THORN
1. Mrs. Thorn's narrative of the battle, "Mrs. Thorn's War Story," is taken from the Gettysburg *Times*, 2 July 1938.
2. This confrontation is marked by a monument on the Baltimore Pike. It reads: NEAR THIS SPOT ON JUNE 26TH 1863 FELL PRIVATE GEROGE W. SANDOE AN ADVANCE SCOUT OF A COMPANY OF VOLUNTEER CAVALRY AFTERWARDS CO. B 21ST PENNSYL-VANIA CAVALRY. THE FIRST UNION SOLDIER KILLED AT GETTYSBURG. Sandoe was from Adams County, Pennsylvania.
3. Rock Creek Bridge was a railroad bridge on the eastern edge of Gettysburg. There was no battle at York. In fact, a deputation from York came out to the Confederates who were camped outside of town to surrender the town. Transportation and communication objects were considered legitimate military targets.
4. The McMillan House was and still is on Seminary Ridge. The Springs Hotel which was not present at the time of the battle but built later was west of the McPherson farm between Chambersburg and Fairfield Roads but closer to the former.
5. "Coon Town" or Kuhn Town was an area around the Kuhn brick works in the southwest quadrant of Gettysburg. The Poor House, or Almshouse, was on the Harrisburg Pike, in the area of what is now Barlow's Knoll. The knoll was the extreme right flank of the XI Corps line on July 1.
6. Musser's farmhouse was south of Evergreen Cemetery on Baltimore Pike near where Rock Creek crosses it.
7. The Henry Beitler farm was south of White Church on the Baltimore Pike.
8. Burials in the National Cemetery began October 26, 1863, and continued through March 1864.

9. This baby, Rose Meade [after the General], lived only to age 14. Mrs. Thorn would have five more children, Peter in 1868, Lillie in 1871, Ezra in 1873, Louisa in 1876, and Emory in 1882.

Fogg

1. Pension records, written by E. F. Williams, Field Agent U.S. Christian Commission, from Culpeper, Va., April 9th, 1864
2. Moore 116-117
3. Signed by John S. Godfrey, Lt. Col. And Chief Quartermaster, Center Grand Division [under Burnside's command the army was temporarily divided into three grand divisions] Army of the Potomac to the Office of the Quartermaster Department.
4. The letter from Hooker was written on June 5th, 1865 to Mrs. Fogg in Louisville, KY. Meade's letter was written on September 25, 1865. Both were testimonials in Mrs. Fogg's pension records.
5. Pension records
6. "Today this 162 acre farm is located along Goulden Road about one mile southwest of White Church. In July of 1863, it was just east of the Sixth Corps hospital (at the Trostle farm) and about three-quarters of a mile directly south of the Second Corps hospitals which partly occupied the Schwartz farm. Fiscel's farm, like the Third Corps site, seemed to be a medical mixture; with parts of the Fifth, Third and Sixth Corps' wounded within its boundaries." Coco 98
7. Moore, 123-124
8. Letter by Rufus Ingalls, Brig. Gen., Chief Quartermaster, from the Office of the Chief Quartermaster, Armies Operating Against Richmond, Va., City Point, Va., August 28th, 1864.
9. Pension submission
10. Hugh is buried at the Cave Hill National Cemetery, Louisville, KY, grave 3951, Row 2, Sec. B

Husband

1. Moore 290-91. Mary Morris Husband's name is often written as Husbands. However, the census and her pension records refer to her as Husband.
2. Brockett & Vaughn 291
3. The following is a capsule of Henry Morris Husband's service records:
   Enlisted in Co. A, 23rd PA (3 mos) from Philadelphia April 18, 1861, mustered July 31, 1861. Age given as 20.
   Mustered in Co. I, 99th PA from Philadelphia Jan. 18, 1862 for 3 years. Age given as 21.
   Jan. 1862 deserted from Chestnut Hill Hospital, Philadelphia.
   Was at Second Bull Run Aug. 29-30.
   Was at Chantilly Sept. 1, 1862.
   Sept. 1862 "absent without leave from Charles City C.H., VA"
   Oct. 1862 Fairfax C.H. "deserted."
   Enlisted under the name Morris H. Husband [the sly boots] in Co. B, 114th PA on Sept. 15, 1862. Rec'd bounty of $25.
   Nov. 1862 "absent without leave since Oct. 11, 1862."
   Was at Fredericksburg Dec. 13, 1862.
   Dec. 1862 Falmouth deserted.
   Jan. 1863 Falmouth Va. "gain" from desertion.
   Forfeited pay from Nov. 9, 1862 to Jan. 7, 1863 "absent without leave."
   From a letter of Major Chandler of the 114th PA: "Personally appeared before me Private Morris Husband of Co. B One hundred and fourteenth regiment Penn Vols on the following charge 'Absent without leave.' To which charge the prisoner plead 'Guilty' upon investigation I find that the prisoner had left his regiment and remained absent about five weeks, during which time he had visited Philadelphia without any permission from his superior officers. Therefore sentence him the said Private Morris Husbands of Co. B One hundred and fourteenth regiment Penn Vols to forfeit to whole of one months pay for the month of January 1863 and wear upon all drills and guard duties, his knapsack loaded to its fullest capacity this for the space of one month."
   March 1863 transferred to 99th as deserter by order of Gen. Birney
   Was at Chancellorsville May 3, 1863

July 1, 1863 Emmitsburg, MD deserted.

July 9, 1863 he was admitted to Mower General Hospital Chestnut Hill with a gunshot wound right foot.

Aug. 1863 was in Mower USA hospital and Chestnut Hill hospital, Philadelphia

Oct. 10, 1863 deserted and was admitted to same hospital

Oct. 29, 1863 with gunshot wound right foot and deserted Nov. 9, 1863. "He was tried before a general court martial for desertion, specification. In this that he did desert the same or about the first day of July 1863 at or near Emmittsburg [sic], Md. while his company and regt. were on the march (being his second offense). He was found guilty of the charge and sentenced to be shot to death with musketry at such time and place as the general commanding may direct. The proceedings findings and sentence were approved by proper authorities and forwarded to the President for his action."

Extract from Special Orders NO. 560 form the War Department: "The sentence of the General Court Martial Convened in the Army of the Potomac in the case of Private H. Morris Husband 99th Pa. Vols. tried for desertion is by direction of the President hereby disapproved and the accused will be at once returned to duty." Dated Dec. 18, 1863.

Dec. 31, 1863 from Descriptive list of deserters: "Joined from desertion. Tried by Ge. Ct. Mt. Sent. To be shot. Pardoned by Pres. of U. S. and returned to duty Dec. 17, 1863."

Jan. 29, 1864 re-enlisted at Brandy Station for 3 years.

Received $300 bounty which 2 installments were supposed to be forfeited but there is no record of forfeit.

From a letter from the colonel of the 99th: "Private Husband enlisted as a Veteran in January last, and accompanied his Regiment to Philadelphia on Veteran furlough. During his stay at home he was taken sick, and sent to Germantown Hospital from which place he subsequently transferred to Chestnut Hill Hospital Pa. While in the latter place he received a pass to visit his friends in Philadelphia and failing to report at the proper time was reported as a deserter, and finally apprehended Oct. 22/64 after an absence of 5 weeks.

I do not believe Husbands had any intention of deserting as it does not appear that he made any effort to conceal himself or his whereabouts but I am of the opinion that he was on a 'spree' (as he himself states for the first few days of his absence) and was then afraid to return to Hospital. He appears to be very penitent at present and promises to do his best in the future.

I would respectfully request that I may be allowed to forward charges of absence with out leave against him instead of desertion."

March & April 1864 at Cuyler USA Gen. Hosp. Germantown, returned to duty 5/31/64.

April 1864 absent without leave in Philadelphia since March 22, 1864.

May 1864 absent sick at Germantown Hospital and furloughed.

June 10, 1864 admitted to Mower general hospital at Chestnut Hill with sunstroke.

Sept. 1864 "absent in arrest" in Pittsburgh while trying to enlist in yet another Pa. unit. The man who arrested him was from the 121st Provost Guard and rec'd $30 which Henry had to pay back to the government. "The prisoner obstinately denies being the man and denies having ever been in service."

Oct. 1864 absent in arrest Petersburg. Application for removal of charges of absence without leave of March 22, 1864 and desertion of August 11, 1864 has been denied. By 1867 all charges were removed from record.

4. Moore, 319, 323
5. Brockett & Vaughn 297
6. Moore 323
7. Biddle & Dickinson, *Notable Women of Pennsylvania*, (Philadelphia, University of Pennsylvania Press, 1942) 154
8. Pension record H.R. 5894, 48th Congress
9. John Husband's pension records
10. Moore 316-17
11. Brockett & Vaughn, 293-94
12. Brocket & Vaughn, 294

13. Pension, Dr. John A. Douglass
14. Brockett & Vaughn 294-95. According to the American Heritage Dictionary miasma is a "poisonous atmosphere formerly thought to rise from swamps and putrid matter and cause disease."
15. Henry Morris Husband's war records
16. Pension, statement by Frederick N. Knapp of the Sanitary Commission.
17. Maxwell 252
18. Hancock 67
19. Moore 326-27
20. Hancock, 114, 118, 120, 121
21. Moore 329
22. Pension

Harris

1. *Fifth Semi-Annual Report of the Ladies Aid Society of Philadelphia* with Letters and Extracts from Letters from the Secretary of the Society Written from Various Places While Attending to the Sick and Wounded of the Union Army (Philadelphia: C. Sherman & Sons, 1863) 13. Quote from a letter written at Gettysburg on July 9, 1863 to her husband.
2. *Fifth Semi-Annual Report* 12
3. Hancock 10, written in a letter dated July 7
4. Abijah was an aide who worked with Mrs. Harris through many battles and to whom she referred to in her letters as "Abijah the poet."
5. Probably Charlotte Bradford from Pennsylvania. There was no battle at Frederick, Maryland
6. *Fifth Semi-Annual Report* 13-14
7. Mrs. Joel Jones, President of the Society
8. *Fifth Semi-Annual Report* 14
9. *Third Semi-Annual Report of the Ladies Aid Society of Philadelphia with Letters and Copious Extracts of Letters from the Secretary of the Society* (Philadelphia: C. Sherman & Sons, 1862)
10. Brockett & Vaughn 149
11. Moore 176
12. *Third Semi-Annual* 23
13. *Third Semi-Annual* 47
14. *Fourth Semi-Annual* 17, 18 written January 15, 1863
15. *Third Semi-Annual* 43. The "landing" is most likely Harrison's Landing
16. *Fifth Semi-Annual Report* 15
17. *Fifth Semi-Annual Report* 17
18. Moore 205
19. *Third Semi-Annual* 45
20. *Third Semi-Annual* 50
21. *Fifth Semi-Annual* 15
22. Rev. D. K. Turner, *History of Neshaminy Presbyterian Church of Warwick* (Philadelphia: Culberton & Bache, 1876) 352-53
23. *Third Semi-Annual* 50
24. *Third Semi-Annual* 23
25. *Fourth Semi-Annual* 27
26. *Third Semi-Annual* 50
27. *Fourth Semi-Annual* 11
28. *Third Semi-Annual* 52, 57-59
29. *Fourth Semi-Annual* 16
30. *Fourth Semi-Annual* 16, 18, 19, 23
31. *Fifth Semi-Annual* 5
32. *Third Semi-Annual* 45, 46
33. *Fourth Semi-Annual* 12-13
34. *Third Semi-Annual* 27-28
35. *Third Semi-Annual* 21-23, 25

36. Moore 212
37. William Meronie, *Harris (or Herris), Miller, and Dunlop,* privately printed, 1920, 94
38. "Obituary," *Democratic Watchman,* Bellfonte, Pa., 12 December 1902

LEE

1. Excerpt from a letter written to Mrs. Lee by Mrs. Mary D. Ripley whose son, Thomas, had recently died. [Moore 166]
2. Greenbie 134, 135
3. Moore 150
4. Moore 151
5. Moore 152
6. Brockett & Vaughn 486
7. Moore 160
8. Brockett & Vaughn 486
9. Hancock, 53, 58
10. Brockett & Vaughn 486
11. Hancock 78, 79, 82
12. Hancock 99, 101
13. Hancock 104, 111, 112
14. Hancock 123, 125, 136
15. Hancock 176
16. Moore 168
17. Brockett & Vaughn 488
18. Greenbie 133
19. Moore 148

JULY FIFTH THROUGH JULY EIGHTH

1. Broadhead privately published "In order to aid the Sanitary commission in its holy work of succoring the wounded of the Union army, 75 copies—3/8 of the edition—will be presented to the Great Central Fair now open in Philadelphia," 16-17, 18
2. McGuire 229
3. Mary Elizabeth Montfort and her mother cared for the wounded at the railroad station when they discovered her mortally wounded father. "Father looked at me and said, 'Mary Elizabeth,' then he closed his eyes. He had been hit by a shell. There was a big hole in his side. Mother told me to go home and take care of Grandma and Jennie. I kissed him and walked toward the door..." "The Daily Intelligence," Doylestown, Sat. 30 May 1959, Vol. LXXIII, No. 127.
4. Greenbie 169-70
5. Written by Mr. John Y. Foster for *Harpers Weekly,* Feb. 1864
6. Maxwell 209, 210
7. Maxwell 211-213
8. Broadhead 25. It was not usually admitted that the government did not supply its wounded with necessary supplies and care, or that the various private agencies were doing the government's job. In a letter at which Mrs. Harris would have snorted had she engaged in such behavior, that was published in the Sanitary Commission Bulletin, Vol, 1, written by General Meade after the battle of Gettysburg, he expressed his view: "Now, although his government is most liberal and generous in all its provisions for the sick and wounded, yet it is impossible to keep *constantly on hand either the personnel or supplies* required in an emergency of this kind. In addition to the difficulty at Gettysburg, I was compelled to pursue the retreating foe, and, as I expected, in a few days, to have another battle at some distance point, it was absolutely necessary that I should carry away the greater portion of my Surgeons and medical supplies, so that the wounded at Gettysburg were, in a measure, dependent upon such extra assistance as the Government could hastily collect and upon the generous aid so cheerfully and promptly afforded by the Sanitary and Christian Commissions, and the various State and Soldiers' Aid Societies. [368] In the same bulletin was a letter written by another influential person, Mr. John Seymour, brother to the war governor of New York, who put it bluntly: "The soldiers would have starved to death without their aid." It was after Gettysburg that each army division was assigned one wagon of the Sani-

tary Commission's. After two years of rising to all emergencies, their agents enjoyed a more welcome situation in the military. Any such nationwide agency was impossible in the South due to invasion and poor transportation. Had the public of the North not been so forthcoming and the armies left dependent on the government, war casualties could have approached the million mark and the outcome of the war may have been quite different.

9. Broadhead 26
10. Nellie E. Aughinbaugh, *Personal Experiences of a Young Girl During the battle of Gettysburg*, from a narrative at the Adams County Historical Society. Speaker was Col. H.S. Huidelkoper.
11. Aughinbaugh
12. Alice Powers, Gettysburg *Compiler*, 1 July 1903.

SISTER CAMILLA O'KEEFE

1. Ellen Ryan Jolly, *Nuns of the Battlefield* (Providence, RI: The Providence Visitor Press, 1927) 67
2. Jolly 61
3. George Barton, *Angels of the Battlefield* (Philadelphia: The Catholic Art Pubishing Co., 1898) 114
4. Sister Camilla O'Keefe's narrative, unpublished, St. Joseph's Archives, Emmitsburg, MD
5. Barton 133
6. O'Keefe's narrative
7. Barton 133
8. O'Keefe's narrative
9. The number of Sisters having served at Gettysburg from Emmitsburg including the ones that came on the 6th varies from 20 to 28 and with another group arriving from Baltimore, also on the 6th, the total nuns nursing in the hospitals was somewhere around 40. The following is a list obtained from the archivist at St. Joseph's of the Sisters from Emmitsburg who attended the wounded at Gettysburg:

Sister May Oswald Spalding	Sister Catherine Rectenwald
Sister Angela Walsh	Sister Matilda Coskery
Sister Annie McShane	Sister Anselim Shaw
Sister Raphael Smith	Sister Baptists Dowds
Sister Gertrude Balfe	Sister Susanna Webb
Sister Aloysia Ring	Sister Gabrielle Rigney
Sister Mary Elizabeth Schroeder	Sister Maria Landry
Sister Ann Simeon Norris	Sister Annie Ewers
Sister Geneivieve Dodthage	Sister Walburga Gehring
Sister Victorine Petry	Sister Euphemia Blickensop
Sister Mary Ann Streckel	Sister Camilla O'Keefe
Sister Adele Durm	Sister Catherine Reddy
Sister Loretto Mullery	Sister Philip Barry
Sister Petronilla Breen	Sister Clotilda O'Neil
Sister Ameliana Schroeder	Sister Valentine Latouraudais
Sister Mary Farell	Sister Maria Mulkern
Sister Mary Catherine Chrismer	Sister Mary Shaw
Sister Mary Joseph Murphy	Sister Anastasia Felix
Sister Eliza McDonough	Sister Serena Klimkiewicz
Sister Henrietta Casey	Sister Jane Stokes

10. Barton 133-34
11. O'Keefe's narrative
12. Barton 135-36
13. This is the McClellan House which was a hotel on the square of Gettysburg.
14. O'Keefe's narrative
15. Barton 137
16. The Pennsylvania College is now the Gettysburg College. The main building in 1863 housed wounded Confederates, the estimated number varies widely from 600 to 900.
17. Barton 138

18. O'Keefe's narrative
19. Jolly 62-63
20. O'Keefe's narrative
21. A similar coincidence took place in a hospital in New Orleans. A Sister from Kentucky found her wounded brother whom she had not seen since they were orphaned years before. In this case, however, though the soldier was able to recognize his sister, he died shortly thereafter.
22. Barton 21
23. Barton 207
24. Barton 207
25. Barton 238. Even patients who were used to the Sisters' attire did not understand their garb. This incident took place in a D. C. hospital: "One day a poor fellow obtained a pass and spent the entire day in the city and returned at twilight looking sad and fatigued. A Sister of his ward asked him if he was suffering, and he replied, 'No, Sister; but I am tired and vexed. I received my pass early to-day and walked through every street in Washington trying to buy one of those while bonnets for you and did not find a single one for sale.'" [Barton 66] Another incident told of a soldier gone shopping for a dress for his favorite Sister.
26. O'Keefe's narrative
27. O'Keefe's narrative
28. O'Keefe's narrative. Point Lookout was a hospital until the battle of Gettysburg. Confederate prisoners began arriving in August of 1863. It was a permanent, open air prison with tents that was known to be "hell on earth."
29. Barton 108
30. The monument was unveiled in 1924. The inscription reads: "They comforted the dying, nursed the wounded, carried hope to the imprisoned, gave in His name a drink of water to the thirsty...In the memory and in honor of The Various Orders of Sisters who gave their services as nurses on battlefield and in hospitals during the Civil War." There are 11 figures representing the following orders: Sisters of Charity, Daughters of Charity of St. Vincent de Paul, Sisters of St. Dominic, Sisters of the Poor of St. Francis, Sisters of the Holy Cross, Sisters of St. Joseph, Sisters of Mercy, Sisters of Our Lady of Mercy, Sisters of Our Lady of Mt. Carmel, Sisters of Providence, and Sisters of St. Ursula.
31. Barton 21
32. Jolly 58
33. Barton 101
34. Jolly 59-60
35. Barton 36
36. Barton 44
37. Barton 32
38. Barton 93
39. Barton 95
40. Barton 96
41. Barton 98-99. This situation was repeated in New Orleans:

> ...[T]he train steamed into the Crescent City, and the [Union] officers went to seek their commanders and the sisters their patients, who were in a small town on the Mississippi River. Sister S— divided her small forces of nurses with such rare good judgement and executive ability that in twenty-four hours all of the sick and wounded men were resting comfortable. Suddenly came the order to depart and the Union troops all left the town, taking with them such of the convalescent patients as were able to bear the strain of travel. Twelve hours later a portion of the Confederate army entered the town, bringing several hundred of their sick and wounded. Sister S—, thinking that the call to duty in this instance was no less imperative than it had been in the case of the Union men the day before, started for the hospital, where the wounded Confederates had been carried.
>
> One of the Union surgeons who had remained behind with his wounded men, placed a detaining hand upon her arm.
>
> "Where are you going?" he said.

"To look after these men," she replied.

"That is impossible," he said. "you are in the service of the United States Government, and you are not permitted to serve under the enemy. We have no objection to your nursing the wounded Confederates, but it must be under the auspices of our generals. The Union forces will probably regain possession of this town before nightfall, and then you can wait upon both sides alike."

"But I insist," and the eyes of the usually mild-mannered Sister sparkled as she stamped her foot in an emphatic manner. "I know nothing of technical military rules, but I insist upon my right to nurse these poor men."

"I regret very much being placed in such a position," said the surgeon gently, "but I am here representing the Government."

"And I," responded the Sister, "am here representing something greater than the Government."

"What is that?" he asked in an incredulous tone.

"Humanity!" was the quiet reply.

The officer—a brave man obeying his orders—did not utter another word, but bowing his head opened the door and admitted the Sister and her companions into the presence of the sick." [Barton 390-392] Sister S—is the Sister who found her brother from Kentucky in this number of wounded.

42. Barton 99-100. The fifty additional nurses were most likely serving with the 100,000 additional men that McClellan believed Lincoln was withholding.

43. Barton 57, 58

44. "The name upon the cross over the grave was the name of the sister in the world. She was known in religion by the title of Sister Louise." [Barton 60]

45. Barton 58, 60

46. Barton iii. A lustrum is five years.

47. Barton 216.

HANCOCK

1. Unless otherwise stated, all quotes in this chapter are taken from *South After Gettysburg*, a compilation of Miss Hancock's letters from the war and afterwards from her school in South Carolina. The letters were compiled by Henrietta Stratton Jaque, privately printed, 1937, p. 14

2. p. 4

3. p. 5

4. p. 6

5. p. 7

6. pp. 8, 9

7. p. 10

8. p. 14

9. pp. 10-12, 14, 15

10. pp. 14-16, 18

11. pp. 11, 13, 21. Some of the nurses from the war era spoke of doubts about their feelings if they were asked to work with wounded enemy soldiers, but all were able to do so with varying degrees of compassion. With the exception of Mrs. Anna Holstein who wrote her book soon after the war with fresh memories of the returning Union men from Andersonville Prison, Miss Hancock is the only nurse represented in this work that would always harbor hatred for the South and its people. In 1864 on the march from Fredericksburg to City Point, Cornelia wrote home: "Tonight we halted at a village called Newtown, went into a Secesh house, found a nice bed and room to sleep. They told us they have nothing to eat. We sent back to the train for rations and had the colored people to get us a good supper which we ate upon their table. The women are bitter Secessionists—one said her husband is a commissary in the Rebel army. We think he furnishes rations to the guerilla bands and I was not disposed to show them any favours but true to some people's ideas of right they wanted to take Sanitary stuff and give those rebels to live on because they said they were starving. There was a splendid side saddle that I want to confiscate for I know that has been smuggled from the North. There was not a man in our crowd who had spunk enough to take it...Protecting Secesh property is entirely played out with me...[Later] Nothing was to be

seen but the densest clouds of smoke, a burning slave pen, and the ruins of the Court House. Stopped at a house just a little way beyond where the most wholesale destruction of property was going forward. I do not like to see wanton destruction but a dignified order to burn I enjoy and it is right, I believe." [101, 118]. "I hate them very badly indeed." [171] Her feelings towards the end of the war were unaltered as she traveled south through Richmond to South Carolina in 1866. "It was laughable to see and hear the poor secesh getting along; they are so poorly clothed; talk so thick, and most of their houses and bridges are burned. The most forlorn country I ever have seen…I suppose the sparseness of their clothes make them look so very bad. But they really look starved in their faces." [192-3] "I talk to all I can get a chance [to] when I am in a safe place. I like to hear them speak of their ruin." [198] Cornelia's Quaker family took her to task for these types of comments.

12. pp. 11, 14, 16, 19-21, 23, 24
13. pp. 15, 18. The following is a letter Miss Hancock received from an anonymous patient: "TO OUR SOLDIER'S FRIEND, MISS HANCOCK,

You will please excuse a Soldier for writing a few lines to you to express our thankfulness for your kindness to our poor wounded comrades after the late battle. You little know the pleasure a Soldier feels in seeing a woman at camp. I only wish that we were able to express our gratitude in a different manner, but 'Uncle Sam' happens to be in debt to us and until he 'comes down' with his greenbacks, we are not able to do any more. You will never be forgotten by us for we often this of your kind acts and remember them with pleasure. Please excuse a Soldier for taking the liberty to write to you, for although we are Soldiers we know how to appreciate a kind act. Your sincere friend." [17]

14. pp. 19-21
15. pp 19, 21, 22
16. p. 22
17. pp 22, 24
18. p. 26
19. pp. 27, 28
20. Hancock pension records.
21. pp. 60, 64, 71
22. pp. 60, 61, 71
23. pp. 67, 69
24. p. 69
25. pp. 62, 65
26. pp. 61-63, 65, 66, 73
27. p. 67
28. pp. 74, 76, 85
29. p. 76
30. pp. 73, 74
31. p. 84
32. pp. 77, 87
33. pp. 89, 92, 94
34. p. 105. This was written by a Dr. Vanderpool.
35. pp. 102, 136
36. pp. 136-137
37. p. 104
38. p. 137
39. pp. 109, 119
40. Pension
41. Dr. Dudley in Hancock's pension
42. pp. 123, 126, 127, 157, 161
43. p. 133
44. pp. 135-35, 1 44
45. p. 140
46. p. xii
47. p. 249

McKay

1. McKay vii
2. McKay 51
3. McKay 51-53
4. McKay 53-56
5. Brockett & Vaughn 514
6. Moore 279
7. McKay 159-60
8. McKay ix
9. McKay 13-14
10. McKay 22
11. McKay 21
12. McKay 22, 23
13. McKay 28
14. McKay 29
15. McKay 29
16. McKay 30
17. McKay 30-33
18. McKay 34-36
19. McKay 38
20. McKay 39
21. McKay 39, 40
22. McKay 43
23. McKay 112-114
24. McKay 64-66
25. McKay 81, 82
26. McKay 98, 99
27. McKay 103, 104
28. McKay 119-120
29. McKay, 116, 119. Another Sanitary Commission worker noted the male nurses, who "are themselves convalescent soldiers," in a letter concerning boxes delivered to the Commission. "There are, it is true, female nurses in service of the hospitals who do all that they can do. But those peculiar attentions which none but a wife, a mother, or a sister can with propriety give, are bestowed by their brother convalescent soldiers, who are detailed for such duty. And when I have seen these poor fellows, themselves still needing nursing, (for as soon as they are strong they are sent to the 'front') wearily dragging themselves up and down the two, three or four long flights of stairs, carrying food, water, or medicines, and attending to their frequent and most necessary wants; oftentimes called from their own meals, waiting upon them in their turn day and night, and always so kind, so patient; my eyes have filled with gratitude, and I have thought that if mothers and friends at home only knew how their sons and brothers were nursed by these noble fellows, there would be no more boxes sent to the Commission marked 'not for the nurses...' J. T. Ingram, The U. S. Sanitary Commission Bulletin, Vol. I, p. 102.
30. McKay 127-129
31. McKay 131
32. McKay 142
33. McKay 158, 159
34. *The History of Waterford, Oxford County, Maine*, A Compilation of Addresses, Records, and Proceedings, published at the direction of the Town (Portland, ME: Hoyt, Fogg, and Donham, 1879) 264.

HOLSTEIN

1. All quotations are from Mrs. Holstein's book *Three Years in Field Hospitals in the Army of the Potomac* (Philadelphia: J.B. Lippincott & Co., 1867) 11
2. pp. 26, 27
3. pp. 30-37

4. This was "Luther White, Co. K, 20th Massachusetts, from Boston; he was wounded by a piece of shell, which tore off part of his ear, and shattered his jaw, laid bare one side of the throat. After the battle, remained for three days unconscious, then rallied, and again sank away until he died,—it was thought, and carried to the grave." p. 42
5. pp. 38-44, 49
6. Letter in pension records, private act #141, 52nd Congress.
7. Pension
8. Hancock 26
9. pp. 49-54
10. p. 58
11. pp. 69, 70
12. pp. 76, 77, 80
13. pp. 85, 86
14. Biddle and Dickenson, 166, 167

Dada / Hall

1. Brockett & Vaughn, 438. From a letter written by Dada in March 1865.
2. This was the oldest American foreign missionary society in the United States, organized in 1810. It was required that at least one-third of its members be women.
3. Brockett & Vaughn, 431-32
4. Brockett & Vaughn 433
5. Brockett & Vaughn 434
6. Brockett & Vaughn 435
7. Harriet Dada was most likely at the George Bushman farm. The First Corps had their divisions in different hospitals but Susan Hall was probably at the Adams Express Office, a building in town near the railroad Station.
8. Brockett & Vaughn 436
9. Hall pension records
10. Brockett & Vaughn 436, 437
11. Brockett & Vaughn 438
12. Brockett & Vaughn 439
13. Robert Barry pension records
14. Robert Barry pension records

Remainder of July

1. *Gettysburg Compiler*, 1 July 1903, unidentified woman
2. Coco 167, 168
3. Broadhead 28, 29
4. Bucklin 31, from the introduction signed only by the letters S.L.C.

Woolsey

1. *Letters of a Family During the War 1861-1865*, compiled by Georgeanna Woolsey, (privately printed, 1899) 531
2. Woolsey 526
3. Moore 130-31. The entire tract of *Three Weeks at Gettysburg* is reprinted in Moore's *Women of the War*.
4. Woolsey 527-528
5. Moore 132
6. Woolsey 530-31
7. Moore 132-37
8. Woolsey 528-29
9. Woolsey 535
10. Moore 137-39
11. Moore 139
12. Woolsey 533
13. Moore 139-40
14. Woolsey 529-30

15. Moore 144-42
16. Moore 142-44
17. Woolsey 531
18. Moore 145-46
19. Woolsey 532
20. Moore 146
21. Woolsey 534. As late as May 1864 this pamphlet would haunt the Woolsey family. Caroline Woolsey wrote Georgy at the time: "Miss E. M. wants to know if I wrote those everlasting Three Weeks at Gettysburg. Having read them, she cannot stay at home, and would like a little information as to what was needed for a nurse…she is the second anxious inquirer this morning. We think of opening a branch office for information…What it is to be the sister of an authoress!" [597] "We think of adding, 'Army Gen'l Directory' to our door-plate, so many people of all sorts come to us for information…" [600]
22. Woolsey 62
23. Woolsey 78
24. Woolsey 69-70
25. Woolsey 77
26. Woolsey 79-82
27. Woolsey 89
28. Woolsey 85-86
29. Woolsey 106
30. Woolsey 113
31. Woolsey 114
32. Woolsey 117
33. Woolsey 119-20
34. Woolsey 120
35. Woolsey 142-44
36. Woolsey 131
37. Woolsey 147
38. Woolsey 316
39. Woolsey 331
40. Woolsey 360-61
41. Woolsey 428
42. Woolsey 383
43. Woolsey 449
44. Woolsey 481
45. Woolsey 531-32
46. Woolsey 535
47. Woolsey 542-43
48. Woolsey 545-56
49. Woolsey 549
50. Woolsey 582
51. Woolsey 593
52. Woolsey 588, 591-92
53. Woolsey 617
54. Woolsey 619, 620
55. Woolsey 619, 620
56. Woolsey 622
57. Woolsey 714

JONES

1. Pension submission file, in a letter dated Feb. 5, 1917, to the Commissioner of Pensions. With the exception of one newspaper interview, Miss Jones' narrative is pieced together from the many "proofs" and letters in her extensive pension file. For clarity, some spelling has been corrected and abbreviations spelled out.
2. Clarissa probably means the Provost Marshal. There have been no facts found as to the identity of Mrs. C.F. Jones, "noted rebel woman."

3.   This would be Pvt. George W. Presgraves. He and his three brothers all enlisted on July 10, 1861 at Mt. Gilead in Co. I, 8th Virginia which was in Garnett's Brigade, Pickett's Division and took part in Pickett's Charge on July 3. According to his war records, he was taken prisoner at Gettysburg but made his escape and went home. He was listed at one point as a deserter but the muster rolls noted him as "absent, taken prisoner" through the year of 1864. He took an oath of allegiance and was "released" June 20, 1865. The brother he was nursing was Lt. John R. Presgraves who died of wounds on July 8. The other two brothers were taken prisoner at Gettysburg. The records state that Cpl. James R. "was paroled" and William T. was incarcerated at Ft. Delaware and exchanged Oct. 30, 1864. The Presgraves brothers were from Loudon County, Virginia, not from around the James River as Miss Jones recollected.
4.   Philadelphia "North American," Sunday, June 29, 1913, Special Section, p. 4
5.   Elizabeth Logan, Clarissa's 35 year old sister, died on May 5, 1864 of miasmas [wasted away]. She left three girls for Clarissa to care for; Lydia age 8, Elizabeth age 7, and Clarissa J. age 3. As of 1860 Elizabeth's husband, Daniel, was in the Philadelphia County Prison for larceny.

BELL

1.   A letter of Annie Bell Stubb's in her pension records.
2.   Pension
3.   Coco 103

SOUDER

1.   Mrs. Edmund Souder, *Letters from the Battlefield of Gettysburg* (Caxton Press of C. Sherman, Son & Co., 1864) 8. All quotations are from this book.
2.   Souder 11
3.   Souder 12-14
4.   Souder 15
5.   Souder 45. *Who Will Care for Mother Now* was written by Charles Carroll Sawyer, who also wrote *When This Cruel War is Over*. Both songs were very popular with both armies. The words to the song that so moved Emily are as follows:

> Why am I so weak and weary?
> See how faint my heated breath!
> All around to me seems darkness
> Tell me, comrades, is this death?
> Ah! how well I know your answer;
> To my fate I meekly bow,
> If you'll only tell me truly,
> Who will care for mother now?

> Chorus:
> Soon with angels I'll be marching
> With bright laurels on my brow,
> I have for my country fallen,
> Who will care for mother now?

> Who will comfort her in sorrow?
> Who will dry the falling tear?
> Gently smooth her wrinkled forehead?
> Who will whisper words of cheer?
> Even now I think I see her,
> Kneeling, praying for me, how
> Can I leave her in her anguish?
> Who will care for mother now?

6.   Souder 21, 22
7.   Souder 15
8.   The 1860 census listed Emily Souder's children as Emily age 22, Stephen age 20, Sarah age 18, Edward age 11, Fanny age 8, Mary age 4, and Sallie age 1. There was a Capt. Stephen

Souder of the correct age who enlisted in a three month unit for the "existing emergency." He enlisted in Philadelphia on June 18, 1863 and mustered out in that city on August 1, 1863. This may have been Emily's eldest son.

9. Souder 16, 22
10. Souder 16, 17, 38
11. Souder 23
12. Souder 17, 47
13. Souder 35
14. Souder 26, 53
15. Souder 26, 55
16. Souder 49, 51
17. Souder 17, 24, 25
18. Souder 18, 26
19. Souder 18
20. Souder 23, 24, 44
21. Souder 28, 38, 63, 64
22. Souder 32
23. Souder 56, 57
24. Souder 34, 59
25. Souder 61, 62
26. Souder 133
27. Souder 137
28. Souder 137-142

SMITH

1. Holland 102
2. There was only one Smith family in Greencastle who were white in 1860. They had moved to the area from Maryland where Mary was born. The year before the war, her father, Jacob, and mother, Ana, had eight children ranging from age one to eighteen. Mary Alice was 16, and Sarah, or "Sadie," the sister mentioned, was 18.
3. Holland 101
4. Pension application.

BRADY

1. Moore 50. This quote is from a soldier Mrs. Brady met on the street car in Philadelphia in 1863.
2. The 1860 census show the Brady household as; Edward Brady, age 42 who was a real estate agent and lawyer, Mary A. age 39, Hugh age 13, Marion age 9, Ed age 8, Margaret age 6, and William age 3. Three other women lived there, ages 42, 65, and 75, all from Ireland, Mary's birthplace.
3. Moore 38
4. Brockett & Vaughn 647, 648
5. Moore 46
6. Brockett & Vaughn 648-49
7. Moore 46
8. Brockett & Vaughn 649
9. Moore 49
10. Moore 49
11. Brockett & Vaughn 649
12. Moore 51
13. *The Public Ledger*, 30 May 1864
14. Moore 75
15. The last stanza from "Soldiers at Home," author unknown, *Confederate Veteran*, Vol. 39, 235

BUCKLIN

1. Sophronia E. Bucklin, *In Hospital and Camp* (Philadelphia: John E. Potter & Co., 1869) 34
2. Bucklin 33, 35

GOLDSBOROUGH

1. A stanza from a poem written by Effie Goldsborough found in the papers of the Provost Marshal file and used as evidence for the charge of treason.

2. A Gettysburg civilian recalled: "Four such ladies from Baltimore were at our house for a few days. They were brought to us and introduced by Dr. John Swope who was then living in the town. One was Mrs. Banks and the name of another was Mrs. Warrington. I do not recall the name of the other two, a lady and her daughter, and am not sure that we ever knew. They were very delightful ladies and were well supplied with money. They spend the whole day out on the field in the hospitals where the Confederate wounded were. We did not suspect their intentions at first, but when they tried to buy up men's civilian clothes, and even women's clothing, we began to understand what they were about. As soon as my father learned what their real mission was, he insisted that mother send them away. He would not tolerate any Confederate sympathizers in our house. He had seen too much of what our brave men had suffered because of the war, especially in the Battle of Gettysburg.

    The ladies begged very earnestly to be allowed to stay, saying that they were much pleased with their accommodations. They especially liked mother's tea and hot biscuits, and in fact everything she put on the table. Mother was sorry to send them away as they were willing to pay well for every attention. They even offered to increase the amount, but father was relentless. He was not willing to sacrifice his principles, even though the losses he had suffered during the war made ready money very desirable. The four ladies left our home very reluctantly and we could not help wondering whether they found another place they liked." Narrative by Mrs. Jacob A. Clutz, "The Battle of Gettysburg," *Pennsylvania History*, Vol. V, No. 3 (Philadelphia; University of Pennsylvania Press, July 1938)

    No doubt some clothing was procured with the intent of aiding the prisoners to escape, but there was a general and desperate need among the Confederate wounded for clean clothing.

3. From an unidentified periodical written by an unnamed prisoner in the GNMP files entitled "College Hospital in Gettysburg," dated Feb. 1867, pp. 290-292, 294.

4. Mrs. R. P. McCormick (Effie's sister Mona), *The Banishment of Miss Eupehmia Goldsborough*, "Looking back to the days of 1863." Believed to have been printed in a journal for a Confederate Relief Bazaar in 1898. Southern Marylanders continued to help Confederate men and women after the war by raising money for the destitute and organizing networks of seamstresses in order for them to earn money. Food and clothing were sent South for years after the war. In the late 1865 General Robert E. Lee wrote: "I am fully aware of the many repeated acts of sympathy and relief bestowed by the generous citizens of Baltimore upon the people of the South, acts which will always be remembered, but which can never be repaid, and which will forever stand as monuments of their Christian charity and kindness. I know, too, that by their munificence they have brought loss and suffering on themselves, for which I trust God will reward them." And again in 1866 when he received the gift of a gown: "I beg that you will express to them my grateful thanks for this mark of kindness, which I shall value most highly in remembrances of the munificent bounty bestowed on thousands of destitute women and children by the 'Association for the Relief of Southern Sufferers' the fruits of which shall live long after those who have received it have mouldered into dust." Dawson 37.

5. From an obituary written by Mona McCormick

6. Banishment

7. Capt. George H. Jony, Co. D, 22nd Ga.

8. Sgt. Julian Bellou, Co. M, 2nd Fla.

9. Banishment

10. Phoebe Yates Pember, *A Southern Woman's Story* (St. Simons Island, GA: Mockingbird Books, Inc. 1959) 43.

11. Obituary

12. Banishment

13. The Provost Marshal records on Miss Goldsborough contains the following order to Lt. Col. Fish dated November 23, 1863:

    "I am directed by the General Commanding to enclose to you for your perusal a letter addressed by a Rebel prisoner to Miss E.M. Goldsborough, 49 North East corner Cortland

& Mulberry Streets with the instructions that you at once send a discreet officer with sufficient guard to the house indicated, arrest Miss Goldsborough, search the house in every part, take possession of all papers and any contraband or suspicious articles, search the persons of the inmates and retain in custody Miss Goldsborough until further notice.

The General desires that you will conduct the matter with much secrecy and dispatch as to take by surprise all the inmates in the house and to possess yourself of all evidence that there is in the house of the intercourse of its inmates with the Rebels."

The other papers in the Goldsborough file, all written by Effie, consisted mainly of letters and poems, all of which left no doubt to her allegiance. One poem was six pages of intense feeling about her cousin General Robert Garnett's death, another her reaction to General Benjamin Butler's [from whom she would soon receive personal degradation] infamous "woman order." In both of these poems she calls Northern women to task for their men's treatment of the "Southern sisters:"

"To give the sisters' home to flame,
To slaughter and to women's shame."

Letters found were ones written to and received from Confederate prisoners. On the day of her arrest, Effie had written a letter to a Confederate officer, presumably unable to send it before the provost came. In it she said, "I fear I am *implicated most seriously* in the *attempted* escape of a prisoner, a *letter directive* was found on his person and probably I shall go to 'sweet Dixie' sooner than *you*—however, I am not one *bit afraid* to *defy* the whole *Yankee nation. Send me where they will* I am *able & willing to suffer hardships & loss* for *myself* for the sake of a *Country & people that I love* but probably it will *all blow over* & my friends may be *unnecessarily alarmed* at my sake."

Also contained in her file were lists of men who died at Gettysburg, lists of women's names with no explanation noted, and lists of historical figures. The latter had so many dashes, underlines, and addition uncalled for letters it must have been thought coded, and indeed, it probably was.

14. Goldsborough Provost Marshal Records "Papers of Miss E. Goldsborough containing much that is disloyal—Treasonable Plans and letters & Traitorous Poetry."

15. Banishment

16. Gen. Ben Butler, aka "Spoons" for his passion for Southern silverware and "Beast" for his "Woman Order" while occupation commander of New Orleans, was abhorred by Southerners, disliked by many Northerners, and disapproved of by Europeans. He managed to offend almost everyone. Southern females seemed his especial prey, including a six year old girl who was arrested and interrogated by him in Annapolis. Butler was notorious in Maryland and indeed throughout the South as indicated by his likeness painted on the receptacle bowls of commodes.

17. Obituary

18. Obituary

19. Effie would recall this instance on a train Oct. 23rd, 1866. She wrote in her diary for that day: "On the train a lady approached me with some question in regard to the train reaching Baltimore. She proved to be the sister of Gen. Mulford, U.S. who commanded the U.S. Truce boat, Steamer New York. The only Yankee gentleman I ever met. Received great kindness at his hands while a prisoner in his charge for which I shall ever be profoundly grateful. Found Miss M much of a lady. She had often heard her brother speak of me. I told her of his polite attention and kindness when I was in so much sorrow. For my life I could not help crying as I thought and spoke of my sadness and lonely desolate condition, and of his kindness to me under such circumstances."

20. Banishment

21. Banishment. One of the letters Miss Goldsborough close to keep was the following:

Lewisburg, Va. Jan. 5, 1864

Miss Goldsborough, I have just received a letter from my brother in Richmond announcing your arrival but as he failed to mention the first name, I don't know that I have the pleasure of your acquaintance. But as we are both from old Maryland and I have been absent so long, my great anxiety for the welfare of my dear friends induces me to write this letter and if it be congenial to your feelings I would be most happy to receive an answer that I may know something of my friends. Brother mentions that you brought Uncle Howe's picture over. I hope you left him well and that the picture was intended for me. Congratulations on your safe arrival in the land of living, I remain with highest regards,

R. Chew Jones, Lt. Enrolling Officer
Greenbrier County, VA.

22. Obituary
23. Banishment
24. Obituary
25. Two Houston brothers served in Co. K on the 11th Va. This was Andrew as Thomas was imprisoned at Johnson's Island at the time. The brothers and indeed the whole Houston clan became close friends of Miss Effie's after her banishment and remained so as they are mention frequently in her diaries of the subsequent years. Tom Houston was an almost constant companion during Effie's visits to Virginia after the war and their relationship appeared to be unique. Nurses' and patients' narratives indicate the unusual bond produced by their mutual experience of care and healing.

On August 13, 1863 Tom Houston entered the following poem in the Hospital Books

Away with care
And dull Despair!
Let no one dare disturb us!
Tonight we'll drink
And never think
Of those that may observe us!
Then boys fill up
The rebel cup
Tho' captive chains do bind us!
Drink deep—drink deep!
And wake from sleep
Mem'ry of those behind us.
Here's to Miss G.
The girl of my song
Her heart's all right
May her life be long!
May her bright eye
Have no cause for tears!
May her proud soul
Be bowed by no fears!
God bless her now
God bless her always
We'll think of her, boys
In all coming days!
Then fill your glass
With glorious wine
And drink with me—
"This Creature divine!"

26. This is almost certainly Lt. Col. R.W. Martin of the 53rd Va., who signed her Hospital Book. He was wounded in Pickett's Charge. He listed his home address as Pittsylvania C.H., a place Miss Effie would visit in later years.
27. Some of Miss Effie's Gettysburg patients wound up in Johnson's Island. In her Hospital Book there is a notation "Lt. Col. James R. Herbert of the 1st Maryland Infantry, Sept. 10, 1863, left hand." In Miss Effie's effects is a letter from Johnson's Island dated Nov. 11, 1863 from Col. Herbert.

My dear Miss Goldsborough,

I cannot refrain from dropping you a few lines from my present abode expressing my admiration for your many kind acts and devotion to the poor wounded soldiers at Gettysburg,

470

you and your collaborators, Miss McKee, Miss Branson, Miss Long, and others will never be forgotten. May God bless you all and I am sure he will. Well, I supposed you would like to hear of your patients. As far as I know they are all doing well and if they could see you, or get some of the milk punch made by your own fair hands they would be as happy as possible under the circumstances. We are all very comfortable here but expect very cold weather ere long, but we will grin and bear it. What on earth has become of Major G? [Major Wm. W. Goldsborough, 1st Md. Batt.] How is his wound? I have written but have got no answer. I have not heard from him since I came here. He knows that until lately I have been unable to use my hand or I would have written to him often. Give my love to his mother who was just as kind to me as my own mother. Write me [if] you can find him, and just as long a letter as you please. I can receive it. Has Dr. Goldsborough got home from Libby Prison yet? I hope so, especially on his brother's account. We amuse ourselves here in various ways, chess, backgammon, checks, cards, etc. It will be entirely too cold for the Major at this place. This winter it would certainly kill him. And Lt. Ferguson got well, I hope and trust he did. I never saw anyone bear such suffering with more Christian fortitude. He is a bold man. How are all the girls? You can kiss them for me [if] you chose and if they submit. I believe when this "Cruel war is over" I will make love to all and no one in particular. I am rather afraid of the 'Dear creatures,' would you believe it? But 'tis a fact. But I would be glad if you would make as many as possible write. I am sure if they knew with how much pleasure they are read they would write. You, I know, have so many correspondents, more agreeable ones, I can only claim a very small share of your thoughts. With many wishes for your happiness,

    I remain your friend

28. A diary entry read: "Tuesday, Feb. 12th 67. Dear Fenton came this morning, bless her heart. I was so glad to see her. Thinner than when I last saw her Saturday, March 25th, 1865 in Richmond just one week before the surrender. We had a talk and a cry over the days that are gone, Confederate times that can never return. " Diaries of Southern women record the end of life as they knew it with profound grief. Mary Chestnut of South Carolina wrote: "We are shut in here—turned with our faces to a dead wall. No mails. A letter is sometimes brought by a man on horseback, traveling through the wilderness made by Sherman. All RR's destroyed—bridges gone. We are cut off from the world—to eat out our own hearts." Southern bereavement would last for generations. The entire region suffered economically, politically, socially and culturally almost until WW II.

29. Banishment
30. Banishment
31. Obituary

CONCLUSION

1. Sanitary Commission Bulletin, Vol. II, p. 616

Bibliography

Books

Alleman, Tillie Pierce. *At Gettysburg or What A Girl Saw and Heard of the Battle.* W. Lake Borland, New York, 1889.

Barton, George. *Angels of the Battlefield.* The Catholic Art Publishing Co., Philadelphia, Pa., 1898.

Beers, Fannie A. *Memories.* J.B. Lippencott Co., Philadelphia, 1888.

Biddle and Dickinson. *Notable Women of Pennsylvania.* University of Pennyslvania Press, Philadelphia, 1942.

Blackford, Susan Leigh, compiler. *Letters from Lee's Army.* Chas. Scribner's and Son, New York, 1947.

Blanton, DeAnne, and Cook, Lauren, *They Fought Like Demons*, Louisiana State University Press, Baton Rouge, LA, 2002

Boatner, Mark M. III. *Civil War Dictionary.* David McKay Co. Inc., New York, 1959.

Boyd, Belle. *Belle Boyd in Camp and Prison.* ed. Carroll Curtis Davis, Thomas Yoseloff, Cranbury, New Jersey, 1968.

Broadhead, Sally. *Diary of a Lady of Gettysburg.* limited printing, copy available in GNMP Civilian folder.

Brockett & Vaughn. *Women's Work in the Civil War.* R.H. Curran, Boston, 1867.

Bucklin, Sophronia. *In Hospital and Camp.* J.E. Potter, Phila., 1869.

Burton, O.V. *In My Father's House Are Many Mansions, Family and Community in Edgefield County,* S.C. University of North Carolina Press, Chapel Hill, 1985.

Caldwell, J.F.J. *The History of a Brigade of South Carolinians knownfirst as Gregg's and subsequently as "McGowan's Brigade."* King & Biard, Philadelphia, 1866.

Carter, Robert G. *Four Brothers in Blue.* University of Texas Press, Austin & London.

Chapman, John A. *History of Edgefield County from the Earliest Settlements to 1897.* The Reprint Co., Spartanburg, South Carolina, 1988.

Coco, Gregory A. *A Vast Sea of Misery.* Thomas Publications, Gettysburg, Pennsylvania, 1988.

Confederate Veteran series. Compiliation of Addresses, Records, and Proceedings, *The History of Waterford, Oxford County, Maine.* Published at the direction of the town by Hoyt, Fogg, and Donham, Portland, Maine, 1879.

Crotty, Daniel G. *Four Years Campaigning with the Army of the Potomac.* Dysart Bros & Co., Grand Rapids, Michigan, 1874.

Dawson, Capt. Francis W. *Our Women of the War.* an address, Charleston, S.C., 1887.

Edmonds, S. Emma E. *Nurse and Spy in the Union Army.* W.S. Williams & Co., Hartford, Conn, 1865.

Fremantle, Lt. Col. *Three Months in the Southern States.* John Bradburn, New York, 1864.

Gamder, Capt. and Brevet Lt. Col. Ira B. *Recollections of A Boy Member of Co. I, Fourteenth Maine Volunteers,* 1861-1865. Lewiston Journal Co., Lewiston, Maine, 1902.

Gordon, General John B. *Reminscences of the Civil War.* Charles Scribner and Sons, New York, 1903.

Greenbie, Marjorie Barstow. *Lincoln's Daughters of Mercy.* G.P. Putnam's Sons, New York, 1944.

Hancock, Cornelia. *South After Gettysburg.* ed. Henrietta Stratton Jacquette, Stratton, Cowell Co., 1937.

Haynes, Martin A. *A History of the Second Regiment, New Hampshire Volunteer Infantry in the War of the Rebellion.* Co. I, Lakeport, New Hampshire, 1896

Holland, Mary A. Gardner. *Our Army Nurses.* B. Wilkins & Co., Boston, 1895.

Holstein, Anna Morris. *Three Years in Field Hospitals in the Army of the Potomac.* J.B. Lippincott & Co., Philadelphia, 1867.

Houghton, Edwin B. *The Campaigns of the 17th Maine.* Short & Loring, Portland, Maine, 1866.

Hum, Ethel Alice. *Wisconsin Women in the War Between the States.* Wisconsin History Commission, 1911.

Johnston, J. W. *The True Story of "Jennie" Wade.* (with the endorsement of her sister, Georgia Wade McClellan), published by J.W. Johnston, Rochester, New York, no date.

Jolly, Ellen Ryan. *Nuns of the Battlefield.* The Providence Visitor Press, Providence, R.I., 1927.

Jones, Terry L. *Lee's Tigers.* Louisiana State University Press, Baton Rouge & London, 1985.

Lauter, Don Richard, "Once Upon a Time in the East…Arabella Wharton Griffith Barlow,"*The Journal of Women's Civil War History,* Vol. I, Thomas Publications, Gettysburg, PA, 2001

Livermore, Mary. *My Story of the War.* A.D. Worthington & Co., Hartford, Conn, 1895.

Maher, Sister Mary Denis, *To Bind Up the Wounds: Catholic Sister Nurses in the U. S. Civil War,* Greenwood Press, Inc., Westport, CT, 1989.

Massey, M. E. *Bonnet Brigades.* Knopf, New York, 1966.

Maxwell, William Quentin. *Lincoln's Fifth Wheel.* Longmans, Green & Co., New York, 1956.

McGuire, Judith. *Diary of a Southern Refugee.* E.J. Hale, New York, 1867.

McKay, Charlotte. *Stories of Hospital and Camp.* Clayton, Tensen, & Hoffelfinger, Philadelphia, 1876.

Meroni, William. *Harris* (or *Herris), Miller, and Dunlop,* privately printed, 1920.

Mulholland, Brevet Major General St. Clair A. *The Story of the 116th Regiment Pennsylvania Infantry.* F. McManus, Jr. & Co., Philadelphia, no date.

Pember, Phoebe Yates. *A Southern Woman's Story.* Mockingbird Books, Inc. St. Simons Island, Georgia, 1959.

Phister, Frederick. *New York in the War of the Rebellion 1861-1865.* D.E. Lyns Co., Albany, New York, 1912.

Poe, Clarence ed. *True Tales of the South at War; How the Soldiers Fought and Families Lived 1861-1865.* The University of North Carolina Press, Chapel Hill, 1961.

Rauscher, Frank. *Music on the March* 1862-65 *with the Army of the Potomac.* Press of Wm. F. Fell & Co., Philadelphia, 1892.

Reed, Wm. Howell. *Hospital Life in the Army of the Potomac,* Boston, 1866.

The Sanitary Commission Bulletins, three volumes, located at the Library of Congress.

Schultz, Jane E., ed., *This Birth Place of Souls: The Civil War Nursing Diary of Harriet Eaton,* Oxford University Press, 2011

Simpkins & Patton. *The Women of the Confederacy.* Garrett & Massie Inc., Richmond and New York, 1936.

Souder, Mrs. Edmund. *Leaves from the Battlefield of Gettysburg.* Caxton Press of C. Sherman, Son & Co., Philadelphia, 1864.

Storrick, W.C. *Gettysburg, The Place, The Battle, The Outcome.* Harrisburg, 1932.

Tunnard, William H. *A Southern Record-the History of the Third Regiment Louisiana Infantry.* Baton Rouge, Louisiana, 1866.

Turner, Rev. D.K. *History of Neshaminy Presbyterian Church of Warwick.* Culbertson & Bache, Philadelphia, 1876.

United Daughters of the Confederacy, South Carolina Division, *South Carolina Women in the Confederacy.* two volumes, Columbia, S.C., The State Company, 1903-07.

Velazquez, Loreta Janeta. *The Woman in Battle.* Dustin, Gilman, & Co., Richmond, 1876.

Waite, Major Otis F.K. *New Hampshire in the Rebellion.* N.H. Tacy, Chase, & Co., Claremont, New Hampshire, 1870.

The War of the Rebellion Official Records of the Union and the Confederate Armies.

Welch, Richard F., *The Boy General: The Life and Careers of Francis Channing Barlow,* Associated University Press, Cranbury, NJ, 2003

Woodward, C. Vann, editor. *Mary Chestnut's Civil War.* Yale University Press, New Haven and London, 1981.

Woolsey, Georgiana, compiler. *Letters of a Family During the War 1861-1865.* privately printed, 1899.

Young, Agatha. *Woman and the Crisis.* McDowell, Oblensky, New York, 1959.

Newspapers and Journals

Atlanta *Journal*

Augusta *Chronicle*

Augusta *Herald*

"Buffalo Medical & Surgical Journal," *Reminiscences of Field-Hospital Service with the Army of the Potomac.* W.W. Potter, New York, October and November 1889.

Daily Picayune, New Orleans

Democratic Watchman, Bellefonte, Pa.
Gettysburg Compiler
Gettysburg *Star and Sentinel*
Harpers Weekly
Holland's Magazine
Louisiana History
Military Images
New York *Herald*
North American, Philadelphia
The North American Review
Philadelphia *Inquirer*
Pittsburg *Dispatch*
The Press, Philadelphia
The Public Ledger, Philadelphia
Semi-Annual Report of the Ladies Aid Society of Philadelphia, 1862 and 1863.
Seventeenth Publication of the Oswego County Historical Society.
South Carolina Historical Society Papers, Charleston, S.C.
Syracuse *Herald*
Syracuse *Journal*
United Daughters of the Confederacy magazine, Richmond, Virginia.
"Old and New," Mrs. P. M. Clapp, *Helen Gilson: A Memorial.* April and May 1872.

Unpublished letters, manuscripts, and collections

Blake Collection, U.S. Army War College, Carlisle, Pennsylvania.
Fanny Gordon Letters, Georgia Department of Archives and History.
Francis Channing Barlow Civil War letters, 1861-1865, Massachusetts Historical Society.
Civilian Folders, Gettysburg National Military Park.
John Gordon Papers, Hargrett Rare Book and Manuscript Library, University of Georgia Libraries.
Louisiana Historical Association Confederate Records Collection, Tulane University, New Orleans.
McCormick, Mona, *The Banishment of Miss Euphemia Goldsborough* and *Obituary,* in possession of descendants.
Pension files, The National Archives.
Sister Camilla narrative, St. Jospeh's Archives, Emmitsburg, MD.

Index

Fogg, Isabella 197-203
Folly Island 84, 173
Frederick, MD 8, 166, 214, 235, 253, 266, 267, 268, 294, 295, 308, 419
Fredericksburg 1, 22, 23, 24, 25, 38, 64, 87, 93, 95, 124, 169, 171, 172, 174, 175, 176, 199, 200, 208, 222, 231, 232, 235, 264, 284, 295, 296, 299, 302, 308, 353, 356, 454

Garlach, Anna 52-56
George Bushman farm 363
Gibbons, Miss 355
Gilson, Helen 24, 162-183, 208
Goldsborough, Euphemia 407-437
Gordon, Frances 26-37
Grant, Mrs. S. J. 33

Hall, Susan 320-330
Hampton hospital 215
Hancock, Cornelia 23, 232, 272-289, 315
Harpers Ferry 47, 207, 230, 235, 236, 274, 325, 367
Harris, Dr. 298
Harris, Ellen 212-226
Harrison's Landing 21, 89, 91, 92, 180, 205, 225, 229
Hilton Head, SC 84, 85
Hodges, Jennie 151
Holmes, Dr. F. S. 199
Holstein, Anna 277, 308-319
Horne, Lucinda 38-42
Hubbard, Dr. 77
Husband(s), Mary 204-211, 286, 318

Jacob Schwartz farm 290
Jacobs, Julia 184
Janes, Dr. Henry 331
Janvier, Dr. 78
Jones, Clarissa 355-362
Josiah Benner farm 18
Judiciary Square hospital 391, 392

Kirby, Mrs. William 384

LaCroix, Sister Regina 270
Lacy House hospital 230
Lee, Mary 227-233
Lee, Mrs. Hugh 32
Lincoln, Abraham, 50, 232, 238, 245, 306, 316, 345, 349, 378, 404
Livermore, Mary 151, 154
Louisville, KY 202, 384
Lutheran Seminary hospital 262

Maher, Sister Mary Denis 265
Mayre Mansion hospital 175
McAllister, Mary 43-51
McClellan, Georgia 142, 143, 144, 147
McDonald, Dr. Alexander 97, 253
McGuire, Judith 6, 8, 252
McKay, Charlotte 290-307
Means, Dr. T.A. 17
Methodist Church hospital 261
Michael Fiscel Farm 200
Miller, Dr. 289
Miller, Josephine 148-150
Montfort, Mary 252
Moore, Jane 234-251
Morris Island 84, 173
Murfreesboro 325, 326, 328
Myers, Sallie 131-134

Nashville, TN 325, 367
National Cemetery 316, 403, 404
Newton, Jane Eliza 344
Nightingale, Florence 113, 157, 165

O'Keefe, Sister Camille 256-271

Palmer, Mrs. Ora 252
Pennsylvania College hospital 260, 410, 412, 414, 416
Philadelphia Ladies Aid Society 205, 208, 212, 215, 217, 223